THE WORLD OF BAROQUE MUSIC

THE
WORLD
OF
BAROQUE
MUSIC

New Perspectives

Edited by George B. Stauffer

INDIANA UNIVERSITY PRESS
Bloomington & Indianapolis

This book is a publication of
Indiana University Press
601 North Morton Street
Bloomington, IN 47404-3797 USA

http://iupress.indiana.edu

Telephone orders   800-842-6796
Fax orders   812-855-7931
Orders by e-mail   iuporder@indiana.edu

Library of Congress Cataloging-in-Publication Data

The world of baroque music : new perspectives / edited by George B.
    Stauffer.
        p. cm.
    Includes bibliographical references and index.
    ISBN 0-253-34798-X (cloth : alk. paper)
    1. Music—17th century.   2. Music—18th century.   I. Stauffer,
George B., date.
ML193.W67 2006
780.9′032—dc22
2006008084
1 2 3 4 5 11 10 09 08 07 06

In celebration of the life of
Gabe M. Wiener and his love of music

Contents

Contents

Preface

If there is one thing that we can say with complete certainty about the music of the Baroque Era, it is that we still have much to learn. The intense interest in the pre-1750 repertory and the revival of historical instruments and practices since the end of World War II have taught us a great deal about the Baroque, its culture, its music, and its composers. And yet one senses that we are still viewing a picture painted with no more than the broadest of brush strokes. Once we look more closely at the portrait, we see the coarseness of the lines and the lack of detail. It is clear that we need new perspectives.

One way we can gain these perspectives is by considering Baroque music in its full context, taking into account the economic, sociological, political, and cultural climate in which it prospered. Often this is best achieved by looking carefully at segments of the repertory that have been unjustly overlooked, and examining how these meritorious works fit in with the well-known masterpieces. No one was more committed to this approach than the late Gabe M. Wiener, founder and director of PGM Recordings. A skilled audio engineer with a B.A. degree from Columbia University, Gabe launched PGM in 1993 with the goal of creating a series of recordings that would offer new perspectives on Baroque music. His refined recordings of Salamone Rossi's Hebraic motets, Santiago de Murcia's guitar pieces, Barbara Strozzi's cantatas, and other gems opened new vistas into the Baroque. The compact discs attracted great interest among scholars and performers and spurred listeners to consider old issues afresh. Gabe's untimely death in April 1997 cut short the life and work of an impassioned champion of Baroque music and deprived us of additional recordings.

Using Gabe's compact discs as a springboard for discussion, the essays in the present volume explore in depth the matters raised in the music. This book is not a broad survey of the Baroque repertory. Rather, it concentrates on a number of critical developments that led to the creation and flowering of a new musical idiom—an idiom that was both cosmopolitan and immensely popular. In the opening chapter Craig Monson explores the private world of the Elizabethan lute song, whose calculated intimacy represented the last great flourish of Renaissance gallantry. In a related essay, Barbara Russano Hanning shows how the Italian monodic song carried forth the Elizabethan notion of intimacy, but in a new way, one that showed unprecedented sensitivity to the words of the text. Equally novel breakthroughs occurred simultaneously in the realm of instrumental writing, as Mary Oleskiewicz demonstrates in her discussion of the rise of Italian chamber music.

How the new Baroque style fit into the economic and political culture of its time is the topic of essays that follow. In Chapter 4, Kerala J. Snyder scrutinizes Buxtehude's vocal music and the way in which it mirrored the municipal aspirations of the prosperous seventeenth-century seaport of Lübeck, in North Germany. In a chapter on music at the French court, I look at a cultural establishment that was the polar opposite from that in Lübeck. In Paris, municipal forces had no say in the development of music—the king alone was the final arbiter of artistic taste. In Chapter 6, a stimulating essay on Jewish music, Michael Beckerman explores the life and works of Salamone Rossi, whose motets and instrumental works bridged the gap between the Renaissance and the Baroque. The challenges Rossi faced as an outsider in the musical establishment were similar to those encountered by the female singer and composer Barbara Strozzi. Yet as Wendy Heller points out in Chapter 7, Strozzi, too, managed to overcome challenging odds to write brilliant works.

Contrasting with the public worlds of Lübeck, Paris, Mantua, and Venice was the private world of the guitar. Still, as Victor Coelho points out in his essay, the guitar was also one of the most egalitarian instruments of the Baroque, embracing a wide range of popular and classical idioms. In Chapter 9 David Schulenberg traces the evolution of keyboard music in the seventeenth century in Northern Europe, from Sweelinck and his students to Böhm, Kuhnau, and others. Bach's propensity for recycling old scores is the topic of Chapter 10: Just how original were his late vocal and instrumental works, when most of the music they contain stems from earlier compositions? Equally stimulating questions can be posed about Bach's masterpiece the St. John Passion. As Daniel R. Melamed stresses in Chapter 11, we may not know this work as well as we thought. And finally, in the concluding chapter, Gerard Béhague traces the travels of the Baroque to the New World, giving a vivid portrait of eighteenth-century music in Mexico and Brazil.

The insights into the economic, sociological, political, and cultural trends of the time presented by these chapters, accompanied by the illuminating recordings of Gabe M. Wiener, offer us a window into the world of Baroque music. They underline its rich fabric and help to explain the broad currents that led to the universal embracement of Baroque style, both in the seventeenth and eighteenth centuries and in our own time. It is hoped that the present volume will be used by scholars, teachers, students, performers, and other interested readers, for—to paraphrase the motto of PGM Recordings, *Pro Gloria Musicae*—the Glory of Baroque Music.

This book would not have been possible without the assistance of a number of institutions and people. I would like to thank the Performing Arts Library of the New York Public Library and the Blanche and Irving Laurie Music Library at Rutgers University, New Brunswick, N.J., for allowing me to use their collections. I would like to extend special gratitude to Michael and Zena Wiener and their daughter Jenny, whose encouragement and financial support through the Gabe M. Wiener Foundation made this project possible. I am indebted, too, to Gayle Sherwood and Donna M. Wilson, music editors at Indiana University Press, for backing this volume and providing editorial guidance on many issues. David Chapman, Ph.D. candidate and double-bass player extraordinaire at Rutgers University, tracked down the illustrations and permissions and compiled the index, and David Oliver, formerly of PGM Recordings, helped with technical advice on the CDs. I want to extend thanks to Chris Wilson for setting the music examples and to David Anderson for copyediting the finished manuscript. In addition, a residency at the Liguria Study Center provided by the Bogliasco Foundation gave greatly appreciated time for final editorial touches. I also owe a significant debt to the contributors to this volume. Esteemed friends and experts in their field, they provided not only the texts to the chapters in this book but also stimulating discussions about the issues raised by the topics and the accompanying compact discs.

Finally, I owe a posthumous thanks to Gabe M. Wiener, with whom I worked closely first as a mentor, during his Columbia years, and then as a colleague, during his PGM years. Our collaboration on PGM 115, "The Uncommon Bach," for the American Bach Society was an uncommonly fulfilling experience. For the recordings that accompany this book, and the new perspectives they bring to Baroque music, we are in Gabe's debt.

George B. Stauffer
New Brunswick, N.J.
January 2006

THE WORLD OF BAROQUE MUSIC

CHAPTER ONE

Songs of Shakespeare's England

Craig Monson

After being at the pains of scoring several of Dowlands compositions, I have been equally disappointed and astonished at his scanty abilities in counterpoint, and the great reputation he acquired with his contemporaries, which has been courteously continued to him, either by indolence or ignorance of those who have had occasion to speak of him, and who took it for granted that his title to fame, as a profound musician, was well founded. . . . Jones, Corkine, and Adson [also composed] Ayres; but all so much alike, so unmarked, unmeaning, and vapid, that there is not sufficient difference of style, melody, or modulation in them to enable the most penetrating critic to assign them to one composer more than another. And it would be as vain for a cultivated and refined ear to hope for amusement in them, as a plagiarist to seek for plunder. (Burney 1789, 1: 117, 262)

THE EIGHTEENTH-CENTURY MUSIC HISTORIAN Charles Burney seems as frequently out of tune as in tune with the "ancient music" he examined and described. Although later writers scarcely approached the harshness of Burney's judgments, sixteenth-century solo song, in both England and Italy, rarely seems to have fared particularly well at their hands, either. For in wide-ranging general histories, the solo song of this period is commonly eclipsed, first by the sixteenth-century madrigal (whose emphasis on counterpoint and emotional expression resonates with nineteenth-century aesthetic values), and then by the birth and rise of opera (the forerunner of music drama). As Nigel Fortune aptly put it, "Opera, like a thick hedge, hides monody from the historian" (Fortune 1953, 172).

This is not to say that sixteenth-century song has been neglected. The English lute ayre (or lute air), in particular, has garnered substantial interest beyond the field of music. The superior literary quality of some lute ayre texts, and the fact that the songbooks represent a significant repository of late-sixteenth-century and early seventeenth-century verse, have drawn many scholars of English literature to the repertory. For nonspecialists and wider audiences, however, late-sixteenth- and early seventeenth-century song has remained largely hidden territory, overshadowed by the madrigal.

It is therefore useful to recall Castiglione's oft-quoted words from The Book of the Courtier (*Il libro del Corteggiano;* 1528), as conveyed to Elizabethan readers by Sir Thomas Hoby in 1561:

Methink . . . pricksong [that is, vocal polyphony] is a fair music, so it be done upon the book surely and after a good sort. But to sing to the lute is much better, because all the sweetness consisteth in one alone, and a man is much more heedful and understandeth better the feat manner and the air or vein of it when ears are not busied in hearing more than one voice; and beside, every little error is soon perceived, which happeneth not in singing with company, for one beareth out another. But singing to the lute with the ditty (methink) is more pleasant than the rest, for it addeth to the wordes such a grace and strength that it is a great wonder. (Strunk 1998, 3: 50)

In both England and Italy accompanied solo song represented a more widely practiced and esteemed aspect of musical life than we often recognize today. English solo song of the "lute ayre" variety steps more openly into the limelight during the flurry of music publishing that got underway after the expiration of William Byrd's monopoly on English music printing in 1596. Byrd's disinterest in the lute may have been a factor in the small number of lute publications and the total absence of lute-song editions before that date. John Dowland's *First Booke of Songes or Ayres of fowre partes with Tableture for the lute* (1597), a landmark publication that went through at least five editions in its first fifteen years, initiated a flood of song prints and reprints that swelled to some three dozen by the last reprinting of the *First Booke* in 1613. William Corkine, in the dedication to his own *Ayres,* published in 1610 at the height of this brief "boom," could exclaim rather extravagantly, "It was long before the vse of Notes and Tableture came in to our English Presse, but hauing found the way, there are few Nations yeeld more Impressions in that kind then ours" (Sternfeld 1968). After 1613 the tide ebbed just as quickly, with only half-a-dozen additional lute-ayre publications surfacing over the next decade. Most were of mixed content.

Early Elizabethan Song

The fact that English solo song left limited traces before this publishing boom does not mean it was less widely practiced than other secular musical forms, such as the more familiar madrigal. It is significant that as early as 1561 Thomas Hoby had chosen to translate Castiglione's phrase "il cantare alla viola" as "to sing to the lute," which suggests that by the earliest years in the reign of Elizabeth I (ruled 1558–1603), voice and lute already represented the commonly recognized medium for solo song (see Plate 1).

Apart from Hoby, numerous other literary references offer our chief witness that accompanied solo singing was common long before the prints, and that the lute was perceived as the expected accompaniment. A talent for solo singing and playing the lute almost invariably was ascribed to royalty—except for Henry VIII's fourth wife, the "Flanders mare" Anne of Cleves, who could "not syng nor pleye enye instrument, for they take it heere in Germanye for a rebuke and an occasion of lightnesse that great ladyes shuld be lernyd or have enye knowledge of musike" (Boyd 1974, 17). By contrast, Viscount Chateaubriant, courtier of Francis I, recalled with customary hyperbole that Anne Boleyn, "besides singing like a syren, accompanying herself on the lute, she harped better than King David and handled cleverly both flute and rebec." Mary Queen of Scots, according to Brantôme, "had a very good and delicate voice, for she sang very well, tuning her voice to the lute, which she played with assurance with her fair, white hand and with those beautiful fingers, so well formed" (Poulton 1982, 185).

As for Elizabeth I, her tutor Roger Ascham's claim in 1550 that "in music she is very skilful but does not greatly delight" may reflect an attitude toward music he hoped to promote rather than the reality frequently documented in other sources (see Plate 2). William Camden wrote in 1615 that "neither did she neglect Musicke, so farre forth as might beseeme a Princesse, being able to sing and play on the Lute prettily and sweetly" (Boyd 1974, 7). Camden's view was regularly repeated both in public and private comments, such as Virginio Orsino, Duke of Bracciano's private report in 1601 that "Before I depart [from London] she wishes to enjoy me again, in private; and I hope from the speech I have had with her that she will favour me by playing and singing" (Monson 1989, 332). It does not matter whether every queen and princess actually did sing to the lute. What is important is that variations on this theme make clear that it was perceived as appropriately regal behavior, worthy of emulation by others.

Further references confirm the practice of accompanied song beyond these loftiest circles. Thomas Whythorne's autobiography provides several descriptions of his own singing, not only to the lute, but also to the virginals, and of his teaching the same techniques to others at exactly the time of Hoby's translation of The Book of the Courtier. William Webbe's *A Discourse of English Poetrie* (1586), on the other hand, attests to a lighter, more elusive style of song:

> Neither is there anie tune or stroke which may be sung or plaide on instruments, which hath not some poetical ditties framed according to the numbers thereof: some to Rogero [that is, the old Italian *aria di Ruggiero*, a musical scheme for singing poems or playing instrumental variations—see discussion in Chapter 2] . . . to Galliardes, to Pavines, to Iygges, to Brawles [that is, popular dance forms], to all manner of tunes which everie Fidler knowes better then myself. (Spink 1974, 17)

This was the kind of song-making Sir Philip Sidney had in mind for his *Certain Sonnetts,* eight of which were characterized as expressly conceived to preexistent melodies (Spencer 1995, 594n). Webbe's description suggests a freer, improvisatory style of singing verses to familiar tunes, less likely to leave traces in print, akin to traditions in Italy such as those of the *improvvisatori,* who sang poems to schematic melodic formulae.

Private Musicke

Virginio Orsino's remark, cited above, touches upon one of the most interesting and telling aspects of Elizabethan song and its cultural context: "she wishes to enjoy me again, *in private;* and I hope . . . that she will favour me by singing and playing" (emphasis added). Private music-making among royalty and the gentry was acceptable within their own social circle. But practitioners of solo song seem to intensify that turn of mind in a way that contrasts with attitudes toward other musical genres. Solo song remains a reflection of intimacy and staged seclusion, a close and rather closed collaboration of poet, composer, performer, and audience, to the studied exclusion of a wider public. By extension, song also becomes an expressive vehicle for artful, personal negotiation and dialogic play—whether serious or in jest, "real" or staged—within that private sphere.

Thomas Whythorne, the poet and composer whose fascinating autobiography offers a rare entry directly into the world and mind of an Elizabethan musician (Figure 1-1), captures something of the particularly intimate environment and uses of English Renaissance song. Most intriguing, the account articulates Whythorne's view of song's role in the delicate play of interpersonal relations, most notably romance:

> In these days [c. 1550] I used to sing my songs and sonnets sometime to the lute and sometimes to the virginals, whereby I might tell my tale with my voice as well as by word or writing. And sometimes it should be the better heard because the music joined therewith did sometimes draw the mind of the hearer to be the more attentive to the song. Also if it were not to be well taken, yet in as much as it was sung, there could not so much hurt be found as had been in the case of my writing being delivered to her to read. For singing of such songs and ditties was a thing common in those days. (Osborn 1961, 51)

["Craig Monson"]

Figure 1-1. Thomas Whythorne, *Duos, or songs for two voices, composed and made by Thomas Whythorne* (1590). By permission of the British Library.

4

Whythorne's description of his initial attempts at wooing a lawyer's daughter not long afterwards reveals how he put theory into practice: "At this time I had gotten two or three pretty ditties made of love, the which because I dared not deliver to her in writing, for fear of after claps, I would sing them oftentimes unto her on the virginals or lute, by the which I made my first entrance into my suit unto her. And as I saw how she liked to hear them, then would I enter into talk of the same matter" (Osborn 1961, 77).

This was not merely some clever, writerly conceit. Variations on this theme turn up more than once, notably at the highest level of British society, in courtiers' delicate dealings with the aging, ever virgin Queen Elizabeth I. Sir Henry Wotton, sometime confidential secretary to Robert Devereux, Earl of Essex, recalled, for example: "There was another time long after, when Sir *Fulke Grevill* (late Lord Brooke) . . . had almost super-induced into favour the Earle of *Southampton;* which yet being timely discovered, my Lord of Essex chose to evaporate his thoughts in a Sonnet (being his common way) to be sung before the Queene, (as it was) by one Hales, in whose voyce she took some pleasure" (Poulton 1982, 227).

Daniel Batchelar's "To plead my faith where faith hath no reward," published in Robert Dowland's *A Musical Banquet* twenty-five years later, when both Elizabeth and Essex were dead, is headed "The Right Honourable Robert, Earle of Essex" and includes the lines "I loved her whom all the world admir'de/I was refus'de of her that can love none." The song certainly calls to mind the situation Wotten described. John Dowland's "Can shee excuse my wrongs," titled in an instrumental version "The Earle of Essex Galliard," has also been viewed as a product of Elizabeth and Essex's turbulent relationship.

The same musical stratagem could still be invoked at the very end of Elizabeth's reign, as William Brown, secretary and court agent to Gilbert Talbot, Earl of Shrewsbury, reported on September 18, 1602:

> I send your Lordship here inclosed some verses compounded by Mr Secretary [Sir Robert Cecil], who got Hales to frame a ditty to it. The occasion was, as I hear, that the young Lady of Darby wearing about her neck, in her bosom, a picture which was in a dainty tablet; the Queen espying itt, asked what fyne jewell that was? The Lady Darby was curious to excuse the shewing of it; but the Queen wold have it, and, opening it, and finding it to be Mr. Secretary's, snatcht it away, and tyed itt upon her shoe, and walked long with it there; then took it thence and pinned itt on her elbow, and wore it there sometime also; which Mr. Secretary being told of, made these verses, and had Hales to sing them in his chamber. It was told her Ma[jes]ty that Mr. Secretary had rare musick, and song; she would needes hear them; and so this ditty was soung which you see first written. More verses there be lykewise, wherof som, or all, wer lykewyse soung. I do boldly send these things to your Lo[rdship]. Which I wold not do to any else, for I heare they are very secrett. Some of the verses argue, that he repynes not, thoghe her Ma[jes]ty please to grace others, and contents himself with the favour he hath. (Monson 1989, 333)

Throughout the Elizabethan period, then, solo song remained an effective mediator in the most delicate forms of personal discourse. The sense of intimacy, the air of secrecy, most obvious in the Robert Cecil example, also recalls in striking and interesting ways the courtly experiments with song in late-Renaissance Italy. In the 1570s and 1580s, the so-called *musiche segrete* (private music), first established by Duke Alfonso I at Ferrara, and subsequently emulated at the courts of Florence, Mantua, and Rome, explored new styles of virtuoso solo singing, whose music and texts were so assiduously guarded that Anthony Newcomb has recently characterized other courts' attempts to borrow Ferrarese practice as "cultural espionage" (Newcomb 1980, 53). These English examples convey a carefully fostered sense of intimacy that seems greatly intensified and more directly personal than their Italian

Figure 1-2. Frontispiece from *Select Ayres and Dialogues* (1659). Reproduced by permission of The Huntington Library, San Marino, California.

equivalents. This sense of confidentiality also seems to characterize the world of the English lute ayre (Figure 1-2) much more than that of the rival Elizabethan madrigal. Indeed, music historian Daniel Fischlin has gone so far as to term the private space of the lute ayre "an alternative form of staged interiority" (Fischlin 1998, 21). The contrast between the cited uses of courtly solo song as a means of private negotiation with Elizabeth and the overt, public manner of madrigals in *Triumphs of Oriana,* likewise directed toward the aging Virgin Queen, underlines the different aesthetic contexts of Elizabethan and Jacobean solo song and the polyphonic madrigal.

Dedications and "letters to the reader" of lute ayre and madrigal or polyphonic part-song publications, which suggest how composers wanted themselves and their works to be received by the public, generally confirm this dichotomy. The dedication, "Epistle to the Reader," and "Reasons briefly set down by th'auctor, to perswade euery one to learne to sing" of William Byrd's 1588 *Psalmes, Sonets & Songs* establish a pattern for subsequent "madrigal" prints. The "Reasons" publicly proclaim to a wider world the virtues of music at a time when polyphonic singing was coming into its own among English amateurs. Such sweeping defenses responded to long-standing, deep-seated suspicions planted in the minds of the patriciate and middle classes for a good fifty years by the likes of Thomas Elyot and Roger Ascham:

> But in this commendation of music, I would not be thought to allure noble men to have too much delectation therein, that in playing and singing only, they should put their whole study and felicity: as did the emperor Nero. . . . It were therefore better, that no music were taught to a noble man, than by exact knowledge thereof, he should have therein inordinate delight: and by that be elicited to wantonness, abandoning gravity and the necessary endurance and office in the public weal to him committed. (Thomas Elyot, *The Boke of the Governour,* 1531, quoted in Poulton 1982, 203–204)

> Too much music marreth men's manners, saith Galen, although some men will say that it doth not so, but rather recreateth and maketh quick a man's mind. . . . And even so in a manner these instruments make a man's wit so soft and smooth, so tender and queasy, that they be less able to brook strong and tough study. Wits be not sharpened, but rather dulled and made blunt with such sweet softness, even as good edges be blunter, which men whet upon soft chalk stones. (Roger Ascham, *Toxophilus, The schole of shootinge,* 1545, quoted in Poulton 1982, 203–204)

Half a century later, Thomas Coryat returned to the same theme of music's effeminizing potential in describing Venetian courtesans' singing to the lute: "Moreover shee will endevour to enchaunt thee partly with her melodious notes that shee warbles out upon her lute, which shee fingers with as laudable a stroake as many men that are excellent professors in the noble science of Musicke; and partly with the heart-tempting harmony of her voice" (Rosenthal 1992, 75).

Byrd and other composers of secular polyphony obviously had such condemnations in mind when they recommended their published works to dedicatees as private, spiritual refreshment, to be presented after weightier business had been concluded:

> I hope that (by this occasion) these poore songs of myne might happely yeeld some sweetnesse, repose, and recreation unto your Lordships mind, after your dayly paines & cares in the high affaires of the Common Wealth. (Byrd, *Psalmes, Sonets & Songs* [1588], dedication)

> [Accept] these my poore travells in that Art . . . as seruants redy to give your L. delight, after you haue bene forewearied in affayres of great importance. (Byrd, *Songs of Sundrie Natures* [1589], dedication)

> They were solely entended for your Honors priuate recreation, after your tedious im-
> ployments in the affayres of the common-wealth. (Thomas Bateson, *Second Set of
> Madrigals* [1618], dedication)

From the very beginning of its vogue, the solo song represents these same themes in a
more private way, as a much more intimate musical enterprise. And there are fewer attempts
to justify music in general. In the very year when the spate of lute ayre publications began,
Thomas Morley aptly drew the distinction between "public" polyphonic madrigal and "private" lute song. His *Canzonets, or Little Short Aers to five and six Voices* (1597), a collection of
secular vocal polyphony, also included an alternative version for solo voice and lute. In the
dedication Morley points out, "I have also set them Tablature wise to the Lute in the Cantus
booke for one to sing and plaie alone *when your Lordship would retire yourselfe and bee more
private*" (emphasis added). The remarks echo Byrd's words regarding his polyphonic songs,
but now are rearticulated specifically in terms of the lute ayre as the vehicle for solitary
music-making. Twenty-five years later, in the last stages of this song tradition, Martin Peer-
son still chose to title his rather peripheral and eclectic song collection of 1620 *Private Musicke*. Walter Porter's *Madrigales and Ayres* (1632), occasionally cited as the very end of the tradition, but in fact having in many respects left it behind, still speaks this common language:
"Retreats from the World are settings forward for Heauen, . . . For which cause I haue employed my best endeauours to serue your Honor in your sweet Solitarinesse (as Sir *Philip Syd-
ney* cals the fruition of his owne) with my best abilitie" (dedication to John Lord Digby of
Sherburne, Earle of Bristol).

The language of the prefatory material to books of ayres from the 1590s to 1632 rings the
changes on such themes of solitude, frequently with a personal quality, often at greater length
than madrigal book prefaces, creating an air of interchange and collaboration among members of a genteel circle, where gentleman poets provide the words made into songs for their
special purposes and delectation, rather after the manner of the Earl of Essex's and the Earl of
Salisbury's privileged artistic collaborations with Robert Hale. By publishing, the composer
reluctantly presents the fruits of this insiders' world to a wider public.

The prolific Robert Jones, who published both madrigals and lute ayres, usefully exemplifies this madrigal–lute ayre distinction. Although the dedication to his *First Set of Madrigals* (1607) offers the usual general praises of music, comparable to those from "madrigal"
prints quoted earlier, his lutebook prefaces speak a different language. When he first ventures
into print, Jones cites the encouragement of his collaborators, the aristocratic providers of the
poetry—"their idle ditties (as they will needes haue me call them)," as the composer puts it
in his carefully crafted suggestion of intimacy:

> I confesse I was not unwilling to embrace the conceits of such gentlemen as were earnest
> to haue me apparell these ditties for them; which though they intended for their priuate
> recreation, neuer meaning they should come into the light, were yet content upon in-
> treaty to make the incouragements of this my first aduenture, whereuppon I was almost
> glad to make my small skill knowne to the world. (Robert Jones, *First Booke of Songes or
> Ayres*, 1600)

This was a common justification for publication among song composers (and some
madrigal composers, too). Dowland had likewise acknowledged private, noble complicity in
the creation of his *First Booke of Songes or Ayres* (1597), with a concluding, rather elliptical
phrase suggesting the intimacy of an "in" joke shared with his aristocratic collaborators:
"How hard an enterprise it is in this skilfull and curious age to commit our priuate labours to

the publike view, mine owne disabilitie, and others hard successe doe too well assure me: . . . The Courtly iudgement I hope will not be seuere against them, *being it selfe a party*" (emphasis added).

In his second lute ayre publication, Jones was bold enough this time to act on his own initiative: "Let me be a Bird in your Cage, to sing to my selfe and you. . . . If the Ditties dislike thee, 'tis my fault that was so bold to publish the priuate contentment of divers Gentlemen without their consents, though (I hope) not against their wils: therein if thou find anie thing to meet with thy desire, thank me; for they were neuer meant thee" (Robert Jones, *The Second Booke of Songs and Ayres,* 1601, dedication to Sir Henry Leonard and "To the Reader"). The line from the dedication conveys the sense of familiarity and privacy the solo song commonly fosters, while the concluding remark to the reader clearly articulates the separation of insider (composer and aristocratic poet) and outsider (the eventual purchaser of the songbook).

John Donne, on the other hand, offers in "The Triple Fool" a witty perspective on the poet's sometimes unwilling and unwitting participation in the creative process and the public dissemination of the results, as well as another variation on the theme observed above of "evaporating his thoughts" in verse, subsequently set to music. Having penned a poem to free himself from love's pains, the poet remarks,

> But when I have done so,
> Some man, his art and voice to show,
>   Doth Set and sing my paine,
> And by delighting many, frees againe
>   Griefe, which verse did restraine.
>   (Walls 1984, 237)

Songbook prefaces also suggest an aesthetic community whose members often knew each other's work, and sometimes penned commendations of each other's volumes (Campion writes for Dowland in 1597; Dowland, William Leighton, and John Welton write for Alison in 1599; five anonymous authors praise Greaves in 1604; Ben Jonson, Thomas Campion, and Nathaniel Tomkins write for Ferrabosco in 1609; and Henry Peacham lauds Robert Dowland in 1610). Moreover, the insiders read each other's prefaces. Robert Jones's remark in the preface to his *First Booke* of 1600, for example, that "I cannot thinke it necessary to make my trauels, or my bringing up arguments to perswade you that I have a good opinion of my selfe," reads like a slightly backhanded allusion to Dowland's self-promoting, prolix description of his country hopping and his name dropping in his own *First Booke* of 1597.

Lutebook prefaces could in fact take on a polemical quality that goes quite beyond Jones's subtler barbs and his general tendency to carp at critics. Dowland is notably prone to lapse into this mode, in both general and particular ways. Thomas Campion, too, could turn a lutebook preface into a soapbox, both when he mocks the common disdain of publication ("Others taste nothing that comes forth in Print, as if *Catullus* or *Martials* Epigrammes were the worse for being printed"; *First Booke of Ayres,* c. 1613), and most notably in his oft-quoted diatribe against madrigalism that appeared in Philip Rosseter's *A Booke of Ayres* (1601):

A naked Ayre without guide, or prop, or colour but his owne, is easily censured of everie eare, and requires so much the more inuention to make it please. . . . But there are some who to appeare the more deepe, and singular in their iudgement, will admit no Musicke but that which is long, intricate, bated with fuge, chaind with sincopation, and where the nature of everie word is precisely exprest in the Note, like the old exploded action in Comedies, when if they did pronounce *Memeni,* they would point to the hinder part of their heads, if *Video,* put their finger in their eye. But such childish obseruing of words is altogether ridiculous, and we ought to maintaine as well in Notes, as in action a manly cariage, gracing no word, but that which is eminent, and emphaticall.

The opening of Campion's comment has been recognized as an echo of Castiglione's much cited observations on the chief virtues of solo song eighty years earlier, while his mockery of madrigalism has been compared to the new theories concerning monody of the Florentine Camerata (Greer 1992, 162, 154). But it also resonates more locally and immediately within Campion's own circle, as the poet-composer's piqued response to Thomas Morley's recent *Plaine and Easie Introduction to Practical Music* (1597). There the madrigal is praised and madrigalian word-painting is espoused with the sort of detail that Campion pans—to the total neglect of the lute ayre, which Morley leaves unmentioned.

Robert Jones

Campion and John Dowland are most commonly invoked in discussions of the lute ayre. They should not blind us to the other songwriters, however, who enriched the repertory with works well worth repeated hearings, and who widen our view of the ayre in interesting ways. Robert Jones was among the more prolific lute ayre composers—and also among the more voluble in his prefaces, as we have seen. He was not among the most talented musically, however, as later critics have pointed out (Burney 1789; Spink 1974; Brown 2000). Indeed, Jones himself was sensitive to his musical shortcomings, judging by comments in his *First Booke* of 1601: "I will not saie my next shall be better, but I will promise to take more paines to shew more points of musicke [that is, imitation], which now I could not do, because my chiefest care was to fit the Note to the word." But infelicities that may stand out on paper, particularly by comparison with the most adept lutenist songwriters such as Dowland, pass quickly by, largely unnoticed, in the moment of sensitive performance.

Jones's *Second Booke* (1601) fulfilled his earlier promise of weightier music to come. The final song in the collection, "Come sorrow, come" (Sampler CD 1, track 1), reveals his conscious emulation of older English traditions of serious song. The text's spurning of pleasure and "vaine shews" in favor of sorrow, virtue, and grief recalls the themes, if not the poetic forms, of the sober, sententious verse that had regularly appeared in older Elizabethan song, notably William Byrd's:

Come sorrow, come sweet scayle,
by the which we ascend to the heauenlie place
where vertue sitteth smyling,
to see how some looke pale
with feare to beholde thy ill fauoured face,
vain shewes their sence beguiling,
for mirth hath no assurance
nor warrantie of durance.

Hence pleasures, flie, sweete baite,
On the which they may iustly be said to be fooles,
That surfet by much tasting,
Like theeues you lie in waite,
Most subtillie how to prepare sillie soules,
or sorrowes euerlasting.
Wise griefes haue ioyfull turnings,
Nice pleasures ende in mournings.

Jones therefore chose the musical style appropriate to the decorum of his text, that of the old consort song for solo voice and consort of viols. The song unfolds with measured gravity, often in stately whole notes and half notes, a hallmark of that venerable, serious style. This is most conspicuous in the expansive, fourfold statement of the opening invocation (Example 1-1). "More points of musicke," promised in the *First Booke,* regularly appear in the extended imitative interludes that separate sections of the text, another characteristic feature of the consort song since Byrd's time. In his espousal here of the consort song style for serious words Jones is in step with other ayre composers such as Michael Cavendish, Thomas Morley, John Danyel, and John Dowland, who likewise betray the influence of that time-honored tradition in their occasional use of slow and stately vocal declamation and of expansive, imitative introductions and interludes. The same can also be seen in Jones's own "Over these brookes" from his *Second Booke* (PGM 112).

On the other hand, "Come sorrow, come" indulges in a level of textual depiction uncommon in the traditional consort song, and it does this with an enthusiasm bound to have made Thomas Campion wince. The strings of suspended dissonances at the opening were a usual musical trope for "sorrow." Jones's vocal line setting "scayle . . . by which we ascend" is more patently pictorial, treading resolutely and obviously up the scale, predictably imitated by the accompaniment. The long-held, monotone breves in the voice on "durance," contrasting with the accompaniment's busy quarter-note motion, bring the song to a literal-minded close (Example 1-2).

"Come sorrow, come" calls to mind not only the sober themes of the acknowledged master of the doleful lute ayre, John Dowland, but also the title of one of his best known serious songs, "Sorrow, stay." Several details of Dowland's setting suggest that it may have been ringing in Jones's ear as he composed his own "Come sorrow, come." The repeated suspensions of Dowland's opening gesture, "Sorrow, sorrow stay," echo and reecho rather prolixly in Jones's "Come sorrow, come," sometimes at Dowland's pitch level, as if Jones were trying to do Dowland one better (compare Examples 1-1 and 1-3).

Interestingly enough, Dowland had also employed literal-minded word painting: a scalar descent on "But down, down, down, down I fall"—which Jones reverses at "scayle by which we ascend." Dowland subsequently employs a rising figure to illustrate "down and arise," which in its final statement involves essentially the same rising figure, at the same pitch, leading to the same drawn-out breves on D that reappear in Jones's song at "no warrantie of durance" (compare Examples 1-2 and 1-4). Jones's busy bass line below the held D in the voice also duplicates the simpler of Dowland's two statements of the equivalent passage almost exactly. Jones's "Come sorrow, come" thus looks very much like a "friendly aemulation" of Dowland's "Sorrow, stay," following the customary practice of creating the closest resemblances to the beginning and end of his model. Jones thus clearly demonstrates that this "pseudo-consort song" style was the acknowledged medium of the serious lute ayre, and John Dowland, the acknowledged master.

The more expansive, serious lute song finds a very attractive foil in much lighter and more common contributions to the form, provided in great numbers by the likes of Robert Jones, William Corkine, and Thomas Campion, who offered an apt description of the light ayre: "Short Ayres, if they be skillfully framed, and naturally exprest, are like quicke and good Epigrammes in Poesie, many of them shewing as much artifice, and breeding as great difficultie, as a larger Poeme" (*First Booke of Ayres,* c. 1613).

In the preface to his *Fourth Booke of Ayres* (c. 1617), Campion tried for a second time to capture the essence of the light ayre by an analogy to gold leaf: "The Apothecaries have

Example 1-1. Jones: "Come sorrow, come," mm. 1–14.

Bookes of Gold, whose leaves being opened are so light as that they are subject to be shaken with the least breath, yet, rightly handled, they serve both for ornament and use; such are light *Ayres*."

Both Campion and Jones seem most at home with the light ayre, whose airy style is artfully captured by Robert Jones's "My love is neither young nor old" (Sampler CD 1, track 2), a musical trifle scarcely twenty bars long, also from his *Second Booke* (1601):

Example 1-2. Jones: "Come sorrow, come," mm. 66–70.

My loue is neither yoong nor olde,
not fiery hot nor frozen colde,
but fresh and faire as springing brier,
blooming the fruit of loues desire,
not snowy white nor rosie red,
but faire enough for sheepheards bed,
and such a loue was neuer seene,
on hill or dale or countrey greene.

For such a gossamer text, cut from the same cloth as dozens of other light ayre verses, the elaborate, highly rhetorical idiom of madrigal or more serious song would be indecorous. Jones aptly chooses an ultra-simple, uncomplicated idiom, in which musical interest clearly centers in the vocal line, syllabically wed to the words—thumbprints of the light ayre (Example 1-5). The accompaniment commonly adheres to the accepted style—straightforward and homophonic, dancing lightly in triple time, usually right in step with the voice. Even in this facile style, it seems that Jones cannot resist fulfilling his promise of "more points of Musicke" from the *First Booke* preface. He adds the odd whiff of imitation, very lightly touched, first when bass trips after the voice at "Not fiery hot, nor frozen cold," then again when the outer voices of the accompaniment quickly toss in the melodic snippet for "But fresh and fair" before it crops up in the voice.

The melody takes on a regular, schematic quality, common in light ayres, thanks to short rhythmic figures that recur from line to line and section to section. Simple melodic sequence

Example 1-3. Dowland: "Sorrow, stay," mm. 1–2.

also enhances the sense of comfortable predictability, first to reflect the repetition of "blooming the fruit" and to prepare a modest climax before the end of the line. Another trifling sequence picks up the parallelism of "Not snowy white, nor rosey red," then carries over into line 6. This phrase gains additional momentum from the accompaniment's continuation of the previous little rising sequence from lines 4–5. This all adds up to a happy articulation of the song's primary internal division at the end of line 6.

The final couplet is repeated whole, for emphasis, as so often happens in these slight, schematic songs. The melody's leap to g", the very top of its range, satisfyingly completes the motion of the earlier rising sequences that dominated the second half of the song, and combines with the immediate, precipitous drop through d" to g' (the very bottom of the vocal range) to underscore lightly the accompanying text, "On hill or dale," a whimsical bit of artifice we happily hear again in the automatic repetition. "Skillfully framed, and naturally exprest" (as Campion might describe it), Jones's modest music aptly illustrates in notes the essence of the light ayre as well as Campion's pithy characterization in words, a style that likewise reappears slightly more expansively in "Fie, fie what a coile is here" (PGM 112) and "Love is a bable" (PGM 112) from Jones's *Second Booke*.

In Jones's songs the accompaniment did not always feature the familiar lute, but, rather, the viol. Robert Jones was the first to introduce into print the lyra viol—the viola da gamba whose performance style involved, not a single musical line, but a polyphonic texture, and whose music was notated in tablature, similar to the lute, rather than conventional staff notation (Figure 1-3). The lyra viol provided an appropriate, alternative accompanying instrument in Jones's *Second Booke of Songs and Ayres* (1601), "set out to the Lute, the base Violl the playne way, or the Base by tableture after the leero fashion."

Performances of "lute ayres" could in fact involve a wide variety of performing combinations, as songbook title pages make clear. Dowland's *First Booke* established the general pattern:

> *THE FIRST BOOKE of Songes or Ayres of fowre partes with Tableture for the Lute: So made that all the partes together, or either of them seuerally may be song to the Lute, Orpherian or Viol de gambo.*

It is interesting that Dowland's title page seems to favor the part-song versions of these airs, since the phrase is given pride of place in the title. Possibly this was a cautionary gesture, since the songbook was launched against the still rising tide of current "madrigal" prints. The

Example 1-4. Dowland: "Sorrow, stay," mm. 28b–37.

formatting of the volume includes soprano with lute tablature below it on the left-hand opening and the alto, tenor, and bass texted parts, each facing a different direction, on the right-hand opening, permitting simultaneous performance, a format that would become commonplace (Figure 1-4). Morley's 1597 *Canzonets* follow a similar tack, for they were published both as five- or six-part vocal polyphony and as solos with lute accompaniment. This provides another interesting parallel to sixteenth-century Italian practices of solo singing, where the comparably lightweight polyphonic *villanella,* which served as a model for Morley, might be performed in this alternative manner, as an accompanied solo.

A number of Dowland's lower "vocal" parts are awkward, however, in both their text underlay and their vocal writing, and probably were originally conceived as lute songs pure and simple, subsequently rearranged to cash in on the established craze for part singing. Thomas

Example 1-5. Jones: "My love is neither young nor old," mm. 1–18.

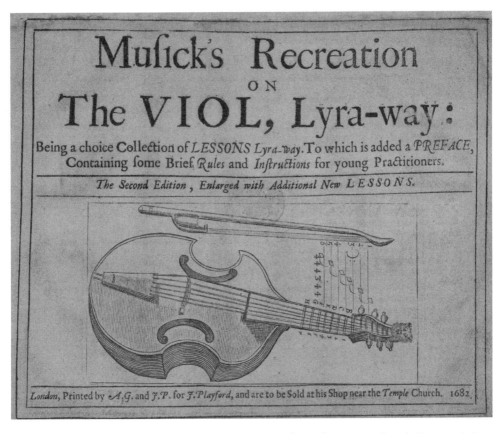

Figure 1-3. Title page from *Musick's Recreation on the Viol, Lyra-way* (1682). By permission of the British Library.

Campion admitted as much about his own songs in the preface to his *First Booke of Ayres* (c. 1613),

> These Ayres were for the most part framed at first for one voyce with the Lute, or Violl, but upon occasion, they haue since beene filled with more parts, which who so please may use, who like not may leaue. Yet doe wee daily obserue, that when any shall sing a Treble to an Instrument, the standers by will be offring at an inward part out of their owne nature; and true or false, out it must, though to the peruerting of the whole harmonie.

An interesting insight into the realities of early Jacobean performance!

Viol Passions

The viola da gamba was rarely absent from title pages. Beginning with Dowland's *First Booke* and continuing more prominently with Jones's works, it became a popular accompanying instrument. By the turn of the century, viol accompaniment was becoming increasingly common, so much so that it even began to challenge the hegemony of the lute. By far the greatest enthusiast for the viol in this context was Tobias Hume, one of the most imaginative and "fantastical" English musicians of the age. Hume first attempted rather belligerently to invade the ranks of published song composers in 1605, proclaiming, "My Life hath beene a Souldier, and my idlenes addicted to Musicke, . . . My Profession being, as my Education hath beene, Armes, the onely effeminate part of me, hath beene Musicke." Hume seems to have been an interloper in the "insiders' world" of the lute ayre, someone who would never fit in. He continues his assault by bluntly firing off volleys at his various musical peers, an act that cannot have won him many friends: "my studies are far from seruile imitations" (a jibe at English madrigalists' aping of Italian fashions?)—"I robbe no others inuentions" (Could Hume have recognized Morley's recent borrowings from Gastoldi and Anerio in his *Ballets* of 1595?)—"I take no Italian Note to an English dittie" (A swipe at Nicholas Yonge's *Musica Transalpina* and Thomas Watson's *Italian Madrigals Englished?*)—"or filch fragments of Songs to stuffe out my volumes" (a salvo at Thomas Morley, Thomas Weelkes, Michael East, or other composers in whose publications tacet musical borrowings appear, sometimes with remarkable frequency?).

Hume's greatest musical enthusiasm also cannot have endeared him to many lutenist songwriters. He was a passionate aficionado of the lyra viol. In the few songs appearing amid numerous solo works for lyra viol in his *First Part of Ayres* (1605) and *Captaine Humes Poeticall Musicke* (1607), Hume replaces the lute with as many as three viols, and proclaims, "And from henceforth, the statefull instrument *Gambo Violl,* shall with ease yeeld full various and as deuicefull Musicke as the Lute. For here I protest the Trinitie of Musicke, parts, Passion and Diuision, to be as gracefully united in the *Gambo Violl,* as in the most receiued Instrument that is, which here with a Souldiers Resolution, I give up to the acceptance of al noble dispositions."

To John Dowland, of course, these were fighting words, prompting him to call fellow lutenists to arms in another polemical offensive that opened *A Pilgrimes Solace* (1612): "Here vnder their owne noses hath beene published a Booke in defence of the Viol de Gamba, wherein not onely all other the best and principall Instruments haue beene abased, but especially the Lute by name. [He then quotes Hume directly.] . . . Which Imputation, me thinkes, the learneder sort of Musitians ought not to let passe vnanswered." This said, one or more viols in consort nevertheless remained a common accompanimental alternative for performing the lute ayre repertory.

Hume also showed singular invention in challenging and extending the conventional technique of the viol in ways that seem quite Baroque in the search for effect and probably raised the eyebrows of his contemporaries. For vocal accompaniment, he recommended double stringing the viol's three lowest strings, to enrich the sonority: "If you will heare the Viol de Gambo in his true Maiestie, to play parts, and singing thereto, then string him with nine strings, your three Basses double as the lute, which is to be plaide on with as much ease as your Violl of six stringes."

Appropriately, the warrior-turned-composer opens his 1605 collection with an "over the top," programmatic battle song, "I Sing the praise of honor'd wars." Well-tutored Jacobeans' initial amusement at this portentous play on the opening of Vergil's *Aeneid,* "Arma virumque cano," must have waxed at Hume's enthusiastic depiction of "The great Ordenance" with sharp strokes on the bottom open string as the voice exclaims, "Harke, harke, shootes and wounds abound." Rapid fire, repeated sixteenth-notes are marked "Kettle Drumme," to which the voice responds, "the drums allarum sound: the Captaines crye za za za." Later in the collection Hume earns a place for himself as a pioneer in the use of *col legno* when he concludes the instrumental piece, "Harke, Harke," with a series of three-to-six-note chords and the note "Drum this with the back of your Bow." Pizzicato also crops up in vari-

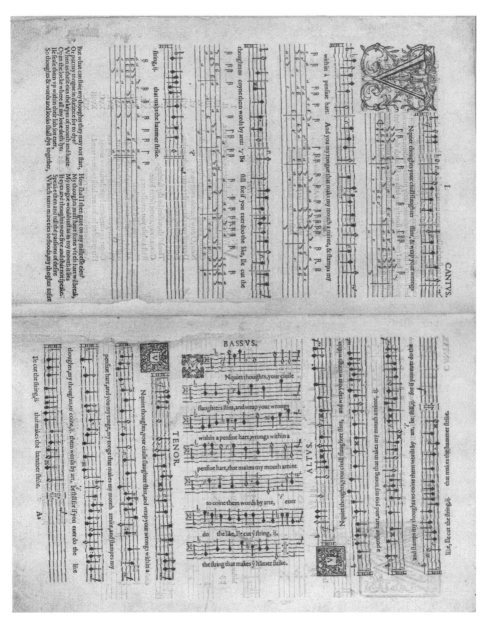

Figure 1-4. "Unquiet thoughts," from John Dowland, *The First Booke of Songes or Ayres* (1597). By permission of the British Library.

Figure 1-5. "Fain would I change that note," from Captaine Tobias Hume, *First Part of Ayres* (1605), pizzicato passage ("You must play one straine with your Fingers . . ."). By permission of the British Library.

ous songs. "Fain would I change that note" (PGM 112) requires the viol accompanist to alternate between plucking and bowing the strings: "You must play one straine with your Fingers, the other with your Bow, and so continue to the end" (Figure 1-5).

In "Alas poore men, why striue you to liue long," Hume attempts to transform a solo song into a sort of pseudo–verse anthem, the very fashionable ecclesiastical form of the time, where vocal solos with organ accompaniment alternate with full choruses. The composer notes, "The Imitation of Church Musicke, singing to the Organes, but here you must vse the Viole de Gambo for the Organe, playing the burthen strongly with the Bow, singing lowde; your Preludiums and verses are to be plaide with your fingers, singing thereto not ouer lowde, your Bow euer in your hand."

Hume's most singular conception of accompanied solo song appears under the title "The pashion of Musicke" (Sampler CD 1, track 3) in his otherwise rather less eccentric *Poeticall Musicke* of 1607. In this piece for two lyra viols, bass viol, and treble viol, the top, textless part bears the additional note, "This part is for the treble viole or the voice." Possibly the older Elizabethan tradition of singing "viol" fantasies "to the bare note," using solmization syllables, rather than playing them on instruments, prompted Hume's unusual vocal treatment. He offers no clue to his intended manner of vocal performance: *solfège* syllables or a single vowel. But such a strange "song without words" spawned no imitations among Hume's peers, or, indeed, among subsequent Baroque composers. Apart from a certain number of mid-eighteenth- and nineteenth-century *vocalises,* the technique—like other of Hume's wilder fancies—would have to await the 1900s to capture composers' imaginations.

Less musically extravagant is the opening song of *Poeticall Musicke,* "Cease leaden slumber dreaming" (Sampler CD 1, track 4), which nevertheless is headed rather portentously "A new Musicke made for the Queenes *most Excellent Maiestie, and my New-yeeres Gift to her* HIGHNES." Hume dedicated the entire collection to Anne of Denmark, wife of King James I and the center of courtly artistic enterprise, with a handwritten note in the dedication copy (preserved in the British Library), "I doe in all humylitie beseech your Ma[jes]tie that you woulde bee pleased to heare this Musick by mee; hauing excellent Instruments to performe itt." From Queen Anne he received "according to her highnes comandment and pleasure: 100 s[hillings]" for his pains (Morrow, Harris, and Traficante 2000, 11: 823).

Hume offers no clue as to what he conceived as "new" in this "new Musicke"—perhaps the unusually rich texture of three bass viols (two played lyra fashion) and voice first introduced here, an innovative combination that reappears later in the collection in other pieces such as "The pashion of Musicke." Here it is further enriched by "the Meane Lute to play the Ground if you please."

Unequivocally "new" is the form of the text, which offers a rare Jacobean example of free verse:

> Cease leaden slumber dreaming,
> my Genius presents
> the cause of sweet musickes meaning,
> now which breedes my soules content,
> and bids my Muse awake, awake,
> to heare sweete musickes note,
> that cherefully glads me so cherefully:
>
> Me thought as I lay sleeping
> dreames did enchaunt me
> with the prayse of musicke and her worth

and her eternisht fame,
but now I find indeed
my leaden windowes open,
that cherefully comforts full cherefully.

Night gloomy vaile to the morn
dreames affricht, no more no more
where sweet musicke is now still appearing,
leaue passions to perplexe,
for now my soule delights
in musicks harmony,
whose heauenly noyse,
glads soules with tongue and voyce,
for now my soule delights in heauenly noyse
of musickes sweetest joyes.

The meter and number of syllables per line fluctuate according to the length of the musical phrases, while the text setting betrays little interest in rhyme or "just note and accent": strong syllables often fall on weak beats, and lines sometimes begin or end in odd metrical positions. This suggests that "Cease leaden slumber dreaming" may have begun life as an instrumental piece such as "The pashion of Musicke," discussed earlier. There are, of course, any number of lute ayres that had originally been conceived as instrumental works—John Dowland's "Flow my tears," arranged from his wildly popular *Pavanna Lachrimae,* is probably the best-known example. The composer-arrangers generally show some concern with more obvious coordination of poetic and musical metrics. Hume does, however, craft successive stanzas consistently to move from nocturnal, dreamy slumber to cheerful wakefulness, fostered by music's power to awaken delight and solace—as Hume pretentiously puts it, "my Genius presents the cause of sweet musickes meaning."

This convincingly matches the movement of the music, which opens with a somber, imitative texture in "white notes," recalling old consort song viol accompaniments, condensed here onto two lyra viols and bass. Together with the slow-moving vocal part, laden with suspensions, it captures convincingly the gloomy, dream-fraught sleep that characterizes the beginning of all three stanzas. Then, once music "bids my Muse awake," the movement is enlivened by a characteristic turn from half notes to quarters and eighths, a quickening of the harmonic pace, and the introduction of a texture shot through with imitations on a quick, falling dotted figure reminiscent of the sprightly canzonet.

The Italian Manner

For all their striking details, however, the musical style of Hume's ayres continues to sound essentially traditional, a characterization that fits the overwhelming majority of the lute ayre repertory, which remains largely untouched by the more striking developments in solo song occurring in Italy. Examples of the innovative Italian vocal style did find their way across the Channel, however, and even into a few English song publications. Giulio Caccini's popular "Amarilli mia bella" was included in Robert Dowland's *Musical Banquet* of 1610, together with three other more or less up-do-date Italian songs. Angelo Notari's *Prime Musiche Nuove* (1613) offered additional Italian vocal pieces in various solo and duet styles. Even Robert Jones tried his hand at Italian in "Ite, caldi sospiri" and "S'amor non è" (which concluded his *A Musicall Dreame* of 1609), but with little apparent comprehension of the Italian "new music," to judge by the results. John Dowland did likewise in "Lasso! vita mia" from *A Pil-*

grimes Solace (1612), offering a hybrid of Italianate declamatory intensity and traditional English contrapuntal accompaniment.

Strikingly Italianate declamation, supported by simple, continuo-like chords, had had its moments even in Dowland's earlier songs, and later works from *A Pilgrimes Solace* take that style about as far as the composer went with it. "Tell me true love," for example, opens with a declamatory vocal line, delicately ornamented and momentarily seeming to speak the text above a largely chordal accompaniment, which hints at Italian practice. Yet the song remains firmly connected to its English roots by the frequent return to contrapuntally active accompaniment and, most notably, by the conclusion for four-part chorus, repeating the end of the solo section. This practice clearly recalls the old Elizabethan consort anthem or verse anthem traditions. Comparable five-part choral conclusions appear in the two other solo songs most akin to Italian monody in their occasional declamatory phrases and moments of continuo-like accompaniment, "Welcome black night" and "Cease these false sports."

Both of these pieces, which appear toward the end of Dowland's songwriting career in *A Pilgrimes Solace,* have a much more public aspect about them and less of the intimacy that generally characterizes the lute ayre. They may, in fact, have been intended for the wedding celebration of Lord Walden, the composer's patron, and dedicatee of the collection (Doughtie 1970, 618). It is in this more public atmosphere that the vocal elements of the emerging Baroque seem more readily to have found a place (though even there it is a long time before they seem very thoroughly at home). In the realm of more ceremonial, heroic, public spectacle such as plays, masques, and similar, larger-scale courtly collaborations of Inigo Jones and Ben Jonson, broader, more overt effects were required to reach a wider audience in less intimate halls.

Such searches led to musical solutions more closely akin to Italian musical innovation of the early 1600s. Singer-songwriters Alfonso Ferrabosco II and Nicholas Lanier led in the composition of these newfangled songs, with their more static basses, more chordal accompaniments, more *parlando* vocal lines, and often high levels of virtuoso vocal ornamentation. They were perceived, or remembered, as novel and Italianate. Recalling Lanier's music for the masque *Lovers Made Men* (1617), the Caroline edition of Ben Jonson's works claimed that "*the whole Maske was sung (after the Italian manner)* Stylo recitativo" (Spink 1974, 46). In the absence of the music, it is hard to say how much of the Italian manner it betrayed. Ian Spink has remarked that "one gets the impression that Italianate composers such as Ferrabosco and Lanier had not so much heard the 'new music' as heard *about* it" (Spink, 43).

Dowland also perceived this as something new. The preface to *A Pilgrimes Solace,* where he also inveighs against Tobias Hume for his promotion of the upstart viola da gamba, seems likewise to recognize these innovative vocal trends, and the fact that he was out of step with them.

> So haue I againe found strange entertainment since my returne; especially by the opposition of two sorts of people that shroude themselues vnder the title of Musitians. The first are some simple Cantors, or vocall singers, who though they seeme excellent in their blinde Diuision-making, are meerely ignorant, euen in the first elements of Musicke, . . . yet doe these fellowes giue their verdict of me behinde my backe, and say, what I doe is after the old manner.

After *A Pilgrimes Solace* Dowland never again ventured into print. By the time he penned the preface, the wave of lute ayre publication had crested. In comparison to newfangled notions of Italianate "recitative musicke," the delicate, refined subtleties of the lute ayre, conceived for privy chambers, seemed "after the old manner." It would be in the imposing, more public spaces such as Inigo Jones's Banqueting Hall at Whitehall that broader, bolder musical gestures, calculated to dazzle a wider audience, would find a place, in an art more characteristically "Baroque."

BIBLIOGRAPHY

Boyd, Morrison Comegys. 1974. *Elizabethan Music and Musical Criticism.* Philadelphia: University of Pennsylvania Press.

Brown, David. 2000. "Robert Jones." In *The New Grove Dictionary of Music and Musicians,* ed. Stanley Sadie, 2nd ed., 11:197–198. London: Macmillan.

Burney, Charles. [1789] 1957. *A General History of Music from the Earliest Ages to the Present Period*, ed. Frank Mercer. Reprint, New York: Dover.

Doughtie, Edward. 1970. *Lyrics from English Ayres 1596–1622.* Cambridge, Mass.: Harvard University Press.

Fischlin, Daniel. 1998. *In Small Proportions: A Poetics of the English Ayre 1596–1622.* Detroit: Wayne State University Press.

Fortune, Nigel. 1953. "Italian Secular Monody from 1600 to 1635: An Introductory Survey." *Musical Quarterly* 39: 171–95.

Greer, David. 1992. "Vocal Music I: Up to 1660." In *Music in Britain: The Seventeenth Century,* ed. Ian Spink, 138–174. Oxford: Blackwell.

Monson, Craig. 1989. "Elizabethan London." In *The Renaissance: From the 1470s to the End of the 16th Century*, ed. Iain Fenlon, 304–340. London: Macmillan.

Morrow, Michael, Collette Harris, and Frank Traficante. 2000. "Tobias Hume." In *The New Grove Dictionary of Music and Musicians,* ed. Stanley Sadie, 2nd ed., 11: 822–823. London: Macmillan.

Newcomb, Anthony. 1980. *The Madrigal at Ferrara 1579–1597.* Princeton, N.J.: Princeton University Press.

Osborn, James M. 1961. *The Autobiography of Thomas Whythorne.* Oxford: Clarendon Press.

Poulton, Diana. 1982. *John Dowland.* London: Faber and Faber.

Rosenthal, Margaret F. 1992. *The Honest Courtesan: Veronica Franco, Citizen and Writer in Sixteenth-Century Venice.* Chicago: University of Chicago Press.

Spencer, Robert. 1984. "Performance Style of the English Lute Ayre, c. 1600." *Lute Society Journal* 24: 55–68.

———. 1995. "Dowland's Dance-Songs: Those of His Compositions Which Exist in Two Versions, Songs and Instrumental Dances." In *Le concert des voix et des instruments à la Renaissance,* ed. Jean-Michel Vaccaro, 587–600. Paris: CNRS Éditions.

Spink, Ian. 1974. *English Song Dowland to Purcell.* New York: Scribner's.

Sternfeld, F. W., ed. 1968. *English Lute Songs, 1597–1632; A Collection of Facsimile Reprints.* Menston, Eng.: Scholar Press.

Strunk, Oliver. 1998. *Strunk's Source Readings in Music History,* ed. Gary Tomlinson, rev. ed., vol. 3. New York: W. W. Norton.

Walls, Peter. 1984. "'Music and Sweet Poetry'? Verse for English Lute Song and Continuo Song." *Music and Letters* 65: 237–254.

CHAPTER TWO

Love's New Voice:
Italian Monodic Song

Barbara Russano Hanning

From the beginning of human existence, singing has been a natural outlet for the expression of feelings. Probably even before the development of language, the utterances of the human voice gave vent to basic emotions—the wails of lament, the howls of pain, the giggles of joy, the quivering of fear. When combined with language, singing became a powerful means of communicating not only generalized feelings but also the most personal and subtle sentiments. By heightening and coloring the words, the singing voice can render their meaning with a force greater than they have when merely spoken. Moreover, at least since the advent of recorded history, attitudes toward singing have also reflected the cultural and intellectual concerns peculiar to a given time and place. For example, during the Middle Ages, Saint Augustine and other bishops of the Church were troubled by the sensuality of the voice in the performance of religious chant, whereas during the Renaissance the ability to sing well and effortlessly was viewed as one of the traits of the perfect courtier.

Song in Renaissance Florence

In the court culture of sixteenth-century Florence, the art of singing took on very special significance. Its position of centrality in the elite music-making of the time arose from the philosophical and intellectual conviction that the human voice, through music, provided the link between the earthly world and the cosmos. Because it was thought that the individual was connected to the entire universe through harmony—a notion uncannily similar to the most recent theories in physics about the basic substance of all matter, that is, microscopic, oscillating loops of string, called "superstrings" (Greene 1999, chapter 6)—it followed that the best way to express this connection was by giving voice to song (Tomlinson 1999, 9–14). Moreover, the artful singer could embody or control others' awareness of their connection to these invisible realms. By employing certain patterns of correspondence between micro- and macrocosm, between the motions of the human soul and the hidden concordances of the cosmos, the singer could manipulate the auditor's responses.

In general terms, this control was achieved via the Aristotelian concept of imitation or mimesis: the idea that a work of art (or in this case, a song), by observing and mimicking the motions of nature—that is, the behavior and actions of the human subject—had the ability to envoice psychological and moral reality and the power to make that reality present to others. The composer-singer, then, became the expressive agent of artistic power and the medium through which the audience-listener experienced a connection to that reality as well as to a broader, supersensible universe. That is why the driving force behind the vocal repertories of the early Baroque period was first and foremost to unleash and enable the emotional and ethical powers of song.

Let us examine the context of singing and song in sixteenth-century Florence more closely.

The Florentine Camerata

While the geographical birthplace of the new ideas about vocal music was Florence, the foremost city of the Italian Renaissance, their proximate cause was humanism, the most characteristic intellectual movement of the period. Basically, humanism involved the retrieval and revival of the culture of antiquity: the discovery of ancient works by Greco-Roman sculptors and architects and the translation of plays, poems, and treatises by Greek and Roman authors about science, mathematics, philosophy, politics, rhetoric, and, last but not least, music. This led to a reexamination of ideas about the structure of the cosmos, the nature of science, and the place of the arts in society. With regard to music, it stimulated new thinking on matters such as tuning and intervals, tonal systems and the modes, the relationship between words and music, and the connections between sounding and silent harmony, body and mind, human spirit and the universe.

Such neoclassical ideas were explored by a group of Florentine noblemen and literati who gathered around Count Giovanni de' Bardi (1534–1612) in the 1570s and 1580s. Bardi hosted this informal academy, later referred to as the Florentine Camerata (circle or coterie) or more precisely Bardi's Camerata, at his palace in Florence, where meetings were devoted to discussions about the arts and sciences in general and the virtues of ancient music in particular. Central to the discussions about ancient music were the opinions of Girolamo Mei (1519–1594), a learned Florentine scholar working in Rome who had studied every ancient musical treatise then available. He was also a classical philologist and editor of a number of Greek tragedies. In response to questions from Bardi and his friends, Mei engaged in a lively correspondence with them beginning in 1572, and his letters often appeared on the agenda of the group's meetings, where they served as a catalyst for the radical ideas about solo singing and dramatic music that we now associate with the Camerata (Palisca 1989).

Mei believed that performances of Greek tragedy had regularly been sung throughout—the actors' parts as well as the choruses—and that it was precisely the songful delivery of the words that proved so moving to ancient audiences. In his view, the Greeks had obtained extraordinarily powerful effects with their music because it had consisted of a single melody, whether sung by a soloist with or without accompaniment, or by a chorus. In either case, the performance was monodic (from the Greek *monos,* alone, and *aidein,* to sing)—that is, it consisted of a single line. And monody, he reasoned, could convey the message of the text through the natural expressiveness of the voice—via the register, rhythms, and contours of its utterance—far better than the contrived delivery of a polyphonic texture, as in the contemporary Italian madrigal, where simultaneous voices competed with one another for the listener's attention.

Galilei's Reforms

As the authoritative elder statesman of the Camerata, Mei profoundly influenced Bardi and his colleague Vincenzo Galilei (c. 1530–1591), who became the chief spokesman of the group through the publication in 1581 of his *Dialogo della musica antica e della moderna* (Dialogue on Ancient and Modern Music, so-called because it was couched in the typical form for didactic Renaissance treatises, that of a dialogue between two parties, in this case Bardi and another member of the Camerata, Piero Strozzi). Vincenzo, a lutenist, singer, composer, and theorist, came from a prominent Florentine family and was the father of the famous astronomer and physicist Galileo Galilei. The elder Galilei enjoyed the support of Count Bardi, who had sent him to Venice twenty years earlier to study with the renowned theorist and counterpoint teacher Gioseffe Zarlino.

After being influenced by Mei, however, Galilei disavowed the theory and practice of vocal counterpoint that had been codified by Zarlino in the mid-sixteenth century and published in his treatise *Le istitutione harmoniche* (Harmonic Foundations, 1558). Galilei proposed instead to revive the Greek ideal of the union of music and poetry through monody, the ancient style of singing. In the *Dialogo,* Galilei argued that only monody could accomplish music's true purpose, which was to move the listener's affections and not merely to give pleasure. Like Mei, Galilei was persuaded that the semantic and emotional message of the text was impaired by counterpoint: if, as in the fashionable madrigals and motets of the time, some voices were low and others high in register, some rose while simultaneously others descended, some moved in slow notes together with others in faster rhythms, then not only were the words distorted and the music's efficacy neutralized, but also the resulting web of contradictory impressions confused the listener and served merely to show off the cleverness of the composer and the skillfulness of the performers.

Plato had taught that song (*melos*) was comprised of words, rhythm, and pitch, in that order. It followed that poetry and music were practically synonymous and that song arose from an innate harmony within words that was muted in normal speech. For this reason, Galilei advocated the art of oratory as a model for modern musicians, urging them to imitate the manner in which successful actors delivered their lines on stage:

> In what range, high or low, how loudly or softly, how rapidly or slowly they enunciate their words . . . how one speaks when infuriated or excited; how a married woman speaks, how a girl, . . . how a lover . . . how one speaks when lamenting, when crying out, when afraid, and when exulting with joy. From these diverse observations, . . . one can deduce the way that best suits the expression of whatever meanings or emotions may come to hand. (Weiss and Taruskin 1984, 67–68)

For Galilei it is clear that "how one speaks" the words reveals their underlying emotion. For the *performers* of monody, it became a question of "how one sings" the words to disclose their innate significance. And by extension, *composers* of monody had to discover how to fashion a song so that, rather than making the music adapt to the meaning of the words, they allowed the hidden harmony of the words themselves to suggest the contours, accents, and rhythms of the music. If they succeeded in doing that, the meaning inherent in the words would be revealed, in a sense, instinctively.

The dichotomy between old and new implied in the title of Galilei's *Dialogo* requires some explanation. Galilei equated the binaries "ancient" and "modern" with "old" (in the sense of "antique" or "classical") and "new" (in the sense of au courant or fashionably modern), respectively, and he championed the qualities of the old as worthy of adoption by new or modern composers—that is, his contemporaries, whose works he thought did not measure up to the ideals of Greek music. In this way Galilei and Bardi's generation were privileging the "ancient" style over the "modern," perhaps for the first time in music history, as Renaissance artists and sculptors had already done when they rediscovered and emulated the marble statues and architectural ruins of antiquity.

After the turn of the century, however, the "new" or "modern" style of music was redefined to include those composers, like Giulio Caccini, Sigismondo d'India, and Claudio Monteverdi, who (as we shall see) had internalized the doctrines of the older generation and put them into practice, either by rejecting counterpoint altogether or by modifying its orthodox rules to allow for a more expressive "second practice." Thus, during the first decade of the seventeenth century Galilei's "moderns" were further stigmatized by the practitioners of the "new music" for being old-fashioned composers of the conservative polyphonic school.

The New Music

Le nuove musiche (New [Pieces of] Music), printed in 1602, was in fact the title of a path-breaking collection of solo songs "from which it is plausible and convenient to date the inception of genuine monody" (Fortune 1980). These were written by Giulio Caccini (1551–1618), Bardi's young protégé in the Florentine Camerata. Although Galilei had given the ideas of the Camerata their fullest literary expression, Caccini was among the first to realize them concretely in musical terms. At the time of the *Dialogo*'s publication, Mei was an infirm sixty-two-year-old musicologist, Bardi and Galilei were approaching fifty and had already done their best thinking on the subject of ancient music, and Caccini was a thirty-year-old singer from Rome in the prime of his career. Caccini had performed some of his songs for Bardi's circle and boasted in the foreword to *Le nuove musiche* that they had been received "with warm approval." By the time of their publication in 1602, however, Mei and Galilei were dead, Bardi had moved to Rome, and the Camerata had disbanded, whereas Caccini was well established in Florence as one of the leading composer-singers at court and *the* principal teacher of the new style of solo singing. In some ways, his 1602 collection of songs with its lengthy and meticulous preface about the art of singing was a monument to his mentors as well as a legacy to his students, among whom were many members of his own family.

Oral Traditions

Solo song was not new in Florence at the turn of the century. Indeed, Italian Renaissance culture had a long and venerable tradition of improvised solo singing. Among many musicians less familiar to us but renowned in their day, the painter Leonardo da Vinci (1452–1519) was famous for improvising songs and accompanying himself on the lira da braccio (a bowed stringed instrument, shaped like a violin and held on the shoulder; Figure 2-1). According to Vasari's biography of the artist, Leonardo "devoted much effort to music; above all, he determined to learn how to play the lira, since by nature he possessed a lofty and graceful spirit; he sang divinely, improvising his own accompaniment on the lira" (Winternitz 1982, xxiii). From Baldassare Castiglione's Book of the Courtier (1528) we learn that the ideal courtier had to be able to sing well from notated music (*cantar bene al libro*)—what we call singing at sight—as well as be skilled at improvised singing (*cantare alla viola per recitare*).

The notated music Castiglione had in mind undoubtedly included sacred and secular polyphony (the Latin motets, French chansons, and Italian madrigals that began to appear in printed collections during the early sixteenth century) as well as the North Italian frottola, a simpler and more popular type of part-song that was usually written for four voices but often performed by a soloist with instrumental accompaniment. Castiglione clearly reserved his highest praise for the second category, the skill of improvising songs *alla viola* (Haar 1983, 170–175). This type of song belonged to the older and far nobler oral tradition, one that included Leonardo, to be sure, but also dated back to the legendary bards of antiquity such as Apollo and Orpheus, who not only invented their own rhymes but also fused them with lyric melody (improvised to the lyre) in the heat of performance.

The new Italian monody at the beginning of the seventeenth century, then, had roots in an oral tradition of improvised solo singing which, by its very nature, focused on the per-

Figure 2-1.   Recitation "alla viola" (c. 1500). Vienna, Austrian National Library, Manuscript and Incunabula Department, *Sign. Ink. 5.G.9.* Reprinted with permission.

former. Whether singing one's own poetry or that of someone else from memory, it was the performer who made the connection between poetry and music palpable for the listener and bridged the gap between the significance of the words and the convincing communication of their meaning to an audience. The performer's voice and the vocal rendition of the words were at the center of the listener's experience of a song. Indeed, before the advent of printing and the spread of literacy, oral performance was the essential condition of poetry as well as of music. In both the process of creating it and of rendering it perceptible, the poet moved in a world that was primarily auditory rather than optical, and operated in sound and time rather than in architectonic form and space (Hanson 2003). This was the context for the magnificent epic poems of the Middle Ages and Renaissance.

In the sixteenth century performers known as *cantastorie,* or singers of tales, songfully recited from memory portions of works such as Boiardo's *Orlando innamorato* and Ariosto's *Orlando furioso;* some singers were known to invent their own stories and lyrics in rhyme. They also either devised original melodies or relied on stock tunes, called *arie,* that functioned as frameworks for poems having a specific structure, such as the *ottave rime* (eight-line stanzas) of the epic, or the sections of a sonnet (more will be said about ottava rima below). This repertory of arie comprised the melodic-harmonic shapes that served as a formal basis for communicating the poem. But in another sense, because the singer, like any good orator, delivered the words in a distinctive individual manner, with variation and embellishment, the performance itself gave the music "aria," that is, character and persuasive force.

Vincenzo Galilei, himself a *cantastorie,* was keenly aware of this oral tradition and the subtle and flexible dialogue that took place between performer and audience. Therefore, he urged the revival not only of ancient monody but also of the traditional manner of singing strophic poetry *su l'aria,* in the quasi-improvisational style of the performers of epic poems. This was not at all contradictory to Mei's or Bardi's teachings, for the words were still regarded as being in themselves music: meaningful tonal substance with varying rhythm, pitch, and inflection. Even though the syllables were guided in their musical succession by the "fixed" melodic contour and given harmonic progression of a suitable aria, accompanied only by a few simple chords, yet the details of their delivery were enormously varied and differed with each stanza as the performer calculated their effect and observed their impact on the listeners. Caccini's *Nuove musiche* must be understood against the background of this oral culture, one in which the originality of the musico-poetic effort lay at least partially in the manner in which the singer related to his audience and was influenced by their response.

Caccini's Monodies

Caccini's epoch-making collection consists of twenty-two songs for solo voice, representing two distinct poetic forms then in use by the fashionable poets of the day: the madrigal and the air. The madrigal, characteristic of Giambattista Guarini (author of the highly influential pastoral tragicomedy *Il pastor fido,* The Faithful Shepherd), is a brief lyric poem with mixed seven- and eleven-syllable lines. Musically, it was set in a through-composed fashion (see, for example, "Amarilli mia bella," Sampler CD 1, track 5). This gave the composer-singer the opportunity to fashion the song according to the changing sentiments of the poem, with its varying accents, grammatical inflections, and semantic progression.

The air (Caccini himself used the word *aria*) is characteristic of Gabriello Chiabrera, a court poet and important force behind the classicizing of Italian poetry after Greek models. It is a lengthy poem comprised of several strophes, each having the same number of lines. The lines are uniform in their meter and rhyme patterns (see, for example, "Belle rose porporine," PGM 103). In an air, the music of the first stanza serves for all subsequent strophes, with the understanding that the performer may inflect the melody slightly differently with each repetition, or may vary it substantially, depending upon the pacing and mood of the poem. "Chi mi confort'ahimè" (PGM 103) is a good example of the latter: the progressive rhyme scheme (ABA BCB CDC, etc.) invites the performer to depart increasingly from the written music, until the final stanza, which closes the progression with an end rhyme (EFEF) in the traditional pattern of *terze rime,* and therefore requires Caccini to provide different music.

Caccini's airs are, on the whole, less affective and more playful than the madrigals. He wrote them, he said, to provide a way of occasionally relieving depression. In this type of lively air, exemplified by "Belle rose porporine" (on a canzonet text by Chiabrera), the embellishments tend to be repeated from one stanza to another: because they accentuate the same syllables in each line according to meter rather than meaning, they remain valid for all stanzas.

While the airs may be seen to provide a link, however tenuous, with the time-honored Italian tradition of improvised singing *a la viola,* Caccini's *madrigals* deliberately break with the past. A true pupil of Bardi and Galilei, Caccini vehemently criticizes the polyphonic madrigal of the sixteenth century for being ineffectual and bankrupt of expression: "Having observed . . . that such music and musicians afforded no pleasure beyond that which pleasant sounds could give—solely to the sense of hearing, since they could not move the intellect without the words being understood—it occurred to me to introduce a kind of music in which one could, as it were, speak musically" (Hitchcock in Caccini 1970, 44).

In his preface to the collection, Caccini continues to articulate the key elements of his new style, which may be summarized as follows: enabling the words to be understood by "speaking in tones," following Plato and other philosophers ("according to whom music consists of speech, rhythm, and, lastly pitch—not the contrary"); focusing on the power of the solo voice "to move the affect of the soul" and "to imitate the ideas behind the words" by "hiding the art of counterpoint" and avoiding harmonic complication; and finally, "employing . . . a certain noble *sprezzatura*" or effortless grace through which the performer is able to convince us of the sincerity and naturalness of the sentiments being expressed (the word was coined by Castiglione, in his Book of the Courtier, to connote an unforced manner, the opposite of affectation). All of this is to be accomplished in a bare, two-voiced texture polarized between voice and bass, with the lower part acting as support for the upper rather than standing as an equal participant. Caccini, incidentally, played his own accompaniments on the archlute (also known as the chitarrone) or theorbo, which is the only instrument he mentions in his preface (see Plates 3 and 4).

Many historians have suggested that Caccini's claims for innovation be taken with a grain of salt, given the preexistence of solo singing as a performance style, his reputation for vanity, and the intense competition among musicians at the Florentine court (Carter 1984). What does seem incontrovertible, however, is his role at the turn of the century in transforming the entire premise of composition by rejecting the artifice of part-writing, with its pictorialisms, metaphors, antitheses, concetti, and the other devices characteristic of the polyphonic madrigal, in favor of a simple vocal line that declaimed the text clearly and flexibly above a spare chordal accompaniment. Quite remarkably, he even transformed the look of music on the printed page, inventing an economical notation in score format and coding the "hidden" inner voices with figures that indicated the desired intervals above the unobtrusive bass notes or basso continuo (Figure 2-2). And it was through monody, perhaps more than through any other medium, that the new Baroque style based on the basso continuo texture spread throughout Italy.

In keeping with Caccini's emphasis on the solo voice and his preeminence as a virtuoso singer was his preoccupation with embellishment. He devised a new vocabulary of words to describe his special array of ornaments, and he created symbols to denote their placement in the music. In his view, ornaments were key to "moving the affections." Caccini had two objectives in publishing these pieces and the didactic discourse that forms the preface. First, he wished to ensure that the songs were performed properly, especially with regard to the judicious application of ornaments. Second, he was determined to explain the theory behind his new style of composition as well as the artistry behind his impeccable manner of performing his songs. Thus, during the course of his lengthy preface, Caccini speaks in turn as a voice teacher, as a singer and vocal coach, and also as a composer (Hitchcock 1970, 389). Indeed, he manages to reconcile and integrate two apparently antithetical realities: his career as a virtuoso singer and his commitment to the Platonic ideals of the Camerata.

The very opening of Caccini's madrigal "Amarilli mia bella" (Sampler CD 1, track 5) illustrates several essential features of his new style. Instead of rising—a more usual way for a melody to begin—the first phrase ("My beautiful Amaryllis") falls from its highest point, outlining a descending fourth. Rhetorically, the poet addresses the beloved, claiming her attention with an exclamation. Musically, the melody bursts forth with a long note at the top

Figure 2-2. "Amarilli mia bella," from Giulio Caccini, *Le nuove musiche* (1602). By permission of the British Library.

32

Example 2-1.   Caccini: "Amarilli mia bella," mm. 1–10.

of its range—only once does the voice go higher by a step, and that not until the final phrase in a kind of delirium of lyricism. The line then cascades down through successive leaps of adjacent fourths before landing on "bella," a perfect fourth below its starting point (Example 2-1).

In keeping with his principles of speaking in tones and imitating the ideas behind the words, Caccini not only follows the declamation of the syllables but also fashions the melodic contour to convey their emotional impact. This he does by mimicking the enthusiastic delivery of a lover anxious to make his point, with the question "Don't you believe that you are my love?" The effect is further enhanced in performance by the application of one of Caccini's trademark and most subtle ornaments, the *esclamazione,* which he defines as "a certain strengthening [or reinforcement] of the relaxed voice" (this is interpreted on the recording as a gentle attack on the opening note, with a vocal tone that grows more urgent as it progresses). By avoiding more ostentatious ornaments (such as roulades and other rapid figuration) and their excessive use, adhering to a fairly narrow range (as befits the ordinary speaking voice), and employing word repetition only for rhetorical emphasis rather than for purely musical elaboration, Caccini the composer as well as Caccini the performer allows the words to "speak" for themselves.

In a sense, Caccini is a transitional figure in the art of song, personifying a crucial moment in the progression from orality to literacy: the moment when the focus shifts from performer to composer, when the singer becomes the interpreter of the composer's fixed musical notation, and the composer attempts to control the musical performance to a higher degree than ever before. Caccini acknowledges this on the title page of his second collection of songs, published in 1614: "New [Pieces of] Music and a New Way of Writing Them Down . . . in which all the subtleties of this art can be learned without having to hear the composer sing" (Figure 2-3). In effect, Caccini the *composer,* having analyzed and adapted the art of Caccini the *singer,* manifests a new attitude toward what had been an oral tradition. As a result, his new pieces, after being performed and circulated for more than a decade and finally published as examples for all to study, have become frozen performances, waiting to be newly envoiced.

Figure 2-3. Title page from Giulio Caccini, *Nuove musiche e nuova maniera . . .* (1614). By permission of the British Library.

Example 2-2. D'India: "Cruda Amarilli," mm. 1–8.

D'India's Contributions

The Sicilian nobleman Sigismondo d'India (c. 1582–1629) must have encountered Caccini during his 1608 visit to Florence, where his own Caccini-style madrigals were performed and admired before being published in his first collection of songs (*Le musiche,* 1609). By this time, monody was all the rage, and d'India composed every kind of song found in the early seventeenth-century monodic repertory, including arias, strophic variations, dramatic laments (like "Piange madonna," PGM 103), and dance-like canzonettas. Unlike Caccini, however, d'India did not confine his efforts to solo song but also continued the practice of writing polyphonic madrigals in the style of older contemporaries such as Jacques de Wert, Don Carlo Gesualdo, Luca Marenzio, and Claudio Monteverdi.

However, the opening of d'India's monodic setting of the famous Guarini text "Cruda Amarilli" ("Cruel Amaryllis"; Sampler CD 1, track 6) immediately reveals a kinship with Caccini (Example 2-2). The exclamatory address of the beloved, the descending melodic contour (again outlining a perfect fourth), and the declamatory rhythms are all reminiscent of the beginning of Caccini's "Amarilli mia bella" (see Example 2-1), although the texts ultimately have very different sentiments. Consequently, d'India knowingly indulges in a typical *concetto* of the polyphonic madrigalist when he inflects the word "cruda" (cruel) with a dissonant harmony (as Monteverdi had done in his polyphonic setting of the same text, published a few years earlier). D'India also emulates Caccini's practice of writing out his ornaments, making them an integral part of the composition rather than entrusting their placement to the performer. In general, however, d'India's style is more extravagant and audacious than Caccini's, since it includes more word repetition and chromaticism. Still, d'India's goal is the same as that of his Florentine colleague: to move the affections of the soul.

The Spread of Monody

Monody remained centered in Florence until 1620 or so, and the success of Caccini's publication was a major factor in the genre's popularity. From Florence the new vocal style traveled to Venice and other northern Italian cities, as well as to Rome, where Caccini spent time as Bardi's secretary in 1592 and where his performances had inspired interest in his songs even before they were published. By the middle of the seventeenth century more than a hundred composers, both professionals and amateurs, had produced entire volumes of monodies, in some cases as many as six each.

The strophic aria, with its noble ancestry in the sixteenth-century oral tradition, gradually became more popular than the solo madrigal, which faded away in the early 1630s. This concentration on the aria goes hand in hand with the rise of instrumental music during the early Baroque Period, for both depended heavily on the idea of successive variations, which in turn reflected a new interest in structure and formal expansion. In instrumental music, where the absence of a text presented composers with the challenge of organizing their works in a logical and meaningful fashion, theme and variations proved to be an especially effective way of imparting coherence to a lengthy formal design.

Frescobaldi's Song Publications

It is not surprising, then, that the chief exponent of instrumental music in Rome, Girolamo Frescobaldi (1583–1643), published among his vocal works two volumes of *Arie musicali*. The collections contain a total of forty-three compositions, including many examples of strophic variations. Frescobaldi was lured to Florence by Ferdinando II, Grand Duke of Tuscany, who made "the prince of Italian organists" the most highly paid musician at the Medici court between 1628 and 1634, a period when Florence was suffering a dire economic crisis as well as outbreaks of plague. Nonetheless, Frescobaldi published both volumes of his *Arie* in 1630, during the peak of the bleak times. It may be that he was inspired by that city's distinctive musical history and, more specifically, by its song culture. In any case, the printing of two volumes of song simultaneously was an unusual move, even granting the popularity of the genre (Gallico in Gallico and Patuzzi 1998; Hammond 1977; Hill 1987). In dedicating one of the volumes to Grand Duke Ferdinando, the composer acknowledged that it was "fruit born of the benevolent influence" of his Florentine patron, whose emblem appears on the title page (Figure 2-4). That is not to suggest that Frescobaldi had never composed monody until he came to Florence. On the contrary, there is ample evidence that he had assimilated the new style in Rome and, after cultivating it there, brought it back to Florence in full bloom. Thus began a new stage in solo chamber singing in both Rome and Florence.

Some of the different types of strophic aria forms represented in Frescobaldi's *Arie musicali* also appear in his keyboard compositions. Such is the case with the Ruggiero, one of the stock tunes used for singing an *ottava rima,* an eight-line poetic stanza employed as the main unit in epic poetry. The performer reciting the epic verses could follow the same melodic outline—and, if accompanied, the same harmonic progressions—for stanza after stanza, improvising variations as necessary and appropriate (Ruggiero was, in fact, the name of a legendary heroic knight in epics by Boiardo, Ariosto, and Tasso, and the aria may have been associated with one or more of Ruggiero's stanzas). The bass and harmony of the air are always recognizable in Frescobaldi's variations on the Ruggiero theme, but the melody is often obscured by figuration. This is the case with the aria "Ti lascio, anima mia" from Frescobaldi's second volume of *Arie musicali* (PGM 103). The piece is subtitled "Sopra l'aria di Ruggieri" (on the Ruggiero air). The poem upon which the song is composed consists of a single stanza of eight lines, with the rhyme scheme AB AB AB CC. Each line has eleven syllables. This is the poetic form of the time-honored ottava, but in this case the verse is not taken from an epic. Rather, it is a *partenza,* a type of lyric poem dating from the Middle Ages that describes the anguish of secret lovers who must part at dawn:

Figure 2-4.   Frontispiece from Girolamo Frescobaldi, *Primo libro d'arie . . .* (1630). Reprinted by permission of Studio per Edizione Scelte, Florence.

Ti lascio, anima mia, giunta è quell'hora.	A	PRIMA PARTE
L'hora, Ohimè, che mi chiama alla partita.	B	

(I leave you, my soul, the hour has come.
The hour, alas, that summons my departure.)

Io parto io parto, Ohimè, convien ch'io mora,	A	SECONDA PARTE
perchè convien partir da te, mia vita.	B	

(I leave, alas, convinced that I will die
because I am forced to part from you, my life.)

Ah pur troppo è 'l dolor ch'entro m'accora;	A	TERZA PARTE
non mi dar col tuo duol nova ferita.	B	

(Ah! Grief already penetrates me all too well;
do not give me, through your sorrow, a new wound.)

Deh non languir, cor mio, ch'al mio partire	C	QUARTA PARTE
mi duole il tuo dolor più che 'l morire.	C	

(Oh! Do not languish, my love, for at my parting
your suffering grieves me more than death.)

The musical structure, however, is not affected by the nonepic nature of its context; the poem still fits into the musical design of the Ruggiero. The traditional aria di Ruggiero has four phrases, ending respectively on the bass notes G, D, D, and G (Example 2-3, a). Frescobaldi superimposes the poem on this preexistent structure, using a half line of verse for each phrase of the music. Thus, the first pair of lines "uses up" one complete statement of the aria, and every subsequent pair requires a repetition of that music (Example 2-3, b). In the score Frescobaldi designates each repetition of the aria *parte,* or variation. Each *parte* is the same length (that is, four phrases long) and has the same harmonic structure. The melody, however, is varied. Thus each *parte* constitutes a different variation on the aria di Ruggiero. Only the last section has an optional extension, a repetition of the final line of the poem, set to phrases three and four of the aria.

Thus Frescobaldi's song, an aria for solo voice and basso continuo, is a composed set of variations, or *partite,* on a preexistent theme, the *aria di Ruggiero.* In this way, it resembles the improvised elaborations of the old *cantastorie.* As with many a jazz tune, the harmonies remain the same, but the melody is gracefully varied and flexibly ornamented according to the changing accents and meaning of the text. Like Caccini, Frescobaldi avoids meaningless word repetition and notates a large number of rhythmically elastic ornaments, carefully placing them either on accented syllables at the end of each verse or on affective words, such as "Ohimè" (alas), "parto" (I leave), "mora" (I may die), and so forth. Unlike Caccini, however, Frescobaldi employs a good deal of chromaticism in his melody (particularly in the third and fourth variations), a feature that betrays his Ferrarese origins.

Although Frescobaldi also wrote madrigals and other types of monody, and chamber works for two and three voices with basso continuo, he deployed the variations procedure we have just discussed to compose many of the vocal arie in his collections (see PGM 103), using the Ruggiero and similar popular patterns such as the romanesca and passacaglia. Most importantly for the development of instrumental music, Frescobaldi borrowed many of the vocal harmonic formulas for his keyboard works, enabling him to write relatively long sets of variations (his partite have as many as twelve or more sections) that explored the expressive and technical possibilities of the instrument without having to sacrifice logic or coherence.

Example 2-3.   a) The Ruggiero theme; b) Frescobaldi: "Ti lascio, anima mia," mm. 1–8.

Instrumental Music

Although some instrumental music had its origins in time-honored vocal forms like the aria, other types had roots in dance music or in the idiom of specific instruments. Such is the case with the collections of music for theorbo by the prolific composer and performer Johann Hieronymous (Giovanni Girolamo) Kapsberger (c. 1580–1651), a colleague of Frescobaldi's in Rome. Kapsberger was most responsible for the development of the theorbo as a solo instrument. In fact, his output for theorbo parallels Frescobaldi's for harpsichord in its expressive virtuosity, its daring originality, and its exploitation of the instrument's idiomatic qualities. A successor to the Renaissance lute and guitar, the theorbo was related to the archlute (a large lute) or chitarrone (meaning big guitar). As such, it had a wider range and greater volume and versatility than its smaller counterparts. It was recognized as the ideal portable instrument for a solo singer's self-accompaniment as well as a stunning vehicle for a solo player's virtuosic performance (see Plates 5 and 6). Like the lute, the theorbo used the system of notation known as tablature, which shows not the pitch of each sound (as in normal score notation) but rather the position of the fingers on the strings, graphically represented by parallel horizontal lines, and, more precisely, on the frets required to produce each pitch (Figure 2-5).

Kapsberger's *Libro primo d'intavolatura di chitarone* (1604), the first of his seven collections published for theorbo and lute, begins appropriately with a toccata (from *toccare,* to touch or play), a seemingly spontaneous "warm-up" piece that serves to display the breadth and sonoric capabilities of the instrument (PGM 103). The toccata's opening arpeggios soon dissolve into an introspective, tuneful section with more complicated textures that provide both a melody and harmonic support. Both segments demonstrate the idiomatic style of broken-chord figuration common to the lute, chitarrone, and other plucked string instruments. Hence the toccata exemplifies the type of Baroque instrumental piece that seems to have sprung from the qualities that reside in the instrument on which it was performed.

Other pieces, such as sonatas for violin or other bowed instruments capable of producing a singing tone, imitated the new monodic style of solo song, with its graceful and expressive ornaments. Like solo song, the sonatas required a basso continuo accompaniment. Still another category of instrumental composition was dance music, which was adopted equally for solo and ensemble performance. Kapsberger's *Libro primo* contains several dance pieces— stately passamezzos followed by lively gagliards—that retain all the rhythmic and motivic regularity of the genre (PGM 103). Like the partite discussed above, these too are often extended in length through the process of harmonic variations on a bass pattern. Kapsberger's Passamezzo (PGM 103), for instance, includes three equally long variations in contrasting styles. The last displays a shift to minor mode. It is likely that the variations were originally improvised by the composer and then notated (or "intabulated") and published (Figure 2-5), a tradition that survived until Bach's day.

The gradual progression from improvisation to composition in instrumental music parallels the progression from oral to written performance in vocal music. Both developments reflect the productive tension that existed between spontaneity on the one hand and fixed musical content on the other. In a sense, monody was a meeting ground between the oral tradition and the notated tradition because it represented, at least initially, the composer's written interpretation of an oral performance. But monody encompassed many different styles of solo singing: from Caccini's quasi-improvisational aria "Chi mi confort'ahimè" (PGM 103) to the lyrical madrigal "Amarilli mia bella" (Sampler CD 1, track 5) to the lively, dance-like, strophic song "Belle rose porporine" (PGM 103). All reflected the humanist goals of imitating, expressing, and arousing the emotions—emotions that stem from the rhythmic patterns and melodic inflections of the natural voice.

Figure 2-5. Lute tablature from Johann Hieronymous Kapsberger, *Libro primo d'intavolatura di chitarone* (1604). Courtesy of the Irving S. Gilmore Music Library, Yale University, New Haven, Connecticut.

Peri's Theory of Recitative

The most radical solution to the problem of envoicing the emotions implied by a given text was the invention of recitative, the species of monody which sought to eradicate altogether the distinction between speaking and singing, between words and music. It did so by synthesizing speaking and singing into an inseparable whole, thus creating a language that was sui generis—more than speech, but less than song. As Jacopo Peri explained in the preface to his first opera, *Euridice,* published in Florence in 1600:

> Discarding every other manner of singing hitherto heard, I devoted myself wholly to seeking out the kind of imitation necessary for these poems. And I considered that the kind of voice that the ancients assigned to singing, which they called diastematic (that is, sustained or suspended), could at times be hastened and made to take an intermediate course, lying between the slow and sustained movements of song and the swift and rapid movements of speech, and that it could be adapted to my purpose . . . and made to approach that other kind of voice, which they called continuous. . . . I recognized likewise that in our speech some words are so intoned that harmony can be based upon them, and that in the course of speaking we pass through many others that are not so intoned. . . . Keeping in mind those inflections and accents that serve us in our grief, in our joy, and in similar states, I made the bass move in time with these, either faster or slower according to the affections. (Adapted from Brown's translation of Peri 1600, facing Plate II)

It is apparent that Peri's theory of recitative was based on an interpretation of the mechanics of sounding speech, which he believed (in good humanist fashion, along with Bardi's Camerata before him) could reveal the state of mind of the speaker. The goal of the new theatrical style, or *stile rappresentativo,* was to imitate or capture those qualities of delivery that betrayed the affections with which the words were uttered. In the view of Peri and his Florentine colleagues, the style was capable of representing or acting out the emotions in music. And the principal tool for accomplishing this goal was recitative. Peri's preface to *Euridice,* like Caccini's preface to *Le nuove musiche,* articulated not only a belief in the principles of ancient rhetoric but also a new analytic attitude toward vocal performance. The result was a specifically musical realization of sounding speech, one that Peri managed to encode in notation in the printed score.

Monteverdi's Operatic Style

Opera spread from Florence, where it was exclusively a court entertainment, to Rome, and eventually to Venice, where the first public operas were produced as commercial ventures in the 1630s. Claudio Monteverdi (1567–1643) must have obtained and studied a copy of the score of Peri's *Euridice,* for a comparison between that work and Monteverdi's early operas (*Orfeo,* 1607, and *Arianna,* 1608) reveals that he understood and pursued the premises and techniques of Peri's recitative style. A further link between the two composers is their close collaboration with the same librettist, court poet Ottavio Rinuccini (1562–1621), who established with *Euridice* and *Arianna* many of the lasting conventions of dramatic *poesia per musica.* By the time Monteverdi completed his last operas, *Il ritorno d'Ulisse in patria* (The Return of Ulysses to His Homeland, 1641) and *L'incoronazione di Poppea* (The Coronation of Poppea, 1642), he had profoundly refined the medium of recitative, imbuing it with great flexibility and dramatic power.

Penelope's opening monologue from Act 1 of *Il ritorno d'Ulisse,* "Di misera Regina" (PGM 103), illustrates this well, since it ranges over a broad spectrum of emotions. At first, the long-suffering Penelope broods over her seemingly endless separation from Ulysses, her self-pity gradually giving way to anger and resentment at the thought that her enforced chastity was indirectly caused by the errant ways of Helen of Troy. The low range, lethargic pace, and descending lines of the music underscore her misery and depressed state. The slug-gish harmonies, too, reflect her somber mood, which is emphasized by dissonance on the re-peated word "mai" (never) and her exclamation "lunga ahi troppo" (ah, too long!—a com-ment on the duration of her misfortune). As she rehearses the events that have reduced her to this point, however, her voice rises, her speech becomes more agitated, the stepwise melody admits larger intervals, and the harmonies quicken. Her accusations become bitter:

Ulisse accorto e saggio,	Ulysses cunning and wise,
tu che punir gli adulteri ti vanti	you, who boasted of punishing adulterers:
aguzzi l'armi e susciti le fiamme	you hone your weapons and fan the flames [of war]
per vendicar gl'errori	in order to avenge the errant ways
d'una profuga Greca;	of a fugitive Grecian woman;

These words are hurled at her absent spouse in a breathless torrent of elided verses, and she reaches the highest point of her melody so far, before she succumbs once more to despair:

e intanto lasci	at the same time leaving
la tua casta consorte	your own chaste consort
fra nemici rivali	amid enemy rivals
in dubbio dell'honore,	in dubious honor and
in forse a morte.	perhaps in mortal danger.

Finally, at the end of this first phase of her monologue, Penelope briefly suppresses her feel-ings and reflects more calmly on her situation: "Ogni partenza attende desiato ritorno, Tu sol del tuo tornar perdesti il giorno" (Every departure expects the desired return; you alone have failed to come back). The idea of Ulysses' return becomes a refrain that recurs several times and serves to hold together an otherwise rambling piece. Musically set to brief moments of lyricism, it also reminds us that Penelope is clinging to the fragile hope of Ulysses' homecoming.

Monteverdi thus traces the progress of Penelope's emotions by painstakingly reflecting in the musical score every aspect of the singer's recitation: how slowly or quickly to utter the syl-lables, when to stammer in word repetition or to spew out a flood of syllables fluently, when to breathe and for how long, when to raise or lower the voice's register, how to mimic a sob, a sigh, an exclamation. In short, he is a consummate master of recitative, carefully analyzing and faithfully reproducing the nuances of the voice as it, in turn, divulges the passions of the speaker's soul.

The Development of the Aria

Although a wonderful example of expressive recitative, Penelope's monologue is often called an aria by historians, in the sense that it is a set dramatic piece that serves to introduce us to Penelope's character and portray her state of mind. However, by the late seventeenth and early eighteenth centuries, arias in an opera, cantata, or oratorio had become virtuosic vehi-cles for singers and musical elaborations of a single passion—rage, lament, desire, joy, and so forth. Each passion was associated with a certain set of musical attributes. As such, arias were unified in content and repetitive in form (often they were set over an ostinato bass or cast in the rounded da-capo form of A-B-A). They also made use of a minimal amount of text—sometimes only four lines of poetry, which was expanded via the repetition of individual words and phrases. The aria functioned as a musical portrait of a particular emotion, much as a cinematic close-up or a slow-motion effect in film today permits a lyrical moment to be arrested and amplified outside the framework of the plot. It was a musical freeze-frame.

The increasingly long and conventionalized aria became the psychological and expressive focus of opera. Recitative, by contrast, lost its original function as sounding speech capable of providing insight into the character's soul and stirring the listener's affections. Rather, recitative became a convenient vehicle for the perfunctory delivery of large segments of text, facilitating the forward motion of the drama. Thus, the musical styles of recitative and aria diverged. Though they were originally contiguous on an imaginary line that stretched between the opposite poles of speech and song—one style being essentially songful recitation, the other, speech-like song—they eventually moved away from one another and took up positions at either end of the musical continuum, in keeping with their newly polarized functions.

The Chamber Cantata

The initial stage of this polarization may be seen in monodic chamber cantatas of the mid-seventeenth century by composers such as Luigi Rossi (1597–1653) and Giacomo Carissimi (1605–1674) in Rome and Barbara Strozzi (1619–1677) in Venice. As settings of intimate poetic texts, these works were still indebted to Caccini, since they are characterized by intense lyricism projected by a solo voice over a simple basso continuo. The chamber cantata "Lagrime mie" by Barbara Strozzi illustrates this style well (Sampler CD 1, track 7). Although the work contains both recitative and aria, as is typical for chamber cantatas of the period, the distinction between the two styles is not always clear-cut. Rather, the styles sometimes merge fluidly into one another and sometimes pull apart, depending on the shape and content of the poetry. Thus it is especially important to understand the structure and meaning of the piece's text, which is probably by Giulio Strozzi (1583–1652), a prominent figure in Venetian intellectual and musical circles who also may have been Barbara's adoptive father (see Chapter 7). For convenience, the continuous stream of varied verses has been grouped into five sections below. In a later cantata, by Alessandro Scarlatti, for example, the groups might have formed the basis for a series of separate recitative and aria movements. Here they are only subtly differentiated in musical style. (The letters and numbers to the right of the poetry indicate the rhyme scheme and the number of syllables in each line of verse. Uppercase and lowercase letters also conventionally indicate the longer and shorter lines, respectively.)

1.	Lagrime mie, a che vi trattenete?	A 11
	Perchè non isfogate il fier' dolore	B 11
	che mi toglie 'l respiro e opprime il core?	B 11
	(My tears, what holds you back?	
	Why don't you vent the fierce pain	
	that takes away my breath and weighs on my heart?)	
2a.	Lidia, che tant'adoro,	c 7
	perchè un guardo pietoso, ahimè, mi donò	D 11
	il paterno rigor l'imprigionò.	D 7
	(Lydia, whom I adore so much,	
	because, alas, she gave me a pitying look	
	was imprisoned by her harsh father.)	
2b.	Tra due mura rinchiusa	e 7
	sta la bella innocente,	f 7
	dove giunger non può raggio di sole;	G 11
	e quel che più mi duole	g 7
	ed accresc'il mio mal, tormenti, e pene,	H 11

è che per mia cagione	i 7
prova male il mio bene.	h 7

(Locked up between two walls
the innocent beauty remains
where no ray of sunshine can penetrate;
and what pains me most
and worsens my sickness, torments, and suffering
is that because of me
my beloved suffers.)

3.	E voi, lumi dolente, non piangete?	A 11
	Lagrime mie, a che vi trattenete?	A 11

(And you, my grieving eyes, you do not weep?
My tears, what holds you back?)

"aria" 4a.	Lidia, ahimè, veggo mancarmi,	j 8
	l'idol mio, che tanto adoro,	k 8
	stà colei tra dure marmi;	j 8
	per cui spiro e pur non moro?	k 8

(Lydia, alas! I see you are lost to me;
my idol, whom I so adore,
remains between hard marble walls;
for her I sigh, yet do not die?)

4b.	Se la morte m'è gradita,	l 8
	hor che son privo di speme,	m 8
	deh! toglieteme la vita,	l 8
	(ve ne prego) aspre mie pene.	m 8

(Since I welcome death,
now that I'm deprived of hope,
oh! take away my life—
I beg you—my harsh torment.)

5a.	Ma ben m'accorgo, che per tormentarmi	N 11
	maggiormente, la sorte	o 7
	mi niega anco la morte.	o 7

(Still, I realize that to torment me
the more, fate
even denies me death.)

5b.	Se dunqu'è vero, o Dio,	p 7
	e sol del pianto mio,	p 7
	il rio destino ha sete,	a 7
	Lagrime mie, a che vi trattenete?	A 11

(If then it is true, O God,
that only for my tears
does cruel fate thirst,
then, tears of mine, why do you hold back?)

The poetry is a mixture of madrigal and aria verse. The madrigal verse uses seven- and eleven-syllable lines with no regular rhyme scheme. The aria verse employs stanzas of equal lines, in this case eight syllables each, with a regular pattern of rhyme (here assigned the interlacing scheme j k j k, l m l m). Indeed, the composer herself writes the word "aria" in the score over the fourth section, where the same music serves for both stanzas of text (4a and 4b, in the diagram).

The first section, in which the distraught lover addresses his tears, begins with an astonishingly doleful wail. This bursts upon the ear at the top of the vocal register and makes its way downward over a stationary harmony, faltering in its syncopated rhythms and prolonging the most excruciating dissonances. We have seen this opening contour before, in madrigals by Caccini and d'India, but never before have the words been so protracted, the effect so stunning, the affect so close to lamentation. Is it recitative or aria? It has the rhythmic flexibility and harmonic language of the most expressive recitative. Yet it betrays the word repetition and intervallic melodic motion associated with aria.

In the second section, a narration about the imprisoned beloved, there is similar ambiguity. The first sentence (2a) is tunefully set, with graceful melismas on "adoro" and "pietoso," and a striking, scalewise descent on "rigor." The second sentence partakes more of the speech-like quality of recitation, but the static bass line characteristic of recitative yields to more rapid harmonic motion as the section progresses. In fact, this type of melodious speech, or speech-like melody, is often called *arioso,* which reflects the aria-like lyricism of the melody where it departs from the short note values and repeated pitches imitative of ordinary speech.

However, the music of the next two lines (section 3) shifts into triple meter, which is *never* a feature of recitative, expressive or otherwise. And the degree of sequential motivic play as well as word repetition indicates that the music has swung away from speech and moved toward song: "E voi lumi dolenti, dolenti, e voi lumi dolenti, dolenti." The bass, too, abandons the realm of recitative and progresses purposefully downward by step, outlining three tetrachords (two diatonic and one chromatic), until the text of the opening line returns and the reprise of the wailing music reinforces the narrator's distress.

At this point, halfway through the work, the poetic and musical styles converge into the section that Strozzi calls an "aria" (section 4)—a strophic song with regular phrases, steady rhythms, and melodic and harmonic motion that remains independent of the words without distorting them. It reflects the lover's interior drama as he entertains soothing thoughts about death as a welcome escape. But the calmer mood is broken poetically by the word "ma" (but), which opens the last section, and musically by the reversion to recitative style, as the poet realizes that his longing for death is to remain unfulfilled. However, once again, just as at the midpoint of the cantata, the composer slips into lilting triple meter, with sequential melodic and harmonic motion and lyrical word repetition. This leads to the third and final invocation of tears, which will provide the desired release from grief. Thus the cantata ends as it began, with a compelling cry of lament. This supplies symmetry and closure to a work that explores the gamut of emotions between despair and resignation.

Together with other mid-century composers, Barbara Strozzi composed, published, and presumably performed many such intimate chamber cantatas for solo voice. Each one represents a miniature drama that movingly captures and projects the mostly tormented sentiments of love's new voice.

Conclusion

From the beginning of the seventeenth century and well into the eighteenth, the single most consequential force in the world of Baroque music was the singer, whether performing in private chambers, on stage, or even in church (for the new music had gained a foothold in the sacred repertory as well). Once opera became fashionable, singers were worshipped like the rock stars of today and sometimes commanded fees more than twice as high as those paid to composers. Although composers could achieve international recognition through opera, they nevertheless had to bow to the wishes and whims of their singers. The larger-than-life heroes of the operatic stage were a far cry from the interpreters of Caccini's intimate monodies, who had given voice to the link between the sensible and supersensible worlds.

Singers came to exercise a kind of magic over their listeners. The first wave of performers, versed in the traditions of Renaissance poetry and song, engaged in an elite, courtly type of music-making, one in which the natural alliance between word and tone was paramount and required no props. The second wave, the virtuosic voices of early modern opera, transformed song into an almost purely tonal representation of passion and relied as well on spectacle and gesture (Tomlinson 1999, 51). These performers, singers of Italian aria, in which the text had already been reduced to minimal significance, transcended and dissolved the words into pure, spellbinding lyricism. In so doing, they captivated a public eager to submit to the mysterious, metaphysical powers of song.

BIBLIOGRAPHY

Caccini, Giulio. [1602] 1970. *Le nuove musiche*. Reprint, with introduction and notes, ed. H. Wiley Hitchcock. Madison, Wisc.: A-R Editions.

Carter, Tim. 1984. "On the Composition and Performance of *Le nuove musiche*." *Early Music* 12: 208–217.

Fortune, Nigel. 1980. "Monody." In *The New Grove Dictionary of Music and musicians,* ed. Stanley Sadie, 12:497. London: Macmillan..

Gallico, Claudio, and Stefano Patuzzi, eds. 1998. *Girolamo Frescobaldi, Arie musicali,* with Introduction, *Monumenti musicali italiani,* vol. XXI. Milan: Zerboni.

Greene, Brian. 1999. *The Elegant Universe: Superstrings, Hidden Dimensions, and the Quest for the Ultimate Theory.* New York: W. W. Norton.

Haar, James. 1983. "The Courtier as Musician: Castiglione's View of the Science and Art of Music." In *Castiglione: The Ideal and the Real in Renaissance Culture,* ed. Robert W. Hanning and David Rosand, 165–189. New Haven, Conn.: Yale University Press.

Hammond, Frederick. 1978. "Girolamo Frescobaldi in Florence." In *Essays Presented to Myron P. Gilmore,* ed. Sergio Bertelli and Gloria Ramakus, 405–419. Florence: La Nuova Italia.

Hansen, Jette Barnholdt. 2003. "From Invention to Interpretation." *The Journal of Musicology* 20: 556–596.

Hill, John W. 1987. "Frescobaldi's *Arie* and the Musical Circle around Cardinal Montalto." In *Frescobaldi Studies,* ed. Alexander Silbiger, 157–194. Durham, N.C.: Duke University Press.

Hitchcock, H. Wiley. 1970. "Vocal Ornamentation in Caccini's *Nuove musiche*." *Musical Quarterly* 56: 389–404.

Palisca, Claude V. 1989. *The Florentine Camerata: Documentary Studies and Translations.* New Haven, Conn.: Yale University Press.

Peri, Jacopo. [1600] 1981. *Euridice,* ed. Howard Mayer Brown. Madison, Wisc.: A-R Editions.

Tomlinson, Gary. 1999. *Metaphysical Song: An Essay on Opera.* Princeton, N.J.: Princeton University Press.

Weiss, Piero, and Richard Taruskin, eds. 1984. *Music in the Western World: A History in Documents.* New York: Schirmer.

Winternitz, Emanuel. 1982. *Leonardo da Vinci as a Musician.* New Haven, Conn.: Yale University Press.

CHAPTER THREE

The Rise of Italian Chamber Music

Mary Oleskiewicz

BAROQUE ITALY WITNESSED THE FIRST EFFLORESCENCE of chamber music composed in a truly instrumental idiom. In the course of the seventeenth century, Italian composers developed new genres of music for instrumental ensemble, including the sonata and concerto. These genres were carried abroad by Italian violinists, first to Germany and later to England and France. Although the term "concerto" was first used around 1600 to describe a work combining voices and instruments, by the eighteenth century it denoted an instrumental piece that featured a soloist or group of soloists playing together with a larger ensemble.

Today we think of the sonata as chamber music and the concerto as orchestral music. During the Baroque, however, music was commonly classified by the venue in which it was performed rather than the size of the ensemble that played it. *Musica per camera,* music for the chamber, was anything played at home, whether in a small drawing room, private studio, or grand palace. Both concertos and sonatas might fall into this category. *Musica per chiesa,* music for the church, was anything played in a church or chapel during a liturgical service. Concertos and sonatas were heard in this context, too. Thus the sonata and concerto were fundamental forms employed in both secular and sacred music-making.

Instruments, Practices, and Genres

INSTRUMENTS

The most popular instruments of the Baroque were the bowed strings of the violin family. These prevailed above all in Italy, where by the mid-seventeenth century the viola da gamba had become obsolete. Distinguished by its frets and six strings, the gamba was unable to compete in brilliance and agility with the violin. Only the bass viola da gamba continued in limited use into the later Baroque, especially in France, England, and Germany, where J. S. Bach and a few others still wrote Italianate sonatas for it. By 1600 in Italy the northern city of Cremona already had established itself as the European capital of violin making. It is no coincidence that the regions surrounding Cremona (Plate 7) produced many of the earliest violin makers, violinists, and composers. Still prized today are instruments by the foremost makers of the time: the Amati, Beronzi, Guarneri, Ruggieri, and Stradivari families (Figure 3-1).

The violin was sometimes referred to as the viola da braccio (arm viol) to distinguish it from the viola da gamba (leg viol). Like the viols, violins were built in several sizes. All might be termed viole da braccio, even the large bass instrument, which like the later cello was played in upright position. The size and tuning of the bass violin raises questions throughout the period. Seventeenth-century parts frequently call for violone or bass viola da braccio,

Figure 3-1. Viola made by Andrea Guarneri (1664). National Music Museum: America's Shrine to Music, University of South Dakota. Photograph by Bill Willroth, Sr.

both probably referring to a bass violin slightly larger than the cello (Plate 8). The cello, or more properly the violoncello, emerged during the 1660s. It was smaller and more manageable than the old violone, which it replaced as the standard bass instrument by the eighteenth century. Meanwhile, the term violone came to be applied to even larger instruments—forerunners of the modern double bass. These sounded an octave lower than written and were commonly recommended for performances in large spaces, to double the cello and reinforce the bass line.

Relatively few wind instruments are called for in Italian scores from the early Baroque. The most important wind instrument in the early seventeenth century was the cornetto, which is often named as a possible substitute for the violin. The cornetto has a slender, crescent-shaped body whose holes are fingered like those of a recorder or flute (Plate 9). The detachable, cup-shaped mouthpiece resembles that of a trumpet. The sound of the cornetto beautifully combines aspects of the trumpet, flute, and human voice, though the instrument is notoriously difficult to play. Early Baroque composers nevertheless exploited its highest register, calling upon skilled players to perform florid passagework with the same agility as a violinist or vocalist. Surviving cornettos of ivory (as shown) may have originated in Venice, whereas more typical wooden examples with leather covering were produced in Nuremberg.

Other woodwinds were little used in chamber music before their transformation by French and Netherlandish makers during the second half of the seventeenth century. Until the 1660s, the oboe existed only in the form of the shawm, a loud double-reed instrument used chiefly for outdoor performances (especially military occasions). It was unsuited for chamber music, since it could not combine satisfactorily with softer instruments. Shortly after instrument makers developed the oboe, the recorder and transverse flute were completely redesigned to achieve similar subtlety and versatility. Likewise, a new bass double-reed instrument, the bassoon, emerged from the older dulcian. The new instruments possessed a warm, flexible tone, and they gave players ready capability to produce full chromatic scales as well as considerable dynamic variation. Each blended easily with strings and other woodwinds and could produce the highly nuanced ornaments and articulations prized in Baroque performance. By 1700 the oboe and bassoon were in use throughout much of Italy, Germany, and England. The redesigned transverse flute soon gained wide acceptance as well, especially in northern Europe.

Baroque brass instruments found more limited use in chamber music, even though they were somewhat smaller and quieter than modern counterparts. The natural trumpet of the Baroque Era lacked valves (in this sense it resembled the modern bugle), and until the publication of Girolamo Fantini's important trumpet method *Modo per imparare a sonare di tromba* (Method for Learning to Play the Trumpet) in 1638, it apparently was used primarily as a signaling or heraldic instrument (Plate 10). Trumpeters belonged to exclusive guilds and were employed for special civic, court, and military events, although on festive occasions they might also play in churches and other venues. One of the principal centers of trumpet and trombone making during the period was Nuremberg, close to mines where silver and other metals were especially abundant. In the Baroque, trombones had a very different function from that of trumpets. They were viewed primarily as church instruments, used chiefly in choral music and in a significant number of seventeenth-century chamber works. Trombones were built in a variety of sizes, but in ensemble music the soprano and alto parts were often taken by the cornetto, which blended particularly well with tenor and bass trombones.

Virtually all Baroque music included a chordal accompaniment furnished either by a keyboard instrument or a plucked stringed instrument. The keyboard instruments included harpsichords and organs, large and small. The stringed instruments included the lute, which was especially popular in the form known as the chittarone, an instrument whose extra bass strings were ideal for continuo playing (see Chapter 1). The harp and guitar were also available for chordal accompaniment, but they are rarely specified in scores (see Chapter 8).

SCORING

Prior to the Baroque, relatively few composers wrote instrumental music, and those who did rarely called for specific instruments. It was common practice to leave the choice to the performer. Remnants of this practice continued after 1600, but most Baroque composers scored their music quite carefully, a fact that belies the modern notion that instrumentation is unimportant in this repertory. When composers gave the performer a choice—the option to substitute cornetto for violin in many early sonatas, for instance, or flute or oboe for violin in later ones—this fact was usually noted on title pages or in performance parts. Dependable reproductions of certain older Baroque instruments, such as the bass violin, can be difficult to come by, and thus performers sometimes compromise by using a cello for early Baroque bass parts.

Idiomatic writing for specific instruments is one of the fundamental characteristics of Baroque music. Its roots can be traced to the elaborate instrumental traditions of late Renaissance Venice, where sumptuously scored vocal and instrumental works might call for as many as thirty musicians or more. At the same time, in Rome, Florence, and other Italian cities a new, intimate style of chamber music was coming into vogue. Characterized by monodic textures—solo voice with simple chordal accompaniment—this style incorporated declamatory text expression and refined virtuoso embellishment. As Giulio Caccini explained in the preface to his *Nuove musiche* (New Music) of 1601, the purpose of this innovative style was to move the listener, to stir the affections of the soul. Caccini describes the performance of the solo part in some detail, illustrating new types of vocal ornaments that would soon become standard fare in instrumental performance (see Example 3-2). He also describes the accompaniment, notated as a bass line with numerical figures and other symbols. This so-called figured bass allowed the lute or keyboard player to improvise appropriate harmony in the form of chords or simple counterpoint. An accompanying part of this type came to be known as basso continuo, or simply continuo.

Within a few years, contemporaries of Caccini such as Claudio Monteverdi published vocal duets and trios with continuo accompaniment. All three scorings—vocal solos, duets, and trios—can be found in the madrigals of Luzzasco Luzzaschi (1545?–1607), published in 1601 but possibly written several decades earlier for the Three Ladies of Ferrara, the famous trio of singers whose virtuosity inspired much early Baroque performance and composition. Vocal music such as this could be translated readily to instruments, and by 1610 the Milanese composer Giovanni Paolo Cima (c. 1570–1622) appended sonatas for two, three, and four instruments to the end of his *Concerti ecclesiastici* (1610), a large collection of sacred vocal works. Apart from their instrumental designations, the sonatas are virtually indistinguishable in style and idiom from the vocal duos, trios, and quartets found earlier in the same collection. However, within a few years composers began to publish purely instrumental volumes whose works displayed a distinctly instrumental idiom.

Today the terminology of the early sonatas is easily misunderstood. A sonata a due always included two melody instruments, high or low, plus continuo. A sonata a tre called for three instruments, typically two violins and a violone, plus continuo. The violone part is usually similar to but not necessarily identical to the continuo part. In many places it became customary to add melodic bass instruments to the continuo, which was initially played by a chordal instrument alone. The melodic instruments doubled the bass line, thus lending additional foundation support to the ensemble. By 1700 a solo sonata, the descendant of the sonata a uno, was typically performed by three musicians, a soloist and two continuo players. A trio sonata, the descendent of both the sonata a due and the sonata a tre, was typically performed by four musicians, two soloists and two players in the continuo group. A quartet sonata included three melody instruments plus continuo, although many early eighteenth-century quartets are really closer to the sonata a tre, in which the third solo part is for a melodic bass instrument only partially independent of the basso continuo. Oddly enough, solo sonatas for one melody instrument and continuo were relatively rare in the early Baroque. The sonata a due and the sonata a tre were much more common throughout the seventeenth century.

In sonatas and concertos, the precise makeup of the continuo group was often unspecified. Chordal support was usually provided by harpsichord or organ, though in many areas a lute of some type was preferred, particularly during the seventeenth century. Although we associate the organ with sacred music, small instruments were found in many wealthy homes in Italy and provided continuo support in secular as well as sacred works. The cello was the most common doubling instrument, though the viola da gamba and violone were also used. As late as Bach's Brandenburg Concertos (1721), the term continuo could still designate a part for a single unspecified keyboard instrument, with separate parts for cello, bassoon, or other melodic bass instrument. Importantly, by the end of the Baroque the new fortepiano (invented around 1700 in Florence) came into use as a continuo instrument, favored by many for its ability to produce expressive dynamics.

PATRONS

Public concerts in the modern sense were rare during the Baroque. Most Italian chamber music was written either for the private enjoyment of wealthy music lovers, who often played instruments themselves, or for liturgical use in church. In Roman Catholic countries sonatas and concertos were commonly performed during church services, in which it became common practice to substitute instrumental compositions for certain sections of the liturgy that were normally sung, such as the Introit or Gradual. The great churches of Venice, Rome, Bologna, and other cities, large monasteries, and the chapels of rulers made splendid use of instrumental music, especially on high feast days. Sonatas and concertos were also frequent fare in public theaters, private homes, and palaces. The learned academies that burgeoned in seventeenth-century Italy, as well as religious confraternities, merchant guilds, and other civic organizations frequently sponsored private concerts, sometimes commissioning new musical works. Some academies were specifically devoted to music, most notably the Accademia Filarmonica of Bologna, whose membership included numerous composers. Other academies, such as the Arcadian Academy of the Roman Cardinal Pietro Ottoboni, were primarily groups of literary figures or members of the nobility. Musicians might perform for them, but few were admitted as members. An exception was Arcangelo Corelli (1653–1713), who joined the Arcadian Academy under the pseudonym "Arcomélo" (all members adopted names of ancient Greek "shepherds"; Allsop 1999, 57).

In Italy vast amounts of private wealth sustained the arts, including music, even during times of economic hardship or foreign invasion. Several ruling houses specifically supported the composition and performance of instrumental music during this period. These included the Gonzaga family of Mantua (until 1630), the Este family of Modena, the Farnese family of Parma, and the Medici family of Florence. In Venice, the elected doge supported extravagant musical affairs. In Rome, the papacy generally eschewed instrumental music, but the papal Barbarini family were nevertheless significant musical patrons. The importation of Italian musicians by Austrian and German royalty helped disseminate Italian music and playing styles north of the Alps. In the sixteenth century it had been fashionable in Italy to import Flemish and French musicians. In the Baroque the tables were turned, as Italian music and musicians became the rage throughout Europe. A further source of patronage was the European merchant class, whose members now enjoyed the means and leisure to study music and musical instruments. Composers and publishers rushed to meet an insatiable demand for instruction manuals and collections of music that were accessible to amateur players. In northern Europe publishers such as Estienne Roger in Amsterdam and John Walsh in London issued Italian chamber music in editions that were circulated throughout Europe.

GENRES

The terms "sonata" and "concerto" may seem self-explanatory today, but until the eighteenth century the distinguishing features of these genres had not yet fully crystallized. Composers used numerous terms to describe their instrumental works, sometimes in seemingly contradictory ways. Labels applied in the early Baroque to pieces resembling the sonata, for instance, include canzona, sinfonia, capriccio, fantasia, ricercar, and toccata. These terms reflect the various roots of the Baroque sonata, and it will be helpful to examine the most important of these in turn to understand fully the sonata's genesis in the seventeenth century.

THE CANZONA

Of the sixteenth-century genres that might be viewed as predecessors to the sonata, the most closely related is the canzona, which remained in use through the mid-seventeenth century or so. The Italian word *canzona* or *canzone,* which literally means "song," was often applied to the polyphonic French chanson of the sixteenth century. Instrumental arrangements of such pieces were sometimes designated *canzone francesi* (French songs), such as those by the Venetian organist Andrea Gabrieli (c. 1510–1586), who created embellished keyboard arrangements of chansons by Rolande de Lassus and others. By the end of the sixteenth century the term was being applied to original instrumental pieces. Although some of these pieces imitate the style of the French polyphonic chanson, many do not, apart from a repeated-note motive in dactylic rhythm that often appears at the beginnings of phrases (Example 3-1).

Seventeenth-century canzonas, which were written for solo keyboard as well as instrumental ensemble, usually contain two or more sections. The sections normally alternate between imitative and homophonic textures and employ contrasting meters. The first section, in duple time, normally leads to a second, in triple meter. It is often said that the sonata evolved from the canzona, drawing from it the concept of a multisectional or multimove-

Example 3-1.   Thomas Crequillon, *Pour ung plaisir,* mm. 1–4.

ment plan. Yet the two coexisted through the middle of the seventeenth century. Some composers published collections containing both types of works, clearly suggesting that the terms designated distinct types of pieces. Others, notably Girolamo Frescobaldi (1583–1643) and Tarquinio Merula (c. 1594–1665), focused chiefly on canzonas, a conservative approach possibly related to the fact that both were keyboard players. Sonatas for keyboard would not become common until the eighteenth century.

DANCE MUSIC AND THE SINFONIA

Dance music forms another genre that continued in an unbroken tradition from the late Renaissance through the Baroque. Italian dances of the late-sixteenth century that continue to appear in early Baroque settings include the balletto, pavana (pavane), gagliardo (galliard), and corrente. By the late seventeenth century the individual dance types that had appeared in large numbers in earlier publications were being grouped into ordered series. Such a series of dance movements, now described by the French term *suite,* was sometimes designated instead a *sonata da camera* (chamber sonata), as Corelli's opus 2 trio sonatas.

The first movement of such a suite was sometimes a nondance movement called a *sinfonia,* although this term, like sonata, could designate almost any instrumental composition. Sinfonia seems to have been applied particularly to instrumental pieces within larger vocal works, such as operas. Hence the word could also be used as a synonym for ritornello, in reference to a short, recurring instrumental passage that separated the stanzas of a strophic song or aria. Sinfonias of this type might be composed and published separately from the arias themselves. A more substantial type of sinfonia containing several sections closely resembled not only the contemporary canzona but also the short instrumental compositions that served as introductions—overtures in the modern sense—to early operas and oratorios. From the last quarter of the seventeenth century onward, composers in Bologna used the label sinfonia for pieces that seem indistinguishable from their sonatas. This is especially true of works for trumpets, strings, and continuo.

THE SONATA

The word *sonata* literally means anything played on an instrument. It stems from the Italian word *sonare,* to sound. By the eighteenth century, the term sonata denoted a relatively ambitious instrumental work comprising several self-contained movements. Earlier examples are shorter and more loosely structured. Ensemble works labeled sonata first appear around 1600 in collections by Giovanni Gabrieli, Salomone Rossi (see Chapter 6), and others. Gabrieli's early sonatas, published in 1597, are large polychoral works. Rossi's first published sonata, included in a print of 1607, is a brief contrapuntal piece that closely resembles a four-part ricercar (Harrán 1999). Characteristics that soon would become typical of the early sonata appear in Cima's *Concerti ecclesiatici,* published in 1610. Cima's sonatas contain several short sections of contrasting meters or characters, like the contemporary canzona. The individual sections include both imitative or fugal passages and virtuoso figuration. One of Cima's pieces is frequently described as the first violin sonata, although it is actually a sonata a due for violin and violone.

As sonatas proliferated in the decades following these early publications, they assumed a broad variety of shapes and forms. Only toward the end of the seventeenth century did the sections generally become long enough to be described as movements. The movements might occur in any number, and they might be written in many different styles, from simple dances to strict fugues. Although the earliest sonatas were mostly intended for church performance, the so-called *sonata da chiesa,* or church sonata, with four movements in the sequence slow-fast-slow-fast, did not emerge as a distinct type of sonata until the eighteenth century. The sonata da chiesa was by no means associated solely with liturgical services, however. It was often performed in secular contexts as well. In addition, the sonata da chiesa is often said to have been codified by Corelli, yet he never used the term, and the four-movement pattern is not particularly prominent in his works. On the other hand, the *sonata da camera,* or chamber sonata, is often described today as the secular antithesis of the church sonata, since it usually consists of a series of dance movements. Corelli used the term for his opus 2 trios, as we have seen. But a clear distinction between church and chamber sonatas probably never existed for Corelli or his contemporaries. Indeed, there appears to have been a great intermingling of styles and functions.

THE CONCERTO

The word *concerto* and its derivatives are fraught with even greater ambiguity than sonata. The term, which originally meant "consort" (ensemble) or "concert," came to invoke the idea of contrasting musical forces: voices versus instruments, or a soloist (or soloists) contrasted by a larger ensemble. The earliest works labeled "concerto" were sacred vocal compositions for voices and instruments. Only in the late-seventeenth century was the term first applied to exclusively instrumental works, and even in the eighteenth century it could still denote a piece for instruments and voices (Bach labeled many of his cantatas "concerto"). Moreover, throughout this period the terms concerto and sonata were sometimes used interchangeably.

By about 1700 several distinct types of concerto had emerged. Most consisted of three movements in the order fast-slow-fast. These included works for four-part string ensemble and continuo, without soloist, and often performed with multiple players on each part (today this type of piece is commonly termed a concerto a quattro), works for a single soloist pitted against a larger ensemble (this is now termed a solo concerto), and works for several soloists together with a larger ensemble (now called a group concerto or concerto grosso). These distinctions were rarely made at the time, however, and a single work might contain different movements representing each type of concerto. Moreover, one should probably divide the third category into the true concerto grosso, which is, in a sense, a sort of expanded trio sonata (as we shall see shortly), and the group concerto as written by Vivaldi, which is like a solo concerto, but with multiple soloists. Common to all types is an extroverted, virtuoso style characterized by lively figuration or passagework, transparent textures, and occasional dramatic gestures.

Composers and Works

The early Baroque is of special interest in the present survey, since it witnessed the invention and initial proliferation of the sonata and related instrumental genres. For this reason, and because the instrumental music from the seventeenth century is relatively unfamiliar, we will devote special attention to this era, focusing in particular on the sonatas and similar works produced in the important North Italian musical centers of Venice, Mantua, and Bologna.

VENICE, 1600–1650

During the first three decades of the seventeenth century, Venice was the unrivaled center of instrumental music. No other city could match its publications of instrumental music and the number of composers who cultivated the new style. Throughout the Baroque, Venetian musical life was shaped in large part by the intimate relationship between church and state within the Republic. Both instrumental and vocal music thrived because the Basilica of St.

Mark fell under the jurisdiction of the civic authorities. Technically, it was the private chapel of the ruling doge and not the seat of an ecclesiastical see. Located in the center of the city and connected directly to the doge's palace, St. Mark's served as a public stage for official pageantry, ritual, and political display. Numerous Venetian civic holidays, observed in tandem with important religious feasts, and frequent events honoring distinguished visitors or marking affairs of state provided ample opportunity for lavish musical performances that were equal to those at any royal court chapel in Europe.

The hiring of salaried instrumental players contributed immensely to the development of musical style at St. Mark's. In 1568 Girolamo Dalla Casa (c. 1543–1601), a virtuoso cornettist, was hired as maestro de' concerti to head instrumental music. He was succeeded by Giovanni Bassano (d. 1617), whose responsibilities included the performance of Giovanni Gabrieli's instrumental works. The core ensemble at St. Mark's consisted of two cornettists and two trombonists (one of which played bass trombone). String players and other freelance musicians were brought in as needed. In 1614 sixteen salaried players were engaged to form the basilica's first permanent "orchestra" (Selfridge-Field 1994, 15).

Giovanni Gabrieli

Venetian composers were the first to write sacred works with parts specifically designated for instruments. The availability of virtuoso instrumentalists, together with the unique architecture of the sanctuary of St. Mark's, which is thought to have encouraged the disposition of performing musicians at various locations within the building, led Giovanni Gabrieli (c. 1553–1612) to experiment imaginatively with polychoral textures in a significant portion of his music. The result, around 1600, was a compositional style that placed large choirs of instruments on an equal footing with large choirs of voices. The resulting concertato style became a hallmark of Baroque music

Gabrieli's famous motet *In ecclesiis,* from the posthumously published *Symphoniae Sacrae* (1615), beautifully illustrates the new concertato scoring. Juxtaposing a six-part instrumental choir against two four-part vocal choirs, the work opens with vocal monody that alternates with an Alleluia refrain sung by the second choir. Then, in a passage marked "sinfonia," Gabrieli majestically introduces the crown jewel of the Venetian polychoral style—the instrumental choir. The sinfonia begins with a canzona-like motive set in a thick homophonic texture. This leads to a passage of imitative polyphony (Example 3-2). All three choirs then alternate and combine in pairs in a virtual kaleidoscope of textures and colors that emulates the opulence of St. Mark's itself.

Gabrieli's volumes of *Sacrae Symphonie* also include purely instrumental music in the form of canzonas and sonatas. Both were intended for performance during church services and are scored for three to twenty-two parts, plus organ. The forces are divided into as many as five choirs. Gabrieli seems to have used the term sonata for works that were more serious and contrapuntal than the canzona. His canzonas are generally lighter and chanson-like, with lively, less-strictly contrapuntal textures. There is often some sort of reprise or recurring section. Gabrieli's *Sonata pian' e forte,* arguably his most famous instrumental work, is from the volume of *Sacrae Symphoniae* published in 1597. It is scored for two instrumental choirs, one led by cornetto and the other by viola, with trombones on the lower parts. The title is uniquely appropriate, for not only are dynamics piano and forte clearly notated (itself an unusual practice for the time), but the work seems to have been the first in which dynamics serve as the basis for compositional organization. Quiet passages alternating with loud ones form the building blocks of the sonata's architecture. Two canzonas in the same collection also display the structural use of echoes, which became a favorite of later composers. The ex-

Example 3-2. Giovanni Gabrieli, *In ecclesiis*, mm. 26b–30 (without organ bass).

pressive and lyrical *Sonata con tre violini* from the posthumous 1615 collection is also worth mentioning, since it is the only piece by Gabrieli for three violins and organ continuo (with optional melodic bass instrument). It may have been written in imitation of vocal works such as Luzzaschi's madrigals for three sopranos and keyboard, which employ similar types of *groppi* and ornamental figures (Example 3-3).

Castello

By 1621, when Dario Castello (fl. early 1600s) published the first of his two books of instrumental music, sonatas for small combinations of instruments had become a common feature of the Venetian repertory. The title of his second book, issued in 1629, conjures up the latest trends in the new Italian instrumental style: *Sonate concertate in stil moderno per sonar nel organo overo clavicembalo con diversi instrumenti* (Concerted Sonatas in the Modern Style, for Playing with an Organ or Harpsichord on Diverse Instruments). The instruments required in the individual sonatas are mostly those available at St. Mark's—that is, cornettos, trombones, and strings—where these pieces may have been first performed. This volume opens with two extraordinary sonatas for unspecified soprano instrument (presumably violin or cornetto) and continuo, followed by fifteen pieces for larger forces. The last calls for pairs of violins and cornetti "in echo."

Sonata II of the second book concludes with brilliant arpeggios and florid *groppi* (Example 3-4a). The treble elaboration of the final plagal cadence introduces the dissonant interval of the tritone as the soloist trills between c#″ and d″ over bass G. The effect may strike

Example 3-3. a) Giovanni Gabrieli, *Sonata con tre violini*, mm. 24–28; b) Luzzasco Luzzaschi, *Occhi del pianto mio*, mm. 39–40 (without keyboard accompaniment).

the modern listener as exotic, but in fact the gesture is a heightened version of a figure common in contemporary organ music (Example 3-4b). The repeated notes in thirty-seconds that immediately precede the final chord are a notated example of Giulio Caccini's *trillo,* a kind of intense vibrato frequently used by early Baroque singers to ornament the penultimate note of a cadence. Both effects are examples of *bizzarria,* that is, virtuoso extravagance cultivated throughout the Baroque by Italian composers, especially those in Venice.

Marini

By the mid-seventeenth century the sonata was no longer a novelty. Composers increasingly focused their attention on the violin, incorporating more idiomatic string writing into their works in place of the somewhat generic style still found in music by composers such as Castello. From the 1620s until his death some forty years later, the most important figure in this development was the Brescian violinist Biagio Marini (c. 1587–1663).

Marini served as violinist under Monteverdi at St. Mark's from 1615 to 1618. After brief

Example 3-4.   a) Castello, Sonata II *a soprano solo* (Book 2), conclusion; b) Andrea Gabrieli *Intonatione del quarto tono* (published 1593), conclusion.

appointments at Brescia (1620) and at the Farnese court in Parma (1621) he became Kapellmeister at the Wittelsbach court of Neuburg on the Danube (1623–1649). During this time he also traveled extensively, helping to disseminate the North Italian style of virtuoso violin playing across Germany. Marini composed sacred and secular vocal music, but he is best known today for his five collections of inventive and virtuosic chamber works that helped to establish a truly idiomatic string style.

While still in Venice Marini issued his first work, the *Affetti musicali,* opus 1 (1617), a seminal volume of sinfonias, canzonas, sonatas, and dances for one-to-three parts with basso continuo. One of the largest and most significant works in the volume is *La Foscarina,* a sonata a tre for two violins or cornetti with bass trombone or bassoon and continuo (Sampler CD 1, track 8). The sonata is especially interesting from a formal standpoint, with its long sections and its extended, nearly literal recapitulation of the opening material capped by a rhythmically energetic codetta. Even more striking, however, is a passage that seems to call for a type of bow vibrato—the first such incident in a published composition (Example 3-5, a). This innovation occurs within a harmonically unstable passage of half-note chords that contrast with the rushing counterpoint found elsewhere in the piece. The technique probably involved dividing each half note into repeated sixteenths, played in a single, uninterrupted bow stroke to produce the effect of a throbbing vibrato (Example 3-5, b). Markings in the bass and continuo parts appear to call for corresponding effects with the phrase *metti il tremolo* (Pull the tremolo), directing the organist to draw the tremulant stop that would produce similar pulsations.

Marini's second volume of sonatas, opus 8, appeared in Venice in 1629. It is his most extensive and imaginative collection, with a wide variety of compositional types. This is clear from the title: *Sonate, symphonie, canzoni, pass' emezzi, baletti, corenti, gagliardi, e retornelli.* The works introduce novel compositional ideas and make new technical demands on the performer, especially in a group of pieces specifically for violin that are advertised on the vol-

Example 3-5. a) Marini, Sonata *La Foscarina* from *Affetti musicali,* op. 1, mm. 71–74; b) presumed "realization" of bow vibrato.

a)

b)

Example 3-6. Marini, *Sonata quarta per il violino per sonar con due corde,* from op. 8, mm. 40b–45.

ume's title page as "curious and modern inventions." One of these, the *Sonata quarta per il violino per sonar con due corde,* fulfills the promise of modern inventions particularly well through an extended passage in double stops (Example 3-6). Equally "curious" effects occur in the *Sonata seconda d'Inventione,* a work that requires *scordatura,* the intentional mistuning of the violin to produce special effects. After playing the opening phrase, the violinist rests for seven measures and, while the continuo plays alone, retunes the e" string down to c". This makes possible the performance of an extraordinary passage in parallel thirds that would be otherwise virtually unplayable. After the passage, the violinist is instructed to return the e" string to its normal tuning. No doubt such a trick was particularly striking in live performance. Even the very first work in the collection, the *Sonata prima a doi violini* (PGM 118), presents a novel effect borrowed from *La Viena* (PGM 118), a *sonata in dialogo* by Salomone Rossi. Here a dialogue is created by upper voices that exchange several solo phrases before proceeding as a duo.

Another invention of opus 8 is the widespread use of verbal indications of the type that we now term expression marks. Among these is the word *affetti* (affections), which occurs not only in the title of the collection but within the parts, printed over simple melodic passages consisting of half notes. This indication may imply that the performer is expected to improvise embellishments. The tempo markings *tardo* and *presto* also appear in opus 8. In the *Sonata con due corde,* for instance, the continuo plays sustained chords while the violin alternates between tempos in an improvisatory passage suggestive of monodic recitative (Example 3-7).

The *Sonata in ecco* for three violins and continuo is perhaps the most theatrical work in the volume. As we have seen, echo effects were not Marini's invention. Although there were numerous instrumental precedents, Marini's sonata is closer in style to vocal models found in stage works, such as Peri's "Dunque fra torbid' onde" for three tenors from the intermedi for *La Pellegrina* (1589). Marini's sonata is based on the showy display of the first violin, whose brilliant phrase endings are cleverly imitated in turn by the second and third violins. A stage direction within the parts indicates that the first violin should play loudly and remain visible to the audience, whereas the second and third violins should be unseen throughout the work. The score includes the dynamic markings *forte, piano,* and *più piano,* which help create the echoes.

Marini's last published collection for instrumental ensemble, *Per ogni sorte d'stromento musicale* (For All Sorts of Instruments), opus 22 (Venice, 1655), contains, as the remainder of the title indicates, all sorts of church and chamber sonatas, for two, three, and four parts. The volume's varied content, however, shows that word sonata could still mean simply "piece." Exceptionally, Marini included guitar notation (*alfabeto*—see Chapter 8) as an optional addition or alternative to the basso continuo in the many dances and sinfonias—but not in five

Example 3-7. Marini, *Sonata quarta per il violino per sonar con due corde,* from op. 8, mm. 51–56.

sonatas and a *passacaglio* for two, three, and four strings with continuo. Other novelties include a sonata a 3, subtitled *sopra Fuggi dolente core,* which is in fact a multisectional canzona on the popular melody "Flee, Sad Heart" that Smetana later used in *The Moldau.* The concluding *Passacaglio* is not a simple set of variations on a ground bass, as the title might suggest. Rather, it wanders through varying tonalities in several distinct sections, like Frescobaldi's famous *Cento partite sopra passacagli* for keyboard (1637), making some remarkable harmonic juxtapositions along the way. The passacaglia proper is framed by an opening introduction and a closing finale. This design recalls Monteverdi's famous *Lamento della ninfa,* published in 1638. Here, too, one can sense Marini's love of theatrical models.

MANTUA, 1600–1650

At the beginning of the seventeenth century, the duchy of Mantua was second only to Venice in its production of instrumental music and the trio sonata in particular. The dukes of the Gonzaga family showered lavish patronage on the city's musicians, whose circle of vibrant string players included several notable composers. The most significant of these was Monteverdi.

Monteverdi

Although Claudio Monteverdi (1567–1643) was described as a player of the viola da braccio, he apparently wrote no independent instrumental compositions. He is nevertheless important for his pioneering use of instruments in several vocal works. His opera *Orfeo* (1607) has long been celebrated for its extensive use of instruments in highly imaginative scorings. Perhaps most interesting from an instrumental standpoint is the Toccata that opens the work. Scored for five trumpets and drums, it is an elaborate version of a traditional polyphonic fanfare, incorporating a heraldic melody used at German courts and probably known to Mantuan court trumpeters. The Toccata closely resembles a less elaborately scored fanfare from the *Modo per imparare a sonare di tromba* (1638), a treatise on trumpet playing by the Florentine court trumpeter Girolamo Fantini. Monteverdi later reused the Toccata in the response "Domine ad adiuvandum" that opens the Vespers Collection of 1610.

Monteverdi's sole work labeled sonata is the *Sonata sopra Sancta Maria ora pro nobis*, published as part of the Vespers Collection. The scoring includes pairs of violins, cornetts, and trombones (or one trombone and a viola da brazzo), a bass for viola da brazzo or trombone doppio, and organ continuo. A soprano voice repeats a brief Gregorian melody eleven times (the litany "Holy Mary, pray for us") while the instruments play what is in effect a multisectional canzona, including a reprise, in the style of Gabrieli.

Salamone Rossi

Salamone Rossi (1570–c. 1630), a contemporary of Monteverdi's, was one of several Jewish musicians who worked for the Gonzaga court (see Chapter 6). Rossi published four books of instrumental music, which appeared in Venice between 1607 and 1622. The last two volumes contain some of the most modern and distinctive instrumental works of the early Baroque. Rossi's first two books contain canzonas, sinfonias, dance movements, and a single sonata. These works are scored primarily for two violins and chitarrone. The dances include correntes, ballettos, and galliards such as the lively *Galliarda detta la Zambalina* (Sampler CD 1, track 9), whose title, following the custom of the time, refers to the work's dedicatee. Whereas the dances are mainly homophonic in texture, the sinfonias often incorporate simple imitations. *Sinfonia seconda* from Book 2 (Sampler CD 1, track 10) resembles a miniature version of one of Rossi's sonatas in its close imitative treatment of the opening subject (Example 3-8) and its incorporation of a distinct, if brief, triple-time passage in its second half.

Rossi has been considered an important figure in the development of the trio sonata, although the term is applied to his works somewhat anachronistically. However, his third and fourth books are devoted almost exclusively to works for two violins and chitarrone. Compared to the sinfonias, the sonatas are lengthier, more serious works that take the form of a series of variations or else are cast in binary form with repeated sections. Their cogent formal organization sets them apart from other early sonatas. However, Rossi's sonatas resemble those of his contemporaries insofar as the second part of the binary structure often incorporates several short passages in contrasting meters and textures, as in the *Sonata detta La Moderna* of Book 3 (PGM 118) and the first two sonatas from Book 4 (PGM 118). The *Sonata in dialogo detta La Viena* from Book 4 (PGM 118) presents a conversation between the two upper parts, which alternate in extended rhapsodic solo phrases.

The variation sonatas are among Rossi's lengthiest instrumental pieces. Some are con-

Example 3-8. Rossi, Sinfonia seconda, book 2, mm. 1–4.

structed over well-known ground basses, such as in *Sonata decima sopra l'aria di Romanesca* from Book 4 (PGM 118). Here the upper parts introduce distinctive motives and rhythms in varying textures over twelve statements of an ostinato bass. A notable feature of this sonata is the irregularly resolved dissonance in the first measure, a rare reference in Rossi's work to Monteverdi's "Second Practice," which allowed the rules of counterpoint to be broken for expressive purposes. Two other sonatas from Book 4 take a different approach to variation: the treble parts weave increasingly ornate embellishments around repetitions of a folk-like tune. This approach can be observed clearly in the *Sonata quinta sopra un aria francese* (PGM 118).

Buonamente

Giovanni Baptiste Buonamente (d. 1643) is often credited with being a student of Rossi's. Although it remains to be proven whether or not this is true, his works bear the clear stamp of Rossi's influence. A Franciscan monk, Buonamente began his career in Mantua before leaving in 1626 to serve the emperor Ferdinand II in Vienna, making him one of the first Italians to carry the culture of the sonata northward over the Alps. By 1632 he was back in Italy, working as maestro di cappella in 1633 at the Franciscan center of Assisi. In the meantime, he evidently continued to supply music to the Gonzaga household in Mantua. In a letter of 1627 he states that he sent the duke "a new solo violin sonata that I hope Your Highness will be pleased to play without ornamentation. For the convenience of the young desiring to adorn it with passaggi, I have made it not too difficult" (Newman 1972, 37).

The sonata mentioned in the letter has not been identified, and Buonamente's first three collections of instrumental music are lost. The remaining four volumes, published between 1626 and 1637, contain the usual assortment of Italian instrumental pieces, including sonatas, sinfonias, and dances. Book 6 of 1636 is exceptional, for it contains exclusively sonatas and canzonas for two to six instruments with basso continuo. The first sonata of Book 7 is entitled *La Monteverde*, although from a stylistic standpoint it has no obvious connection to its dedicatee. The *Sonata a tre violini* (Sampler CD 1, track 11) is an especially well-wrought work in three sections. The opening section, in duple meter, leads to a central section in triple time. The final section recapitulates the thematic material of the first, concluding with dramatic upward-rushing scales.

BOLOGNA, 1650–1700

The flow of Venetian instrumental publications diminished after 1629, reflecting the economic depression caused by the Thirty Years War (1618–1648) as well as the long-term political and economic decline of Venice itself. In the decades that followed, the heterogeneous collections of the early Baroque were replaced by more homogeneous publications, often containing a dozen works: twelve solo sonatas da chiesa, twelve trio sonatas da camera, and so forth. The multisectional sonata was gradually supplanted by sonatas with self-contained movements, and rhapsodic, improvisatory writing was abandoned in favor of regular phrases that develop clearly articulated motives through such means as the sequence and balanced exchanges between parts. The new developments were eventually picked up by Venetian composers. But they began elsewhere.

After the decline of Venice, Bologna became the leading center of sonata composition in the seventeenth century. The city's cultivation of instrumental music can be attributed to a number of factors: the presence of virtuoso string and wind players affiliated with the church of San Petronio, the founding of the Accademia Filarmonica in 1666, and the special penchant of Bolognese composers to write not only new types of string pieces but also virtuoso works for one or two trumpets with three- or four-part string ensemble.

The Bolognese Trumpet Sonata

The natural trumpets of the Renaissance and Baroque were confined to the notes of the harmonic series, limiting their performance to simple fanfares and signals except in the highest part of their range, where special techniques allowed greater melodic possibilities. Composers of the day not only had to understand the technical limitations of the trumpet, but also had to invent new types of melodic writing to take advantage of the instrument's unique features. Among the first writers for the trumpet were Maurizio Cazzati (c. 1620–1677) and other Bolognese composers, who, beginning in the 1660s, created a large repertory of works for one or two trumpets and strings. Many of the pieces were performed on ceremonial occasions at the Church of San Petronio. In addition, such works were regularly played during church services, often before the opening Kyrie. Many were no doubt inspired by the gifted trumpeter, Giovanni Pellegrino Brandi, who participated at San Petronio at festive events between 1679 and 1699.

Although the Bolognese works were not unique—composers elsewhere also began to incorporate trumpet parts into sonatas and opera sinfonias at about the same time—their catchy melodies and rhythms give them special appeal. Moreover, in searching for effective ways to introduce the trumpet soloists into these works, composers hit upon new types of scoring that led to the creation of a new genre, the solo concerto. In a typical scheme the strings play alone at first, the trumpet or trumpets enter dramatically a bit later, and then the two join in antiphonal exchanges (Example 3-9).

Numerous sonatas and sinfonias with trumpet survive in various scorings, including solo sonatas with basso continuo as well as large polychoral works. Many were used in performances with a large string ensemble, as documented by the survival of multiple copies of each string part. Composers elsewhere soon began to produce similar works. In Austria, imperial court violinist Johann Heinrich Schmelzer (c. 1620–1680) preceded Cazzati in the publication of Italian-style sonatas with trumpet. His *Sacro-profanus concentus musicus fidium* appeared in 1659 in Nuremberg, a town well known for its trumpet makers. Within a few years, Heinrich Biber (1644–1704), in Salzburg, was composing wonderfully majestic sonatas containing up to eight trumpet parts, with and without strings.

Bolognese Cello Sonatas

Bologna was further remarkable for producing some of the earliest chamber works specifically for the cello. Although large bass stringed instruments with tunings similar to those of the cello had existed since the sixteenth century, those instruments were somewhat larger. The cello as we know it today came into existence only in the 1660s, thanks to technical advances that made it possible to construct a smaller instrument at bass pitch (Bonta 1977). Among the important virtuosos in Bologna who cultivated the new instrument were Domenico Gabrielli (1651–1690) and his student Giuseppe Maria Jacchini (c. 1663–1727). Both were members of the San Petronio capella and composed some of the earliest sonatas for cello and continuo as well as trumpet sonatas and sinfonias whose slow movements call for solo cello. Gabrielli also wrote ricercars for unaccompanied cello. The earliest printed music for solo cello appeared some years later, in the form of *12 Ricercate* (1687) by the Bolognese organist Giovanni Battista Degli Antonii (1660–after 1696). The works by Gabrielli and Degli Antonii join a handful of pieces by Marini, Biber, and others to form a small repertory of music for unaccompanied violin and cello that preceded J. S. Bach's famous contributions to the genre.

Example 3-9. Torelli, Sonata in D Major for Trumpet, Strings, and Continuo, G. 5, movement 2, mm. 1–7 (ripieno violoncello and *violone* omitted).

TORELLI AND THE CONCERTO

Among the most important composers to emerge in Bologna was the Veronese-born violinist Giuseppe Torelli (1658–1709). Torelli worked in Bologna from 1681 until the temporary disbandment of the San Petronio orchestra in 1696. He then traveled northward, working in Ansbach and Vienna before returning to San Petronio in 1701. His compositions include solo and trio sonatas for strings and trumpet sonatas and sinfonias. He also contributed the first important examples of a new genre, the concerto. In addition, his later orchestral music also incorporates the oboe, an instrument new to Italian composers of the time.

Torelli published six instrumental collections between 1686 and 1698. The *Sonate a tre,* opus 1 (1686), and *Sinfonie,* opus 3 (1687), are traditional collections of sonatas. They contain works in three parts, plus a few pieces a due and a quattro, all with continuo. The *Concerto da camera,* opus 2 (1686), and the *Concertino per camera,* opus 4 (after 1687), are suites of dances in binary form, scored for string trio (two violins and basso) or string duo (violin and cello). Neither collection includes a figured basso continuo. Here the word concerto seems to imply "concert" or "consort," as it probably still did in Torelli's *Sinfonie a tre e concerti a quattro,* opus 5 (1692), and *Concerto musicali,* opus 6 (1698).

In retrospect, however, we can see in the last two publications the beginnings of a new genre, some of whose innovative traits—contrast of timbres, solo-tutti exchange, and the use of incipient ritornello in certain movements—had already appeared in unpublished trumpet works (Example 3-9). Opus 5 reflects the instrumental performance practices of San Petronio in asking for multiple string parts for the six concerti a quattro to produce a large ensemble. True solo-tutti contrast emerges in two concertos from opus 6, whose first violin part contains the word "solo" at various points, indicating that the two or three doubling violins on the part should be silent until the appearance of the word "tutti." These two works, numbers 6 and 12 of opus 6, can be considered the first solo violin concertos. In Torelli's opus 8, published posthumously in 1709, the system of solo-tutti notation is extended to all twelve concertos. Six pieces include solo markings for the first violin, and six pieces include solo markings for the first and second violins.

Corelli

Another product of Bologna was Arcangelo Corelli (1653–1713), arguably the most influential violinist-composer of the Baroque. In Corelli's time, Rome was ruled by the Pope, who also controlled much territory elsewhere, including Bologna. Thus it was natural for the young Corelli, born near Bologna, to gravitate to Rome. He arrived by 1675 and soon enjoyed patronage at the highest levels, first from the exiled Queen Christina of Sweden and then, from 1683 until his death, from Cardinal Benedetto Pamphilii, a member of one of the great papal families. Corelli participated regularly in private concerts and academies and directed numerous public performances of oratorios and other works. Many of these events involved large ensembles of thirty, forty, even sixty players, presumably performing music that included Corelli's concerti grossi. Yet we also know that Corelli also participated in intimate chamber performances. It was here that he demonstrated his brilliance as a soloist.

Corelli apparently focused exclusively on sonatas and concertos, the only type of music that survives in his six published collections (Table 3-1). The first four collections contain church and chamber sonatas, although Corelli did not apply the expression *da chiesa* to the former, as we have seen. Corelli's most recent biographer prefers to call the church sonatas "free sonatas" instead (Allsop 1999, 69). By the same token, only the dance pieces of opus 2 are designated sonate da camera. All six collections were enormously successful and were reprinted in numerous editions that circulated throughout Europe well into the eighteenth century. Scarcely a composer in Germany, France, or England escaped the influence of Corelli's music.

Corelli's sonatas stand apart from most earlier works through their classical restraint, poise, and symmetry. On the printed pages one seeks in vain for the rhapsodic outbursts that characterize string music by earlier composers. Nevertheless, the first six sonatas of opus 5 offer considerable technical challenges, especially in their fugal movements, which alternate between contrapuntal textures in double and triple stops and virtuoso passagework in quick notes. The adagios of opus 5 and other collections present opportunities for the improvisation of embellishments. Corelli's playing appears to have been quite impassioned, to judge from the famous report of a contemporary: "Whilst [Corelli] was playing on the violin it was usual for his countenance to be distorted, his eyes to become red as fire, and his eyeballs to roll as in agony" (Newman 1972, 158).

At the same time, Corelli's forty-eight trio sonatas resemble those of his older contemporaries at Bologna. This is especially evident in the elegant counterpoint of their fugal movements, which are based on short but memorable themes. In such movements Corelli employed certain formulaic devices, including chains of suspensions (Example 3-10, a) and a type of shocking cadence that is often called the "Corelli clash" (Example 3-10, b), even though it can be found in the works of his predecessors. Corelli's tremendous success lies in

Table 3-1.		
The Published Works of Arcangelo Corelli		
Opus 1	*Sonate a tre, doi violini, e violone, o arcileuto, col basso per l'organo* [4 partbooks]	Rome, 1681
Opus 2	*Sonate da camera a tre, doi violini, e violone, o cimbalo* [3 partbooks]	Rome, 1685
Opus 3	*Sonate a tre, doi violini, e violone, o arcileuto col basso per l'organo* [4 partbooks]	Rome, 1689
Opus 4	*Sonate a tre* [3 partbooks]	Rome, 1694
Opus 5	*Sonate a violino e violone o cimbalo* [score]	Rome, 1700
Opus 6	*Concerti grossi per due violini e violoncello obbligati e due altri violini, viola e basso di concerto grosso ad arbitrio che si potranno raddoppiare* [7 partbooks]	Amsterdam, 1714

the fact that he was able to incorporate such formulas effortlessly into pieces that at once sound familiar yet fresh.

Opus 5 is Corelli's only music for solo violin and basso continuo. The twelve works are divided evenly between free sonatas and chamber sonatas. The collection is virtually without precedent, for published sonatas for violin and continuo had been rare and no earlier ones closely resemble these in style. Within the first year of publication the sonatas of opus 5 were reprinted as far away as London (Table 3-2). Two years later the last six sonatas appeared in

Example 3-10. Corelli, Sonata *da camera a tre* in D Major, op. 2, no. 1, a) movement 1, mm. 5b–8a; b) movement 2, mm. 7–8.

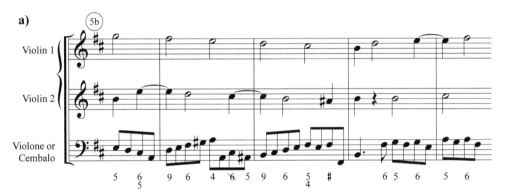

Table 3-2.
Editions of the Opus 5 Sonatas Published during Corelli's Lifetime

1700	*Sonate a Violino e Violone o Cimbalo*	Rome: Gasparo Pietra Santa
1700	*Sonate a Violino e Violone o Cimbalo*	Bologna: Marino Silvani
1700	*XII Sonatas by Arcangelo Corelli, his V opera*	London: John Walsh
1700	*Sonate a Violino e Violone o Cimbalo*	Amsterdam: Estienne Roger
1702	*Six Solos for a Flute and a Bass by Archangelo Corelli Being The second part of his Fifth Opera Containing Preludes Allmands Corrants Iiggs Sarabands Gavotts With the Spanish Folly The whole exactly Transpos'd and made fitt for a Flute and a Bass with the aprobation of severall Eminent Masters*	London: John Walsh
1708	*Sonate a Violino e Violone o Cimbalo*	Paris: Claude Massard de La Tour
1709	*Sonate a Violino e Violone o Cimbalo . . . nouvelle édition mise en meilleur ordre et corrigée d'un gran nombre de fautes*	Amsterdam: Pierre Mortier
1710	*Sonate a Violino e Violone o Cimbalo . . . troisième édition ou l'on a joint les agréemens des Adagio de cet ouvrage, composez par Mr. A. Corelli, comme il les joue*	Amsterdam: Estienne Roger
1711	*XII Sonata's or solo's for a Violin, a bass Violin or Harpsichord compos'd by Arcangelo Corelli, his fifth opera, this edition has ye advantage of haveing ye graces to all ye adagio's and other places where the author thought proper by Arcangelo Corelli*	London: J. Walsh and J. Hare

London in arrangements for recorder ("flute" in the English terminology of the day). Of special interest is the Roger edition issued in Amsterdam in 1710. It contains the first six sonatas with elegant, highly florid embellishments printed on a third staff above the original violin part (Figure 3-2). The publisher's claim that the embellishments were "composed by Mr. A. Corelli as he plays them" has often been questioned. But it has recently received support from the discovery of a contract between Roger and Corelli (Allsop 1999, 60). The edition thus provides priceless evidence for historical performance style.

The virtuoso elements of opus 5 became part and parcel of the solo concertos that other composers were beginning to write. Yet Corelli never wrote concertos of this type. The twelve works published posthumously in opus 6 are concerti grossi, that is, ensemble pieces without soloists. They are scored like Torelli's opus 8, but they use the ensemble quite differently. The two solo violins and the cello provide all the essential material. The remaining instruments—two additional violins, viola, and basso continuo—serve as ripieno instruments, reinforcing the three main parts and occasionally filling out the harmony. These concertos therefore also can be performed as sonate a tre—that is, as sonatas for two violins, cello, and organ or harpsichord continuo. By the same token, some of Corelli's trio sonatas could have been expanded into orchestral works by the addition of ripieno parts. Certainly this approach was practiced in Germany, where Georg Muffat (1653–1704) published a collection of trios in the Corelli style (*Armonico tributo*, 1682) in which he marked optional doublings within the solo parts. This convention continued well into the eighteenth century in Dresden, where the court violinist Johann Pisendel (1687–1755) arranged trio sonatas by Telemann and others for orchestral forces.

The twelve concertos of Corelli's opus 6 can be divided into two groups. Eight of the concertos contain abstract movements and fugues. The other four concertos feature series of dance movements. The most famous piece in the collection is No. 8, known as the "Christ-

Figure 3-2. Opening of movement 1, Arcangelo Corelli, Sonata in C Major for Violin and Continuo, op. 5, no. 3, from Walsh's reprint of the 1710 Amsterdam edition. Marcellene and Walter Mayhall Collection. Courtesy of Walter Mayhall.

mas" Concerto because it was intended for performance in church on the *notte di Natale,* Christmas Eve. Yet this work, now viewed as the epitome of the church concerto, contains several dance movements, including an optional concluding pastorale. This movement is a sort of slow jig, in which the ripieno instruments imitate the *zampogna,* a type of folksy bagpipe played by Italian peasants. The pastorale would become a popular genre in the eighteenth century (and remain so in the nineteenth as well, through Beethoven's Sixth Symphony and other works).

Handel

Among Corelli's many admirers was the young George Frideric Handel (1785–1759). The two met in 1707 or 1708 in Rome, where Corelli had led a performance of one of Handel's early oratorios. After settling in England in 1712, Handel devoted the next three decades to the composition of operas. Yet by the 1720s, Handel had also written at least dozen solo sonatas and a dozen trio sonatas, and probably a number of concertos as well. These works, which circulated among musical connoisseurs via manuscript copies, included a few pieces for woodwind instruments—flute, recorder, and oboe—that were cultivated by a growing number of amateur players. In a scenario that was common in the days before copyright, the London publisher John Walsh obtained a number of Handel's sonatas and issued them in a pirated edition without the composer's consent or cooperation. Walsh, who also published a number of unauthorized editions of Corelli's sonatas, even provided his print of Handel's solo sonatas with a fake title page, claiming it was the work of an Amsterdam publisher. Walsh included several works by other composers in the set, presumably because he could not locate twelve authentic pieces. Moreover, to make Handel's relatively difficult flute sonatas more saleable to amateurs, Walsh transposed them to easier keys. Walsh would go on to publish pirated sets of trio sonatas and concertos as well. Among these are the six concertos for two oboes, strings, and continuo. Much of the music is drawn from instrumental movements in Handel's operas and other works, and it is difficult to tell whether or not it reflects the composer's intentions.

To this day, many players know Handel's sonatas and concertos from the dubious arrangements published by Walsh. Several spurious sonatas also continue to be played as Handel's works, while the more challenging original versions of several pieces remain little known. These include Handel's flute sonatas, such as the Sonata in D Minor, HWV 367a, and the Trio Sonata for Flute, Violin, and Continuo in C Minor, HWV 386a (Oleskiewicz 1999–2000, 1030–1031). The authentic Handel sonatas, though strongly influenced by works of Corelli, are far from being colorless imitations. They contain highly inventive passages, such as the rushing Furioso movement of the D-Minor flute sonata (published by Walsh in B minor) or the aria-like Adagio of the C-Minor Trio Sonata, in which the flute is accompanied by the violin playing in double stops.

Handel's most inventive homage to Corelli can be found in the twelve concerti grossi published in 1739 as his opus 6 (the same opus number as Corelli's set). By then the Roman-style concerto grosso was practically forgotten, having been superseded by the more popular Venetian solo concerto. Yet Handel revivified the old genre through a remarkable combination of old-fashioned counterpoint and up-to-date scoring. He included fugues, even one based on a theme by his old German teacher Friedrich Wilhelm Zachow (1663–1712). But he also presented original transformations of traditional Baroque dances, such as the chaconne that appears in the middle of the sixth concerto. This movement, one of the composer's favorites, bears the title "Musette," which—like Corelli's Christmas pastorale—refers to a bagpipe-like instrument imitated by the string accompaniment. A more direct imitation of the Christmas pastorale occurs in the sinfonia entitled "Pifa" from the *Messiah,* which was composed a year or two later.

Following the precedent in Corelli's concerti grossi, Handel occasionally singles out the first concertino violin for special virtuoso treatment in his opus 6 concertos. Also significant are the six concertos for organ and strings, opus 4 (1738). Among the first keyboard concertos on record, the pieces were originally composed by Handel for his own use as instrumental interludes during oratorio performances. Yet they, too, belong largely to the Roman tradition, and many movements are essentially organ pieces with optional string reinforcement. For true soloistic writing within a larger instrumental ensemble, one must look elsewhere, especially to the distinct tradition that had been developing since the turn of the century in Venice.

VENICE AFTER 1650

Despite its declining political and economic importance, Venice remained the leading musical city in Italy through the end of the Baroque. During the first half of the eighteenth century Venice was especially known for its *ospedali,* charitable institutions that combined features of orphanages and convents and often raised money through public concerts by their members. The most famous of these was the Ospedali della Pietà, whose all-female ensemble achieved considerable acclaim. Through much of the early eighteenth century the ensemble was led by violinist Antonio Vivaldi (1678–1741), who became the most famous Italian composer of his day.

Vivaldi

Vivaldi is sometimes said to have studied with Giovanni Legrenzi (1626–1690), a major Venetian composer of operas and instrumental music. Although this no longer seems likely, Vivaldi undoubtedly knew Legrenzi's works, which include several sets of sonatas for strings and continuo. But Vivaldi's distinctive style owes more to the forthright virtuosity and inventive scoring of the Bolognese composers, as well as to opera. Venetian opera at the time was dominated by solo singers who were renowned for their beautiful embellishment of slow arias and their bravura performance of rapid passagework in quick ones. Vivaldi called on his instrumental players to do the same. Although he composed operas, solo sonatas, and trio sonatas, he is best known for his innovative concertos, especially the two hundred or so for his own instrument, the violin.

Vivaldi's first published set of concertos, *L'estro armonico* (The Harmonic Whim), opus 3, appeared in 1711. The set contains twelve masterful concertos with three distinct types of scoring: four solo concertos for violin, strings, and continuo; four double concertos for two violins, strings, and continuo; and four concertos for four violins, two violas, and two cellos. The last are sometimes termed "chamber concertos," since all the instruments serve as equal partners (there are no separate ripieno parts). Vivaldi was not the first to write these types of concertos—all three are found among the works of Torelli and other Venetians such as Tomaso Albinoni (1671–1751) and the Marcello brothers Alessandro (1684–1750) and Benedetto (1686–1739). It was Vivaldi, however, who would most influence other composers, including J. S. Bach, who arranged several concertos of opus 3 as well as other works circulating in manuscript as keyboard transcriptions or concertos.

What distinguishes the Venetian concertos and the works of Vivaldi in particular is their incorporation of elements drawn from the operatic aria. Most movements, especially the outer ones in quick tempos, open with a ritornello for the entire ensemble. This ritornello returns at the end of the movement and, in shortened form, several times in between. The ritornello frames contrasting episodes dominated by the soloist or soloists. The result, known today as ritornello form, became the basic building block for most later Baroque and early Classical concertos. Vivaldi brought the ritornello form to a remarkable state of refinement, and added to it incisive, declamatory themes, clear and logical harmonic plans, and compelling motoric rhythms. These qualities were emulated by composers throughout Europe, including J. S. Bach and Jean-Marie Leclair (1697–1764), whose concertos represent inventive personal adaptations of the Vivaldi style within their respective German and French traditions.

Vivaldi's best-known concertos are the four that open opus 8, a set of twelve works published around 1725. Known today as "The Four Seasons" and scored for solo violin, strings, and continuo, these concertos were accompanied in the original publication by four sonnets describing spring, summer, autumn, and winter. Although undistinguished as poetry, the sonnets nevertheless present distinctive images that are cleverly represented in the music by special effects. Among these are chirping motifs played by violins to imitate birds in the opening movement of the Spring Concerto, double stops imitating hunting horns in the last movement of the Autumn Concerto, and loud, staccato notes in the viola to imitate a barking dog that disturbs the soloist's melody in the slow movement of the Spring Concerto (Examples 3-11 and 3-12, a-b).

THE VENETIAN STYLE IN GERMANY

Among Vivaldi's younger contemporaries in Venice was the violinist Francesco Maria Veracini (1690–1768). Veracini was one of a number of eighteenth-century violin virtuosos

Example 3-11. Vivaldi, "Spring" Concerto in E Major, op. 8, no. 1, movement 1, mm. 59–63: "Canto degl'uccelli: *Tornan' di nuovo al lor canoro incanto*" (Song of the Birds: They turn again to their enchanting song).

Example 3-12. Vivaldi, a) "Autumn" Concerto in F, op. 8, no. 3, movement 3, mm. 30–35: "La caccia: *I cacciator' alla nov'alba a caccia/Con corni, schioppi, e canni escono fuore*" (The Hunt: The hunters, at the first crack of dawn, / With horns, guns, and shot, go forth to the hunt); b) "Spring," movement 2, mm. 1–3: the solo violin part is labeled "Il caparo che dorme" (The Sleeping Goatherd), the ripieno violins are labeled "Mormorio di frondi e piante" (The Murmuring Fronds and Plants) and the viola, labeled "Il cane che grida" (The Barking Dog), also contains the indication "si deve suonare sempre molto forte e strappato" (to be played always very loudly, forcing the string).

a)

b)

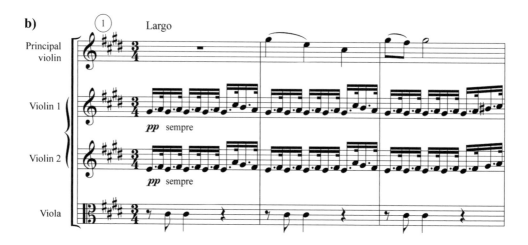

who, following the path of Corelli and Vivaldi, enriched the violin repertory with sonatas that increasingly stretched the technical and interpretive limits of the instrument. Veracini traveled from his native Florence to play at St. Mark's in Venice in 1711 and 1712. Later journeys brought him to London, Düsseldorf, and Dresden.

Dresden was the seat of the Saxon Elector, who at the time was also King of Poland. During the first half of the century the Saxon court boasted one of the finest musical establishments in Europe (see Chapter 5). Its large orchestra included a host of eminent virtuosos, such as violinist Johann Georg Pisendel, flutists Pierre-Gabriel Buffardin and Johann Joachim Quantz, and lutenist Silvius Leopold Weiss. Among Veracini's works is a set of twelve sonatas for violin or recorder and continuo, preserved in a manuscript sent from Venice to the Saxon Elector in 1716. The work was surely intended to draw the Elector's attention to Veracini's skills, and it appears to have succeeded. Veracini joined the court in the following year and remained until 1722, when, according to one account, he "leapt from a

Example 3-13. Quantz, Sonata in C Minor for Flute and Continuo, QV 1: 14, movement 1, mm. 1–8.

third-story window in a fit of madness brought on by too much application to music and reading of alchemy" (Hill 2003).

Collections of woodwind sonatas would soon become a staple of the German repertory. The extraordinarily prolific Georg Philipp Telemann (1681–1767), for instance, composed dozens of woodwind sonatas alongside concertos and other Italian-style works. Veracini's Dresden set is one of the earliest examples of the genre, however, although its use of violinistic figuration suggests that the recorder option was an afterthought. Nevertheless the pieces show inventive features such as in the use of da capo form, borrowed from the operatic aria, as the basis for allegro movements (Sampler CD 1, track 12).

Flautist Johann Joachim Quantz (1697–1773) of the Dresden ensemble traveled to Italy and London, meeting Vivaldi and Handel before returning to write a distinctive repertory that reflects their influence. Quantz is best known for his numerous flute sonatas and concertos composed in Dresden and Berlin, many for the Prussian king Frederick the Great (1712–1786). Frederick was himself a flutist and composer, receiving his early training from Quantz. Quantz joined him in Berlin in 1741 and later dedicated his famous treatise on flute playing, *Versuch einer Anweisung die Flöte traversiere zu spielen* (On Playing the Transverse Flute, 1752), to his royal patron.

Today Quantz is strongly identified with a so-called Berlin style, which is characterized by highly expressive solo writing (Example 3-13). His younger colleagues in Berlin, including Bach's son Carl Philipp Emanuel (1714–1788), adopted a similar style in their sonatas and concertos and thus extended the Italian Baroque tradition well into the second half of the century. The origins of this style, however, lay in Dresden, where Quantz derived it from the Italian style that dominated music there (Oleskiewicz 1999, 81–83).

Quantz's early works are very much in the spirit of Vivaldi. Among these is a recently discovered Quartet in D Major for Flute, Violin, Viola, and Continuo, in which the flutist acts like the soloist in a concerto, playing brilliant solos introduced by ritornellos (Oleskiewicz 2003; Example 3-14). In the five other quartets that follow in the collection, the flute, violin, and viola serve as equal partners in a more old-fashioned, contrapuntal texture. The contrast between sonatas in concerto style and those in fugal style would later be delineated by Johann Adolph Scheibe (1708–1776), a writer best known for his negative critique of the music of J. S. Bach.

Bach, like Handel, was primarily a composer of vocal and keyboard music. Yet his sonatas and concertos also extended the Italian instrumental tradition. Although removed in

Example 3-14. Quantz, Quartet no. 1 in D Major for Flute, Violin, Viola, and Continuo, movement 3, mm. 21–28.

time, place, and style from the works of Italian composers, his monumental music would have been inconceivable without the foundation laid by Marini, Castello, Torelli, Corelli, and Vivaldi. Indeed, the emergence of Italian chamber music during the Baroque is nothing less than the emergence of instrumental music as we know it today.

BIBLIOGRAPHY

Allsop, Peter. 1992. *The Italian "Trio" Sonata from Its Origins until Corelli.* Oxford: Clarendon Press.
————. 1999. *Arcangelo Corelli: New Orpheus of Our Times.* Oxford: Oxford University Press.
Bonta, Stephen. 1977. "From Violone to Violoncello: A Question of Strings?" *Journal of the American Musical Instrument Society* 3: 64–99.

Harrán, Don. 1999. *Salamone Rossi: Jewish Musician in Late Renaissance Mantua.* Oxford: Oxford University Press.

Hill, John Walter. 2003. "Veracini, Giovanni Maria." In *The New Grove Dictionary of Music Online,* ed. Laura Macy. http://www.grovemusic.com (accessed July 14).

Mann, Alfred. 1996. *Handel: The Orchestral Music.* New York: Schirmer Books.

Newman, William S. 1972. *The Sonata in the Baroque Era.* 3rd ed. New York: W. W. Norton.

Oleskiewicz, Mary. 1999. "The Trio in Bach's *Musical Offering:* A Salute to Frederick's Tastes and Quantz's Flutes?" In *Bach Perspectives, Volume 4: The Music of J. S. Bach: Analysis and Interpretation,* ed. David Schulenberg, 79–110. Lincoln: University of Nebraska Press.

————. 1999–2000. Review of *Georg Friedrich Händel: Elf Sonaten für Flöte und Basso continuo,* new edition by Terence Best. *Music Library Association Notes* 56: 1028–1032.

————. 2003. "Quantz's *Quatuors* and Other Works Newly Discovered." *Early Music* 31 (2003): 484–505.

Quantz, Johann Joachim. [1752] 2000. *Versuch einer Anweisung die flöte traversiere zu spielen,* ed. Hans-Peter Schmitz. Kassel: Bärenreiter Verlag. Translated in 2001 by Edward R. Reilly as *On Playing the Flute.* Reissue of 2nd ed. Boston: Northeastern University Press.

Selfridge-Field, Eleanor. 1994. *Venetian Instrumental Music From Gabrieli to Vivaldi.* 3rd rev. ed. New York: Dover.

Talbot, Michael. 1992. *Vivaldi.* New York: Schirmer Books.

CHAPTER FOUR

Music for Church and Community: Buxtehude in Lübeck

Kerala J. Snyder

IN THE AUTUMN OF 1705, the twenty-year-old Johann Sebastian Bach requested a one-month leave of absence from his position as organist of the New Church in Arnstadt and set out by foot on a journey to North Germany. When he returned four months later and was asked where he had been for so long, he replied that he had "been to Lübeck in order to comprehend one thing and another about his art" (David, Mendel, and Wolff 1998, 46). Enigmatic as his answer was, it is nevertheless clear that he had broader goals in mind than merely to study organ performance with Dieterich Buxtehude (c. 1637–1707), the organist of St. Mary's Church in Lübeck and one of the leading musicians of North Germany. The timing of Bach's trip suggests that he wanted to be present in Lübeck for the Abendmusik season, a series of concerts that Buxtehude presented to the community every year on the last two Sundays of Trinity and the second, third, and fourth Sundays of Advent, running between November 15 and December 20 in 1705. It must have been the dual thrust of Buxtehude's music-making, which served both to enhance worship in the church and to entertain the larger community, that attracted the young Bach to travel more than two hundred miles to study with him.

The City of Lübeck and St. Mary's Church

Lübeck was a major seaport at that time, situated on the Trave River just a few miles inland from the Baltic Sea. It had risen to a position of great power and wealth during the late Middle Ages as the head of the league of German cities known as the Hansa, which then dominated north European trade. By the time Buxtehude arrived in 1668, however, the Hansa was essentially defunct, and Lübeck had yielded much of its former importance to Hamburg, which was better situated for the growing Atlantic trade and more receptive to new ideas. Still, Lübeck, with a population of about 27,000, remained a center for wholesale trade, shipbuilding, and shipping, and the trading relationships developed during the Hanseatic time were maintained and even expanded, extending from the Mediterranean to Greenland and Russia and even as far as the Caribbean. Lübeck's leading businessmen still commanded considerable wealth.

Lübeck's distinguished brick-Gothic cityscape, which Matthäus Merian depicted in an engraving published in 1641 (Figure 4-1), is still largely visible today. In the center of Merian's view from the west we see the twin towers of St. Mary's Church, the official church of the city council and the parish church of the city's most important businessmen. To its left is a smaller church with a spire but no tower; this is St. Catherine's, formerly part of a Franciscan

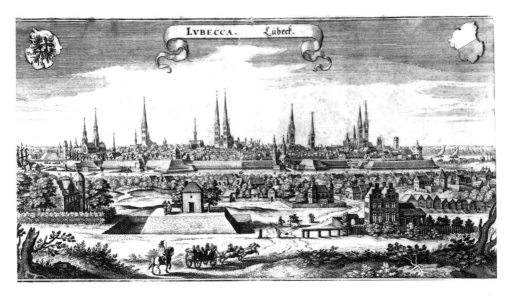

Figure 4-1. Lübeck, view of the city from the west. Engraving by Matthäus Merian (1641). Used with permission of the St. Annen Museum, Lübeck.

monastery that became the city's Latin school with the Lutheran Reformation. Here the cantor taught music, and the choir of the school sang regularly at the church services of St. Mary's. The other twin-towered church, at the southern end of the city, is the Cathedral, and north of it are the single towers of the other three parish churches: St. Peter's, St. Aegidien, and St. Jakobi. The two churches at the far left of the engraving were never principal churches and were torn down during the nineteenth century. St. Mary's, St. Peter's, and the Cathedral suffered severe damage during World War II, but they have been rebuilt. An imposing city hall, scarcely visible in the engraving, stands on the spacious marketplace just to the south of St. Mary's. This inner city is quite small, and one can easily walk from St. Jakobi to the Cathedral in twenty minutes.

St. Mary's, like most medieval churches, had a long and complicated architectural history, achieving its final form as a high-Gothic basilica during the years 1260–1350, the period of ascendancy for both Lübeck and the Hansa. This style had been developed in France using stone; in Lübeck the normal building material was brick, and St. Mary's became one of the first churches in which the high-Gothic style was executed in this material. The church exerted a powerful influence in the spread of the brick-Gothic style throughout the Baltic region. One of the largest places of worship in Germany, St. Mary's measures 341 feet in length, 190 feet in width, and the vaulting of its nave, supported by flying buttresses, is 126 feet high. Its reconstructed exterior (Plate 11) differs little from the church that Buxtehude knew.

St. Mary's had functioned as the official church of the Lübeck city council since 1286, when the council had gained the right to chose its head pastor, independently of the bishop. A distinction between church and state did not exist at that time; the church bell called the council into session, and its members assembled in their special pews in St. Mary's before proceeding as a group across the church yard to the city hall. Much city business was conducted within the walls of the church, including the execution of contracts and the recording of documents, and the treasures and archives of both the city and the Hansa were kept there.

When Lübeck adopted the Reformation in 1530, St. Mary's became even more important, because Lübeck was a free imperial city, and under the Lutheran system of church government the city council presided over all the churches in Lübeck. The superintendent that the council appointed to fulfill this responsibility preached regularly at St. Mary's. At least one of the superintendents was a friend to Buxtehude.

The Organs of St. Mary's

Important Hanseatic cities such as Lübeck, Hamburg, Königsberg (now Kaliningrad, Russia), Bremen, Danzig (now Gdansk, Poland), Lüneburg, Stade, Stralsund, and Rostock all boasted large organs in their churches. Next to an impressive city hall, a magnificent organ case on the west wall of a large church offered the merchants of these trading cities the best opportunity to display their collective wealth. According to a list of organ specifications published by Johann Mattheson in 1721, all these cities had three-manual organs, and each of Hamburg's four principal churches had a four-manual organ (Mattheson 1721). In addition to the many registers of pipes commanded by their manual keyboards, these organs contained large, independent pedal divisions, typical of the North German style of organ building.

The beautiful two-story case of the large organ in St. Mary's Church, Lübeck (Figure 4-2), completed in 1518 by Bartold Hering, originally housed a two-manual instrument, which was expanded to three manuals in 1561. When Buxtehude assumed the duties of organist in 1668, its most recent renovation had been completed in 1641 by the Lübeck organ builder Friedrich Stellwagen, just prior to the arrival of Franz Tunder, Buxtehude's predecessor as organist. In 1687 Arp Schnitger, the leading North German organ builder of the seventeenth century, completed his first masterpiece in Hamburg, at St. Nicholas's Church. The instrument contained sixty-seven stops on four manuals and pedal. After inspecting the St. Nicholas organ, Buxtehude began a long and ultimately fruitless attempt to convince the directors of St. Mary's to hire Schnitger to renovate the large organ there. Schnitger did build a three-manual organ, completed in 1699, for the Lübeck Cathedral, and the St. Mary's organ received a small renovation by Otto Dieterich Richborn in 1704, bringing its total number of stops to fifty-two. Its pedal division contained fifteen stops, including two thirty-two-foot stops, which sounded two octaves below normal pitch. Many of Buxtehude's praeludia (see Chapter 9) contain dazzling virtuoso passages for solo pedal. With other minor renovations, the large organ survived until 1851, when Johann Friedrich Schulze began the installation of a new organ behind Hering's façade. Both the organ and the façade were destroyed in the Allied bombing of 1942.

Like many other churches in Hanseatic cities, St. Mary's contained a second, "small" organ. With approximately forty stops on three manuals and pedal (its history is not well documented), it would have been considered a large organ anywhere else. This instrument was housed in the "Totentanz" chapel on the north side of St. Mary's, so called because it contained a famous mural of the Dance of Death, originally painted by the Lübeck artist Bernt Notke in 1463. This organ, too, had been renovated by Friedrich Stellwagen, who had also built the Rückpositiv of a sister instrument in Lübeck, the small organ of St. Jakobi, in 1636. Although the Totentanz organ was destroyed in 1942, the St. Jakobi organ survives and now offers a unique example of the sound of a seventeenth-century Lübeck organ. It can be heard on modern recordings.

Buxtehude as Organist

Buxtehude came to Lübeck from Denmark, where had he served as organist of St. Mary's Church in Helsingør (Elsinore) from 1660 to 1668. His father, Hans Buxtehude, also an or-

Figure 4-2. Lübeck, St. Mary's Church, west end before 1942, showing large organ and balconies. Used with permission of the St. Annen Museum, Lübeck.

ganist, had emigrated some time prior to 1641 from Oldesloe, a small city between Lübeck and Hamburg, to Helsingborg, which is now part of Sweden but was Danish at the time. Dieterich Buxtehude was probably born in Helsingborg in 1637 and received most if not all of his training as an organist in Denmark. The course of his life prior to his appointment as organist of St. Mary's Church, Helsingborg, in 1657 or 1658, is not documented, but the family was friendly with Johann Lorentz, Jr., organist of St. Nicholas's Church in Copenhagen, and study with Heinrich Scheidemann in Hamburg or Franz Tunder in Lübeck is also possible. Shortly after becoming a citizen of Lübeck on July 23, 1668, Buxtehude married Tunder's second daughter, Anna Margaretha. Although this was a normal way to secure a position at that time, it is unlikely that the stipulation had been laid down by Tunder himself (as Buxtehude would later do for his successor), since other organists had been auditioned following Tunder's death on November 5, 1667.

Buxtehude's responsibilities as organist in Lübeck are not spelled out in any surviving contract, but he undoubtedly played at the main morning service and the afternoon Vespers service on Sundays and feast days, each of which lasted about three hours, with a one-hour sermon in the middle. William Carr, an English visitor to Lübeck during the mid-1670s, noted that "the people here spend much time in their Churches at devotion, which consists chiefely *[sic]* in singing" (quoted in Snyder 1987, 40). The organist normally did not accompany the congregational singing in Lübeck during Buxtehude's time—that was done by the cantor with his choir—but numerous chorale preludes by Buxtehude suggest the style in which he would have improvised introductions to the hymns.

Lübeck did not have an official hymnal until 1703, very late in Buxtehude's career, and that hymnal, *Lübeckisches Gesangbuch,* contained only the texts of its 303 hymns, not the music. Two years after its publication the cantor Jacob Pagendarm arranged four-part settings of these hymns and had them copied into four manuscript partbooks for the use of the choir. Three of the partbooks have been preserved in the Lübeck archives. A similar soprano partbook from an earlier time (Archiv der Hansestadt, MK Musik 13), probably the 1670s, contains texts and melodies for 110 hymns, and these presumably represent the principal chorales sung at St. Mary's during Buxtehude's tenure. The melodies for all but three of Buxtehude's organ chorale settings, and all of Tunder's, are contained in this manuscript. Approximately half of the hymns stem from the time of the Reformation, including *Erhalt uns Herr bei deinem Wort* (Example 4-1). Martin Luther composed both the melody and the words of this hymn, which may be translated "Lord, keep us steadfast in your word, and control the bloodshed of the Pope and the Turks, who want to displace your son, Jesus Christ, from his throne." Luther's perception of the threats posed by the Roman Catholic Church and the advancing Ottoman Empire were still very much alive in seventeenth-century Lübeck. Later versions of this hymn replace the Pope and the Turks simply with "foes."

Buxtehude's setting of *Erhalt uns Herr,* BuxWV 185 (Example 4-2), can be heard on Harald Vogel's recording on the small organ of St. Jakobi, Lübeck (Vogel 1987). Its manuscript source presents the text on three staves for an organ with two manuals and pedal, so that the highest part, which carries the chorale, can sound as a solo voice on one manual, with a more subdued registration on a second manual for the accompanying middle voices. The bass line is taken in the pedal. Buxtehude seamlessly combines two compositional styles in this very short piece. Following a succinct opening flourish, the top line presents the chorale melody in a highly ornamented form for its first three phrases, in a style similar to that of the improvised Italianate vocal ornamentation taught in treatises on the art of singing. Whenever this voice is present, the resulting homophonic texture resembles that of a solo aria accompanied by basso continuo. During the interludes between chorale phrases, however, the imitative

Example 4-1.   Luther: *Erhalt uns Herr bei deinem Wort.* Archiv der Hansestadt Lübeck, Archiv der Marienkirche, *III: Musik, Nr. 13,* p. 102.

Er - halt uns Herr bey   dei-nem Wort,   und steur des Pabsts und Tür-ken Mord,

die   Je - sum Chri-stum dei - nen Sohn   stür - tzen wol - len von sei - nem Thron.

contrapuntal texture of an organ fugue appears briefly as each of the lower three voices presents the next phrase of the chorale.

Most of Buxtehude's chorale settings resemble *Erhalt uns Herr* and probably represent written-down versions of his improvised hymn introductions during church services at St. Mary's. They differ markedly from his lengthy and varied chorale fantasias, such as *Nun freut euch, lieben Christen g'mein* (BuxWV 210; PGM 104; see Chapter 9 and Snyder 1987, 259–261). Chorale fantasias such as this exploit the possibilities of the North German organ to its fullest, and they appear to have been cultivated only by organists working in Hanseatic cities. Thus the hiring of musicians who could compose and play such extravagant works may have represented yet another means for the merchants to display their collective wealth.

Music for the Liturgy: The Cantor and His Choir

The Lutheran liturgy that surrounded the morning sermon at St. Mary's took its structure from the Roman Catholic Mass. The chants of the proper had been replaced by various German hymns, but the ordinary was still in place. On high feasts, the Kyrie, Gloria, Credo, and Sanctus were sung in Latin; at other times, they might be replaced by their German hymn paraphrases. The Agnus Dei was always sung as the hymn "Christe du Lamm Gottes." The communion service before the altar began with the Credo; during the distribution of communion, hymns were sung or concerted music was performed. The liturgy surrounding the afternoon sermon is less well documented. It included the reading of the epistle for the day, numerous hymns, the singing of the Magnificat in German or Latin, and, on feast days, concerted music both before and after the sermon. The Te Deum, in Latin or in German, could be sung as a part of either the morning or the afternoon service.

The cantor directed the liturgical music of St. Mary's from a choir loft behind the rood screen at the east end of the church (Figure 4-3). Although the church paid the cantor a regular salary, his chief appointment and main income came from his position as a instructor at St. Catherine's School, where he taught Latin and religion as well as music. The choirboys from the school performed regularly at St. Mary's, singing in unison on ordinary Sundays and in polyphony on feast days. The seven members of the Lübeck municipal musicians and three extra instrumentalists received a yearly salary from the church to perform with the cantor, probably only on feast days. Samuel Franck (1633–1679) was serving as cantor when Buxtehude arrived in Lübeck. Franck was married to Franz Tunder's oldest daughter, Sophia, and thus cantor and organist became brothers-in-law when Buxtehude married Anna Margaretha. Jacob Pagendarm (1646–1706) succeeded Franck; he had studied at the universities

Example 4-2. Buxtehude: *Erhalt uns Herr bei deinem Wort,* BuxWV 185.

Example 4-2 (continued).   Buxtehude: *Erhalt uns Herr bei deinem Wort,* BuxWV 185.

of Helmstedt and Wittenberg and had served as cantor in Osnabrück before coming to Lübeck.

A glimpse of the special music that was performed on feast days at St. Mary's can be gained from *Natalitia Sacra,* a booklet that gives the texts and scorings—but not the names of the composers—for the first and second days of Christmas 1682 and New Year's and Epiphany [January 6] 1683 (see Snyder 1987, 89–90, 482–484). On each of these days, the Kyrie and Gloria were performed in Latin in concerted style, with vocal soloists, capella (the choir that reinforced the ensemble of soloists), and instruments. On Christmas Day the Credo and Sanctus were performed with the same forces as the Kyrie and Gloria: eight vocal soloists, eight parts in the capella, and ten instrumentalists. The concerted communion music on free texts for these feast days required far fewer singers and no capella. The afternoon services each presented four vocal works: a motet for eight voices without instruments and a multimovement work with vocal soloists and instruments before the sermon, and usually a Latin Magnificat and German motet afterwards, both with soloists, capella, and instruments. Not one of these works corresponds to a surviving vocal work by Buxtehude. One must remember, however, that his job was that of organist, not cantor.

A large portion of the old choir library of St. Mary's survives in the archive of the Gesellschaft der Musikfreunde in Vienna, which received it as a gift from the city of Lübeck in 1814. With the addition of one volume that remained in Lübeck, it includes a set of parts in manuscript and sixty-nine prints from the years 1546–1674. These sources contain altogether 2,144 separate works (see Snyder 1995). The collection includes 146 Masses or Mass movements by composers such as Hieronymus Praetorius (1616), Christoph Demantius (1619), Georg Vintz (1630), Maurizio Cazzati (1653), Andreas Hammerschmidt (1663), and

Figure 4-3. Lübeck, St. Mary's Church, east end before 1942, showing the choir loft over the rood screen. Used with permission of the St. Annen Museum, Lübeck.

Gulielmo Bart (1674). Many of these pieces show signs of use in performance. The Mass performed on New Year's Day 1683, scored for six vocal soloists, six in the capella, and six instruments could have been Hammerschmidt's Mass XVI for two sopranos, alto, two tenors, and bass (soloists and capella), two violins, four trombones, and continuo. Jacob Pagendarm noted on a title page of the Hammerschmidt Masses that he had purchased these partbooks in 1673, so he must have brought them with him to Lübeck. None of the other three Masses listed in the text booklet correspond in their scoring to those preserved in the old choir library, nor do the Magnificats. Among the other texts only one can be identified from the choir library: the motet *Corde natus ex parentis* for eight voices performed on the afternoon of Christmas Day. This was very likely the setting of this text by Melchior Vulpius contained in the anthology *Florilegium portense* of 1618.

That more of the works performed during that holiday season do not survive in the old choir library is disappointing but not surprising. Pagendarm is known to have been a prolific composer, even if few of his works are extant, so he probably composed many of the pieces himself. Also, there is considerable evidence to suggest that Buxtehude may have directed some of those works—specifically the communion music in the morning service and the second piece in the afternoon service, which made no use of the capella—from the large organ. Two of the municipal musicians received a regular salary for playing from the organ loft, and singers were occasionally paid to sing from that location as well. Although Buxtehude's job as organist did not require him to direct vocal music in the church service, as the leading musician in Lübeck he certainly had the freedom to do so. And the types of texts and scorings found in those two positions in *Natalitia sacra* resemble quite closely those in many of his 122 surviving vocal works.

Buxtehude's *Jubilate Domino*

Buxtehude served St. Mary's not only as organist but also as Werkmeister, or church administrator, and in that capacity he kept the account books of the church. On April 10, 1672, he entered a payment to two visiting singers, an Italian castrato and a bass from Antwerp, who had performed in the Easter services. Although this guest appearance of a castrato seems to have been a unique event during Buxtehude's tenure, it documents performances at a high level of virtuosity at St. Mary's. His *Jubilate Domino*, BuxWV 64, probably composed somewhat later, demands such virtuosity not only from the singer—possibly an Italian castrato but more likely a German male alto familiar with the Italian vocal style—but also from the player of the viola da gamba. In this work, one of his most engaging, Buxtehude pits vocalist against instrumentalist in a virtuosic contest that recalls numerous definitions of the concerto as an artistic battle.

The sacred vocal concerto arose in Italy in the early seventeenth century and was quickly emulated by German Lutheran composers, notably Michael Praetorius (1571–1621), Heinrich Schütz (1585–1672; PGM 109), Johann Hermann Schein (1586–1630), and Samuel Scheidt (1587–1654). Its most salient characteristics are the use of solo singers and the opposition of at least two bodies of sound. Its roots lie in the opposing choruses in the polychoral motet of the late Renaissance, which could be expanded by the addition of solo singers and instruments to form large sacred concertos, such as Giovanni Gabrieli's *Symphoniae sacrae* (1615), or contracted to form small sacred concertos in which only what might have been the top soprano of each chorus remained, supported by a basso continuo, such as Schütz's *Erhöre mich, wenn ich rufe*, SWV 289 (PGM 109). The ultimate reduction was to one voice and continuo, as in Schütz's *Eile mich, Gott, zu erretten*, SWV 282 (PGM 109). But a sacred concerto for solo voice and continuo differs markedly from a typical German sacred aria with the same

Example 4-3. Buxtehude: *Jubilate Domino,* BuxWV 64, mm. 15–19.

scoring. A sacred concerto is nearly always set to a prose text, usually from the Bible, whereas the aria is set to poetry. The prose text is then broken down into short segments that are set to distinctive musical motives and tossed back and forth between the opposing sounding elements, usually producing irregular phrases, whereas the poetic text of the aria tends to produce regular musical phrases corresponding to its poetic lines.

In Buxtehude's hands the stylistic distinction between concerto and aria often became blurred, and *Jubilate Domino* in particular is infused with the longer, melismatic phrases associated with the later Italian aria. The extensive opening sonata for the viola da gamba and continuo does, however, offer an excellent example of the way in which concertato style can be realized even when the scoring is reduced to the bare minimum of one soloist and basso continuo. Concertato interchange of the main motive announced in the first measure begins in the second half of m. 15 (Example 4-3; Sampler CD 1, track 13, at 0:44). This excerpt begins with imitative entrances of the whole motive, followed by a sharing of the motive between gamba and continuo (m. 17), the entrances of the first half of the motive while the other part rests (m. 18), and finally a statement in parallel thirds as the music moves to a cadence in B minor. The rests and parallel motion are typical of concertato texture; the competitors in this metaphorical battle are friendly and polite, often pausing so that the other can be heard. In the measures following the gamba dominates the scene, however, concertizing with itself by means of abrupt shifts of register and concluding the sonata with a downward sweep and wide arpeggios.

Buxtehude drew the words for *Jubilate Domino* from the Latin Bible, Psalm 97:4–6. As in the majority of his preserved vocal works, this text is not linked to a particular feast in the church year. Rather, it is appropriate for any festive season. He set each verse as a separate section of his concerto, articulated by meter changes and full cadences in the tonic:

    1) 4/4, mm. 29–84; CD 1, track 13, at 1:26

        Jubilate Domino omnis terra.   Shout to the Lord, all the earth.
        Cantate et exsultate et psallite.   Sing and rejoice and sing psalms.

    2) 6/8, mm. 85–139; CD 1, track 13, at 4:17

        Psallite Domino in cithara,   Sing psalms to the Lord with the lyre,
        in cithara et voce psalmi.   with the lyre and the sound of a psalm.

3) 4/4, mm. 131–167; CD 1, track 13, at 6:13

    In buccinis et voce tubae,   With trumpets and the sound of a horn,
    jubilate in conspectu regis Domini.   shout in the sight of the Lord, the king.

The first section falls into two parts, articulated by the gamba's exact repetition in mm. 43–55 of the alto's part in mm. 31–43, an unusual occurrence in Buxtehude's vocal music. The beginning of this section shows the concertato style in the interchange between voice and continuo of a repeated-note motive of two sixteenth notes and an eighth, which not only nicely fits the first three syllables of "jubilate" but also comes from the main motive of the sonata. The word "jubilate" is given special treatment with increasingly lengthy melismas, the last of which is derived from the gamba's opening statement in the sonata. And yet this section is aria-like as well because of its lyrical melodic line, regular rhythm, division into two nearly equal parts by text and cadences, and accompaniment by continuo alone. The gamba's repetition of this material emphasizes its melodic richness as it demonstrates that the tune can exist quite independently of its text. Concertato interchange between voice and gamba begins in earnest with the second half of the verse, and the section ends in a stunning sweep by the gamba from d″ down three octaves to D, the instrument's lowest pitch, in the space of three measures.

Stylistic characteristics of the aria and the concerto likewise balance one another in the two remaining sections of *Jubilate Domino*. Aria style is especially prominent in the second section, composed of regular phrases in lilting 6/8 meter over a two-measure quasi-ostinato. Here Buxtehude demonstrates his ability to turn prose into poetry, transforming the psalm verse into dactylic meter by repeating words and omitting the preposition "in": "Psallite, psallite Domino, cithara, cithara, et voce psalmi." Concertato style and virtuosity dominate the final section, beginning with an improvisatory gamba solo and ending with a breathless display of voice and gamba in parallel thirds.

It is the prominent presence of the viola da gamba that distinguishes *Jubilate Domino* as the work of a German composer. The gamba had fallen out of favor in Italy by this time, but it was still very popular in North Germany. Buxtehude called for it frequently in his scorings of vocal works, but he normally used it as a member of the string ensemble. Its role as a solo instrument in *Jubilate Domino* is unique within Buxtehude's vocal works, but not in his oeuvre as a whole; he published two collections of sonatas for violin, viola da gamba, and harpsichord in 1694 and 1696, his only major publications during his lifetime. Despite the fact that the figured bass part is designated for harpsichord in the printed editions, it is quite likely that Buxtehude performed these sonatas from the organ loft during services at St. Mary's. One of them (opus 1, no. 4) exists in an earlier version in manuscript, where the figured-bass part is designated for the organ, and Buxtehude had earlier announced the forthcoming publication of another collection of sonatas suitable for both church and chamber music. The two municipal musicians who performed regularly with him at the organ until 1692, Hans Iwe and Johann Philip Roth, both played violin and viola da gamba.

The gamba also figures prominently in the one known depiction of Buxtehude, Johannes Voorhout's *Domestic Music Scene,* painted in Hamburg in 1674 (Plate 12). In it Johann Adam Reincken sits at the harpsichord, the one figure in the painting who can be identified by means of another portrait. A man seated to his right holds a sheet of music paper containing a canon for eight voices set to a Latin text from Psalm 133—"Behold, how good and how pleasant it is for brethren to dwell together in unity"—followed by an inscription honoring Buxtehude and Reincken as brothers. To Reincken's left is a gamba player, and behind him a singer. The gamba player is now thought to be Buxtehude, and the man with the canon could be Johann Theile, a friend to them both (Snyder 2007). They probably were not playing an existing composition as they posed for this genre painting, but the performing forces are right for *Jubilate Domino,* if the lutenist is also realizing the continuo. The *Jubilate Domino* would be equally at home in the sensual atmosphere of this secular scene as in the organ loft of St. Mary's Church.

Buxtehude's Arias

The *Natalitia Sacra* reveals that on New Year's Day 1683 the afternoon service in St. Mary's included a performance of a musical work, designated "Aria," based on five strophes of *O Jesu süß wer dein gedenckt* (O sweet Jesus, whoever thinks of thee), the German version of the medieval Latin poem *Jesu dulcis memoria.* Among Buxtehude's preserved vocal works are three settings of verses from the Latin poem, BuxWV 56, 57, and 88, but none from the German version. To judge from the surviving text, *O Jesu süß* was scored for three vocal soloists—alto, tenor, and bass—two viole [da braccia], three viole da gamba, and one unspecified instrument, probably a violone. The entire ensemble performed the first and last verses, and each vocal soloist sang one of the inner strophes, accompanied in verse 2 by two gambas and in verses 3 and 4 by two violas and three gambas. A ritornello for six instruments followed the first four verses.

Buxtehude's *O fröhliche Stunden, o herrliche Zeit,* BuxWV 85 (PGM 102), is also designated "Aria" and is constructed similarly to *O Jesu süß.* The text, a poetic account of Christ's triumphant resurrection and thus proper for Eastertide, is taken from Johann Rist's *Neue musicalische Festandachten* of 1655. Buxtehude scored it for four vocal soloists—two sopranos, alto, and bass—and his most typical string ensemble for vocal music: two violins, two violas, and violone. Following an opening sonata whose persistent repeated notes strike a militaristic tone, an ensemble of two sopranos and bass sings verse 1 in a style that resembles the concerto more than the aria—providing another example of Buxtehude's melding of these once-separate genres. Alto and Soprano 1 sing verses 2 and 3 respectively in a style that is more aria-like, followed by a return to concertato texture with the ensembles of verses 4 and 5. In each of these verses the singers are accompanied only by the continuo, followed by varying ritornelli played by the strings. The final verse brings singers and players together in a resounding concertato tutti.

The aria is the central genre within Buxtehude's vocal oeuvre. Forty-one works are either designated as such or have purely strophic texts, and another twenty-seven are contained within his multimovement cantatas. His settings of strophic texts vary from the simplest possible, in which the music is strophic as well, giving only one melody for all of the verses, through strophic variation to completely through-composed works. In almost all of them Buxtehude uses instrumental ritornelli to articulate the separate verses of the poetic text. The scorings for these works likewise vary from one voice with continuo and two violins for the ritornello to a mammoth work such as *Wie wird erneuet, wie wird erfreuet* (BuxWV 110), a polychoral work for a vocal choir of six soloists, probably reinforced by capella (doubling singers) and two instrumental choirs.

Buxtehude's Cantatas

Prior to 1700 the term "cantata" referred mainly to secular music, and it is not found in any of the sources for Buxtehude's vocal music. It is nonetheless a convenient term to designate a work that juxtaposes at least two discrete movements set to different types of texts in contrasting musical styles. Twenty-seven such works by Buxtehude survive, with scoring ranging from one voice to five, all with instruments. His most common type consists of an opening concerto set to a biblical text for all of the singers followed by an aria whose strophic text is related in some way to the biblical words, with successive verses presented by individual singers or smaller ensembles. This type of cantata usually closes with a repetition of the opening concerto, but sometimes a new movement in concerto style to a text such as "Amen" or "Alleluia" is substituted, as occurs in *Herr, wenn ich nur dich habe* (BuxWV 39). In this cantata, set for soprano, two violins, and violone, the aria text actually paraphrases the biblical words:

Concerto

Herr, wenn ich nur dich habe, so frag ich
nichts nach Himmel und Erden. Wenn
mir gleich Leib und Seel verschmacht,
so bist du doch Gott allezeit meines
Herzens Trost und mein Teil.

Lord, there is nothing in heaven or earth
that I desire besides thee. My flesh
and my heart may fail, but God
is the comfort of my heart and
my portion forever.

—Psalm 73:25–26

Aria

1. Wenn ich, Herr Jesu, habe dich,
was frag ich nach dem Himmel,
wie könnte doch vergnügen mich
der schnöden Welt Getümmel?
Wenn mir gleich Leib und Seel verschmacht,
und mich umfaht die Todesnacht,
so bist du doch mein Leben.

1. If I have thee, Lord Jesus,
what do I desire from heaven;
how could the tumult of the
iniquitous world give me pleasure?
If my flesh and heart fail,
and the night of death surrounds me,
you are still my life.

2. Wie wohl muß doch dem Menschen sein,
der Jesum trägt vergraben
in seines Herzens Kämmerlein,
der wird die Fülle haben,
dem fehlt es nicht an einem Gut,
dieweil er Schirm und starke Hut
bei Gott dem Herrn stets findet.
Amen.

2. How happy must be the person
who carries Jesus buried
in the little chamber of his heart,
he will have abundance,
he will not lack a single thing,
as long as he always finds shelter and
strong protection in God the Lord.
Amen.

—Anna Sophia of Hessen-Darmstadt

Buxtehude sets the prose of the biblical text in concertato style (Example 4-4), with voice and instruments exchanging the motive associated with "Herr, wenn ich nur dich habe," frequent text repetition, and the use of word painting with the octave ascent on the word "Himmel" (heaven). At the beginning of the aria (Example 4-5) he underlines the strong textual connection to the concerto with a similar melodic line, a concertato interjection by the instruments, and a repetition of the first phrase. After that, however, he uses absolutely regular musical phrases that mirror the poetic lines to establish aria style before allowing concerto style to break into the aria again. The two verses of the aria are in pure strophic musical form.

The second musical offering at St. Mary's Church on the afternoon of Christmas Day 1682 began with a biblical text, "Unto us a child is born, unto us a son is given" (Isaiah 9:6), performed by five voices and twelve instruments. An aria of five verses followed, beginning with the text "Welcome my light, my Jesus, my life" and sung successively by Soprano 1, Soprano 2, Alto, Tenor, and Bass. The ritornelli between the strophes were based on three different Christmas chorales and scored for twelve instruments: two violins, two violas, two

Example 4-4. Buxtehude: *Herr, wenn ich nur dich habe,* BuxWV 39, opening concerto, mm. 1–11.

Example 4-5. Buxtehude: *Herr, wenn ich nur dich habe,* BuxWV 39, aria, mm. 1–8.

trumpets, two cornetti, three trombones, and dulcian—an ensemble fit for the birthday of a king and requiring all of Lübeck's municipal musicians plus five extra players. At the end of the aria the opening movement was repeated. If Buxtehude composed the music for this lost work, it would add one more example of the concerto-aria cantata to his oeuvre. Buxtehude also composed a few cantatas that include chorale settings as well.

Erfreue dich, Erde!

We can be quite sure that *Erfreue dich, Erde!* ("Rejoice, O Ye Earth!"), BuxWV 26, was never performed at St. Mary's in Lübeck, because this text was written in Stockholm as a sacred contrafactum to a secular cantata that Buxtehude had composed for a wedding. Most of Buxtehude's vocal music is preserved in a collection of manuscripts assembled in Stockholm by Gustav Düben, chapelmaster to the King of Sweden and organist of the German church in Stockholm. Buxtehude documented his friendship with Düben in 1680 by dedicating to him the manuscript of *Membra Jesu,* BuxWV 75, a cycle of seven cantatas. Düben's collection also provides the only source for all of Franz Tunder's vocal music. Düben's sons donated the collection to the Uppsala University Library in 1732, where it remains as one of the most important resources for the study of seventeenth-century music.

Buxtehude had composed the original cantata for the wedding of Joachim von Dalen and Catharine Margarethe Brauer von Hachenburg, which took place in Lübeck on March 14, 1681. Von Dalen was a lawyer, and his bride the daughter of a Bürgermeister. Both belonged to the nobility, which occupied a small but privileged position in Lübeck society. The social classes in seventeenth-century Lübeck were highly stratified, and sumptuary laws governed the conduct of weddings: how many guests one could invite, how many musicians could play, and what sort of food and drink one could serve.

As a musician, Buxtehude belonged to the fourth of six classes, together with lesser wholesalers, retailers, and brewers. At his wedding he was officially permitted thirty-five guests (there were in fact seventy), he could serve cake but not wine, and he would normally have been permitted no more than three musicians plus a player of the positive organ. Von Dalen, as a member of the highest class, was permitted 120 guests (not including those from out of town), wine, a meal of four courses including pastry, fish, game, and roasted meat, and a large ensemble of musicians, including players of trumpets and drums. Thus Buxtehude scored this wedding cantata for four singers (two sopranos, alto, and bass), two violins and violone, two trumpets with timpani, and continuo. The title of the completed work, BuxWV 122, reflects its scoring: *Schlagt Künstler! die Pauken* (Strike the drums, you artists). A libretto was printed for the occasion (Figure 4-4).

The source for this work at Uppsala contains several layers: the original printed libretto, a manuscript sheet with the *Erfreue dich, Erde* text (written on paper used in Stockholm), a set of vocal and instrumental parts with both titles on the cover page and originally only the *Schlagt Künstler* text in the parts (but with a portion of the *Erfreue dich, Erde* text entered later), a tablature with only *Schlagt Künstler* in the title but with the *Erfreue dich, Erde* text, and finally a set of vocal parts with only the *Erfreue dich, Erde* text. It would appear that Buxtehude had sent to Stockholm a copy of the libretto, which Düben kept, and a set of parts, which Düben had copied and then returned. Düben may or may not have used the parts for performance at a wedding in Stockholm, but later he changed the text and wrote the tablature and new set of vocal parts so that he could use the work for a church service there, as Bach would later do with many of his own secular cantatas. The two texts and their English translations may be compared in Table 4-1, a and b. *Schlagt Künstler! die Pauken* can be heard on Magnus Kjellson's recording *Dieterich Buxtehude, Abendmusik* (Kjellson 2001).

Intrad. mit Paucken / Trompet &c.

Das Gerüchte.

Schlagt / Künstler! die Paucken und Saiten
auffs best
Stofft eilend zusammen in eure weitschallende
Silber-Trompeten:
Vermischet das Trummeln auff Kupfernen Trummeln
mit klaren Klareten
Heut feyren zwey Edle ihr Ehliches Fest.

ARIA.

Die Liebe.

Leben ist die Glut der Hertzen
Die von schönen Augen brennt:
Die man lauter süsse Schmertzen,
Liebligkeiten / Hertzens-Schertzen
Und das holde Feuer nennt.
Lieben ist das rechte Leben
Dem diß liebe-Paar ergeben.
Ritornello.

Figure 4-4. Dieterich Buxtehude, *Schlagt Künstler! die Pauken,* BuxWV 122, page from libretto. Uppsala, Universitetsbibliotek, *VMHS 50:15.* Printed with permission.

The text of *Schlagt Künstler* consists of three separate poems with different metrical and rhyme schemes: the opening chorus of four dactylic lines of irregular length, an aria with four strophes of seven-line trochees, and the closing tutti of ten regular dactylic lines. The translator of *Erfreue dich, Erde* retained the original rhyme schemes (with the exception of the fifth line of the fifth strophe of the aria) and the use of allegorical character names in the aria, changing the occasion from a wedding to Christmas or, with a few variant lines, Easter. Buxtehude's musical setting, now *Erfreue dich, Erde* (Sampler CD 1, tracks 14–19), highlights the metrical contrasts of the poetry by giving the four aria verses to a succession of solo singers and casting it in strophic variation form, with the same bass line but differing

Table 4-1a.

Schlagt Künstler! die Pauken: Text

BuxWV 122	BuxWV 122
Intrad. mit Paucken, Trompet &c	*Introduction with drums, trumpet, etc.*
Das Gerüchte	**Fame**
Schlagt, Künstler! die Paucken und Saiten auffs best;	Strike the drums, you artists, and the strings at your best!
Stosst eilend zusammen in eure weitschallende Silber-Trompeten:	Rush to bring together your broadly ringing silver trumpets;
Vermischet das Trummeln auff Kupfernen Trummeln mit klaren Klareten	Blend the drumming of copper drums with the clear clarions,
Heut feyren zwey Edle ihr Ehliches Fest.	Today two nobles celebrate their wedding feast.
ARIA	**ARIA**
[1] **Die Liebe**	**Love**
Lieben ist die Glut der Hertzen	Love is the glow of the hearts
Die von schönen Augen brennt:	that burn for beautiful eyes;
Die man lauter süsse Schmertzen	which is called sweet pain,
Lieblichkeiten, Hertzens-Schertzen	tenderness, heart's frolic,
Und das holde Feuer nennt.	and the dearest fire.
Lieben ist das rechte Leben	Love is the right way to live,
Dem diß liebe Paar ergeben.	to which this loving pair yields.
Ritornello	
[2] **Die Schönheit**	**Beauty**
Schönheit ist das Band der Seelen	Beauty is the ribbon of the souls
Das mit Huld und Wonne bindt:	that binds with devotion and delight,
Das die Seelen zu vermählen,	that weds the souls together
Und mit Anmuth pflegt zu quälen	and tortures them with a
Die der Geist allein empfindt	gracefulness that only the spirit can feel.
Schönheit ist der Liebe Leben,	Beauty is the life of love,
Dem diß schöne Paar ergeben.	to which this fine pair yields.
Ritornello	
[3] **Die Jugend**	**Youth**
Jugend ist der Leim der Liebe,	Youth is the glue of love,
Der die Welt zusammen hält;	that holds the world together,
Wäre der nicht, Ach! wo bliebe,	If it did not, then what would
Was uns zu der Liebe triebe,	continue to drive us to love,
Und durch Liebreitz mehrt die Welt.	and through the charm of love, increase the world.
Jugend ist der Schönheit Leben,	Youth is the life of beauty
Dem diß frische PAAR ergeben!	to which this fresh pair yields.
Ritornello	
[4] **Die Tugend**	**Virtue**
Tugend über alles streichet!	Everything is touched by virtue!
Balsam, Biesam, trinkbar Gold,	Balsam, musk, drinkable gold,
Jugend, Schönheit, Liebe weichet:	youth, beauty, love all give way.
Dieses Edle Paar ihr gleichet	This noble pair mirrors virtue,
Welchem Erd und Himmel hold.	and so is loved by earth and heaven
Tugend ist der Jugend Leben,	Virtue is the life of youth,
Der diß Tugend-Paar ergeben.	to which this virtuous pair yields.
Ritornello	
Touti	**Tutti**
So liebet und lebet viel Zeiten zusammen,	So love and live long ages together,
Vortreffliche Beyde! in lieblichen Flammen.	you excellent pair! in the lovely flames.
Es müssen die Münde, wie Tauben, sich küssen,	Mouth must kiss mouth like doves,
Die Arme die Arme, wie Kletten, umbschliessen.	Arms must embrace arms like cockleburs.
Die Herbst-Zeit bringt Garben dem Säeman und Binder,	The harvest time brings sheaves to the sowers and binders,
Der Sommer die Rosen: Der Winter, die Kinder:	the summer brings the rose, winter brings the children.
Die Rosen den Färten: Die Kinder dem Freyer!	The rose to the garden, the children to the suitor!
Es brenne ohn Ende ohn Ende diß Feuer!	May it burn without end, without end this fire!
Nie hat es an Liebe und Früchten gefehlet,	Never has love and bounty failed
Wo Schönheit und Jugend und Tugend vermählet.	where beauty, youth, and virtue are wed.
Repet. Schlagt Künstler! &c.	*Repeat Schlagt Künstler! &c* [translation: Joel Speerstra]

Table 4-1b.
Erfreue dich Erde!: Text

BuxWV 26	BuxWV 26
Intrad.	*Introduction*
[Tutti]	
Erfreue dich, Erde, du Himmel, erschall!	Rejoice, oh Earth, oh Heaven, resound!
Ihr himmlischen Bürger, laßt eure beweglichsten Stimmen ertönen,	You heavenly hosts, let your most stirring voices sound,
Das Weltgebäu müsse von mutigem Singen und Jauchzen erdröhnen,	so that the world reverberates with your spirited singing and rejoicing,
Ihr Lieder erwidert den fröhlichen Hall.	your songs respond to the joyful sound.
ARIA	**ARIA**
[1] **Die Freude** [Soprano I]	**Joy**
Freud ist die gewünschte Gabe	Joy is the welcome gift
die der Heiland mit sich bringt,	that the Savior brings with him
wenn er kömmt zu euch hinabe	when he descends to you
als ein zarter Menschenknabe	as a tender human child,
leget Schmertz und Leiden abe.	taking away pain and suffering.
In dem Himmel und auf Erden	In heaven and on earth
muss nu Freud die Fülle werden.	joy must now become abundant.
Ritornello	
[2] **Der Friede** [Soprano II]	**Peace**
Fried macht alles voller Freuden,	Peace infuses all with joy,
Friede, der umb Gottes Thron	peace, which always hovers
schwebet stets und was geschieden	around God's throne and reunites what was asunder,
neu vereinigt, weil aus beiden	because God's son comes from
Mensch und Gott wird Gottes Sohn.	both humanity and God.
In dem Himmel und auf Erden	In heaven and on earth
mus aus Friede Freude werden.	joy must come from peace.
Ritornello	
[3] **Die Gnade** [Alto]	**Grace**
Gnade bringt den Fried zuwegen,	Grace brings peace into effect,
Gnade, die der Sohn erwirbt	grace, which the Son obtains
dadurch Heil und aller Segen	so that salvation and blessing
euch Betrübten kommt entgegen,	can come to you sorrowful ones,
Segen, der niemals verdirbt.	blessing that never perishes.
In dem Himmel und auf Erden	In heaven and on earth
soll euch alle Gnade werden.	grace shall come to you all.
Ritornello	
[4] **Die Wahrheit** [Bass]	**Truth**
Wahrheit, welche Gott geschworen,	Truth, which God has promised,
Und darauf er treulich denkt,	and which he faithfully remembers,
hat die Menschen, so verloren,	has now descended to humanity, so lost,
jetzt zum Leben neu geboren	and now born to new life
und in Gottes Huld gesenkt.	in God's graciousness.
In dem Himmel und auf Erden	In heaven and on earth
soll Wahrheit gerümet werden.	shall truth be praised.
Ritornello	
Tutti	**Tutti**
So denket und danket der göttlichen Güte,	So remember and thank the divine goodness
mit freudigem Herzen und dankbarn Gemüte.	with joyful hearts and thankful minds.
Die Freude bestehe, der Kummer vergehe,	Let joy remain, let sorrow vanish;
die Feindschaft vergehe, der Friede bestehe.	let animosity disappear, let peace endure.
Die Gnade vereinige Erden und Himmel:	Let grace unite earth and heaven;
die Ungnad versinke zum Höllengetümmel.	let disgrace sink into the chaos of Hell.
Die Klarheit der Wahrheit ermunter die Sinnen,	Let clarity and truth encourage the senses
Gott freudig zu loben und lieb zu gewinnen.	to praise God joyfully and to love.
Halleluja lasset dem Höchsten zu Ehren	Halleluja, in honor of the Highest,
mit Singen und Klingen in Ewigkeit hören.	let singing and ringing resound eternally.
Erfreue dich Erde! da Capo	*Repeat Erfreue dich Erde!*

melodies, apart from the verses sung by the two sopranos. Buxtehude set the framing movements in concertato style, with the trumpets and timpani pitted against the voices and strings in their interchanges. The work thus provides another example of a concerto-aria cantata, the only one among Buxtehude's preserved wedding compositions, which also include an aria for the wedding of the King of Sweden. That work, *Klinget für Freuden, ihr lärmen Klarinen,* BuxWV 119, is in simple strophic form, although it does, of course, include parts for trumpets, the musical attribute of nobility.

Abendmusiken for Emperors

On May 5, 1705, the Holy Roman Emperor Leopold I died in Vienna, and his son Joseph I succeeded to the imperial throne. To commemorate these events Buxtehude, citizen of the imperial free city of Lübeck, presented two special Abendmusiken concerts later that year, on the second and third of December, a Wednesday and Thursday. Buxtehude himself called the concerts "extraordinary." It was certainly unusual for him to present Abendmusiken on two successive weeknights rather than on Sundays, which suggests that these were in addition to his regular Sunday series for 1705, about which we know nothing. Although the music is lost, the librettos for *Castrum doloris,* BuxWV 134, and *Templum honoris,* BuxWV 135, survive. These are among the Abendmusiken works that the young Johann Sebastian Bach witnessed, and probably performed in, during his visit to Lübeck in the winter of 1705–1706.

The scoring for *Templum honoris* called for two choruses of voices, two choruses of trumpets and timpani, two choruses of horns and oboes, and twenty-five violins. Extraordinary also were the special arrangements for these performances. *Castrum doloris,* like the usual Abendmusiken, was presented from the large organ. To quote from the description in the libretto:

> In an illumination on the recently-repaired and completely gilded large organ, now covered, and decorated with many lamps and lights, is presented the body of his highness the Kaiser in a coffin on the catafalque; at his head the imperial coat of arms, on both sides the royal Hungarian, Bohemian, and other royal coats of arms; above this, a beautifully decorated sky rests on four palm trees, hung with the imperial, royal, and provincial coats of arms; many angels with lights keep watch around it. The two musical choruses by the organ are dressed in black; the trombones and trumpets are muted, and all the other instruments are also muted. (Quoted in Snyder 1987, 69)

The following evening's performance of *Templum honoris* took place at the opposite end of the church. According to the libretto:

> The temple of honor is beautifully decorated and illuminated, surrounded by a strong guard of brave heroes. The path to the temple is bordered with the virtues and the sciences. The folding doors stand open, and inside one can see on the altar the bust of His Holy Roman Imperial Majesty, before which are presented Joy and Gladness with their children, who carry all kinds of trophies, wreaths, and flowers with palm and laurel branches. (Quoted in Snyder 1987, 69)

The librettos for these two oratorios suggest a wide variety of musical genres and styles: choruses (single, double, women's), recitative, arias (mainly strophic, but not always), instrumental selections (a "lamento chiaconetta," a passacaglia played *vivace*), a chorale setting (*Ach wie nichtig! ach wie flüchtig!*), and even the participation of the entire congregation in the singing of a closing chorale (*Nun laßt uns den Leib begraben*), together with both organs. Although written twenty-four years later, the libretto of *Templum honoris* (Figure 4-5) bears a

INTRADA.

Mit 2. Chöre von Paucken und Trompeten;
Worauff
Von allen Chören und Orgeln

Tutti:

Tempel der Ehren! Eröffne Dich weit/
JOSEPH/ dem Käyser/ dem König zu Ehren
Lasset Ihr Chöre! Glückwünschend euch hören/
Jauchzet Ihr Städte / Ihr Länder und Leut!
JOSEPHS Bild wollen wir mitten einsetzen/
JOSEPH / der Feinde Furcht / Unser Ergetzen!
Tempel der Ehren! Eröffne Dich weit.

Das Gerüchte.
Recitat.

Hör / Sterbliches Geschlechte!
Kaum hatte LEOPOLD/
Der Fromme der Gerechte/
Bezahlt der Sünden = Sold/
Und war getreten ab
Vom Hohen Käyser = Throne
Ins tieffe Grab/
Verwechselnd die Irrdsche mit Himmlischer Krone:
Da gantz Germanien von Leid erfüllet/
Sich gantz verhüllet.
Es klagte laut / und überall
Des Väterlichen Käysers = Fall/
Und seine Noth;
Doch ward das Leid gestillet/
Weil JOSEPH noch nicht todt.

B 2   Aria.

Figure 4-5. Dieterich Buxtehude, *Templum honoris*, BuxWV 135, page from libretto. Stadtbibliothek Lübeck. Printed with permission.

striking resemblance to that of *Schlagt Künstler!* (Figure 4-4): both begin with an intrada for timpani and trumpets and introduce "Das Gerüchte" (Fame) as the first in a series of allegorical characters. In 1705 Buxtehude gave that part to a singer of recitative, whereas he assigned it to an opening chorus in *Schlagt Künstler*. Nonetheless, the earlier work may give a hint of how the lost intrada and opening tutti, "Tempel der Ehren!," of *Templum honoris* may have sounded.

The Abendmusiken and the Lübeck Stock Exchange

Franz Tunder, Buxtehude's predecessor, first mentioned "Abendspiele" in 1646, but no one attempted to trace the history of this famous concert series until 1752, when the Cantor of St. Mary's, Caspar Ruetz, wrote the following:

> One can learn nothing definite about the origins of the Lübeck Abendmusiken. I have tried for a long time in vain. Even in the most complete and extensive reports about Lübeck, such as our . . . great historian Jacob von Melle has written, there is nothing about the origins of the Abendmusiken. . . .
>
> I have spoken with a 90-year-old man who can remember that in his youth these concerts were held during the week, on a Thursday. . . . This situation . . . gives some credibility to the tradition regarding the origins of the Abendmusiken. To wit: in former times the citizenry, before going to the stock exchange, had the praiseworthy custom of assembling in St. Mary's Church, and the organist sometimes played something on the organ for their pleasure, to pass the time and to make himself popular with the citizenry. This was well received, and several rich people, who were also lovers of music, gave him gifts. The organist was thus encouraged, first to add a few violins and then singers as well, until finally it had become a large performance, which was moved to the aforementioned Sundays of Trinity and Advent. (Quoted in Snyder 2000, 41)

The tradition that Ruetz recounts can be partially substantiated by historical facts. A stock exchange was established in Lübeck in 1605, whereby a regular time was set for the merchants to meet at a designated part of the marketplace by the city hall to discuss both their private affairs and matters that affected the business community in general. With time they tired of meeting out of doors, and in 1673 a room in the city hall that had formerly been occupied by the clothiers' guild was remodeled to house the *Börse*. It is perfectly reasonable to assume, then, that prior to 1673, particularly in bad weather, the merchants gathered in St. Mary's, the parish church for many of them, before the opening of the stock exchange in the adjoining market. This time period covers all of Tunder's tenure at St. Mary's and the beginning of Buxtehude's.

One of the rich men who sponsored the organist's concerts may have been Mattheus Rodde (1599–1677), a director of St. Mary's Church who stood godfather to Tunder's son Johann Christoph in 1648. His wife served as godmother to Buxtehude's daughter Helena in 1669, and both his son and daughter were godparents to Anna Sophia Buxtehude in 1672. Rodde belonged to a large trading family that has been characterized as a miniature Hansa in itself, with outposts from Lisbon to Russia, headquartered in Lübeck. Unlike some of his Lübeck contemporaries, Rodde was quick to adapt to new economic conditions. He was one of the first Lübeckers to move into the Greenland whaling trade, investing in one-fourteenth of a whaling ship in 1667. This actually combined quite nicely with his wine trade, because the same ship could go to Greenland in the summer and to Portugal in the winter. He also had connections with Sweden: in 1663 he formed part of an official three-man Lübeck trade delegation to Stockholm. It is at the very least a striking coincidence that the first copies of

Tunder's vocal music in the Düben Collection appear to have been copied in Stockholm at this same time. It is quite possible that Rodde brought the exemplars for those copies with him on that trip, thus beginning a commerce in music manuscripts between Lübeck and Stockholm that rose to mammoth proportions during the 1680s, when the majority of Buxtehude's vocal works were written out. There can be no doubt that Mattheus Rodde was rich; his friendship with Tunder and Buxtehude suggests that he was also a lover of music, and thus he was very likely a leading patron of Tunder's and Buxtehude's concerts, and consequently one of the founders of the Lübeck Abendmusiken.

Buxtehude's Music for the Community

Buxtehude must have had ambitious plans for concert-giving at St. Mary's from the very beginning of his tenure there. Within a year of his arrival he had two new balconies installed near the large organ at the west end of the church, each paid for by a single donor. Four small balconies were already in place during Tunder's time; the two closest to the organ in Figure 4-2, a photograph from the 1930s, are filled with organ pipes from the Schulze organ of 1854. The two new balconies from 1669 projected out into the church (see Figure 4-6), and together these six could accommodate about forty singers and instrumentalists. Only one of Buxtehude's surviving works requires enough performers to fill them, *Benedicam Dominum*, BuxWV 113, with six choirs: (1) violins and violone, (2) trumpets and trombones, (3) five vocal soloists, (4) cornetti and dulcian, (5) trombones, and (6) vocal capella. The Abendmusiken were normally presented from the balconies, and patrons received reserved seats in the rood-screen choir loft at the other end of the church (Figure 4-3). Neither the balconies nor the choir loft was rebuilt following their destruction in World War II.

The first public opera house in Germany, founded by Buxtehude's friends Johann Adam Reincken and Johann Theile, among others, opened in Hamburg on January 2, 1678, with Theile's Singspiel *Orontes* as its first official production. It can be no accident, then, that the first evidence for Buxtehude's presentation of a dramatic work in the Abendmusiken dates from December of that year: the libretto of a two-part oratorio, *Die Hochzeit des Lamms* (BuxWV 128; music lost), performed on the second and third Sundays of Advent. Its text gives an embroidered version of the parable of the wise and foolish virgins (Matthew 25: 1–13), using a mixture of biblical passages, familiar chorale texts, and newly composed poetry, but no recitative. The characters are both biblical—Jesus, the wise virgins, the foolish virgins, the angels—and allegorical—the church. The new poetry includes a love duet for Christ and the Church, who is the bride:

Ich bin dein und du bist mein,	I am thine and thou art mine,
Du bist mein und ich bin dein,	Thou art mine and I am thine,
Ewig sol die Liebe seyn	Our love shall be eternal.
	(quoted in Snyder 1987, 62)

Buxtehude had in effect created an opera house for Lübeck in St. Mary's Church. Ten years later Hinrich Elmenhorst, preacher at St. Catherine's Church in Hamburg and a librettist for the Hamburg Opera, wrote: "Musicians understand the word *operas* to mean the compositions of poets and composers performed not only in theaters, but also in churches. . . . In this connection I must mention how the world famous Lübeck musician Diedericus Buxtehude has performed more than one such opera in public churches there in the Abendmusik customary at a certain time of year, whose poetry has been published" (quoted in Snyder 1987, 67).

Figure 4-6. Lübeck, St. Mary's Church before 1942, showing northwest balcony built in 1669. Used with permission of the St. Annen Museum, Lübeck.

The presentation of the Abendmusiken lay completely outside Buxtehude's duties as organist of St. Mary's, and in this respect he acted as the director of music for the city, even if he was not named as such. He organized the entire production, composed the music, raised the necessary funds, chose the singers and instrumentalists, and conducted the performances. In this aspect of his professional life he functioned as a musical entrepreneur, and his experience as Werkmeister of St. Mary's must have qualified him well to manage the business of producing the Abendmusiken. The business community supported his productions both with a collective donation, for which numerous thank-you letters from Buxtehude survive, and as individual patrons. Occasionally the church made a financial contribution to cover a deficit, and it paid to hire extra police to handle the crowds.

As Buxtehude grew older, he began to look for a successor, and the first prospective candidates of whom we know were Johann Mattheson, age twenty-one, and George Frideric Handel, age eighteen, both of whom were employed at the Hamburg Opera. Mattheson relates the story:

> We traveled together on the 17th of August of that year 1703 to Lübeck, and in the coach we composed many double fugues, in our heads, not written down. The privy council president, Magnus von Wedderkopp, had invited me, in order to make me the future successor of the excellent organist Dietrich Buxtehude. So I took Händel along. . . . We listened to that esteemed artist in his St. Mary's Church with dignified attention. However, since he had proposed a marriage condition in the matter, for which neither of us expressed the slightest inclination, we took our leave, after being complemented and entertained. Johann Christian Schieferdecker later applied himself better to the goal, led the bride home after the death of the father Buxtehude, and received the fine position that Johann Paul Kuntzen so laudably fills at the present time. (Mattheson 1740, 94)

Schieferdecker also worked at the Hamburg Opera before going to Lübeck, as an accompanist and composer. Buxtehude died on May 9, 1707, and as his successor at St. Mary's Schieferdecker composed and presented a new Abendmusik every year from 1707 through 1729. The organists of St. Mary's continued to entertain the citizens of Lübeck with Abendmusiken until the Napoleonic wars brought the concerts to an end in 1810.

BIBLIOGRAPHY

Archiv der Hansestadt Lübeck, Archiv der Marienkirche *(MK), III: Musik, Nr. 13.*

David, Hans T., Arthur Mendel, and Christoph Wolff, eds. 1998. *The New Bach Reader.* New York: W. W. Norton.

Mattheson, Johann, ed., 1721. Friedrich Erhard Niedt, *Musicalische Handleitung Anderer Theil, mit einem Anhang von mehr als 60. Orgel-Wercken versehen durch J. Mattheson.* Hamburg: Benjamin Schillers Wittwe und Joh. Christoph Kißner.

————. [1740] 1994. *Grundlage einer Ehren-Pforte.* Reprint, Graz: Akademische Druck- u. Verlagsanstalt.

Snyder, Kerala J. 1986. "To Lübeck in the Steps of J. S. Bach." *Musical Times* 127: 672–677. Reprinted in *Bach: The Journal of the Riemenschneider Bach Institute* 20 (1989): 38–48.

————. 1987. *Dieterich Buxtehude: Organist in Lübeck.* New York: Schirmer Books.

_____. 1995. "Bach, Buxtehude, and the Old Choir Library of St. Mary's in Lübeck." In *Das Früh- werk Johann Sebastian Bachs,* ed. Karl Heller and Hans-Joachim Schulze, 33–47. Cologne: Studio.

_____. 2000. "Franz Tunder's Stock-Exchange Concerts: Prelude to the Lübeck Abendmusiken." In *GOArt Research Reports* 2: 41–57.

_____. 2007. *Dieterich Buxtehude: Organist in Lübeck.* 2nd rev. ed. Rochester, N.Y.: University of Rochester Press.

RECORDINGS

Kjellson, Magnus, conductor. 2001. Göteborg Baroque Arts Ensemble. *Dieterich Buxtehude, Abend- musik.* Intim Musik, IMCD 070.

Vogel, Harald, organist. 1987. *Dietrich Buxtehude Orgelwerke,* vol. 1. Performed on the organs of St. Jakobi, Lübeck, and St. Ludgeri, Norden. Musikproduktion Dabringhaus und Grimm, MD+G L 3268.

CHAPTER FIVE

The Arts and Royal Extravagance: Music at the French Court

George B. Stauffer

IN FRANCE, AS IN NO OTHER COUNTRY, the standards of musical taste, musical style, and musical performance were determined centrally, at the court in Paris and Versailles. First Louis XIII and then, even more firmly, Louis XIV presided over matters musical, making the French Baroque Period one of the most autocratic yet at the same time most refined cultural eras. Just as French court architecture was imitated on a smaller scale in Germany, Austria, England, and Poland, French music was imported by those countries with vigor and delight. But never was a style utilized by so many initiated by so few.

The Establishment of French Baroque Style

France of the early Baroque—that is, between 1600 and 1650 or so—was filled with political turmoil. Religious conflicts between the Roman Catholics and French Protestants (the Huguenots) and political strife between those who wished to join Italy and the Austrian Empire and those who did not produced an atmosphere that was unstable and far from conductive to the arts.

Louis XIII (1601–1643), who ruled from 1610 until his death in 1643, was an accomplished dancer and composer and supported the arts. He retained the tradition of royal chapel musicians that he inherited from his father, Henri IV, and he formally established the virtuoso ensemble the Vingt-Quatre Violons du roi (Twenty-four Violins of the King) in 1626. He had *airs de cour,* or court songs, sung in his private chambers and at public occasions, and he is known to have composed psalms and, now and then, even conducted the royal choir himself. In 1635 he wrote the words and music and devised the choreography for the *Ballet de la Merlaison,* whose music has survived. It shows the king to be a clever composer, tailoring the style of the music to fit the character of each dancer.

But perhaps because he was melancholy and retiring by nature and was ruled by a domineering mother until he was declared of age in 1614, Louis XIII did not take strong steps to enhance the musical establishment he inherited. For him, music appears to have been more of an occasional indulgence than a passion to which he was dedicated in an ongoing way. Large-scale performances took place, sometimes under the king's direction. They were not standard fare, however, and attracted only modest attention abroad.

A critical factor in the development of Baroque French style was territorial unity and the centralization of cultural standards. This came to the fore under Louis XIII's successor, Louis XIV (1638–1715), who ruled from 1643 until 1661 under the guidance of a regent, Cardinal Mazarin, and from 1661 until his death as the absolute authority over political and cultural matters in France. At the urging of Mazarin he studied Italian music and French dance. As king, he expanded music and dance activities at the court to an unprecedented degree. Under his reign, the provinces were neglected at the expense of the court in Paris and Versailles, where the best musicians, dancers, choreographers, singers, and composers in France vied for employment.

Louis XIV played the lute, guitar, and harpsichord. But his great passion was dancing, and it was this love that led to the dance spectacles, held at Versailles, that became legendary during his reign. While dancing in the *Ballet de la nuit* in 1653 (Figure 5-1), he encountered the young Jean-Baptiste Lully, and together these two ambitious figures, king and music master, forged a regal national style. In time, they discouraged the use of Italian idioms and forms in French music and dissuaded court musicians and composers from traveling to Italy. They focused instead on establishing a distinct French practice, a manner of composing and performing that was soon admired and emulated abroad.

Louis formed the Académie royale de danse in 1661 and the Académie royale de musique soon thereafter. He held competitions for open positions in both institutions, and he commonly assumed final say in the outcome. Competition for the Académie posts was fierce, and Louis demonstrated shrewd judgment. In 1693, for instance, he picked François Couperin over six others to become chapel organist and harpsichordist. In addition, Louis insisted that aristocrats throughout France pay homage to his court. For these occasions and other celebrations, he spared no cost in creating accompanying dance and music extravaganzas that were the envy of Europe (Figure 5-2). Foreign diplomats and dignitaries who attended these events carried glowing reports back to their countries. French style, as set forth at the court in Paris and at Versailles, soon became the measure of sophistication and refinement throughout the continent.

Louis XV (1710–1774), Louis XIV's great-grandson and successor, preferred simple pastorals to the ballets, operas, and other entertainments of his predecessor. During his reign (1715–1774), French practice declined.

The Rise of Lully

The establishment of French Baroque style can be credited to the extraordinary collaboration of king and composer, of Louis XIV and Jean-Baptiste Lully (1632–1687). It seems ironic, in retrospect, that Lully was born in Florence and raised in Italy, learning the violin and guitar from local Tuscan teachers. At age fourteen he left Italy for Paris to take up the position of Italian tutor to Louis XIV's cousin Anne-Marie-Louise d'Orléans. In Paris he completed his musical education and probably studied dance with Jean Regnault, who went on to become master of dance to the king in 1651.

After appearing beside Louis XIV in the dance extravaganza *Ballet de la nuit,* Lully received an appointment as court composer of instrumental music, and for the next decade he both danced and composed. As a dancer, he possessed a fine sense of rhythm and precise movements that earned him a place next to the king in ensemble numbers. As a composer, he initially shared the composition of dances and recitatives with others, as was customary at the time. But in 1661 he gained the appointment of superintendent of court music, the highest office available to a musician, and from that point onward he had the option to write complete works himself. Not liking the performances of the Vingt-Quatre Violons du roi, Lully received permission from Louis XIV to form his own band, the Petits Violons du roi (The King's Chamber Violins). Beginning in 1664 he collaborated with Jean Baptiste Molière (1622–1673) on a series of highly successful *comédies-ballets,* which were performed at the court and sometimes included in the spectacular celebrations of the grand festivals. Lully's

Figure 5-1. Louis XIV as the Sun in *Ballet de la nuit* (1653). Cabinet des Estampes, Bibliothèque nationale de France, Paris.

Figure 5-2. Divertissement at Versailles, May 7, 1664, given by Louis XIV to honor his mother, Anne of Austria, and his wife, Queen Marie-Thérèse. Engraving by Israle Silvestre (1670). Austrian National Library.

close ties with Louis XIV are reflected in his Te Deum of 1677, which he composed for the elaborate ceremony accompanying the baptism of his eldest son in Fontainebleau. The king stood as godfather to the child.

But even before the baptism Lully had begun to take firm steps to consolidate his power at the court. In 1671 he obtained exclusive right to present operas throughout France, and in 1672 he purchased the right to set up schools of music wherever he deemed appropriate. That same year Lully took over the directorship of the Académie royale de musique, and together with the librettist Philippe Quinault (1635–1688) he began to compose a new, serious type of French opera, the *tragédie en musique*. *Cadmus et Hermione* of 1673 was the first of a long series of successful works (Figure 5-3).

In 1773 Lully obtained a ban preventing rival companies from using dancers and more than two voices and six violins in their productions. At the same time, the king granted him use of the Royal Theater free of charge. After seeing *Alceste* in 1674, Louis XIV decided to fund Lully's productions. By this point, the sole purpose of the Académie royale de musique and the Académie royale de danse was to stage Lully's works. Because of this association, the Académie royale de musique came to be known as the Opéra. In 1681 Louis XIV appointed Lully royal secretary to the court, and three years later he issued a decree affirming that Lully's monopoly on opera was valid throughout the realm. As a result, until his death in 1687 from an injury suffered while beating time for a performance of his Te Deum, Lully largely determined the course of opera and much other music throughout France. In a sense, he reigned as an absolutist national music director. What is more, the tradition of royal pro-

Figure 5-3. Scene from Jean-Baptiste Lully's *Cadmus et Hermione*. Engraving by François Chauveau (1673). Cabinet des Estampes, Bibliothèque nationale de France, Paris.

tection for court opera continued for more than a century, until the outbreak of the Revolution in 1791.

Lully's works fall into three general categories: the early *ballets de cour,* the *comédies-ballets* of the 1660s, and the *tragedies en musique* of the 1670s and 1680s. The *ballets de cour* consisted of a series of *entrées,* or scenes, each containing a group of dances highlighting a common theme. The music in a *ballet de cour* was normally a pastiche, written by a number of composers. In *Les plaisirs* (1655), *La galanterie du temps* (1656), *Amour malade* (1657), *L'impatience* (1661), and other works, Lully showed himself to be a composer of unusual skill and expressive power. In the *Ballet d'Alcidiane* (1658) he used the French overture for the first time. His moving lament for Ariadne in the *Ballet de la naissance de Vénus* (1665) caused a great sensation. And for the *Ballet des muses* (1666), he composed a Spanish-style piece with harps and guitars. In this way he elevated the quality of music at the court and established the ballet as a noble art.

The *comédie-ballet,* created during the collaboration with Molière from 1664 to 1670, consisted of a comic play with musical intermezzos. The intermezzos were often well integrated into the dramatic action, and they gave Lully the opportunity to write exceedingly amusing scenes for himself and his singers and dancers. The scenes often involved local or exotic humor, such as the Turkish music in *Le bourgeois gentilhomme* of 1670. *Le marriage forcé* (1664), *L'amour médecin* (1665), *Les amants magnifiques* (1670), and other works were immensely successful.

After a falling out with Molière, Lully joined forces with Quinault to forge the *tragédie en musique.* The *tragédie en musique* represented a new operatic genre. It consisted of a prologue and five acts and was more serious and more refined than earlier types of French opera. It was based on the strong literary model of Molière and Corneille, but it featured a simplified plot and tighter dramatic action than the *comédie-ballet.* It contained no unnecessary episodes. Lully limited the length of the *tragédie en musique* to two-and-a-half hours, and he composed music that advanced the plot in a forceful and dynamic way. Lully and Quinault unveiled their new creation in 1673 with *Cadmus et Hermione.* It was followed by *Alceste* (1674), *Isis* (1677), *Phaéton* (1683), *Armide* (1686), and other works that flowed forth regularly until Lully's death. As with the *comédie-ballet,* the expressive quality of Lully's music carried the day. The lengthy Passacaille from Act 5 of *Armide,* based on a four-note descending tetrachord, incorporates instrumental interludes, chorus sections, and solo passages to form a work of remarkable strength and grandeur. It was widely admired and may have been the model for the large opening chorus of Bach's Cantata 78, *Jesu, der du meine Seele,* which is also based on a descending tetrachord theme and shows a similar pattern of alternating vocal and instrumental sections.

The topics for the *tragédies en musique* were chosen by Louis XIV from a list submitted by Quinault. The libretto for each work was then drafted and often revised drastically by Lully, giving him tight control of the plot and action. Tickets for the operas were sold at a wide price range. They included special stage seats, which were reserved for the royal entourage of the king. One could purchase a libretto with a candle for illumination, and season ticket holders often went to the same opera several times. New pieces were premiered before the court in Versailles and then taken to Paris for subsequent performances. There were generally four productions per year, two in the winter and two in the summer.

After Lully

Lully was an effective musician, dancer, dramatist, and entrepreneur. Like Wagner two centuries later, he was also a demanding coach, working directly with his musicians, dancers, actors, and actresses (Wood 1996, 8, 25). He rehearsed all aspects of his productions, and when he died in 1687, the discipline in operatic productions perished with him. French opera declined after his death, and Louis XIV withdrew his support. Lully's legacy remained alive, however, through his compositions, which displayed remarkable staying power. They continued to be performed after his death (Plate 13), both in France and abroad, and in Paris they dominated the repertory until the arrival of Rameau's dramatic works in 1733.

At the same time, harpsichord and organ music flourished through an impressive series of players. Jacques Champion Chambonnières and his pupil Jean-Henri d'Anglebert served as clavecinists to Louis XIV, and François Couperin, called "Le Grand" because of his magisterial playing, served as organist of St.-Gervais and then as organist and harpsichordist to the king (see below).

Marc-Antoine Charpentier (c. 1645–1704), who labored in the shadow of Lully until 1687, was a prolific composer of church music, assembling Masses, antiphons, hymns, psalm settings, and motets in large numbers. His highly successful Te Deum settings were patterned after Lully's famous work of 1677. Charpentier worked as music director at St. Louis and then Sainte-Chapelle. He also composed well-received *tragedies lyriques* for the stage.

The single composer to restore the opera on a grand scale after Lully was Jean-Philippe Rameau (1683–1764). Trained as an organist, composer, and theorist, Rameau held organist positions in Avignon and Lyons before coming to Paris. Although he established a notable reputation as a keyboard composer through his *Livres de pièces de clavessin,* it was his theoretical works that earned him international renown. In *Traité de l'harmonie* (Treatise on Harmony; Paris, 1722), and *Nouveau système de musique théorique* (New System of Music Theory; Paris, 1726) Rameau set forth a new system of harmonic analysis based on the concept of a *basse fundamental*—a fundamental harmonic bass—and root and inverted chord combinations. His work established France as a center for harmonic theory and analysis, a tradition that remained vital at the Paris Conservatory in later centuries. (Nadia Boulanger, the famous twentieth-century teacher and composer, for instance, was an heir to Rameau's practice.)

Rameau turned to dramatic works relatively late in life. *Hippolyte et Aricie,* produced at the Opéra in 1733, received modest praise. But it was the first viable alternative to Lully's *tragédies en musique,* with rich and varied instrumentation, vivid characterization, and deeply expressive melodies. It was the opening work in a long series of successful music-theater compositions, including *Les Indes galantes* (opéra-ballet, 1735), *Castor et Pollux* (tragédie en musique, 1737), *Platée* (comédie-lyrique, 1745), *Zoroastre* (tragédie en musique, 1749), and *Les Sybarites* (acte de ballet, 1753). The success of Rameau's music incurred the wrath of Lully's posthumous supporters, however, and a war of words ensued. Nevertheless, Rameau's works brought to final fruition the French nationalistic tradition of grand opera that had been founded by Lully seven decades earlier.

The Concert spirituel

By the second quarter of the eighteenth century, however, one can observe a shift of interest within Paris from the royal operas and *divertissements* of Lully to more popular, public styles. The most important catalyst in this change was the establishment of public concerts through the Concert spirituel. Established in 1725 through a license obtained from the Opéra by Anne Danican Philidor, the Concert spirituel quickly emerged as the principal forum in France for new music. Philidor's license allowed him to present "public concerts of sacred music" on feast days when the Académie royale de musique was closed (during the seasons of Advent and Lent, for instance). Initially the programs of the Concert spirituel consisted of non-French instrumental and sacred music (set to Latin texts). French music soon entered the repertory as well.

The players of the Concert spirituel were drawn from the orchestra and soloists of the Opéra and other professional organizations in Paris. The ensemble held well-organized rehearsals (an innovation at the time) and presented polished performances. Directors included, in addition to Philidor, Jean-Joseph Mouret, Simon Leduc, and Joseph Legros.

The orchestra of the Concert spirituel grew steadily over the years, from thirty-eight players in 1751 (the first year for which statistics survive) to fifty-two in 1790 (Stauffer 2000, 52). Its choir included forty or so singers, supplemented by a battery of soloists.

The performances of the Concert spirituel commonly featured guest virtuosos, including soloists from Germany, Italy, and other countries as well as France. Over the years, the series hosted such prominent figures as Italian vocalists Giovanni Battista Palmerini, Domenica Annibali, and Caffarelli (the well-known mezzo-soprano castrato); the German tenor Anton Raff; French violinists Jean-Baptiste Anet and Jean-Pierre Guignon (who competed in a musical duel in 1725) and Jean-Marie Leclair; cellists Jean-Pierre and Jean-Louis Duport; and French flautists Michel Blavet and Pierre-Gabriel Buffardin (who traveled from Dresden for his appearances). After the construction of a new organ in 1748, the Parisian organist Claude Balbastre was frequent soloist.

From its start in 1725 until 1784, the Concert spiritual performed in the Salle des Suisses in the Tuileries of the Louvre. The *Mercure de France* described the alterations in the Salle des Suisses made by Philidor in order to accommodate the newly formed orchestra:

> Philidor has had constructed a type of tribune in the large room. It has been placed against the wall on one side of the chamber and measures ten feet high, thirty-six feet across, and nine feet deep. It is capable of holding sixty people and includes a small set of stairs so that it may be mounted easily. This tribune is enclosed by a balustrade enhanced with gold, of which the banisters, in the shape of a lyre, have been placed on a pedestal painted like marble. The wall against which this tribune stands has been done in the best taste. The painting, made by Lemaire on the sketches of Berain, draftsman ordinaire of the King's cabinet, represents an immense vista that is extremely pleasing. Twelve chandeliers and candles beyond number serve as lighting. (Quoted in Stauffer 2000, 52)

It is not difficult to see the influence of the opera at play in the Salle des Suisses: the gold leaf, the painting by Lemaire, and the gaily lighted chandeliers were calculated to win the appeal of an audience weaned on the glitter of the Opéra. Although the proportions of the stage were modest by present-day standards, the Salle des Suisses, as modified by Philidor, was an important forerunner of the modern concert hall. The return of the court of Louis XVI to Paris in 1784 forced the Concert spirituel to vacate the Salle des Suisses and move to the Salle des Machines in the Tuileries, and then, in 1790, to the Salle Favart and the Théâtre de la Porte-St.-Martin, the new home of the Opéra (Anderson 2001, 90).

To a greater extent than the royal court, the Concert spirituel presented programs with an international flavor, introducing works from Germany, Austria, and England. It also served as a critical forum for the early symphony. Repertory included Latin and French motets (including popular works by Michel-Richard de Lalande), cantatas, *airs italiens,* French oratorios, organ concertos, Italian sonatas and concertos (including works by Vivaldi), and pre-Classical and Classical symphonies. In the case of the symphony, the Concert spirituel was a seminal force, featuring first the early works of Joseph Stamitz, François-Joseph Gosec, Simon Leduc, and Joseph Boulogne de Saint-Georges, and then works by

Haydn and Mozart, whose Symphony No. 31 in D Major ("Paris"), K. 297, was written for a performance at the Concert spirituel in 1778. By the French Revolution, when the Concert spirituel ceased operations, the series had presented more than 1,300 concerts, with music by more than 450 composers.

There were competing organizations devoted to public performances: the series by Le Riche de La Pouplinière that ran from 1731 to 1761, the programs of the Société académique des enfants d'Apollon that began in 1741, the Concert des Amateurs, which ran from 1769 to 1781, and the Concert de la Loge Olympique, which commissioned Haydn's "Paris" Symphonies (Nos. 82–87) in 1785–1786. But it was the Concert spirituel that played the central role in nurturing the stylistic transition that led from the Baroque Era to the Classical Period.

French Style

During the Baroque Era, music at the French court set the standard for what became known throughout Europe as "French style." This style was defined by a number of distinct qualities and genres.

The first quality is the emphasis on refined string writing. The Vingt-Quatre Violons du roi, established under Louis XIII and active until 1761, and the Petits Violons du roi, formed by Louis XIV at Lully's request and active until 1715, set a new international standard for string playing. Possibly the first orchestra based solely upon a string ensemble, the Vingt-Quatre Violons brought together professional players to present polished performances for the king. Many of the players were from the Guild of St. Julien, and the long list of illustrious musicians that joined the group includes such notable figures as Marin Marais and Antoine Forqueray. The Vingt-Quatre Violons were formally conducted by a director, beating time with a stick, rather than led informally by the first violinist or the harpsichordist. This, too, sharpened the precision of the ensemble. Lully complained of the Vingt-Quatre Violons' sloppiness and erratic ornamentation and, around 1656, turned to the Petits Violons for his productions. Still, both groups were viewed with envy and imitated at courts large and small throughout Europe.

Equally important was the practice in both ensembles of dividing the players into five parts:

Dessus (first violins)	6 players
Haut-contre (viola)	4 players
Taille (viola)	4 players
Quinte (viola)	4 players
Basse de violon (bass viol)	6 players

This produced a rich middle texture, and it avoided the pronounced polarization of treble and bass found in the four-part scoring of Italian instrumental practice. It was the Italian scoring that eventually prevailed, emerging as the standard during the late Baroque and Classical Periods. Still, up to 1725 or so five-part French texture represented an attractive alternative to Italian scoring (it was used by Bach in his Weimar cantatas of 1714–1716, for instance).

A second quality of French style was the avoidance of regular meters and periodic cadences. The *air de cour* was based on the principle of irregular meters, and even in dance music, French composers preferred to stretch and extend phrases rather than cadence clearly and periodically, in the manner of Italian music. This resulted in asymmetrical units that toyed with the listener's expectations of cadence and closure.

A third trait was the French love for surface gesture in the form of ornamentation, which by the second half of the seventeenth century had evolved into a highly sophisticated system of shorthand symbols. These symbols, indicating "graces" or embellishments, were commonly set forth in tables at the beginning of keyboard publications (see discussion of harpsichord music, below). Italian, English, Dutch, and other national schools utilized embellishments. But the French turned ornamentation into high art, and integrated it fully into the texture of their music. This was made possible by polished ensemble performances (in the Vingt-Quatre Violons tradition), skilled lute and keyboard players, and keyboard instruments with light keyboard actions that facilitated rapid note motion.

Among the genres used at the court, three came to be recognized as distinctly French and were exported with great enthusiasm: the *air de cour,* the overture, and dance music.

The *air de cour* evolved from the polyphonic chanson to become a strophic song with lute or guitar accompaniment. During the first three decades of the seventeenth century, it was the most important vocal form in France. Written mainly for Louis XIII and his court, the *air de cour* was characterized by a simple style and an absence of regular meter. The music was generally syllabic, closely following texts derived from Italian pastorals. There were a number of subtypes, including *airs sérieux* (serious songs), with texts focusing on love, politics, or pastoral scenes, and *airs à boire* (drinking songs), with texts focusing on light or frivolous topics. The *air de cour* was championed by Pierre Guédron, Antoine Boësset, and Etienne Moulinié, whose compositions were published in Paris and disseminated widely.

The invention of the French overture is commonly credited to Lully, but its roots can be traced to Venetian operas of the 1640s and 1650s, which often began with an instrumental piece in two movements, the first in slow duple meter and the second in fast triple meter, much like a pair of contrasting dances in the Renaissance. This type of prefatory piece also appeared in the early *ballet de cour.* Lully developed the form, exploiting and heightening the contrasts between the two sections. In his hands, the opening became a regal, march-like section, whose dotted military rhythms reflected the majesty of the king. Ending on a half cadence, the opening section was generally repeated. The second section was in fast triple or compound meter, with imitative or fugal texture. It, too, was normally repeated. Lully often rounded out his overtures with a short return to the opening material. Lully scored his pieces for five-part strings, with doubling oboes and continuo. He unveiled his form of the overture in the ballet *Alcidiane* of 1658. His *tragedies en musique* commonly contained two overtures, one before the prologue and one before the first act of the opera proper. Lully's form proved to be immensely popular, and it was exported to England, Germany, and other countries receptive to foreign styles. It was viewed as the French alternative to the Italian concerto.

Since dance was extremely popular at the French court—both Louis XIII and Louis XIV were skilled dancers, as we have seen—it became a central part of the French repertory. Each dance had a specific meter, tempo, and rhythmic pattern that mirrored in musical form the nature of the dance steps. Dance music formed the heart of the *ballet de cour* and the *divertissements* of the operas, which contained at least one set of dances per act. For elegant dancing it was necessary for the instrumental players to stress the important beats through downbows and other accents. The precision of the Vingt-Quatre Violons du roi and the Petits Violons du roi enhanced the beauty of the dances and set the standard for the performance of dance music throughout Europe. Dance music was also transferred to solo instruments, such as the lute, harpsichord, viola da gamba, and organ, and listened to with pleasure as a stylized art form.

The principal French dances in the sixteenth century were the pavane (a slow dance in duple meter), galliarde (a fast, leaping dance in triple meter), and allemande (a moderately fast dance in duple meter, normally with an upbeat; see *La Allemanda* by Santiago de Murcia, Sampler CD 2, track 8). The arrival of Baroque style in the seventeenth century ushered in the courante (a moderately fast dance in triple meter, with hemiolas), sarabande (a slow dance, with an accent on the second beat of each measure), gigue (a fast dance in triple or compound meter), loure (a slow gigue), and chaconne and passacaille or passacaglia (slow, large-scale dances in triple meter).

During the late Baroque, new dances with simpler textures and symmetrical phrases rose in popularity: the minuet (a moderately fast dance in triple meter), bourrée (a fast dance, in duple meter, with a single upbeat), gavotte (a fast dance, in duple meter, with a double upbeat), and passepied (a fast dance in triple or compound meter). Also belonging to this group were exotic dances such as the canarie (a fast dance in a variety of meters, from the Canary Islands), musette (a bagpipe dance, in duple meter), tambourin (a tamborine dance in imitation of pipe and tabor), and rigaudon (a lively, duple-meter dance). The new arrivals were often called *galant* dances, since they epitomized the latest in fashionable taste.

Instrument Making: Lute and Harpsichord

The French school of instrument building, as represented by artisans in Paris, displayed unusual sophistication, first in the realm of lute making, and then in the area of harpsichord building.

The lute, inherited from the Renaissance, flourished up to 1640 or so (see Plate 2). Played by both Louis XIII and Louis XIV, the lute continued to be viewed as the most important social instrument of the time. Marin Mersenne, writing in his influential tract *Harmonie universalle* in 1636, could claim that the lute "has taken such a lead over the other stringed instruments, either because honest men gave it this advantage or because of its own excellence and perfection, that one hardly notices the other instruments" (quoted in Anthony 1997, 284).

Lute makers and composers flourished in Paris. The makers included Julien Perichon, Charles Bocquet, and—according to Mersenne—Mercure, Merville, and Bouvier. Composer-performers included Denis and Ennemond Gaultier, Charles and Jacques Hedington (from Scotland), René Mésangeau, and others. Famous collections of lute music included Antoine Francisque's *Le trésor d'Orphée: livre de tablature de luth* (Paris, 1600), Jean-Baptiste Besard's *Thesaurus harmonicus* (Cologne, 1603), and Nicolas Vallet's *Secret des Muses* (Amsterdam, 1615–1619).

By 1640, the love of the bass range, ushered in by the continuo practice of the new Baroque style, put the lute at a disadvantage. Builders responded by creating the theorbo or archlute, a large lute with long neck and bass strings (see Plates 1 and 3 and Chapter 8). But the increased number of strings required constant tuning and made the theorbo difficult to master. The harpsichord was louder, more stable, and capable of accommodating more complex textures, including the imitative writing of fugues. In addition, one could play from staff notation rather than tablature, which was more difficult to learn. From 1640 onward, the harpsichord eclipsed the lute as the string instrument of choice.

Mersenne also gives us valuable information about early French harpsichords. The *Harmonie universelle* includes an illustration of a harpsichord from the third decade of the seventeenth century. It is a single-manual instrument of a Flemish-like design (Figure 5-4), with a disposition of one 8' stop and one 4' stop and a four-octave range of C–c''', much like German harpsichords and organs of the time. By 1650, the leading French builders were constructing instruments with two manuals and a disposition of one 8' and one 4' stop on the lower keyboard and one 8' stop on the upper keyboard. These builders included Jean and

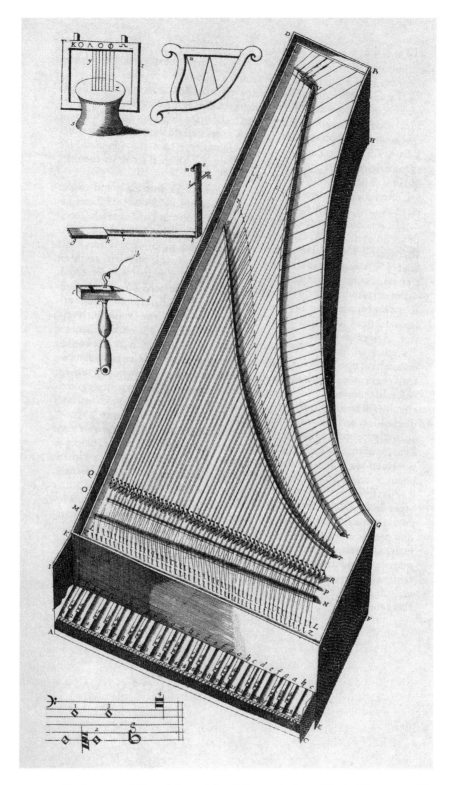

Figure 5-4. Single-manual French harpsichord (c. 1635), from Marin Mersenne, *Harmonie universelle* (Paris, 1636–1637).

Louis Denis, Claude Jacquet, Antoine Vaudry, and Michel Richard, all active in Paris between 1640 and 1680.

The two-manual harpsichords allowed for a new type of work, the *pièce croisée,* which called for intricate crossed-hand passages. Such works first appear in the music of Louis Couperin (c. 1626–1661), who also wrote unusual unmeasured preludes, called *préludes non mesurés* (Figure 5-5), that require the performer to take on the role of composer, sorting and shaping the gestures suggested by the notation. Louis Couperin, together with Nicolas-Antoine Lebègue (c. 1631–1702), Jean-Henri d'Anglebert (c. 1628–1691), and the teacher of all three, Jacques Champion Chambonnières (c. 1601–1672), founded the French school of harpsichord composition. As we noted, Chambonnières and d'Anglebert were clavecinists to Louis XIV.

They were followed by François Couperin, Rameau, and Jean-François Dandrieu (c. 1681–1738). Couperin's *Pièces de clavessin,* issued in four books (1713, 1716, 1722, and 1730), contain 230 dance pieces organized into *ordres* or suites. The pieces are programmatic, with whimsical titles such as "La Gabriéle," "Le rossignol-en-amour" (The Nightingale in Love), "Barricades mystérieuses" (The Mysterious Barricades), "Les Tic-Toc-Choc ou Les Maillotins" (The Tick-Tock Clock or The Little Hammers). Such works foreshadow the short nineteenth-century character pieces of Schumann and others.

The new harpsichord idiom called for the use of *style brisé* (a broken-chord style derived from lute music), copious ornamentation (made possible by the extremely light, delicate keyboard actions of the French instruments), expressive counterpoint, and a rich assortment of keyboard dances. The ornamentation was indicated through an elaborate system of markings, which were commonly indicated in the forewords to harpsichord publications. The so-called French "trill tables" became the standard for harpsichord composers throughout France and abroad, including J. S. Bach, who used the ornament table from d'Anglebert's *Pièces de clavessin* (Paris, 1689; Figure 5-6) as a model for the table that he included in the *Clavierbüchlein* for his eldest son, Wilhelm Friedemann Bach, in 1720.

During the first decades of the eighteenth century two-manual harpsichords became the standard, with a keyboard range that quickly grew from G, B, or C–c''' to F–f''''. Nicholas Blanchet, his son François Etienne, grandson François Etienne, Jr., and François Etienne, Jr.'s pupil Pascal Taskin (who married his teacher's widow) carried the French tradition to dazzling heights. Taskin, especially, created harpsichords that were elegant works of art as well as superb musical instruments (Plate 14). Other Parisian builders included Jean Goermans and his son Jacques, Henri Hemisch and his brother Guillaume, and Jean-Henri Moers. The standard disposition for the late-Baroque French harpsichord was one 8' stop and one 4' on the lower manual, and one 8' stop on the upper manual. After 1750, buff stops were introduced as well as knee levels to control the adding and subtracting of stops. French instruments were richly decorated. With their suave, sophisticated tone and beautiful cases, they served as the principal prototype for the harpsichord revival that took place in the second half of the twentieth century.

Publishing

From the earliest days of the publishing trade Paris stood as one of the principal centers of music printing. In the sixteenth century Pierre Attaingnant issued more than 150 collections of music, using his royal privilege to suppress local competition. During the course of the century, Paris competed with Lyon for the honor of the most important music-publishing center in France. By the end of the century, Paris emerged as the clear winner.

Figure 5-5. Louis Couperin, "Prelude of Mr. Couperin in the style of Mr. Froberger." MS Parville, University of California, Berkeley, Music Library *MS 778*. As shown in Colin Tilney, *The Art of the Unmeasured Prelude* (London: Schott, 1991), vol. 1, 50.

Figure 5-6. Ornament Table from Jean-Henri d'Anglebert, *Pièces de clavessin* (1689).

In the seventeenth century, the Ballard clan played a role in French publishing similar to that of Lully in French music. The dynasty began with Pierre Ballard, who was named *seul imprimeur du roy pour la musique* first by Henri IV and then by Louis XIII. Ballard's son Robert received the title of *seul imprimeur* from Louis XIII in 1639, and Robert and his son Christophe maintained this privilege from Louis XIV until the ruler's death in 1715. By 1700 almost all music in Paris published by movable type was issued by the Ballard firm, including dozens of collections of *chansons pour danser, chansons pour boire, chansonnettes,* and *airs a deux parties.* In addition, the Ballards had the exclusive right to publish the works of Lully. Other composers appearing under the Ballard imprint included Brossard, Campra, Charpentier, the Couperins, Dandrieu, Hotteterre, Lalande, Lebègue, and Montéclair.

Ballard's music monopoly was challenged unsuccessfully by other printers, who eventually worked around the family's royal privilege by turning to copper-plate engraving, which was especially appropriate for instrumental works. The gamba music of Marin Marais, the lute works of the Gaultiers, and the harpsichord works of Chambonnières, Louis Couperin, and others were presented to the public through engraved editions.

Over the course of the eighteenth century over 150 engravers worked in Paris, and music publishing flourished. The high quality and beauty of the engravings (see Figure 5-6), the excellent publicity offered by the engravers and music organizations, and the wide distribution of the finished collections made Paris the European center for music printing.

French Style Abroad

French style was happily embraced abroad, especially in England, Germany, Austria, and Bohemia, where stylistic eclecticism was a natural part of music traditions. In Germany, in particular, dukes, counts, and kings vied to reproduce French practices, building castle complexes on the Versailles model and recruiting musicians who could play in the French manner. The concept of a well-organized, highly disciplined ensemble, in the fashion of the Vingt-Quatre Violons du roi, and elegant French performance gestures such as rich embellishment, overdotting, and *notes inégals* (the playing of even notes unevenly, to add grace to the passage) were especially appealing.

In Dresden, for instance, the Saxon Elector Friedrich August I (ruled 1694–1733) built an opulent residence complex, the Zwinger, on the French court model. For music, August hired a French musician, Jean Baptiste Volumier, to serve as the concertmaster of the royal *Capell- und Cammer-Musique* ensemble. Volumier brought French instrumental practice and vocabulary to the Dresden court and hired French players such as flautist Pierre-Gabriel Buffardin. Works were composed and performed in the French fashion. August I's successor, Friedrich August II (ruled 1733–1763), favored Italian culture, however, and gradually replaced his father's French players and composers with Italian counterparts. Johann David Heinichen's cantata *La bella fiamma ò Tirsi* (The Beautiful Flame, O Tirsi, That Fires for Thee; Sampler CD 1, tracks 20–23) is typical of music performed at the court of August II. It follows the standard Italian cantata format of recitative-aria-recitative-aria and is typical of the works produced in Dresden royal circles after the fall of French style.

French style was exported through music prints produced in Paris (such as the *Pièces de clavessin* of d'Anglebert, Couperin, and Rameau and the *Livres d'orgue* of Boyvin, de Grigny, and Couperin) and Amsterdam (such as the pirated prints of Lully's overtures and other instrumental pieces issued by Estienne Roger). French style was also carried to foreign lands in the seventeenth century by students or followers of Lully. In England, Pelham Humfrey (c. 1647–1674) traveled to Italy and France, where he may have studied with Lully. His verse anthems include movements for string ensemble that are very similar to Lully's writing. In Germany, Georg Muffat (1653–1704) and Johann Sigismund Kusser (1660–1727) studied with Lully in Paris. Muffat's *Florilegium primum* (Augsburg, 1695) and *Florilegium secundum* (Passau, 1698) contain French-style orchestral suites, each prefaced by a French overture. The suites are often in five parts, modeled on the Vingt-Quatre Violons du roi texture. In the preface to *Florilegium primum* Muffat summarized Lully's style for German musicians. In the preface to *Florilegium secundum* he went further, describing in great detail how to perform ballet music "a la Françoise." He included specific instructions for appropriate bowing and ornamentation, and as a result, the *Florilegium* prefaces are among the most important guides for modern players to French Baroque performance practice.

Kusser brought French opera practices to Germany, first as co-director of the Hamburg opera (1695) and then as opera composer in Nuremberg and Augsburg. His *Composition de musique suivant la méthode française* (Stuttgart, 1682), containing six suites for five-part string ensemble, appears to be the first instance in Germany of prefacing a dance suite with a French overture. A third composer, Johann Caspar Ferdinand Fischer (c. 1665–1746), did not study with Lully but adopted his style. His publications of dance music were exceedingly popular and did much to promote French style in Germany and Austria. They included *Le Journal du printemps* (Augsburg, 1695), a series of eight suites for five string instruments and two trumpets, and *Pièces de clavessin* (Schlackenworth, 1696) and *Musicalischer Parnassus* (Augsburg, 1732), both containing keyboard suites in the French manner.

The influence of Lully outside France was immense. His innovative chorus of shiverers in *Isis,* for instance, was later mimicked in England by Henry Purcell (in *King Arthur*) and in Italy by Antonio Vivaldi (in "Winter" of the Four Seasons). Handel, Bach, Telemann, and other composers of the late Baroque readily embraced the tradition of Lully's overture and dance music. Bach's French and English Suites, Partitas, and Orchestral Suites show a direct indebtedness to French dance practice, and his adoption of the French overture enriched his compositional idiom considerably. He followed the lead of Kusser and Muffat in using the overture as a prelude for orchestral suites. But elsewhere he took more novel steps. In the opening chorus of Cantata 61, *Nun komm, der Heiden Heiland,* he used the French overture to commence the church year. In *Clavierübung* III he used the overture to begin a large collection of organ works. And in the Goldberg Variations he used the overture to open the second half of an immense variation set. Finally, in the St. John Passion (see Chapter 11), Bach did not hesitate to turn to a French tombeau, or funeral march, to achieve expressive results. In the aria "Es ist vollbracht" ("It is Finished"; Sampler CD 2, track 21), he used a solo gamba playing in the French fashion, with dotted rhythms and ornamental graces, to create a royal lament for the stricken Christian king, Christ, who has just expired on the cross.

Thus the influence of Lully and his innovations went well beyond the borders of France. French style became an admired model and rich resource for composers throughout Europe. Indeed, from royal courts to public arenas, it became a powerful force in the music of the Baroque Era.

BIBILIOGRAPHY

Anderson, Gordon A., et al. 2001. "Paris." In *New Grove Dictionary of Music and Musicians,* ed. Stanley Sadie, 2nd ed., 19:76–125. London: Macmillan, 2001.
Anthony, James R. 1997. *French Baroque Music from Beaujoyeulx to Rameau.* Rev. ed. Portland: Amadeus Press.
Cessac, Catherine. 1995. *Marc-Antonine Charpentier,* trans. Thomas Glascow. Portland: Amadeus Press.
Christensen, Thomas Street. 1993. *Rameau and Musical Thought in the Enlightenment.* Cambridge: Cambridge University Press.
Dill, Charles. 1998. *Monstrous Opera: Rameau and the Tragic Tradition.* Princeton, N.J.: Princeton University Press.
Heyer, John Hajdu, ed. 1989. *Jean-Baptist Lully and the Music of the French Baroque: Essays in Honor of James R. Anthony.* Cambridge: Cambridge University Press.
———. 2000. *Lully Studies.* Cambridge: Cambridge University Press.
Lesure, François, Claudie Marcel-Dubois, and Denis Laborde. 2001. "France." In *New Grove Dictionary of Music and Musicians,* ed. Stanley Sadie, 2nd ed., 9:140–165. London: Macmillan.
Meller, Wilfrid Howard. 1987. *François Couperin and the French Classical Tradition.* Rev. ed. London: Faber and Faber.
Schulenberg, David. 2000. *Music of the Baroque.* Oxford: Oxford University Press.
Stauffer, George B. 2000. "The Modern Orchestra: A Creation of the Late Eighteenth Century." In *The Orchestra: Origins and Transformations,* ed. Joan Peyser, 41–72. New York: Billboard Books.
Wood, Caroline. 1996. *Music and Drama in the Tragédie en Music, 1673–1715.* New York: Garland.
Zaslaw, Neal. 1987. "Lully's Orchestra." In *Jean-Baptiste Lully: Actes du colloque Saint-Germain-en-Laye et Heidelberg,* ed. Jérome de La Gorce and Herbert Schneider, 539–579. Laaber: Laaber-Verlag.

CHAPTER SIX

The Songs of Solomon (Rossi) as the Search for History

Michael Beckerman

FROM THE MADRIGAL TO THE BERGAMASCA, and from the songs of secular Italy to the Songs of Solomon, it is doubtful that any composer has covered more stylistic and spiritual ground than Salamone Rossi. Working at a time that makes mockery of our attempts to use terms such as "Renaissance" and "Baroque," Rossi combined old and new styles even as he traversed the path between Jewish and Christian worlds.

A resident of the Mantua ghetto, Rossi served the Gonzaga family until his disappearance at the end of the 1620s. His catalog of more than three hundred works contains 150 vocal pieces in Italian, about 130 instrumental works, and around 30 works with Hebrew texts. How should we evaluate his output and his value? There are several standards by which great works and great artists are measured. Perhaps we should remind ourselves that he was a contemporary of Shakespeare and Cervantes, and like the authors of *Hamlet* and *Don Quixote,* Rossi the Jew, also Rossi the Mantuan, managed to combine many worlds in one. In doing so, he amazes us with his power and richness. (Though the very idea of this statement goes starkly against the relativist tendency in place today, no one very much minds the notion of acknowledging, say, that some chefs are better than others, and many who quibble with the notion of quality in the arts certainly find the idea helpful in choosing a surgeon or, say, a teacher for their children.)

And yet how should we investigate and discuss this treasure? Pretending to have authority over either musical works or the past more generally makes us fools before we have even started, but without some authority, we are simply mute. So first we should perhaps admit that we don't know much about music history.

The Mystery of Music History

Read any textbook on American history, pick up a book about the Second World War, browse a timeline in an almanac, or read an in-depth analysis of a single event, and you might think we know a great deal about what happened in the past. In fact, you might take the side of certain philosophers and argue that, if we have a problem writing about what happened long ago or five minutes ago, it is because we have too much information.

My contention is the opposite. The past is almost entirely gone, and we wildly overrate our ability to recapture it. Don't take my word for it. Quick! What happened to you yesterday? Can you rank events in a hierarchy of importance? Is there a single conversation you can remember verbatim, or do you only recall the flavor of the exchange? How did you *feel* yesterday? Can you remember, or are such things inevitably filtered through the way you are feeling today? Do you know what your motivations were in your interactions with your fellow human beings? Did you create documents? Would putting them all together divulge the reality of your existence?

And this was yesterday in *your* life, and it concerns *your* thoughts, and *your* actions, about which you are supposed to have privileged control. Do you have such control? And then imagine doing the same for a particular day last year, five years ago, or twenty. Go further and imagine doing it for someone else's day, thirty years ago, one hundred years ago, or, in the case of Salamone Rossi, almost four hundred years ago.

But, you say, we have many documents to allow us to reconstruct Rossi's past. Yes, but "many" is a relative term. Even if we agreed that we could actually reconstruct the world on the basis of documents, we would have to admit that in the case of Rossi and his time, we certainly have less than one-thousandth of the kinds of documents we would like to reconstruct his life and time better. There is not a single image of this remarkable man, for instance—no family photos where he stands grinning with his arm on his child's shoulder. In fact, our entire claim to be able to understand the past depends on faith, and it *is* a question of faith, that the paltry documents we possess are somehow "representative." And even with all that, we lack any sense of conversations, smells and sights, air quality and elementary sensations. Rossi lived for several billion seconds, and we have records of only the tiniest number of those.

So although historians have constructed a glowing portrait of the "Golden Age of Jewry in Renaissance Mantua" (Figure 6-1), much of it lies in our imagination and competes with a range of historical moments, in particular, the destruction of that ghetto around 1628 and the near-destruction of European Jewry some three hundred years later. The past and the future call back and forth to each other, further roiling the surface and making our investigation more muddied than clear.

In fact, the best metaphor I can come up with for the lost spaces of the past is a billiard ball. It has been proposed—and I do not know the first genius who offered this thought—that if you reduced the earth to the size of a billiard ball, it would be just as smooth as the ball. In other words, Mount Everest, the Marianas Trench, the Empire State Building, you and I, and all the nooks and crannies would vanish completely, and you could run your hands around the old Earth and feel its hard polish. As should be obvious by this time, I believe that is precisely what we do when we settle for some version of the past, and that our simulated, imagined past has all the deep nuance of a polished sphere. Simply put, the real variety of five minutes ago or five hundred years ago, its subtlety, and contradictions of low and high, out and in, and back and forth is largely forgotten.

Having said that, though, I suspect that the reader probably still wants a summary that gives some essential facts about Rossi. Though I cannot write such things at this point, I am happy to supply them. Here is a barrage of Rossi factoids from the internet:

Salamone Rossi (c. 1570–c. 1630)

Italian composer and violinist of Jewish descent. Served at the Mantuan court from 1587 to 1628 and was much respected by the Gonzagas, who exempted him from wearing the yellow badge Jews had to carry on their hats. His output includes four books of sonatas and dances for string ensemble, madrigals, canzonette, music for dramatic productions at Mantua, and Jewish psalms. He was among the earliest composers to cultivate the trio sonata texture in his collections of 1607–1608; he uses binary forms and movements featuring dance rhythms as well as ostinato basses. (www.hoasm.org/IVD/RossiS.html)

Note the sense of authority and ease present in this passage. Although nothing in it, strictly speaking, is false, can we really say that it represents anything like a true portrait of

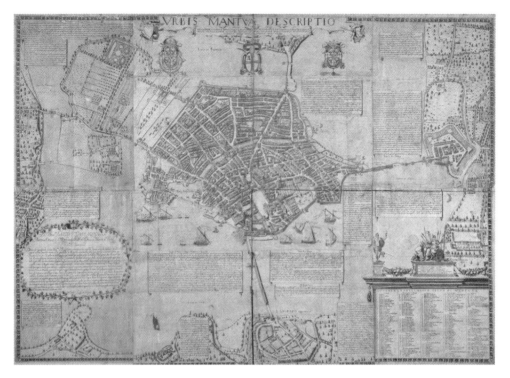

Figure 6-1. Map of Mantua, from Gabriele Bertazzolo (1570–1626), *Urbis Mantue Descriptio.* Mantova, Biblioteca communale, *Stampa Rotolo 1.* Used with permission.

the composer? Especially the last bit. Why speak of binary forms rather than sensuous power of the works? And how do we take the "claim to fame," that he was among the *earliest* composers to write a certain texture? Aren't we really interested in the quality of the works rather than their primacy?

So how do we get around the problems of historical writing and penetrate the past? In our case, we go to one survival of the past that is amazingly rich in information. In fact, it may well contain more information about the past than any diary or painting, any building or fossil. I am talking here about a musical score. Of course, the problem is that it is both disarmingly easy and ridiculously difficult to unpack this information. Let us look at several pieces from Rossi's pen and see what kinds of things lie within.

The Songs of Solomon

Rossi's Songs of Solomon, published in 1623 under the title *Hashirim asher lish'lomo,* is the first collection of polyphony with Hebrew texts available to us (Figure 6-2). Everything we know about it—from its sudden appearance to its novel solution for dealing with the Hebrew alphabet—suggests an extraordinary circumstance. The work comes to us not alone with musical notes, but with commentary, debate, poetry, and florid dedications. Though Rossi is the star of the show, it is clear that Leon da Modena played a major role in the collection's publication, having triumphed as a polemicist and poet. Da Modena points out in his introduction that "old King David" provided "orderly instruction in the rudiments of song" but that in later years, with their wanderings, the Jews had lost contact with the science

Figure 6-2. Title page from Salamone Rossi, Songs of Solomon (c. 1622). Courtesy of the Library of the Jewish Theological Seminary of America.

of music. Advocating an openness to new ways of doing things, da Modena argued that the multitude should "not be afraid to approach this science," but that will have from it "Silver and gold, fields and vineyards, and the Lord will be an eternal light to them." Further details may be found in the section of the introduction titled "Judgment" that features a lengthy debate about the appropriateness of polyphonic music in the synagogue.

Jews and Christians had obviously lived along side each other for centuries, and their patterns of interaction were many and varied. In some ways, though, Rossi's collection seems to be an astonishing intersection of the two different worlds. In his works music for Jewish liturgy not only resembles church music more than ever before, but the sacred and secular show a marked interpenetration.

Historical judgment in artistic matters is often, alas, tied to pedigree and demonstrating "begats" in a traditional form of scholarly storytelling. Rossi's influence in this sphere was slight: the destruction of the ghetto in Mantua and his disappearance more or less coincided chronologically at the end of the 1620s. But Rossi's work provides a model of his art, and perhaps even an argument for later notions of what the expression "Judeo-Christian world" might mean.

The Five-Voice Kaddish

In its various forms and permutations the Kaddish is one of the best-known prayers in the Jewish liturgy. Not only does it weave through the service like a silver thread, occurring in its various forms multiple times, but it has entered the secular world through the efforts of Allen Ginsberg's famous poem and Leonard Bernstein's Third Symphony. Their works were not, however, the first time the Kaddish had interacted with the world of secularized high culture. There are two settings of the Full Kaddish (*Kaddish gamur*) in Rossi's Songs of Solomon. The first of these, for three voices, is somewhat restrained. The second, in which we are interested, is a five-voice setting and very bouncy, or as some would have it, "dance-like." In his new edition of the Songs of Solomon, Don Harrán notes that there may have been a tradition for lively settings of this text (Harrán 1999, 226–227). But Rossi's three-voice realization of the text suggests that a certain range was available.

Looking specifically at Rossi's five-voice Kaddish setting, we must ask: How does its effect come about? How do we come to ascribe an identity to it? We have many possible answers to these questions. We can listen to the setting through the vibrant fairy tale of "the flowering of the Jewish Renaissance in Mantua" we have dabbled in above. I call it a fairy tale not because I disapprove of it—it's a lovely story—but because we so little information about Rossi and his time. We have a written record, to be sure, consisting of musical notation— that is, "the piece"—and a context directly surrounding its composition, consisting of everything from dedicatory poems to remnants of the debate that surrounded this secularized incursion into the synagogue. Opening the lens wider we have information about Jewish society in Mantua, in its glory and ignominy, in its splendor and eventual destruction. We have some old maps and renderings of the ghetto. And on the other side we have notes, over a thousand of them arranged in five-voices, with text underlay. And the contextual equivalent of that is the sum total of our knowledge and our theories of realizing that blueprint. Two large sets of facts, one connected, more or less, to the "real world," once again, with all our theories of history encouraging us to attempt a reimagination, and the world of the notes.

On various levels each presents us with an endless and impossible task. Let's play with Rossi's life. On September 18, 1621, Rossi woke up, got dressed and left his house. Which way did he turn, right or left? What did the air smell like to Rossi? Did he wear his identifying yellow Jewish star, or even think about the fact that, according to documents, he was exempt from wearing it? Was he aware of being a Jew, or was that far less important to him than his life as a composer? Was he happily married? Did he think about sex? What did things *look* like almost four hundred years ago? Did people *see* differently then? And what did the world look like to Rossi? Was he nearsighted or farsighted? Was he a lover of nature like Beethoven, or was he more a Mozart? Was there a smell of cooked meat as he rounded the corner, any corner? Was there ever a problem keeping kosher when he was at court? Was he tall or short, and were his clothes loose or tight fitting? While some of these questions may seem more relevant than others, we have answers to none of them, and in their unanswerableness, they once again form a parallel with questions we ask about his works.

How did Rossi compose his five-voice Kaddish? Did he begin with a tune, something he'd heard in a synagogue, at a dance, or at a country fair? Something whose source is lost forever? Or did he read the text, close his eyes, and hear the "answer" in his mind's ear? As we shall see, Rossi makes slight alterations in the repetitions of sections. Are the changes a response to purely musical needs, or do they relate to an implicit expressive strategy? How does the piece become what it is?

Composing the Kaddish

Rossi's five-voice Kaddish (Sampler CD 2, track 1; Figure 6-3) contains six stanzas, and it is composed of virtual repetitions of musical figures with different texts. Though quite straightforward, the construction of the composition is also somewhat elusive. We might say that each stanza has an opening, a middle, and a cadence. This alone is hardly enough to hold the listener's (or the reader's) interest, but it is in the treatment of the middle bits that Rossi is most enigmatic and subtle, as we shall see.

Is there an apt analogy between music and painting? Is the entire character of a musical composition present at the outset, or is does it take shape slowly, slowly, as if we were allowing our gaze to go from the bottom to the top of a painting? One could argue that the identity of the Kaddish crystallizes in its first seven bars. A smooth and uncomplicated descent of a sixth in the first four bars is "answered" by something more animated and emphatic with shorter note values and syncopations. We can call this phrase A (Example 6-1; CD: 0:00–0:10).

This figure repeats, but only in the first stanza. It is followed by nine measures of something that might be considered quintessential "middleness," which we will label B (Example 6-2; CD: 0:22–0:33). Its identity is less well formed and distinctive. It seems self-effacing, somehow slower, with even note values.

The four-measure figure—let's call it C—acts as a kind of interruption, reasserting the value system of the second part of A with even more emphasis, direction and vitality (Example 6-3; CD: 0:34–0:39).

The stanza concludes with a sensuous Amen, featuring a descent in parallel thirds between soprano and tenor (Example 6-4; CD: 0:40–0:47). This we will label D.

One could argue that by the conclusion of the first stanza, the piece is essentially complete. And yet its six stanzas unfold with variety, in the following manner:

1   A + A + B + C + D
2   A + B + C + D
3   A + B + C + D
4   A + B + D
5   A + B + D
6   A + B + D

As it is evident, the "interruption" of part C, with its aggressive, almost martial turn, disappears in the second half of the piece.

This outline allows us to raise the musical equivalent of questions about Rossi's life and times. How does the identity of the piece form itself? Is the piece essentially present in A, which then repeats (only once, in the first stanza), assuring its primacy, and then simply fleshed out or enhanced by B, C, and D? Does the relatively nondescript B represent the kind of planned self-effacement that allows the work to proceed through time, carrying its origi-

Figure 6-3. Five-part Kaddish, Quinto part, from Salamone Rossi, Songs of Solomon (c. 1622). Courtesy of the Library of the Jewish Theological Seminary of America.

Example 6-1. Rossi: Kaddish, mm. 1–7.

Example 6-2. Rossi: Kaddish, mm. 16–24.

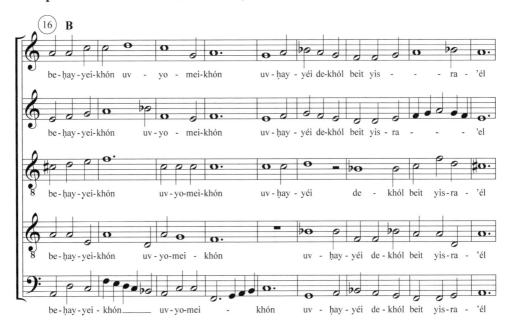

Example 6-3. Rossi: Kaddish, mm. 25–28.

Example 6-4. Rossi: Kaddish, mm. 29–32.

nal character? What of our "interruption," C (and have we already somehow cheated by referring to it as if we understood its role)? Does the cadence itself have real identity, or is it, once again, merely a semistock conclusion to an identity that has already been established?

If these questions are pertinent for individual stanzas, how do they unfold in relation to the composition as a whole? Was the reason to eliminate C for the second half of the piece based on textual grounds, or was the disruptive excitement of it detrimental to the work's gradual movement toward finality? Could there be some symbolic layer of meaning in its disappearance?

Let's look closely at C, since it is the focus of differences in various parts that might have something to do with intention and meaning. After A and B, which seem a bit more distanced and, dare we say, even generic, C has an immediacy about it, as if the camera has suddenly focused closely on an object. By contrast, the gentle and even possibly wistful opening of A gives way here to something declamatory, as if an actual person were forcefully shaping the events. This is the only part where there is anything resembling word painting, or even where the music and the text seem closely related. The words "ba 'agala u vizman kariv" (speedily and shortly) are complemented by the rest in the soprano part, followed by a somewhat breathless upbeat, and the dotted rhythm in the next measure, taken up by all voices. The abruptness is enhanced by the beginning of the cadential D, which treats C as if it had been some type of interruption.

One might argue that it takes the piece three repetitions to finally excise the disruptive C, and that the identity of the piece is ultimately tied to either the quality of the final three stanzas, which lack C, or the process by which C is isolated and removed from the mix.

Let's look for a moment how the piece lays out against the text of the prayer, with congregational responses in parentheses (Table 6-1). It is indeed tempting to imagine that the basic musical materials were generated by the first stanza since they match the music in both mood and shape. We notice how the beginning of the second verse requires the somewhat tortuous elongation of syllables. We might conclude that the composition of this Kaddish has proceeded more or less according to the rules of strophic composition:

1. Set the first stanza beautifully.
2. Select material with enough definition to have character, but enough flexibility to be applied to subsequent stanzas.
3. Unfold the musical template in subsequent stanzas, playing on the flexibility of the material, and taking care to do nothing to draw attention, through irregular or clumsy placement, to the fact there is a "second order" relationship between text and music.

Notice how our forceful C matches up with such phrases as "honored and celebrated" and the personal "That *we* offer this world" (my italics). More obviously the "Amen" of D fits all stanzas except number 2, where its open syllables become filled in.

Is then the absence of C in the last three stanzas simply a textual matter—that is, has Rossi pretty much run out of text and needs to drop *something?* This is possible. But the composer does take real care with the presentation of his musical materials. Note that in the first, double presentation of A in stanza 1 the figuration is slightly different, as if to create a certain asymmetry at the outset. However, it is the kind of asymmetry that is often read as dynamic symmetry by the listener and not noticed. Whether or not this is the case, can we argue that the effect of this choice, and other such choices, creates the identity of the piece, and that this identity may exist apart from the intention of its creator? Finally, would anyone have noticed the disappearance of C, or rather would the singers, and attentive congregants, merely sensed a "rightness" of the setting in regard to its text?

Table 6-1.

Kaddish

Yitgadal veyitkadash shmeih rabba (A)	Magnified and sanctified be His great name
Be'alma divra khiruteih vayamlikh malkhu teih (A)	In the world according to His will may He establish his kingdom
Behayyeikhon uvyomeikhon uvhayyei dekhol beit yisrael (B)	During your life and your days and during the lives of Israel
Ba'agala uvizman kariv (C)	Speedily and shortly
Ve'imru 'amen (D)	And say "Amen"
(Amen. Yehe shmeih rabba mevarakh le'alam ul'almei 'almayya)	(Amen. May His great name be blessed for ever and evermore)
Yitbarrakh veyishtabbah (A)	Blessed and praised
Veyitpaar veyitromam veyitnasse veyit'alle (B)	and glorified and elevated and exalted and extolled
Veyithaddar veyithallal (C)	and honored and celebrated
Shemeih dekudsha berikh hu (D)	be the name of the Holy One, blessed be He
(Amen)	(Amen)
Leeila le'eila min kol birkhata (A)	High above, high above all blessings
Shirata, tushbahata venehemata (B)	Songs, praises, and consolations
Da miran be'alma (C)	That we offer in this world
Ve'imru 'amen (D)	And say "Amen."
(Amen)	(Amen)
Titkabbal tselotehon uva'utehon (A)	May acceptance be granted to the prayers and petitions
Dekhol beit yisrael kadam 'vuhon devishmayya (B)	Of all the House of Israel by their Father who is in heaven
Ve'imru 'amen (D)	And say "Amen"
(Amen)	(Amen)
Yehe shalama rabba min shemayya (A)	May there be peace from heaven
Vehayyim tovim 'aleinu ve'al kol yisra'el (B)	And a good life for all Israel
Ve'imru 'amen (D)	And say "Amen."
(Amen)	(Amen)
Ose shalom bimromav hu berahamav (A)	May He who makes peace on His heights
Ya'ase shalom 'aleinu ve'al kol yisrael (B)	Himself, in His mercy make peace for us and all Israel
Ve'imru 'amen (D)	And say "Amen"
(Amen)	(Amen)

Of course, we may note that my use of a reductive schematic is in no way identical to the "truth" of the Kaddish; it is a kind of limited map, a convenience to draw attention to certain details. Inevitably it also blurs others, most notably, the sense of continuity essential to grasping the piece. Most dangerously, such schemata can permanently distort the manner in which we process the music. But that is the chance we take when we isolate any phenomenon supposedly for the purpose of understanding it more completely.

Of course, once we leave the score, we are back to our old questions. Did Rossi wear bright clothing, and did he smile much? Was any of his dedication tongue-in-cheek? Did he and his champion Leon da Modena really like each other? Were Rossi's liturgical works tried out extensively before publication, and did Rossi himself imagine a sound world based on the acoustics of the synagogue? Did Rossi ever spit when no one was looking? And how many teeth did he have?

The Illusion of Writing

Writing, by its very permanence, implies inevitability. "In 1862 the Bulgarian Parliament was dissolved when Igri Balshangur, leader of the New Republic Party, refused the *dekla* or official parchment at the Twelve Towns Congress" (Popov 1993, 23). Virtually everything in this sentence is false, or made up: there was no Bulgarian Parliament in 1862, no such person as Balshangur, no NRP. Moreover, I'm afraid the *dekla* and the Twelve Towns Congress are products of my imagination as well. But how satisfying they were up there on the page! How perfectly, blissfully, irrelevantly true they seemed, especially when backed up by an equally imaginary bibliographical reference!

We would all like to believe that my writing is truer when I am trying to be true than when I am making everything up. But is it necessarily the case? Attempts to be accurate create apparent certainties where none are possible, and so lull us into a kind of passivity.

Opening the Ark of the Torah

One of the most sacred and festive moments in Jewish ritual involves the opening of the ark and the removal of the torah scroll. In its components this ritual can resemble anything from idol worship to an introspective admiration for a revered collection of great wisdom. To accompany this moment Rossi chooses a *piyyut,* or post-Biblical prayer, written by Matthew of Bologna.

Rossi's Hebrew-texted works are sometimes divided into two categories: those pieces intended for the daily service, such as the Kaddish, and those, like "'Eftah na sefatai" intended for special festivals, such as Rosh Hashanah or Passover.

Following the text of the *piyyut,* Rossi has arranged "'Eftah na sefatai" (Let Me Open My Lips and Respond in Joyous Song; Sampler CD 2, track 2) as a kind of rondo with the first stanza repeated at the end, and a refrain at the end of each stanza. (Notice that by using the word *piyyut,* with its unusual spelling, twice, and now three times, I am establishing authority, and you, too, may be taking some special pleasure in the new terms, feeling initiated into some historical mystery.)

Here is Don Harrán, speaking about two pieces, including "'Eftah":

Similarly, nos. 25 and 27 [the Kaddish and "'Eftah na sefatai"], in Lydian with B-flat, are unusual in their insistent repetition of cadences on the *finalis,* but it must be remembered that these are the only two pieces with a recurring textual-musical refrain. The effect is of a new simplicity, quite unlike the more devious modality of the other 'Songs,' not to speak of the composer's madrigals. With their refrains, the two pieces project an even folklike character. (Harrán 1999, 230)

Ah, "folkish"—what a wonderful constellation of associations are conjured up by this phrase: authentic, physical, primitive, accessible, dance-like, rural, lyrical, lacking in complexity. Whether Rossi intended to be folk-like or not, he does have a different palette in mind for "'Eftah" compared to the Kaddish. Part of the effect of the work and its subtlety involves the use of two choirs, of three and four parts, respectively, to alternate throughout the piece, but then also to join forces as a tutti ensemble, as depicted in the schematic below:

A1 (3-voice choir)	+	A2 (3-voice choir)
A 1 (tutti)	+	A2 (tutti)
B (4-voice choir)	+	A2 (tutti)
C (3-voice choir)	+	A2 (tutti)
D (4-voice choir)	+	A2 (tutti)
E (3-voice choir)	+	A2 (tutti)
F (tutti)	+	A2 (tutti)
G (4-voice choir)	+	A2 (tutti)
A1 (tutti)	+	A2 (tutti)

Example 6-5. Rossi: "'Eftah na sefatai," mm. 1–7.

Here again we have the kind of conflict that must have caught the ear and mind of any sage concerned with preserving Jewish traditions. The first three measures are utterly charming and lively, with a little duet in parallel thirds in the two upper voices (A1 above; Example 6-5; CD: 0:00–0:09).

How can figures that seem so clearly taken from popular song serve a holy function in the sanctuary? Does "sexiness" become "celebratoriness" when the context is changed? Or is the opening coquetry really some kind of "hook"? After all, the eighth notes that appear in the second measure and give the piece its initial sense of lilt disappear completely until a cadence near the end of the composition. The second half of the first phrase is in steady, long note values, which continue into the real refrain (A2, above): "le'el hai 'ashir binsoa' ha'aron" (To living God will I sing during procession with the ark). This refrain, in its first, three-voice appearance, seems to have a downward gravitational pull that is somewhat masked when it is heard in its more festive, seven-voice version for the rest of the composition (Examples 6-6, a; CD: 0:10–0:20, and 6-6, b; CD: 0:32–0:40).

In setting the text Rossi is extraordinarily artful. Each new section offers fresh features, while linking up effortlessly with the refrain. The opening phrases clearly delineate the tonal center of the work—subsequent stanzas explore other territory. So the first departure, "Mehulal 'ekra 'el" (Praised will I call God) plunges us almost immediately into a kind of religious mystery absent from the opening (B above; Example 6-7; CD: 0:40–0:58). The fanfare-like reiteration of F comes to a close, and after a breath that throws the rhythmic structure of the piece into fruitful doubt, we quickly move to an A-major chord on the word "El" (God).

Despite earlier traditions of chromaticism that place this move within the realm of convention, the harmonic fluidity of the language is breathtaking, with the maximum displacement on the symbol of the divine. The rest of the phrase moves blithely and sensuously onward, as if unaware of the depths it had encountered.

Even though the opening seemed to indicate that phrases were regular, beginning without upbeat at the start of each measure, the refrain operates somewhat differently. The accent seems to be on "le El" making the first note a kind of upbeat (see Example 6-6). Perhaps it is simply coincidence that the composer features seven-measure phrase units in his seven-voice composition, but the effect is subtle and powerful. That Rossi creates further effects by mov-

Example 6-6. a) Rossi: " 'Eftah na sefatai," mm. 8b–15; b) Rossi: " 'Eftah na sefatai," mm. 24–30.

a)

b)

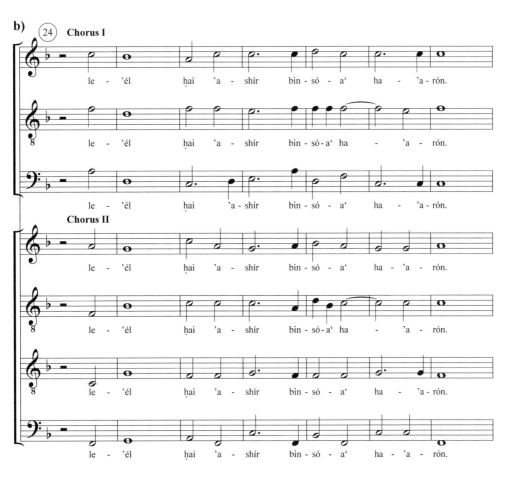

Example 6-7. Rossi: "'Eftah na sefatai," mm. 31–37.

ing the accents around, starting some stanzas on the beat and others as a pickup, is part of his compositional strategy, and part of the way he creates notable effects.

For example, the first four episodes, called B–E in the schematic, function as a group, alternating four- and three-voice settings. Each begins off the beat so that we take it as a "fact" of the composition. This is abruptly shattered when verse F arrives. The text "Hen na'avor" (We will pass on) is squarely on the beat, sounding as if it has come in too soon (Example 6-8; CD: 2:37–2:49).

The effect is magnified by an unexpected return to seven voices instead of a pared-down ensemble, and topped by a movement from the home area of F major to the very distant harmony of D major, the harmonic disjunction clearly identified with "the world beyond."

The last verse, G, seems at first to reassert the pattern by recalling the harmonic motion of B (the move to an A-major chord) and scaling back to four voices. But on the words "na shir" (We will sing) the full ensemble enters with a rare imitative gesture, leading to a cadence featuring the only other eighth notes in the piece.

The final "'Eftah na" combines the opening gesture with cadential (and celebratory?) fanfares in the lower voices (marked "x" in Example 6-9; CD: 3:40–3:51) and eventually another sensuous cadence where a madrigalian descending scale figure in quarter notes eventually takes over the proceedings (Example 6-10; CD: 3:55–4:11). The effect combines celebration and reverence, adoration, and even a certain playfulness.

Though the nature of the tune and its refrain gives the piece an air of "regularity," a quick examination of the text reveals that this is artifice. Nearly every stanza has a different phrase length (Table 6-2), and several of the refrains are a half-beat short, since the following stanza starts on the beat instead of off it. Slight extensions give the impression of expressive additions, and the conclusion is particularly effective in this way.

Let us remind ourselves of our limitations. Do we know why Rossi composed the piece in such a fashion? Was he really just following the shape of the text, or did he artfully imagine how the uneven phrases could paradoxically create the effect of something completely balanced? Did he whistle the tune before he wrote it down, and was he, by any chance, wear-

Example 6-8. Rossi: "'Eftah na sefatai," mm. 118–120.

ing red when he wrote it? Does the downward stepwise motion that characterizes "'Eftah" represent the light, metaphorical or actual, pouring out of the ark, and did Rossi himself glow when he heard this work sung for the first time? How did the synagogue smell?

Why This Piece?

I selected "'Eftah na sefatai" for scrutiny because it is beautiful and accessible at first hearing, and also because it represented Rossi's music for a specific event, the opening of the ark during a time of festival. And it is indeed a lovely piece. But the work also raises questions about the way in which a composer manages the difficult task of making a new musical world comprehensible at first hearing while still allowing parts of itself—and significant parts—to be discovered in future encounters with the material.

The Francese Sonata

All the questions we have asked about history and meaning become amplified when we switch our focus to instrumental music. Rossi's instrumental works divide loosely into three groups: dance pieces (mostly gagliards and correntes), sinfonias, and sonatas. Considered to be among the first instrumental pieces of their kind, Rossi's works are not quite what one

Example 6-9.   Rossi: " 'Eftah na sefatai," mm. 164–165.

might think from their titles. The sinfonias are very short works, and the sonatas rarely exceed five minutes each. The sonatas display trio texture, which was to become very popular during the Baroque Era.

Several hundred years ago there must have been a popular French song. Or perhaps it was not popular at all, but popular only in Mantua. Or popular only in the Jewish community of Mantua—though that seems highly unlikely. Whatever the case, it became the inspiration for Rossi's fifth sonata, also called *Sonata quinta sopra un'Aria francese* (Sonata Five on a French Melody). The tune seems to have otherwise vanished, preserved only in Rossi's musical amber.

It is a variation piece—that is, the sixteen-measure French melody serves as the foundation for elaborations and various changes. Here are some of the things we do not know about the piece.

First, how did it sound in its own time? The performance you will hear (Sampler CD 2, track 3) is quite lovely. Period instruments are used, and the players and ensemble leader have studied old treatises and the latest scholarship for information about contemporary perfor-

Example 6-10.   Rossi: "'Eftah na sefatai," mm. 175–182.

mance practice. Yet we really do not know whether the piece was faster or slower, whether it was phrased more roughly, whether there were longer or shorter pauses between variations, or, in the end, whether the ethos of the composition has actually survived. The piece is simultaneously Michelangelo's David and the Venus di Milo. We also don't know whether listeners in the same room heard the same thing, then or now, or how similar two performances of the same piece might have sounded.

Second, how do we understand instrumental music? Let's look at just the first statement of the theme (Example 6-11; CD: 0:00–0:19). Is it mood or design? Are we participating in lived human events, or looking at lovely shapes on a vase? And our French song: was it a love song, and is there residue of amorous longing in the sensuous way the theme tries to reach upwards, just after the opening, and even higher in the second, parallel statement?

Third, the second half of the theme (Example 6-12; CD: 0:20–0:38) begins almost exactly like the passage we discussed in "'Eftah na sefatai" on" on the words "Mehulal 'ekra 'el" (Praised will I call God; Example 6-7). At that point I suggested there might be a connection between harmonic displacement, musical meaning, and the idea of the divinity. But here there is no almighty. Or is there? The Francese sonata was part of Book IV of Rossi's *Sonata,*

Table 6-2.
" 'Eftah na sefatai"

'Eftah na sefatai ve 'e'ene veron	3[v]	(8) [phrases]
le'el hai 'ashir binsoa' ha'aron 2×		(7)
'Eftah na sefatai ve 'e'ene veron	7	(9)
le'el hai 'ashir binsoa' ha'aron		(7)
Mehulal 'ekra 'el 'et yish'enu yo'el	4	(7)
Uva letsiyyon goel nikra 'az begaron		(7)
Le 'el hai 'ashir binsoa' ha'aron	7	(7)
Tiftah 'erets yesha' litfillat dakh tisha;	3	(9)
Ve yisra'el no sha' ul shon 'ilem taron		(7)
Le'el hai 'ashir binsoa' ha'aron	7	(7)
Tashiv shevutenu le'el hai go'alenu,	4	(7)
Unshallem nedareinu vekhipper 'aharon		(7)
Le'el hai 'ashir binsoa' ha'aron	7	(7)
Yafutsu, 'el 'oyevekham yaronu te'evekha;	3	(8)
Yom tariv 'et rivekha, yashuvu levitsaron		(7)
Le'el hai 'ashir binsoa' ha'aron	7	(6.5)
Hen na'avor ge'ulim velanu 'el 'elim;	7	(9)
Maoz vahayalim yegabber veyitron		(8)
Le'el hai 'ashir binsoa' ha'aron	7	(7)
Hizki na, 'el, tehi venas yagon va hi	4	(6)
na shir Nashir kenam;	7	(10)
Vaihi binsoa' ha'aron.		
Le'el hai 'ashir binsoa' ha'aron	7	(6.5)
'Eftah na sefatai ve 'e'ene veron	7	(9)
le'el hai 'ashir binsoa' ha'aron	7	(10)

Let me open my lips and respond in joyous song
To living God will I sing during the procession with the ark

Let me open my lips and respond in joyous song
To living God will I sing during the procession with the ark

"Praised" will I call God when our deliverance is His will;
with the arrival in Zion of a redeemer we will then cry aloud
To living God will I sing during the procession with the ark

May You open the earth for deliverance, to the prayer of the oppressed may you
hearken; may Israel be saved and the tongue of the dumb rejoice in song
To living God will I sing during the procession with the ark

May you restore our captivity to living God, our redeemer;
We will repay our vows and Aaron will make atonement
To living God will I sing during the procession with the ark

Scattered, God, be Your enemies and joyful in song be your devotees;
On the day You plead Your cause they will return to the stronghold
To living God will I sing during the procession with the ark

Yes, we will pass on, redeemed, having with us the God of gods;
His citadel and power will He fortify to our advantage.
To living God will I sing during the procession with the ark

My strength, God, may You be and with the retreat of despair and woe
We will sing as is said: "so it was during the procession with the ark"
To living God will I sing during the procession with the ark

Let me open my lips and respond in joyous song
To living God will I sing during the procession with the ark

Example 6-11. Rossi: *Sonata quinta sopra un'Aria francese,* mm. 1–9.

sinfonie, gagliarde published in 1622, at just about the same time as the Songs of Solomon. Could there have been any interpenetration of meaning between the two sets?

Finally, what are variations and how do they work? There was a kind of revolution occurring in music around 1600. A concept of sound was increasingly asserting itself, and this new approach involved the invention, between 1550 and 1600, of "functionless" music—that is, of music not for dancing or marching; weddings, funerals, or celebrations; church serv-

Example 6-12. Rossi: *Sonata quinta sopra un'Aria francese,* mm. 10–13.

ices, royal banquets, or an evening of carousing. Rather, this somewhat new music was intended for the performers themselves or groups of attentive listeners. And composers must have asked a question, over and over again: How do I organize my composition if it has no function other than listening or performing? What are the musical equivalents of dramatic shape, narrative structure, and plot?

There were many solutions, as always, at the beginning of what appears to us as an evolutionary curve. But most musicians seemed to understand that musical "plot" involved various kinds of patterned repetition on several levels. While Jan Pieterszoon Sweelinck in Holland and others in Europe were experimenting with pieces titled "ricercare" or "fantasia," usually based on the older principle of imitation—where real or imaginary "voices" enter with similar material at staggered intervals—there was also a surge of interest in variation pieces (see Chapter 9).

Variations work on the principle of varied repetition—they extend, ideally, by combining the familiar with just enough unfamiliar material to retain attention and, perhaps, give the listener the illusion of hearing "old" material for the first time. Sweelinck used intricate quasi-mathematical principles of speed change to suggest certain kinds of instabilities, arrivals, and denouements. Rossi's variations are more intuitive, and at least at first glance, less systematic. Unlike later variation sets, with conspicuous pauses between individual variations, the Francese set flows effortlessly. Indeed, it is sometimes hard for listeners to know where they are within the set. But rest assured: most composers do not care if you know "where you are" in the form. They understand that it is, conversely, the role of form to tell your ear where it is. And your ear knows.

While Rossi does not construct his variations with as much external planning as Sweelinck, there is a general sense of dramatic finish. This is created not by simply using shorter and shorter note values as the piece progresses, but by varying the acceleration to produce something more subtle (Example 6-13; CD: 2:24–3:01). In the end, though, we have the illusion of increased speed, and increased speed creates the illusion of physical excitement.

Is the Francese Sonata Jewish music? Written at the same time, putatively, as the Songs of Solomon, can we argue that the instrumental music is Jewish in any way? Should it be studied in the field of Jewish music? Or should that field include only the Songs? Or is it, like "Russian music," "Czech music," or "French music," a deceptive and potentially misleading field? If Rossi's experience as a Jew was a significant part of his life, and his music reflected his life in any way, the answer should be yes, the expression "Jewish music" is relevant in the Francese Sonata. But though so many years have passed since Rossi's time, and so much thinking about music has taken place, we still cannot answer even such a seemingly simple query. We are gripped by a tender paradox: music seems to do whatever we want it to do, up to a point. But then it goes its own way, and is far beyond our control.

Conclusion

Historical investigations begin in an attempt to understand the past, to use a collection of data to imaginatively reconstruct what no longer exists. But such investigations often end up demonstrating that we know less than we thought we did before beginning the process. In the course of this discussion we have assembled some information about Rossi's life, and we have admitted that not only do we have less than a billionth of what materials we might need to reconstruct Rossi's life in any archival sense, but we do not even have enough to delude ourselves that we know him, as we do so often with other historical figures.

Example 6-13.   Rossi: *Sonata quinta sopra un'Aria francese,* mm. 51–58.

But perhaps there are other ways to know the past. Several years ago, I visited a couple in southern California who have the largest private collection of music boxes in the United States. At one point they walked over to a display case and took out a gold box. Winding it carefully they pressed a small button and it began to play. Given by Napoleon to one of his generals in the first decade of the nineteenth century, it sounded a lovely march. It was my sense at that time, and subsequently, that this was as close to a live performance of nineteenth-century music as one could get. Though I was hard by Disneyland amid the endless LA freeways, I was also in France, standing next to the general as he heard his box for the first time.

Although we do not have mechanical reproductions of Rossi's music, we do, of course, have another kind of technology, far more tantalizing than biographical records. This is a musical score, the blueprint that gives us hints and suggestions of how we might reassemble a living performance. And for all our questions we may conclude that the truest re-creation of the past occurs when we listen to this music.

Rossi's synagogue music is in some ways more limiting in this regard than the Francese Sonata. To some extent our comprehension of it may be dependent on secondary images: the role the music played in the sacred service, its physical place in the synagogue building, and whether or not we are easily lured into issues of Jewish life, particularly in the shadow of events in the twentieth century. With instrumental music we more comfortably revel in abstract patterns that, because they have been worked with such care, are the closest we come to inhabiting any real past. Combining the two together, with concentrated listening, constant skepticism, and arching imagination, it is just possible that we may enter the portal into a truly different world. *Rossi's* world.

BIBLIOGRAPHY

Adler, Israel. 1967. "The Rise of Art Music in the Italian Ghetto: The Influence of Segregation on Jewish Musical Praxis." In *Jewish Medieval and Renaissance Studies,* ed. Alexander Altmann. Cambridge, Mass.: Harvard University Press.

Fenlon, Iain. 2001. "Salamone Rossi." In *The New Grove Dictionary of Music and Musicians,* ed. Stanley Sadie, 2nd ed., 21:731–734. London: Macmillan.

Harrán, Don. 1999. *Salamone Rossi: Jewish Musician in Late Renaissance Mantua.* Oxford: Oxford University Press.

Jacobson, Joshua. 1988. "The Choral Music of Salamone Rossi." *American Choral Review* 30, no. 4: 4–70.

Mostel, Rafael. 2002. "Meet Europe's Hottest Composer, c. 1600: A Devout Ghetto Dweller Named Rossi." *Forward* (Nov. 29): 12.

Newman, Joel, and Fritz Rikko, eds. 1972. *A Thematic Index to the Works of Salamon Rossi.* Hackensack, N.J.: J. Boonin.

Parisi, Susan Helen. 1997. "The Jewish Community and Carnival Entertainment at the Mantuan Court in the Early Baroque." In *Music in Renaissance Cities and Courts: Studies in Honor of Lewis Lockwood,* ed. Jessie Ann Owens and Anthony M. Cummings, 297–305. Warren, Mich.: Harmonie Park Press.

Polak, Emil J. 1993. *Medieval and Renaissance Letter Treatises and Form Letters.* Leiden: E. J. Brill.

Rossi, Salamone. 2003. The Songs of Solomon, ed. by Don Harrán. *Corpus Mensurabilis Musicae,* 100, especially vols. 12, 13a, 13b. Middleton, Wis.: American Institute of Musicology.

Simonsohn, Shlomo. 1977. *History of the Jews in the Duchy of Mantua.* Jerusalem: Israel Academy of Sciences and Humanities.

Twersky, Isadore, and Bernard Septimus, eds. 1987. *Jewish Thought in the Seventeenth Century.* Cambridge, Mass.: Harvard University Center for Jewish Studies.

CHAPTER SEVEN

Usurping the Place of the Muses:
Barbara Strozzi and the Female Composer
in Seventeenth-Century Italy

Wendy Heller

Had she been born in another era she would certainly have usurped or enlarged the place of the muses.

—Giovanni Francesco Loredano on Barbara Strozzi, in a published letter to Domenico Andreis, Venice, 1655

Musical Women in Early Modern Italy

Giovanni Francesco Loredano's description of composer and singer Barbara Strozzi tells us much about the role of the female musician in seventeenth-century Italy. As one of Venice's most distinguished and influential authors, founder of the infamous Accademia degli Incogniti, and one well versed in contemporary opera, Loredano was certainly in a position to recognize Strozzi's extraordinary musical talent. Still, he does not compare her with her professional male counterparts. Instead, he relegates her to an imaginative, fictive realm—an exclusively female sphere—in which she might comfortably dwell. Only as one of the muses, those talented female deities who embodied mankind's greatest literary and artistic accomplishments, might Strozzi have found an appropriate niche. Implicit in his comment is the recognition that her gender excludes her from recognition in her own world as an eminent composer in seventeenth-century Venice.

The dilemma expressed in Loredano's praise is one that would have been familiar to other female musicians who had begun to gain fame in the late sixteenth and seventeenth centuries. Indeed, the difficulties and successes experienced by women composers in early modern Italy were an integral part of the ambivalence with which all female music-making was regarded during this period. On the one hand, a certain amount of musical training was deemed necessary and even desirable for young women, regardless of whether or not they were destined for marriage or the convent. At the same time, female music-making was fraught with moral and social contradictions that were not easily resolved. Aristotelian admonitions on the virtues appropriate to women—namely, silence and chastity—retained their force throughout this period, complicating the lives of women musicians and those who promoted them.

High-placed women in the European courts, for example, were expected to have a certain amount of proficiency in all the arts, which included singing, dancing, and the playing of instruments. In Chapter 6 of the highly influential *Book of the Courtier,* Castiglione notes that music is a worthy and desirable leisure-time activity for a well-educated courtier. But at the same time one of Castiglione's courtiers also claims that not only is music better suited to women, but it can also have a negative, feminizing effect on men. The inference regarding gender and professionalism is clear: while professional male musicians might escape charges of effeminacy, female musicians, because of their femininity, could not escape their amateur status (Newcomb 1985, 101–103).

By the third quarter of the sixteenth century, however, there were numerous exceptions. The high-placed women of dubious moral standing—the so-called *oneste cortegiane* or "honest courtesans"—readily exploited the age-old connections between female music-making and sexual availability to great advantage. Music was an important weapon in the art of seduction, as the Englishman Thomas Coryat (1577–1617) made explicit in his famous description of the Venetian courtesan:

> Moreover shee will endeavor to enchant thee partly with her melodious notes that shee warbles out upon her lute, which shee fingers with as laudable a stroake as many men that are excellent professors in the noble science of Musicke; and partly with that heart-tempting harmony of her voice. Also thou wilt finde the Venetian Cortezan (if shee be a selected woman indeede) a good Rhetorician, and a most elegant discourser, so that if shee cannot move thee with these foresaid delights, shee will assay thy constancy with her Rhetorical tongue. (Coryate 1611)

Daughters and sisters of musicians could take on professional responsibilities without putting their reputations at risk. In other instances, women benefited from the specific musical tastes of a court. This was certainly the case in Ferrara, where several renowned female singers formed the *Concerto delle donne* (Concert of Women), which performed virtuosic music for the pleasure of Duke Alfonso d'Este (Newcomb 1985, 94–100). As the popularity of their singing style grew, professional female singers found themselves in high demand at other North-Italian courts. The great actress, poet, and dramatist Isabella Andreini (1562–1604) also did much to make the comic stage an acceptable venue for a woman. Isabella and her husband Francesco toured the North-Italian courts with the renowned Compagnia dei Gelosi, a commedia dell'arte troupe. In addition, she published a pastoral play and over five hundred poems, many of which were set to music by the best composers of the day (MacNeil 2003).

Women musicians also flourished in sacred institutions, where a musical education was viewed as enhancing rather than detracting from a young woman's spiritual development. Indeed, some of the most important women musicians were trained and raised behind convent walls. Beginning in the late sixteenth century, the girls of the *ospedali* (orphanages) in Venice received a more rigorous musical training than their presumably more fortunate counterparts. This was true at the Pio Ospedale della Pietà, for instance, where Vivaldi was employed much of his life. The performances of the women of the *ospedali* became renowned throughout Europe, and eloquent testimony of their high level of accomplishment is the substantial repertory of music written for them.

Composing Women in Court and Convent

Although one can observe an impressive amount of music-making by women during this period, the role of the female composer takes on a particular complexity. The musical activity deemed acceptable and even desirable for a woman of the court was usually limited to the amateur realm and did not include the composition of music. Inequalities in the education of men and women in the early modern period certainly extended to music, and young girls were less often accorded the kind of rigorous training in counterpoint and composition that would have been unremarkable for young boys (Bowers 1985, 129–133). Again, family situation and social status were of critical importance. Even the most talented women needed to be ideally positioned to pursue a career as a composer.

Such is the case with Francesca Caccini (1587–c. 1641), the daughter of the composer and singer Giulio Caccini, discussed in Chapter 2. Francesca undoubtedly received special training, encouragement, and professional opportunities that would normally have been denied to a woman. The ambiguity with which a female composer was regarded is immediately apparent in two of Francesca's job offers—one from Queen Maria de Medici of France and another from Princess Margherita della Samaglia-Peretti—which included not only a salary but also a dowry to help her attract a husband (Cusick 1993). Francesca spent much of her life in the service of the Medici, writing music for lavish theatrical entertainments. Some of this music has not survived. Caccini also married twice. Her first husband was a court singer, Giovanni Battista Signori, and their daughter Margherita became a singer and later a nun. After Signori's death, Francesca married the Lucchese patron and aristocrat Tomaso Rafaello, with whom she had a son. Rafaello left her a wealthy landowner, yet after his death, she continued to work as a musician—teaching singing, composing, and performing as a singer with her young daughter Margherita. At one point, she refused to let the fifteen-year-old Margherita perform publicly, for fear that it might have limited the young girl's marriage options. Thus, despite Caccini's own professional triumphs as a musician, she was not convinced that this was an appropriate career path for her daughter.

While there are numerous reports of female performers who also composed, our best evidence about the compositional activities of women comes from the publication of their works. Women composers, like their male counterparts, benefited from the growing market for printed music. By the third quarter of the sixteenth century, the North-Italian printing presses provided an outlet for a number of women composers whose work might otherwise have gone unnoticed (Bowers 1985, 162–167). Beginning with Madalena Casaluna's first madrigal book, published in Florence in 1568, Italian printers increased the public's awareness of female composers and heightened their visibility by issuing their works in single-composer volumes. Casaluna's volume was quickly followed by the publication of secular works by such women as Paola Massarenghi and Vittoria and Raffaella Aleotti. Francesca Caccini's *Primo libro delle musiche a una e due voci* (First Music Book for One and Two Voices) was published in 1618, and in 1621 she became the first female composer to publish an opera, *La liberazione di Ruggerio dall'isola d'Alcina*.

The convent was one of the most fertile arenas for female music-making, including composing. In fact, the majority of publications by women composers in the seventeenth century came from inside the convent. By the fifteenth century, the number of women in monastic settings had increased considerably. Convents throughout Italy were filled with women from various levels of society, some with sincere motivations, others who were compelled to enter religious life for financial and personal reasons. For example, families were not always able to supply all of their daughters with sufficient dowries. Since too many marriages in a noble family diluted the family fortune, the convent provided a safe haven in which to deposit women before they became financial or moral liabilities. Forced monachization certainly inspired some dissent, as was expressed most vehemently in print by one of Barbara Strozzi's contemporaries, the Venetian nun Arcangela Tarabotti (Heller 2003, 59–63). Some nuns objected to the stricter rules of *clausura* (closure) and restrictions that were the legacy of the Counter-Reformation. But in an era when women commonly had few options and little say in their own destiny, the convent often provided an acceptable alternative to marriage, even when a true religious calling was lacking.

Recent studies of convent music in Italy provide a vivid and rich picture of the resourcefulness and ingenuity with which the nuns negotiated restrictions and ecclesiastical strictures and the ways they exploited the dramatic potential of seventeenth-century musical language to express quite individualistic notions about female spirituality and religiosity. Craig Monson puts it succinctly: "Within the convent, a socially constructed medium such as music, in which the same words could convey different meanings in different contexts, proved to be a notably valuable, persuasive tool of convent women's culture" (Monson 1995, 40). The fascinating career of Lucrezia Orsina Vizzana (1590–1662) provides an example of the factors that nurtured a musical career in the convent. Vizzana, who had entered the Camaldolese convent of S. Christina in Bologna in 1598 at the age of eight, had the advantage of coming to maturity in a sophisticated musical environment. The S. Christina nuns were the dedicatees for no fewer than four major publications, including Adriano Banchieri's *Messa solenne e otto voce* (Venice, 1599). This underscores the extent to which the S. Christina nuns managed to circumvent ecclesiastical restrictions to produce lavish music (Monson 1995, 50–53).

Vizzana also benefited from the tradition of female mentoring within the convent. She apprenticed with her maternal aunt and organist, Camilla Bombacci, and it is likely that she studied with other musical nuns as well. Vizzana seems to have played the same role for her younger relatives. The fact that she trained entirely within the convent did not preclude her knowledge of the *stile moderno,* or modern style of composition. Her set of motets *Componimenti musicali motetti concertati* (Venice, 1623) clearly shows the extent to which modern musical practices permeated the convent walls (Monson 1995). Indeed, the expressive and highly dramatic setting of texts, which was a hallmark of Monteverdi's break with the *prima prattica,* was an essential part of Vizzana's style—as it was to be for Strozzi, albeit in a secular vein. Vizzana "took her texts seriously," as Monson has put it, and a close reading of music and text tells us much about her artistic voice and her notion of the female spirituality that shaped her life.

The Milanese nun Chiara Margarita Cozzolani (1602–1676), a close contemporary of Strozzi's, is another example of a woman who flourished within a circumscribed and primarily feminine sphere. As described in Robert Kendrick's richly detailed study, Cozzolani came from a prominent merchant family and spent much of her life at the Benedictine monastery of S. Radegonda, one of the foremost female monasteries in the production of seventeenth-century polyphony. She published four volumes of music between 1640 and 1650, not all of which has survived. Most surprisingly, she was allowed to leave the cloister to travel to Venice to sign the dedication and perhaps supervise the publication of one of her works. Might she have met with Barbara Strozzi on that trip? We may never know. Regardless, as in Bologna, the composer-nuns at S. Radegonda were not isolated from seventeenth-century musical innovations. Cozzolani, for example, adopted the modern style of the Lombardian motet, and she emerges as one of the most important Milanese composers of the period, irrespective of her gender (Kendrick 1996, 268–303). She and her colleagues successfully circumvented the various restrictions and edicts that sought to limit music in the convent, bringing considerable fame and glory to Milan. Their ethereal, bodiless voices, emanating from an environment in which musical self-expression was both safe and appropriate, flowed easily from the cloister into the public sphere. Loredano need not have worried about placing the nuns with

PLATE I. *Lady Mary Wroth and Her Archlute* (c. 1620). Reproduced by kind permission of Viscount De L'Isle, from his private collection at Penshurst Place.

PLATE 2. Queen Elizabeth playing the lute, miniature by Nicholas Hilliard (c. 1580). Courtesy of Berkeley Castle, Gloucestershire.

PLATE 3. John Michael Wright (1617–1694), *Lady with a Theorbo* (c. 1675). Oil on canvas. Used by permission of the Columbus Museum of Art, Columbus, Ohio.

PLATE 4. Adriaan van der Werff (1659–1722), *Couple Making Music.* Otto Neumann Gallery, New York. Used with permission.

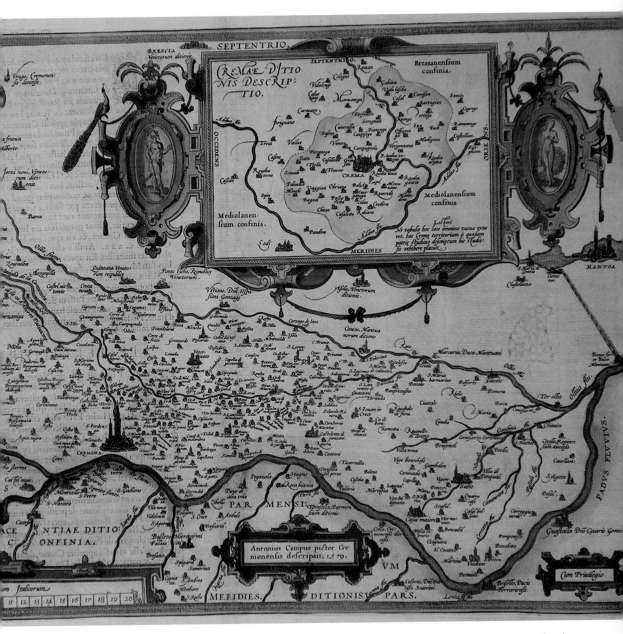

PLATE 7. Cremona and surrounding area. Map dated 1579. Courtesy of Antiquemaps-online.com.

(opposite)
PLATE 5. Bartolomeo Passarotti, *Portrait of a Man Playing a Lute* (1576). Museum of Fine Arts, Boston. Photograph © 2004 Museum of Fine Arts, Boston.

PLATE 6. Theodoor Rombouts, *The Lute Player* (c. 1620). Philadelphia Museum of Art, John G. Johnson Collection.

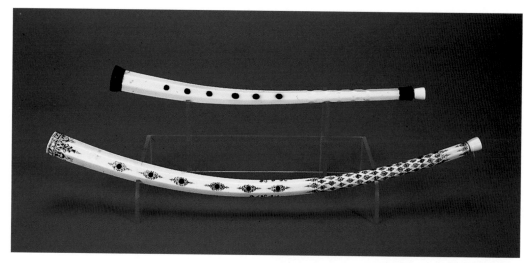

PLATE 8. Bass violin by Andrea Amati (after 1538). National Music Museum, University of South Dakota, Vermillion, South Dakota. Photography by Bill Willroth, Sr.

PLATE 9. Two South-German ivory cornettos (c. 1600). National Music Museum, University of South Dakota, Vermillion, South Dakota. Photography by Simon Spicer.

PLATE 10. Three Baroque trumpets by (*left–right*) Johann Wilhelm Haas (Nuremberg, c. 1690–1710), Paul Hainlein (Nuremberg, 1666), and Johann Wilhelm Haas (Nuremberg, c. 1710–1720). National Music Museum, University of South Dakota, Vermillion, South Dakota. Photography by Simon Spicer.

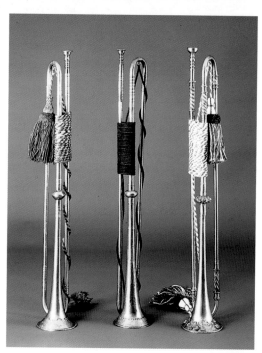

PLATE 11. Lübeck, St. Mary's Church, as reconstructed after World War II. Photo copyright Jutta Brüdern, Braunschweig, Germany.

PLATE 12. Johannes Voorhout, *Domestic Music Scene* (1674), showing Johann Adam Reincken (at the harpsichord) and most probably Dieterich Buxtehude (playing the gamba) and Johann Theile (listening in front, with the canon). Hamburg, Museum für Hamburgische Geschichte. Courtesy of the Museum for Hamburg History.

PLATE 13. Performance of Lully's *Armide* in the Grand Salle of the Palais Royal. Watercolor by Gabriel St. Aubin (mid-eighteenth century). Photograph © 2004 Museum of Fine Arts, Boston.

PLATE 14. French harpsichord built by Pascal Taskin, Paris (1769). Russell Collection, University of Edinburgh. Photo used by permission of the Director of St. Cecilia's Hall.

PLATE 15. Bernardo Strozzi, portrait of Barbara Strozzi (c. 1635). Gemäldegalerie Alte Meister, Staatliche Kunstsammlungen, Dresden.

PLATE 16. Tiberio Tinelli, portrait of Giulio Strozzi (c. 1635). Uffizi Gallery, Florence. Used with permission.

PLATE 17. Giusto Sustermans, Vittoria della Rovere as Flora (c. 1639). By permission of the Collezione d'Arte Cariprato, Galleria deglia Alberti, Prati, Italy.

PLATE 18. Evaristo Baschenis, Agliardi Triptych (c. 1665), Panel 2. Fotografia: Da Re Italy.

PLATE 19. Evaristo Baschenis, Agliardi Triptych (c. 1665), Panel 3. Fotografia: Da Re Italy.

PLATE 20. Johannes Vermeer, *A Young Woman Standing at a Virginal* (c. 1670). The instrument is of the type built by the Ruckers family and other Flemish makers. Although Dutch artists also depicted women seated at such instruments, it was possible to play standing, as shown here and in other illustrations. Photograph copyright National Gallery, London.

PLATE 21. Mathias Grünwald, *The Small Crucifixion* (c. 1511–1520). Oil on panel. Samuel H. Kress Collection. Image © 2004 Board of Trustees, National Gallery of Art, Washington.

PLATE 22. Organs of Mexico City Cathedral. From *Catedrales de Mexico*. Used with permission.

PLATE 23. Igreja do Carmo in Mariana, Minas Gerais. From *Barroco, a alma do Brasil*.

the muses, as they could be counted as members of another female sphere—the angelic choirs of heaven.

Barbara Strozzi and the Venetian Academies

Barbara Strozzi (1619–1677; Plate 15) was trained neither in church nor in court. Instead, she came to maturity in a rather different climate, the "Most Serene Republic" of Venice. Strozzi was born in Venice, the daughter of Isabella Garzoni, a longtime servant of a prominent Venetian, Giulio Strozzi (1583–1652; Plate 16). She was raised as his adopted daughter, and—given that she was to be his sole heir—it is likely that she was his illegitimate child as well (Rosand 1978, 242). As a composer Barbara did not have the institutional protection provided by a convent. Nor was she the daughter of a composer, like Francesca Caccini. Nonetheless, through her adopted father, Barbara Strozzi had access to the centers of literary, artistic, and musical power in Venice, and she seems to have retained her father's links to the Florentine commercial world as well. She studied with no less a teacher than Francesco Cavalli. She performed at her father's house both for informal occasions and for meetings of the musical Accademia degli Unisoni (Society of the Harmonious), and she published eight volumes of vocal music between 1644 and 1664. Seven of these collections were dedicated to secular works; one was devoted to sacred pieces. Thus she not only achieved rare public recognition as a woman musician, but she also became the most prolific composer of secular vocal music in the mid-seventeenth century. Moreover, Strozzi published her works in single-composer volumes, over which she seems to have a great degree of control. Her male counterparts, by comparison, generally printed their works in joint-composer collections.

Recent archival discoveries have opened up other aspects of Strozzi's life (Glixon 1997, 1999). Although she never married, by 1651 she was the mother of four children. At least three of her offspring were probably fathered by a friend of Giulio Strozzi's, Giulio Paolo Vidman, with whom she remained in contact until his death. Of her four children, three took holy orders. She also might have had an intimate relationship with the Duke of Mantua (Glixon 1997, 324–326).

Strozzi also enjoyed considerable financial independence. Whether or not she made her money entirely from her musical activities, she was sufficiently well-off to lend money to the Vidman and Bissari families, both prominent in the Veneto. Her financial dealings brought her into contact not only with academic intellectuals, but also with noble families both in and outside Venice. Despite her professional accomplishments, life could not have been simple for this single mother of four. Before the death of her father, for example, she appealed to the Venetian authorities to be exempted from paying the extra taxes imposed upon the Venetians to fight the Turkish wars. The latter part of her life is less clear. We know that she carefully preserved her adoptive father's manuscripts and portrait, and that her son Giulio Pietro attempted to sell them after her death. She died in Padua at the age of fifty-eight and was buried in the Eremitani Church near the Scrovegni Chapel (Glixon 1999).

Although he was not a musician himself, Giulio Strozzi raised his daughter within a particularly rich artistic environment, providing her with the opportunity to transcend the complex gender politics of seventeenth-century Venice. He was also intimately involved in the production of theater and literature in Venice, in both private and public venues. Giulio Strozzi seems to have had a particular gift for writing librettos and poetry that were suited to the evolving dramatic style favored by composers in the first part of the seventeenth century. He wrote a number of madrigal texts that would be set by Monteverdi, including the drama *Prosperina rapita,* and he also penned the text for the lost opera *La finta pazza Licori.* He was certainly involved in the establishment of public opera in Venice and was the author of four librettos for the Venetian stage, including one of the most widely disseminated operas of the period, Francesco Sacrati's *La finta pazza.*

Barbara's position in the Venetian musical world was influenced in large part not only by Giulio's participation in musical activities, but also by his intense involvement in the Venetian academic and intellectual circles. He was not only a member of the Venetian Accademia degli Incogniti (Society of the Unknown), but also founded and hosted the subgroup of that academy, the Accademia degli Unisoni, which was dedicated to music (Rosand 1978). The Unisoni may well have been a fertile environment for discussions about opera, a sort of laboratory for musical dramatic experimentation. It also provided an opportunity for Barbara to sing both her own compositions and those by other Venetian composers in a circle that, while less public than opera, was by no means completely private.

The somewhat unusual nature of Barbara's involvement with the Unisoni is best understood in the larger context of the Accademia degli Incogniti, its special role in Venetian life, its involvement in the opera industry, and, most notably, its highly idiosyncratic attitudes toward women. Founded in 1630 by the writer and Venetian patrician Giovanni Francesco Loredano (whose comments about Strozzi opened this essay), the Incogniti included nearly all the prominent intellectual patricians of Venice, along with many non-Venetians who were to become active in the Venetian literary-intellectual world. The Incogniti dominated literary life in Venice in the middle part of the century, publishing extensively on topics that ranged from the serious to the seemingly frivolous: histories, poems, letters, plays, short novels, travesties of the classics, as well as opera librettos. Its members also played a prominent role in Venetian political life. Regardless of their often-controversial literary activities, the Incogniti were ardent patriots, active in Venetian government, and strongly committed to the preservation of the state and the perpetuation of the myth of Venice. The Incogniti backed the Republic's well-known propensity to mythologize itself and its origins, to weave fact and fiction into a single fabric that emphasized Venice's unmatched physical beauty, the divinity of its birth, the perfection of its government, and the wisdom and nobility of its leaders.

Contradictory notions about gender played an important role in Venice's self-image (Heller 2003, 2–10). Unlike other North-Italian cities such as Ferrara or Florence, where women could play an active role as musicians or patrons of music, Venetian social life did not revolve around a central court in which high-ranking women participated. Venice's absolute exclusion of women in public life was written into the organization of the Republic. Venice may have prided itself on the availability of all pleasures, marketing itself to the world as Europe's playground, home of the most famous carnival and courtesans, and a place where liberties—sexual and otherwise—might be sampled with minimal interference from the watchful eye of the Inquisition. On the other hand, women and the pleasures that they offered were a distraction for the patriotic male, for whom service to the Republic was the highest calling. It was only by instructing women in those virtues appropriate to their gender that men could engage in the civic service that was so necessary for the well being of the Republic. For women, silence and chastity were valued; for men, eloquence and courage were prized.

The Accademia degli Incogniti and, in particular, Giulio Strozzi's musical subgroup, the Unisoni, understood well how to use opera and music as an expression of Venice's gender ideology. They did so, however, from the sanctity of an almost exclusively male sphere—the Venetian Republic in miniature. The Academy was a meeting place in which women were sometimes admitted, yet in which, as the surviving debates attest, the vices, liabilities, and dangerous attractions of women were among the most popular topics for discussion. The published discourses and satires read at the meetings, the plays, opera librettos, and poems—including those written for Barbara Strozzi—reveal a persistent and seemingly irreconcilable conflict between a physical desire for women and a fascination with their beauty and a profound fear of women's sexual and political power to ensnare men and poison their hearts and souls. In the literary and musical worlds of the Incogniti, female virtue is relative; female self-expression through writing, singing, or self-adornment is suspect; bodies are unstable; and the allure of the erotic is ever present.

Strozzi as Muse

It is in this special world that Barbara Strozzi won acclaim, first as a hostess and singer, then as one of the most prolific composers of Italian secular music in the middle of the seventeenth century. Ellen Rosand's extensive work on Strozzi's life provides a vivid view of the singer's early career and the guiding hand that her father must have provided in presenting her to his Venetian friends and colleagues (Rosand 1978). We know, for example, that Strozzi probably first sang informally in the home of Giulio Strozzi around 1634, at the age of fifteen or so. She is described as Giulio's "virtuossisma cantatrice" in 1635 in the dedication of a set of madrigals by the composer Nicolò Fontei (*Delle bizzarrie poetiche . . . libro secondo*), set to poems penned by Giulio himself. By 1638 she had taken the name of Barbara Strozzi, and she was a featured performer at the meetings of the Accademia degli Unisoni. What we know about these evenings is largely a result of a publication of that academy, *Le veglie de' Signori Unisoni* (The Vigils of the Harmonious Gentlemen), dedicated to Barbara, which mentions not only music, but the various discourses and debating topics that were favored by the Accademia degli Incogniti. Barbara appears to have played a central role in the group's gatherings, as a kind of "mistress of ceremonies," singing songs and reading discourses (Rosand 1978, 244). It is notable that although Strozzi was certainly well known by all of those involved in the opera industry and her career paralleled the development of opera in Venice, she never composed or sang for the Venetian operatic stage.

What is particularly intriguing is the extent to which Barbara became a focus for much of the discourse about women in which the Incogniti so often engaged. This is clear from a number of surviving Incogniti writings, a series of satires in manuscript in the form of dialogues and letters, with a highly libertine tone, in which Strozzi's virtue is called into question in a somewhat playful but nonetheless damning tone. It is indeed difficult to know how to interpret these writings, for although the slander might have been directed at Barbara, these attitudes toward women are evident in numerous other Incogniti publications in which no particular woman was specified. Loredano was particularly fascinated with the "falseness" of female chastity. In one published discourse, he wonders whether or not a woman with only one lover is to be considered chaste. In another he decides that it is chastity itself that most compromises female beauty, as it requires women to keep their eyes downcast and to hide their most appealing charms (Heller 2003, 55–58).

Was Barbara's purity called into question merely because she was an unmarried woman or a musician? Or are we to conclude that the various aspersions on her chastity suggest that she was indeed a courtesan—one of the highly skilled women in the art of love and music who populated Venice, as vividly described by Thomas Coryate? This is certainly the view of Strozzi that is suggested in the portrait painted by Bernardo Strozzi (no relation), in which the erotic implications are quite apparent (Plate 15). Regardless, as the focus of the meetings of the Accademia degli Unisoni and the object of satire within a community that delighted in debating the female question, Barbara was in the position of both representing femininity—

all that was both alluring and dangerous about the female sex—and becoming the spokesperson for the male poets and debaters whose fears and desires she embodied.

To what extent, we might wonder, did she sympathize, delight, and even collude in the gender games that her father and his friends so enjoyed? Can it be that the sense of irony, already a prominent feature of the Incogniti poetry, is even more apparent in Strozzi's settings, in which the female voice was used as the means both to praise and condemn womankind? What is so extraordinary here is that Barbara was in the unique position of using her own voice to express the same erotic obsession and fears of female attachments that was so habitual in Incogniti circles. The marriage between the male and female perspective—the union of her voice with their often ambivalent and overtly misogynist texts—is one of the most fascinating aspects of Strozzi's music.

Barbara Strozzi in Print

Barbara Strozzi published eight volumes of vocal music (Table 7-1). The first, a book of madrigals for two-to-five voices set to her adoptive father's poetry, appeared in 1644. That she would have had the opportunity to publish her works is not surprising. The Incogniti, and in particular Loredano, virtually controlled the Venetian publishing world. Given Giulio Strozzi's strong links with the Incogniti and Venetian musical circles, Barbara was in an ideal position to have her works printed. It is notable that her first book of madrigals coincided with the publications of another prominent Venetian woman, the proto-feminist nun Arcangela Tarabotti. The two editions appeared at a time when the Incogniti interest in the female question was at its height (Heller 2003, chapter 2). The relative novelty of Strozzi's enterprise—music written by a beautiful young singer using texts by her famous father—must have been attractive to the Incogniti and the publishers alike.

Strozzi published only one other volume of music (opus 2) during her father's lifetime. After his death, her professional visibility increased markedly. The dedications of her subsequent volumes to high-placed patrons suggests that she might have been in search of permanent employment or patronage to solidify her family's financial situation (Rosand 1978). Her financial dealings also imply that she was at least moderately successful, even if she was unable to find regular employment as a musician. She also may have sought the patronage of women who would be sympathetic to her unique situation. Her first book of madrigals, for

Table 7-1.
Barbara Strozzi's Published Works

Year	Title	Dedicatee
1644	*Il primo libro di madrigali*, 2–5vv	Vittoria della Rovere, duchess of Tuscany
1651	*Cantate, ariette e duette*, op. 2	Ferdinand III of Austria and Eleonora of Mantua
1654	*Cantate, ariette a una, due, e tre voce*, op. 3 Op. 4 (not extant, possibly never written?)	Ignotae Deae
1655	*Sacri musicali affetti*, libro 1, op. 5	Anne of Austria, archduchess of Innsbruck
1657	*Ariette a voce sola*, op. 6	Francesco Caraffa, prince of Belevedere
1659	*Diporti di Euterpe, overo Cantate e ariette a voce sola*, op. 7	Nicolo Sagredo, doge of Venice
1664	*Arie a voce sola*, op. 8	Electress Sophia of Braunschweig

example, was dedicated to Vittoria della Rovere, the duchess of Tuscany, who had also employed Francesca Caccini (Plate 17). In approaching this most prominent patroness of the arts, Strozzi emphasized her gender with a charmingly self-deprecating tone: "I reverently consecrate this work which all too ardently I send forth into the light to the august name of your highness."

Her last published work was dedicated to another great woman, Electress Sophia of Lüneberg-Braunschweig, the mother of George I of England. Sophia, whose husband Ernst August and brother-in-law Georg William were Venetian opera and carnival enthusiasts, spent part of 1664 in Venice. Sophia's memoirs, unfortunately, make no mention of a meeting with Strozzi. But the Electress was apparently a close friend of the poet Giuseppe Artale, who supplied three texts for Strozzi's final publication, including one in honor of Sophia herself. Certainly a meeting between Sophia and Strozzi was possible. It is notable that some thirteen years passed between Strozzi's final publication and her death. We know nothing about her professional activities during this period.

The titles of the prints of Strozzi's works point to arias and cantatas. But this provides little sense of the stylistic variety of her compositions, which range from small-scale strophic arias to sectional cantatas of considerable length, written for solo voice and small ensembles. In the latter part of her career, in particular, Strozzi was quite free in her approach to strophic texts, using refrains and text repetitions in a highly individualistic and creative manner that disguised the structure of the poetry (Rosand 1978, 260–281). On the whole, Strozzi's cantatas did not depict dramatic situations, with the notable exception of the famous "Lamento sul Rodano severo" (Lament on the Rhone), published in opus 2 and again in opus 3. More often, her cantatas and arias highlighted poetic contrasts in the texts, which often shifted from the serious to the ironic. Free and quasi-improvisational sections were juxtaposed with more highly organized passages, marked not only by metrical shifts but also by changes in tempo and even dynamic indications, suggesting that the composer Strozzi also remained very much the performer. Humor, irony, and sudden alterations of mood are often depicted by contrasting affects, unexpected leaps, dissonances, and chromatic alterations.

Strozzi took particular delight in writing extended melismatic passages for the voice that exploited both the lower and upper ranges of the singer. In such instances the text all but disappears, and the voice assumes an almost instrumental function (Rosand 1978, 273–274). The creation of a stream of pure vocal sound, without interruption by vowel change or consonants, was likely a hallmark of Strozzi's considerable vocal abilities. Like many of her contemporaries, Strozzi was well aware of the expressive potential of different tonal styles. Many of her works can be analyzed quite accurately by using the terminology associated with major-minor tonality, despite the fact that theorists would not fully acknowledge this system until the eighteenth century. Other works, particularly lengthier cantatas organized around shifts between sharp and flat sides of the tonal spectrum, are better explained by invoking the precepts associated with modal-hexachordal theory and the church tones, as described by seventeenth-century theorists (Barnett 2002).

The Unknown Goddess

The care with which Strozzi set her texts—and the unusual dissonance between the male poetry and female singing voices—is evident in several compositions from opus 3, published in 1654 (Figure 7-1). This is the only volume that is not dedicated to a prominent patron. Instead, Strozzi devotes the work to "Ignotae Deae"—the unknown goddess. "Ignoto Deo" or the "unknown God" is a phrase taken from St. Paul (Acts 17:15–34). After St. Paul saw the phrase inscribed upon the altar in Athens, he asserted that it referred to his God, and thus he

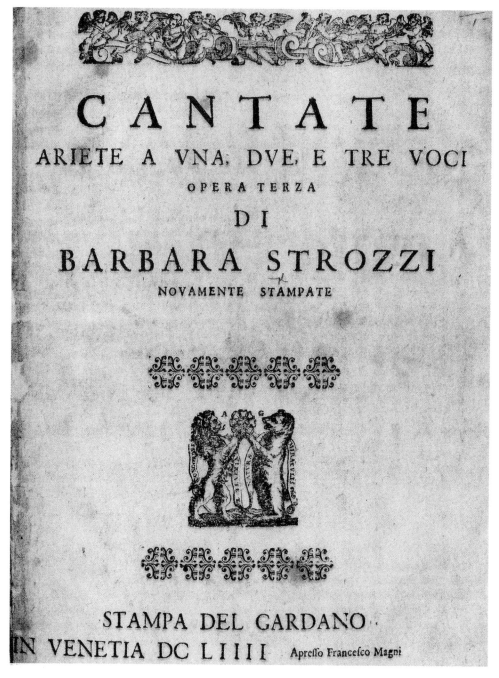

Figure 7-1. Barbara Strozzi, *Cantate, ariete a una, due, e tre voce* (Venice, 1654). By permission of the British Library.

was able to use it to convert many to Christianity. The motto was also adopted by the Accademia degli Incogniti. Loredano, for example, used it on the title page of his *Sei dubbi amorosi,* at the base of a statue of a veiled woman, whose questions had presumably inspired the discourses (Rosand 1978, 248; Figure 7-2).

Might the Incogniti have regarded woman as an object of worship in much the same way that St. Paul referred to his own God? Perhaps this was a sly knowing wink, mocking conventional Christianity in a manner that was compatible with their well-known tendency for heterodoxy? Regardless, Strozzi's transformation of the motto from the masculine to the feminine is suggestive on any number of levels, perhaps indicating the ease with which one could shift from a male to female viewpoint. Strozzi does not give any attributions for the poems in this volume. Rosand has hypothesized that the poems were by Loredano, and they are certainly compatible with his other writings (Rosand 1978). Might we presume that the transformed motto reveals that the volume was dedicated to Loredano and the Incogniti?

"Moralità amorosa" (Loving Morality), set by Strozzi in opus 3, embraces a familiar theme, the fleeting nature of beauty and life (Sampler CD 2, track 4; Figure 7-3). It is a classic sonnet in the style of Petrarch, composed of four strophes. The first two strophes contain four lines, and the second two strophes contain three lines, all of eleven syllables. The rhyme scheme is as follows:

Parte prima (CD: 0:00)

Sorge il mio sol con mattutini albori	a	My sun raises in the early dawn
E, intento a coltivar beltà divine,	b	intent upon cultivating her divine beauties
Con profumi odorosi incensa il crine	b	with fragrant perfume incensing her hair
Per aditar altrui come s'adori.	a	in order to show others how to adorn oneself.

Seconda parte (CD: 1:35)

Poscia con sottilissimi candori	c	Then with the finest white powder,
Sparge dell'aureo capo ogni confine,	b	she spreads to every border of her golden head,
Che di polve di cipri argente e brine	b	thus the dust of silver and frost powders
Fanno officio di smalto in su quegli ori.	c	make an enamel upon her golden hairs.

Terza parte (CD 2:35)

Mentre così la bella man s'impiega	d	While thus the beautiful hand busies itself,
E fra ceneri e fumi il crine involve,	e	and wraps the hair among the ashes and smoke,
In catene di foco il cor mi lega.	d	my heart is entwined in chains of fire.

Quarta parte (CD 3:16)

Che meraviglia è poi se si dissolve	e	What marvel it is then that
La bellezza in brev'ora, e chi mi nega	d	beauty dissolves itself in a brief hour, and who can deny to me
Che fugace non sia, s'è fumo e polve!	e	that it is fleeting, when it is smoke and dust!

Figure 7-2. Frontispiece (by Francesco Ruschi) from Giovanni Francesco Loredano, *Dubbi amorosi* (Venice, 1653–1657). Bodleian Library, *Antiq.f.I.2(3)*. Used by permission of the Bodleian Library, University of Oxford.

The poem opens with the awakening of the beloved in the morning, likening the sun rising in the sky to the perfumed, golden hair of the beloved. The second strophe concerns the silvery white powders that transform her hair into enamel. The third strophe, the terzet, introduces the voice of the poet, who observes how the arranging of the hair by the beautiful hand enchains his heart with fire. The final terzet provides the ironic twist—the beauty so carefully crafted by the beloved, composed of dust and fumes, dissolves and vanishes.

For the poet, the central issue is not merely the fleeting nature of natural beauty, but also the artificial adornments of the hair, expertly contrived by the beloved. The use of the sonnet form is also significant. By choosing the academic and rigorous structure of a poetic genre that traditionally explored the nature of beauty, the poet is emulating the artifice employed by the beloved.

The extent to which this poem focuses on a topic that had become particularly popular among the members of the Accademia degli Incogniti in the mid-1640s—the consequences of female luxury and self-ornamentation—is noteworthy. The controversy came to climax in

Figure 7-3. "Moralità amoroso," from Barbara Strozzi, *Cantate, ariete a una, due, e tre voce* (Venice, 1654). By permission of the British Library.

1644, when the publisher Valvasense printed Francesco Buoninsegni's antifemale discourse, *Contro'l lusso donnesco* (Against Female Luxury), originally presented at an academy in Siena. Valvasense published the discourse with an energetic response by the Venetian nun Arcangela Tarabotti (which was dedicated to Vittoria della Rovere, the dedicatee of Strozzi's opus 1). This, in turn, inspired still another book on female luxuries and fashion, written by a certain Padre Angelico Aprosio. (A more damning condemnation of Tarabotti was never published, likely because of Loredano's intercession on her behalf.)

In Buoninsegni's view, female luxuries, hairdressings, clothing, jewelry, and other adornments were weapons that could conquer the hearts of young men and distract them from the virtue and duty. (In one passage Buoninsegni even uses the same imagery that one finds in "Moralità amoroso," referring to a woman's ornately dressed hair as "her sun.") Tarabotti's enthusiastic defense was based on the premise that self-adornment was one of the fundamental rights of women, an integral part of the way in which women celebrated their God-given beauty. Indeed, implicit in the debate was the fact that luxuries, makeup, powder, and clothing were a vital part of female expression, worthy of praise or condemnation depending on the particular perspective of the viewer.

But what precisely was Barbara Strozzi's point of view on the subject? Indeed, like so many of her settings of Incogniti poems, "Moralità amoroso" presents us with a certain degree of dissonance between the compositional voice and the poetic voice. This somewhat ironic view of female beauty—arguably a parody of the conventional sentiments about the fleeting nature of life and beauty—was, paradoxically, set to music by a woman whose beauty (enhanced by perfumed and powdered hair) and public manner of self-expression were likely to have affected male auditors in precisely the manner predicted in the poem. What happens when the beautiful woman sings about the fleeting and artificial nature of female beauty, and the very act of singing publicly enchains the hearts of the men in precisely the manner desired and feared by the male poet? In this act of musical-poetic ventriloquism we are left wondering if Strozzi herself is in on the joke, colluding in a playful condemnation of women, or perhaps delighting in the discomfort and desire caused by the magical effect of her alluring physical presence and voice.

Strozzi's setting of the text reveals many of the stylistic features already noted in the discussion of Strozzi's "Lagrime mie" in Chapter 2. "Moralità amoroso" is a multisectional work in which the composer exploits virtually all of the various styles in the continuum between recitative and aria to create an expressive response to the poem. Strozzi may not have composed for the Venetian opera or performed on its stage, but clearly her familiarity with contemporary opera and her studies with Cavalli gave her a highly varied palette of musical devices that differentiates her music from that of the early monodists. Consider, for example, the overall organization of "Moralità amoroso." For the most part, the form and tonal design follow the poetic structure. Strozzi divided the work into four parts, one for each strophe. The first, second, and fourth strophes are in duple meter and tonally closed, each beginning and ending in A minor and articulated internally with arrivals on E major and C major. The third strophe, which is entirely in triple meter, begins and ends in C major. The poetic structure is somewhat blurred by the shift to triple meter in the middle section, which belongs to the world of aria rather than recitative. The desired effect is achieved by a calculated shift from the flexible style of the recitative to the rhythmically stricter style of the aria. In the aria section, a single affect is sustained and musical procedures take precedence over text.

Strozzi's artful disposition of the various stylistic possibilities of the recitative and aria complicates rather than simplifies presentation of the text, obscuring somewhat the author's point of view. Consider, for example, the opening of the *prima parte,* a highly improvisatory

Example 7-1. Strozzi: "Moralità amorosa," mm. 1–6.

exploration of the modal octave between e' and e" that provides the primary motivic material that will be exploited throughout the work. The sheer delight in vocal sound so apparent in the wail that opened "Lagrime mie" is used here to a rather different effect. Strozzi provides us with an ascending melisma on the word "sorge" (to rise), a pictorial representation of the rising of the sun, which symbolizes the beloved (Example 7-1).

Strozzi sets this ostensibly improvisatory passage with remarkable sensitivity. The repetition of the word "sorge" inspires the brief scalar run between and a and e', and the words "il mio sol" (my sun) are set syllabically to guarantee their comprehensibility (mm. 3–4). Another melismatic passage—outlining the e' to e" octave—depicts the arrival of dawn, now over an E-major sonority. In m. 6, the description of the beloved's attempts to arrange her hair ("e in tentar a coltivar") initiates the shift to a more organized and deliberate manner of musical expression. The relative harmonic stagnation underlying the opening vocalization is replaced by a walking bass in stepwise quarter notes that accompanies a simplified vocal melody and propels the harmonic motion toward G, arriving on C as the perfuming of the hair commences. This action generates another round of florid singing, now supported by the bass at the tenth. Strozzi soon takes the vocal part beyond the e' to e" octave, however, extending it into the upper register as far as high g", thus establishing a semiotic link between the ornamentation of the hair and its vocal equivalent (Sampler CD 2, track 4, 0:34–47).

For the final line of the strophe ("Per adorar altrui come sa'adori"), Strozzi returns to the stepwise quarter-note motive first introduced by the bass in m. 6. Here the demonstration of the beloved's skills inspires a bit of "learned" imitative counterpoint (Example 7-2). But the composer's sense of irony is made explicit in the setting of "come s'adori" (how to adorn oneself), in which we find the first unexpected dissonances and chromatic alterations, including the use of a tritone and a diminished fourth, as well as a phrygian coloration at the cadence.

The second part of the poem and aria deals with the powdering of the hair, and here Strozzi uses text painting and extended florid passages with lively imitation in the basso continuo. The unrestrained melismas depict the spread of the silvery powders to every portion of the hair, ultimately touching upon high a' for the phrase "ogni confine" (every boundary). As noted above, in the middle of this second part Strozzi shifts to triple meter

Example 7-2. Strozzi: "Moralità amorosa," mm. 17–19.

for the first time (CD, 2:00). The unambiguous use of aria style is particularly apparent in the scalar descent of the bass, a technique used frequently by Strozzi's teacher Francesco Cavalli. The vocal line that opens this section outlines the e'–e" octave once again, and the playful sequences that follow heighten our awareness of the music rather than the text. At the same time, Strozzi does not completely discard local text painting. A sustained A in the vocal line at the end of the section, held for six dotted breves over a moving bass, seems to capture something of the rigid, enameled structure of the lady's hair (CD, 2:27–2:35). For the third strophe (CD, 2:35), set in entirely in triple meter and beginning and ending in C, the aria style is unambiguous throughout. Particularly notable is the expansive madrigalistic gesture for the words "incatene di foco il cor me lega" (my heart entwined in chains of fire), in which the chain of sequences explodes into two extended melismas, reaching into the upper register with abandon (Example 7-3). It is hard to know whose pleasure is being expressed in this expansive aria-like moment. Are we hearing the voice of the poet, the male viewer, whose heart is entwined in the chains of fire? Or perhaps the voice belongs to Strozzi, the female singer, who was rejoicing in the decidedly female gesture of adorning and perfuming her own hair?

In the final strophe, the abrupt shift to recitative and the resulting suppression of emotional expression matches the poet's sudden detour into irony (Example 7-4). Of particular importance is the extent to which Strozzi continues to exploit the e' to e" octave, albeit now in its descending form. For the poem's most important utterance, "si disolve la bellezza in brev'ora" (beauty dissolves in a brief hour), the vocal line descends triadically through the modal octave before concluding on a stark reciting tone. A second scalar descent (mm. 113–144) evokes the flight of beauty, while the final vocal descent, after attempting a noble reach to the f" upper neighbor, falls almost too abruptly to the low e', abandoning the continuo and completing the cadence by itself.

The voice, like beauty, thus fades into the mist, and although the poem may lament the

Example 7-3. Strozzi: "Moralità amorosa," mm. 97–100.

Example 7-4. Strozzi: "Moralità amorosa," mm. 110–117.

artificiality of female beauty, it is the singer whose voice evaporates, leaving behind only smoke and fumes. The result is a work of extraordinary dramatic power and compositional coherence, in which each line is set with vivid detail while an overarching sense of unity is maintained. We might detect here something of Strozzi's own views about female luxury. Her control over the various stylistic options and her sense of irony tells us as much about the beloved's pleasure in self-ornamentation as it does about the fires of desire that consume the lover.

The duet for two equal voices "Begli occhi" (Beautiful Eyes) also calls upon a familiar poetic conceit—the beautiful eyes and kisses that wound and kill (Sampler CD 2, track 5). The form of the poem is idiosyncratic. The initial line that introduces the topic is followed by two strophes of four lines each. A final rhyming couplet functions as a refrain. The concluding pair of eleven-syllable lines conveys the poet's perspective.

Mi ferite, oh begli occhi. (CD, 0:00)	You wound me, o beautiful eyes.
Pensate che farebbono (CD, 0:32)	Think what they do,
Quei baci sì cocenti e mordaci;	those kisses so burning and biting;
Langue l'anima, langue e il	the soul languishes, and the heart
cor vien meno.	fades.
Ahi ch'io vi moro in seno.	Ah, that inside my breast I die for you.
Pensate che farebbono (CD, 1:52)	Think what they do,
Gli strali sì pungenti e mortali;	the sharp and fatal arrows;
Langue l'anima, langue e il	the soul languishes, and the heart
cor vien meno.	fades.
Ahi ch'io vi moro in seno.	Ah, that inside my breast I die for you.
Ma forse non morò senza (CD, 3:14)	But perhaps I will not die without
vendetta	revenge,
Ch'al fin chi morte da la	for in the end he who gives death waits
morte aspetta.	for death.

Example 7-5. Strozzi: "Begli occhi," m. 7.

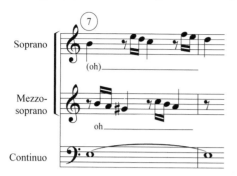

The first two strophes describe unambiguously the wounding kisses and eyes. The lover asks the beloved to imagine the effect of the kisses, which burn and bite, or the eyes which, like fatal, sharp arrows, make the soul languish, the heart fail, and the lover to die within. As in "Moralità amoroso," the final strophe provides an ironic twist: Death is not only unfulfilled desire, but also a metaphor for sexual fulfillment. He who dies of love can actually expect vengeance, because whoever offers death to others must wait patiently for their own fulfillment.

Strozzi's decision to set this as a duet heightens the sense of eroticism. The two singers do not interact in a dramatic sense as two separate characters. Rather, they intertwine as two equal voices—a device borrowed from the love duets of contemporary opera—and form a picture of intimacy. Of note are the frequent crossings of the two voices, the juxtaposition of homophonic and imitative passages, and the suggestive exchange of sigh motives. All of these can be heard in Strozzi's setting of the poem's first line (Example 7-5).

Once again the alternation between triple and duple plays an important structural and expressive role. For the setting of line 2, for example, Strozzi uses triple meter and aria style to mark the shift to the subjunctive mood ("think what they do"). The listener then *hears* how dangerous the beautiful eyes might be (Example 7-6). The pungent biting and burning of the lover's kisses are expressed with dissonance of the ninth between voice 2 and the bass, and the open fourths between the voices (m. 19). Languor in the soul is invoked by a return to chromatic writing (m. 21), and the breathless failing of the heart is highlighted by the fre-

Example 7-6. Strozzi: "Begli occhi," mm. 19–21.

quent textural shifts in the vocal parts and intensification of dissonance at the cadences. Strozzi adheres to the structure of the poem by reusing much of this same musical material for the second strophe, albeit with new musical gestures that accommodate the shift in poetic conceit.

The poet's description of the eye's sharp wounds (as opposed to the biting kisses of the first strophe) is represented by a passage of emphatic descending quarter notes, outlining, for the first time in this predominantly stepwise piece, a triad (C major) in imitative counterpoint. For the final strophe Strozzi utilizes changes in meter that control tempo and underscore both the change in poetic structure and the final ironic twist. A metrical shift between 3/2 and 3 (shown as 3/2 to 6/2 in the published edition) creates what is essentially a ritard that emphasizes the last two lines of the poem "Ch'al fin che morte, dalla morte aspetta" (For in the end he who gives death waits for death). The final repetition of the poem's conclusion, however, is interrupted by a dramatic shift to duple meter that isolates the word "aspetta" (to wait; CD, 3:42). The lover waiting for his or her own death is dramatized by an elaborate, melismatic conclusion in which both voices accelerate to unabashed sixteenth-note runs. The joining of the two voices in parallel motion in a passionate wail on the syllable "as" leaves little doubt as to the sensual nature of the vengeance (Example 7-7).

The wounding power of a woman's eyes is also the topic of a third composition from opus 3, "Cor donata, cor rubato, contrasto tra Filindo, Dori, e Tirsi" (Heart Given, Heart Stolen, Discussion between Filindo, Dori, and Tirsi; Sampler CD 2, track 6). In many respects this is a very different composition from those considered above. Given its old-fashioned tonal style and its similarity to early seventeenth-century madrigals, we might assume that it was written somewhat earlier in Strozzi's career. It is an ostensibly dramatic work. Yet much of the emotion is expressed not by the individual characters, but by the combined effects of the

Example 7-7. Strozzi: "Begli occhi, mm. 92–97.

trio—that is, through dissonance, contrasting textures, tonal excursions, and metrical shifts. At the same time, the alternation between what might be described as action (in this case the interference of Tirsi in the lover's argument) and contemplation (the lovers' joy in their new-found happiness) owes much to the musico-dramatic rhythms of opera.

The first part of the drama concerns the nature of love as manifest in an argument between two lovers, Dori and Filindo. Did she steal his heart, or did he give it willingly? Is the bitter rancor merited? Despite their differing points of view, their words overlap considerably. Even Tirsi, who tries to mediate the dispute, repeats many of the lovers' declarations. The first portion of the text reads as follows:

Filindo: (CD, 0:00)

Ladra, tu ladra crudel,	Thief, you cruel thief,
Mi rubasti il cor, sì, sì	you stole my heart, yes, yes;
Con begl'occhi lo rapi;	with beautiful eyes you kidnapped it;
Mi rubasti il cor, sì, sì	you stole my heart, yes, yes;
Ben è giusto il rancor, aspre le offese.	the rancor is just, the offenses are bitter.
Me' l rubò.	You stole it from me.

Dori:

Tu mendace, tu infedel, no, no	You false one, you unfaithful one, no, no;
Ch' in don, l'hebbe, no'l rubò	as a gift you had it, I did not steal it,
Mi donasti il cor, sì sì	you gave me your heart, yes, yes;
Ben è giusto il rancor, aspre le offese.	the rancor is just, the offenses are bitter.
Me' l donò.	You gave it to me.

Tirsi: (CD, 0:47)

Fermate; lasciate le contese.	Stop; leave off the contest.
Tropp' è ingiusto, il rancor, false le offese.	The rancor is unjust, the offenses are false.
Miracol fu d'amore, cessi l'ingiusta lite.	Love was a miracle, cease the dispute.
No' l donò, no' l rubbò. Fermate,	No, you didn't give it, you didn't steal it.
udite.	Stop, listen.

In the second portion of the drama, Tirsi provides an explanation for their dilemma. Love, in fact, takes the soul from the body and gives it to another: what has happened to them is a natural phenomenon. This seems to satisfy the two lovers, who realize that they live in each other and happily "await their peaceful day in the tomb." Once again, death is used as a metaphor for the act of love, and the tomb represents the soothing aftermath of physical passion.

Tirsi: (CD, 1:48)

Amor, amor che tutto puote un cuore	Love can do anything to a heart,
Un' alma toglie da un seno	it can take the soul from the breast
E' in altro sen l'innesta,	and put it in another.
Se spira humana,	If a man expires,
Salma priva del core.	deprived of his heart,
Opra in amore è questa.	This is the labor of love.

Dori, Filindo, Tirsi: (CD, 2:45)

No'l donò, no'l rapi,	I/you didn't give it, I/you didn't steal it,
Opra è d'amor, sì, sì	it is the work of love, yes, yes;
Vivi tu nel mio seno	You live in my heart (Dori)
Vivo si nel seno	I live in your heart (Filindo)
Spira tu co'l suo core	You die in his heart (Tirsi)
Vivo sì nel tuo seno	I live in your heart (Dori)
Vivi tu nel mio seno	You live in my heart (Filindo)
Vivi tu sì, sì nel suo seno	You live, yes, in her breast (Tirsi)
Tal morte beata/Tal morendo beato	Thus dying happy,
Puoi riamando amata,	one can love and be loved
Rigoder nella tomba il dì sereno.	and enjoy again in the tomb the peaceful day.

Strozzi's setting takes advantage of the various parallelisms and repetitions in the poetic text. The voices overlap in a manner that often obscures the individuality of the two lovers while highlighting the pivotal role of the mediator Tirsi. Drama is again created by shifts in meter and texture, but it is also heightened by the work's tonal organization. The first section is characterized by an ascent from the initial D minor toward sharp-key sonorities, with much of the ensemble singing in D major. The second section, beginning with Tirsi's monologue "Amor, amor," is set unambiguously in the area of flat keys. This leads the lovers to an imitative section in the sharp-key area once again, before the music returns to D minor for the conclusion.

The cantata opens in a highly dramatic fashion, with bold melodic and tonal gestures illustrating the argument (Example 7-8). Against the initial D-minor sonority, Florindo accuses Dori of theft with an impassioned, triadic, despairing cry beginning on a and exploding up through the octave to a'. This is further intensified by the dissonance of the ninth with the sustained B♭ in the bass, before Florindo descends abruptly to another pungent dissonant, C♯, as a mark of Dori's cruelty. This phrygian cadence announces Dori's entrance, in which she outlines an A-minor triad. The argument ensues as Dori's protests in an even eighth-note rhythm, emphasizing A-minor and A-major triads, which contrast with Florindo's sixteenth-note accusations that introduce the E-major sonorities. In this instance, Strozzi uses movement by fifths into the realm of sharp keys (from D minor to the arrival on E major) as a representation of the shifting emotions of the lovers. It is at this point that Tirsi enters to stop the argument, decisively using descending fifths that force the group back to D major (CD, 0:47).

From this point onward, the two protagonists are transformed from the distinctive individual personalities delineated in the opening passage into an ensemble that shares a series of affects. This process reflects the poem's central idea—the unity of the lovers. After Tirsi's intervention, the three singers begin an imitative trio (CD, 1:05) in which the bitterness of the imagined offense is examined as a philosophical construct and expressed through dissonant harmonies (Example 7-9; CD, 1:05). In the center of the work Strozzi provides Tirsi with an elegant and highly expressive monodic passage, in D minor, on the nature of love. His gentle tone is marked tonally by the return to flat sonorities. Of note as well is the stunning descending passage in dotted rhythms that marks the passage of the soul from the lover to the beloved's body (CD, 2:10–2:19).

Tirsi's solo inspires yet another imitative trio, in the sharp-key realm, as all three acknowledge the work of love (CD, 2:46). Strozzi underlines the power of love with an abrupt

Example 7-8. Strozzi: "Cor donato, cor rubato," mm. 1–6.

change to duple meter, which brings the forward motion to a brief halt. This, however, is but a preface to the most explicitly erotic section of the work. Strozzi sets the next portion of text, in which the two lovers acknowledge that they live within each other, over a repeated descending major tetrachord in the bass (CD, 2:59–3:18; Example 7-10). This is a device that is frequently used in Baroque music to express a special state of being, and here the hypnotic effect on the listener is unmistakable. While the minor version was most often used for a lament, Strozzi and her colleagues would certainly have associated the major version with the expression of desire as represented, for example, in the final love duet of Monteverdi's *L'incoronazione di Poppea*.

Strozzi's absolute control over the pacing is apparent in the way in which she once again stops the motion, this time to depict the "blessed death" with a sustained D in the bass, highlighted by the abrupt melodic plunges sung by Filindo and Dori as a last burst of individuality. A final imitative section gives way to the quiet, more homophonic conclusion. All signs of combat are banished in the final measures, as the melodic lines sung by Dori and Filindo descend in parallel thirds under the bass pedal sung by Tirsi, colored by the gentle flat-key inflection of Dori's melodic B♭ (CD, 4:11–end). Strozzi has found a means not only of defining the nature of love, but also of depicting the pain and pleasures that goes with it, as experienced by male and female partners.

Conclusion

What emerges from even a brief study of Strozzi's compositions is a strong sense of her compositional control and skill, her wit, and her sensitivity to poetic and dramatic nuance. From

Example 7-9. Strozzi: "Cor donato, cor rubato," mm. 27–28.

the gentle parody of women's self-adornment in "Moralità amoroso" to the erotic interweaving of the two voices in "Begli occhi" to the passionate, but coolly analytical view of love expressed in "Cor donato, cor rubato," Strozzi deftly interprets her texts with a rich vocabulary of contemporary musical devices, expressing a view of love that is both knowledgeable and playful. The male perspective celebrated in so many of the poems is counteracted by Strozzi's powerful compositional voice, leaving the listener with an unmistakable sense of her presence and her erotic sensibility.

There remain any number of questions about Barbara Strozzi's life and career, many of which are directly related to her gender. Was she a courtesan, paid for her favors, or was she able to achieve economic stability primarily through her musical endeavors? What were her relationships with her prominent patrons? How is it that she was able to present her works to the public in print while still remaining so removed from operatic circles? How might a woman in seventeenth-century Venice have managed family and professional responsibili-

Example 7-10. Strozzi: "Cor donato, cor rubato," mm. 68–69.

ties? And what happened to her musical career in the final decade of her life? Might her daughters in the convent have followed their mother's example and become musicians?

The answers to these questions await further archival discoveries. Meanwhile, we are left to understand Strozzi through her music. Notably, while women singers were gaining new prominence on the Venetian opera stage, Barbara Strozzi managed to penetrate the male-dominated circles of the Venetian academies and present a unique model of female eloquence. In so doing, she defined a special realm in which men and women were equal and willing partners in the art of love and in which the most virulent anti-female sentiments could be tamed by a knowing wink, a bit of irony, perfumed and elegantly dressed hair, and the beautiful sound of a woman's voice. Such was the special power of this feminine muse.

BIBLIOGRAPHY

Barnett, Gregory. 2002. "Tonal Organization in Seventeenth-Century Music Theory." In *The Cambridge History of Western Music Theory*, ed. Thomas Christensen, 411–454. Cambridge: Cambridge University Press.

Bowers, Jane. 1985. "The Emergence of Women Composers in Italy, 1566–1700." In *Women Making Music: The Western Art Tradition, 1150–1950*, ed. Jane Bowers and Judith Tick, 116–176. Urbana: University of Illinois Press.

Coryate, Thomas. 1611. *Coryat's Crudities*. London: William Stansby.

Cusick, Suzanne. 1993. "Thinking from Women's Lives: Francesca Caccini after 1636." *Musical Quarterly* 77: 484–507.

Glixon, Beth L. 1997. "New Light on the Life and Career of Barbara Strozzi." *Musical Quarterly* 81: 311–335.

———. 1999. "More on the Life and Death of Barbara Strozzi." *Musical Quarterly* 83: 134–141.

Heller, Wendy. 2003. *Emblems of Eloquence: Opera and Women's Voices in Seventeenth-Century Venice*. Berkeley: University of California Press.

Kendrick, Robert. 1996. *Celestial Sirens: Nuns and their Music in Early Modern Milan*. Oxford: Oxford University Press.

MacNeil, Anne. 2003. *Music and Women of the Commedia dell'arte in the Late Sixteenth Century*. Oxford: Oxford University Press.

Monson, Craig. 1995. *Disembodied Voices: Music and Culture in an Early Modern Italian Convent*. Berkeley: University of California Press.

Newcomb, Anthony. 1985. "Courtesans, Muses, or Musicians? Professional Women Musicians in Sixteenth-Century Italy." In *Women Making Music: The Western Art Tradition, 1150–1950*, ed. Jane Bowers and Judith Tick, 90–115. Urbana: University of Illinois Press.

Rosand, Ellen. 1978. "Barbara Strozzi, *virtuosissima cantatrice*: The Composer's Voice." *Journal of the American Musicological Society* 31: 241–281.

Strozzi, Barbara. 1997. *Cantate, ariete a una due, e tre voce, opus 3*, ed. Gail Archer. Madison, Wis.: A-R Editions.

Tick, Judith. 2002. "Women in Music." In *The New Grove Dictionary of Music and Musicians*, ed. Stanley Sadie, 2nd ed., 21:511–557. London: Macmillan.

CHAPTER EIGHT

The Baroque Guitar: Players, Paintings, Patrons, and the Public

Victor Coelho

BETWEEN APPROXIMATELY 1600 AND 1730, the guitar emerged as one of the most popular and versatile instruments in Baroque Europe. Although it was criticized by some Baroque writers as being noisy, attracting vulgar listeners (and occasionally players), and having an overall corrupting influence—a commentary that is echoed centuries later in the early reactions to rock guitar—by the mid-seventeenth century the guitar had succeeded in eclipsing the venerable lute, and by the end of the Baroque its considerable influence on style had brought the guitar from the margins of recognition to the center of the musical mainstream.

Similar to the way in which contemporary genres like folk, blues, country, and rock all evolved from simple guitar-based chord patterns, so many important Baroque styles and techniques originated with guitarists. When listening to Bach's monumental Passacaglia in C Minor for organ, or the exquisite Chaconne in D Minor for solo violin—works regarded as two of the crowning achievements of Baroque instrumental music—it is important to remember that both the passacaglia and chaconne forms began as simple strummed dances popularized by Spanish and Italian guitarists, with the first written examples appearing in early seventeenth-century Italian guitar tablatures (Hudson 1982).

The use of the guitar across the broad musical and demographic spectrum during the Baroque invites further comparisons with the mass appeal of the acoustic and electric guitar in our own day (Coelho 2003, 1–5). Like the modern guitar, no other instrument during the Baroque Era was as adaptable to different musical traditions and contexts, from boisterous street music to the elegance of courtly performance, or so accessible to new players. The unusually widespread use of the Baroque guitar thus requires from us a different methodology for studying it as compared to other quintessentially "Baroque" instruments like the harpsichord and organ, whose repertoire was conditioned almost exclusively by either courtly tastes or liturgical needs.

Closer to the spirit and training exhibited by modern rock or blues guitarists, Baroque players flocked to the instrument from all levels of social rank or musical background. They were attracted by a dedicated, simplified notation, an easily learned strumming technique (as opposed to the complexity of lute-style plucking), and a repertoire that did not, at least at first, present many technical demands. Consequently, the profile of a "typical" Baroque guitarist runs the gamut of personalities, from court virtuosos, noblemen, kings, princes, queens, and rich dilettantes to children, university students, young women, painters, priests, missionaries, and merchants, all the way to buskers, traveling comedians, gypsies, barbers, sailors, prostitutes, servants (Mozart's Figaro was a guitarist), and even indigenous peoples from the New World, Africa, and Asia, who encountered the instrument through Spanish, Portuguese, and Dutch colonialism.

The present chapter does not claim to be either a short history of the Baroque guitar or a detailed examination of its performance conventions—several excellent studies have already contributed to these topics (Tyler and Sparks 2002; Russell 2003; Turnbull et al. 2001, for instance). Instead, the following pages will dissect the culture of the Baroque guitar through slices of case studies to place ourselves "within" the world of the Baroque and observe the guitar from a cultural perspective. We will discuss the life and works of two professional guitarists, Francesco Corbetta and Santiago de Murcia, who were crucial in spreading the guitar's influence within and beyond the boundaries of Europe. In addition, we will employ the field of musical iconography to analyze an exceptionally detailed group of paintings by seventeenth-century Italian artist Evaristo Baschenis for information about the instrument's cultural significance, and as a window into the life of a domestic musician. Let us begin, however, by tracing the steps that led to the rapid acceptance of the guitar at the beginning of the Baroque Period and discuss some of the most important characteristics that are unique to the instrument.

The Renaissance Guitar and Lute

Prior to 1600, the most important plucked-string instrument in Europe was the lute, an instrument of Arabic origins that had been used in European music since around the thirteenth century. In sixteenth-century Spain, the lute was a grim reminder of the Muslim domination of the country, lasting until 1492. It was replaced by the vihuela, a guitar-shaped instrument with six courses, or pairs of strings, that was nevertheless tuned exactly like a lute (Griffiths 1989). The lute, with its strong presence in both courtly and domestic circles and its symbolic association with the ancient Greek lyre, was the very symbol of a humanistic and literate culture. It was of seminal importance in the history of Renaissance instrumental music through the quality and diversity of its enormous solo repertory, and it was the preferred instrument for accompanying voices. In fact, one could say that the practice of singing to the lute was perhaps *the* central musical activity of the Renaissance, crossing all boundaries of professional, amateur, court, and home (see Chapter 1). Lute song represented the perfect union of music and poetry, and it was also immensely practical, for it allowed performers to personalize polyphonic madrigals, chansons, and even entire Masses by arranging them for voice and accompaniment.

Contemporary with the sixteenth-century lute was the Renaissance guitar, a relatively small instrument—it would fit into a modern viola case—of four courses. The earliest (and some of the best) works for this instrument are included in a vihuela book of 1536 by the Spaniard Alonso Mudarra. Overall, its repertory was similar but much smaller than that of the lute. But by the middle of the sixteenth century, French composers had produced a sizeable and attractive body of solo works and arrangements of chansons, some of which was of extremely high quality (Tyler and Sparks 2002, 5–29). The works of Albert de Rippe or Guillaume Morlaye, for instance, stand as outstanding examples of this repertory. From 1550, an especially vigorous commercial culture of guitar music was sustained in Paris for almost three decades through the efforts of enterprising publishers working under royal licenses granted by Henry II, an avid guitar fan who may have been introduced to the instrument during the years he spent as a Spanish hostage.

Alfabeto and Mixed Notation

As with lute music, Renaissance guitar music used tablature notation. Using a horizontal staff that represents the *strings* of the instrument, tablature shows where the fingers are placed on the strings and frets of the instrument rather than the actual notes themselves. It is a successful system that is still very much in use today among folk, rock, and country guitarists, many of whom do not read staff notation. But it would be an exaggeration to say that tablature was originally intended only for lutenists and guitarists who couldn't read music. Any Renaissance player who arranged a vocal work for the instrument naturally had to be able to read musical parts. But tablature made contemporary music accessible to everyone, thus creating a cohesive musical culture. In addition, tablature is also perfectly suited for plucked instruments since it shows idiomatic fingering. Indeed, playing from tablature is an essential part of the technique. This fundamental point was not lost on the Baroque guitarists of the next generation as they further adapted tablature to keep up with newer technical demands.

Although other factors are certainly involved, the Baroque guitar is distinguished from its Renaissance counterpart by its greater number of string courses (five, rather than four) and its increased size (and, therefore, its lower pitch; the shorter Renaissance guitar was tuned higher than the Baroque instrument). The five-course Baroque guitar, whose tuning is identical to that of the modern guitar minus the lowest string, was already familiar in Spain by the middle of the sixteenth century. One of the earliest surviving examples of a five-course instrument is dated to 1581. The earliest music for the Baroque guitar dates from 1591, but it was the very popular treatise published five years later by the Spaniard Juan Carlos Amat, the *Guitarra Española,* that can be considered as the first truly influential source for the Baroque guitar. In addition to giving clear instructions for tuning, Amat addresses the issue of notating strummed chords by assigning letter symbols to designate the playing of individual chords (the letter names bear no relation to the actual harmony of the chord).

This tablature became known as *alfabeto,* or alphabet, and it laid the foundation for the notational system for the Baroque guitar. Since Spanish guitar music of this period was almost completely chordal, the *alfabeto* was essentially a shorthand method of notating chords without the need for actually spelling each note of the chord on a staff, as with lute tablature. In *alfabeto,* the guitarist sees the letter and fingers the chord that is associated with it, occasionally adding doublings (that are common to the chord) or dampening strings, as appropriate. This can be observed in manuals such as Gaspar Sanz's *Instrucción de música sobre la guitarra Española* of 1697, which clearly shows how the *alfabeto* translates into chord fingerings (Figure 8-1).

The early Baroque guitar repertory was based almost entirely on strummed works. By around 1630, however, guitarists began using a plucking technique to compose pieces that used scale passages and other textures in conjunction with strummed chords, requiring the use of lute tablature along with *alfabeto.* This combination of systems is known as "mixed tablature." The letter symbols designate the chord shapes to be strummed, as usual, while the lute tablature now notated the individual notes and scales, which were plucked (Figures 8-2 and 8-3). Other important features of Baroque guitar notation were indications for up and down strums, signs for ornaments and slurs, and, on rare occasion, left-hand fingering. It also became necessary for printed books of guitar music to include a preface that explained the notational systems for the complete beginner, including a chart that showed how the *alfabeto* symbols were played on the instrument (Boye 2005).

The invention of *alfabeto* tells us a great deal about the unique characteristics of Baroque guitar performance at the beginning of the Baroque. Amat's treatise, like most of those that were to follow, seeks to describe and formalize an existing practice. Although earlier French guitarists occasionally used strums for certain aspects of their performance, their music is really not that much different from lute compositions, and thus their notation—lute tablature—could not designate strums. Sixteenth-century Spanish guitarists, however, were clearly forging new stylistic paths on the five-course guitar through improvising composi-

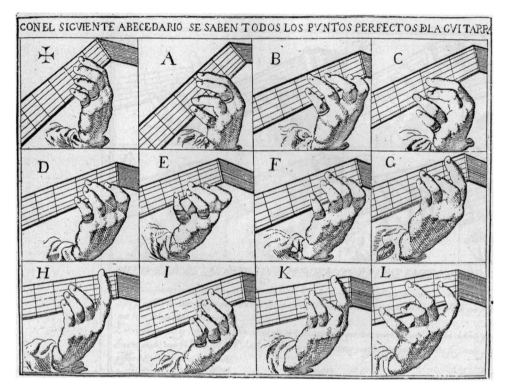

Figure 8-1. "With the following alphabet you will know all the main chords of the guitar," from Gaspar Sanz, *Instrucción de música sobre la guitarra Española,* Libro Segundo (Zaragoza, 1697).

tions on repeated, strummed chord patterns, or providing an entirely strummed accompaniment to songs, in the process bringing techniques from the popular milieu into the world of art music. With Amat's treatise, these improvised techniques received both a theoretical validation and a solid pedagogical method for realization.

Girolamo Montesardo: A Spanish Guitarist in Baroque Italy

The Spanish *alfabeto* system was adopted in Italy chiefly through the Spanish guitarist, singer, composer, and priest Girolamo Montesardo (fl. 1606–1620), whose activities initiated a period during which Italy became the main center for the development of the guitar (Tyler

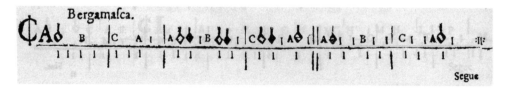

Figure 8-2. *Alfabeto* notation from Antonio Carbonchi, *Le dodici chitarre spostate* (Florence, 1643). Reprinted with the permission of S.P.E.S., Florence.

Figure 8-3. "Mixed" tablature, from Giovanni Battista Granata, *Capricci Armonici* (Bologna, 1646). Reprinted with permission of S.P.E.S., Florence.

and Sparks 2002, 52–56). Montesardo's *Nuova inventione* (New inventions) is the first printed book of music for the five-course guitar, and it was the clearest formulation to date of fingering chords and the up-down strumming technique. The contents of his book illustrate the kinds of pieces that guitarists normally would have improvised. It was like a "standard-rep" of tunes based mostly on well-known, repeated chordal patterns such as the bergamasca, Ruggiero, ballo di Napoli, and so on. The patterns were now presented, however, in *alfabeto*. What the *Nuova inventione* represents, in essence, is the codification of improvised practice. To make a contemporary comparison: an experienced modern guitarist would be completely familiar with such standard chordal schemes as a twelve-bar blues (in any key), the popular early sixties I–vi–IV–V progression, and a shuffle blues, with and without its common I–VI–II–V "turn-around," from years of playing by ear. But a beginner could also learn these progressions with help from a book in which the examples were notated in tablature. Montesardo was providing this help in his publication.

In both France and Italy, the guitar's meteoric rise in popularity was in proportion to the now-receding presence of the lute, the instrument that had dominated instrumental music in these countries throughout the sixteenth century. Although one could argue that the guitar is mostly to "blame" for the gradual decrease in Italian and, to some degree, French lute composition after 1650, there are other reasons as well. By the 1620s, Italian lute music was no longer stylistically or technically attractive to a wide public—a far cry from the previous century, when lute music thrived within a large publishing economy and was successfully marketed to a broad commercial audience. The seventeenth century saw a sharp decrease in Italian lute publications, from over a hundred that appeared between 1507 and 1599, to around twenty. And those that did appear circulated among small erudite groups of nobles and patrons, instead of a broad and international public (Coelho 1995, 4). Whereas sixteenth-century lute books were known for their user-friendly arrangements of popular madrigals, chansons, and attractive dance settings, lute publications in the seventeenth century featured the more subjective, virtuosic forms of the toccata and contained many new techniques set within a highly ornamented and adventurous harmonic language that was frankly beyond the reach—technically and aesthetically—of most players (Coelho 1997a).

Guitar and Voice

In the area of accompanying, lutes continued to flourish after 1600, since they enjoyed a critical role in the new vocal styles of accompanied song and opera (see Chapter 2). The construction of large, extended-neck archlutes (fourteen courses) and theorbos (fourteen to nineteen courses), both with bass strings, reflected the need for more powerful continuo instruments. They were more awkward to play, however, and they opened the door to an increased role—soon to be a frenzy—for the more easily learned guitar. With its fundamentally harmonic orientation, fewer strings, and a notation that was founded on chordal shapes, the guitar seemed born to accompany vocal works, especially rhythmic strophic songs and duets. But this was not an entirely new development. Many of the chordal patterns known by sixteenth-century guitarists, such as the romanesca, Ruggiero, and passamezzo, were also used as accompaniments for simple songs, similar to the way a player today could improvise a three-line blues verse to a twelve-bar, I–IV–I–V progression, where each line of lyric is set to four measures of music.

Thus there was an unbroken tradition of guitar-accompanied song from the Renaissance through the Baroque. Capitalizing on the popularity of the guitar, the most important composers of songs soon began including guitar *alfabeto* in their songbooks to allow for guitar accompaniment, in addition to the conventional bass line in staff notation (Figure 8-4). Nor was the guitar limited to accompanying solo voices. Some of the most high-profile musical events from the first part of the seventeenth century called for guitars to participate along with lutes in continuo ensembles, such as the lavishly staged Florentine *intermedi* of 1597 and 1608, celebrating the marriages of Ferdinando and Cosimo II Medici, respectively. Guitar accompaniment is specified in the music for the Roman, Venetian, and French operas as well. Many guitarists, including Giovanni Paolo Foscarini, Francesco Corbetta, Santiago de Murcia, Nicola Matteis, and Sanz wrote important instructions for playing figured bass on the guitar.

Having traced the development and prosperity of the guitar in seventeenth-century Italy, we can now turn to the questions of who, exactly, were the consumers of this music? To which public was guitar music marketed, and how was this music used? Indeed, what fundamental cultural values were embodied by the guitar? To answer these questions we need to enter the cultural world of the amateur domestic musician. Evaristo Baschenis's fascinating triptych offers us one view of the rich Italian guitar culture of the seventeenth century.

The Guitar and Courtly Life: The Agliardi Triptych

Analogies, metaphors, hidden and conflicting meanings, obsessive attention to detail mixed with tricks of the eye, reality and symbolism, sound and silence, and love and death—these qualities and contradictions abound in the exquisite still-life paintings by the painter, musi-

Figure 8-4. *Alfabeto* guitar accompaniment to a song, from Giovanni Girolamo Kapsperger, *Libro secondo di villanelle* (Rome, 1619). Reprinted with permission of S.P.E.S., Florence.

cian, and priest Evaristo Baschenis (1617–1677). One could say that Baschenis the priest influenced the conviction, precision, faithfulness, and the sanctity of the simple objects found in these works, while Baschenis the musician sought fantasy, passion, and even self-gratification. These two extremes find their common ground in Baschenis the artist.

Of the many hundreds of seventeenth- and eighteenth-century paintings that depict guitars and lutes, the musical portraits by Baschenis are of special importance because of their unusual detail and rich musical symbolism. Let us examine the three panels of Baschenis's largest and most famous work, the Agliardi Triptych, painted around 1665 and named for the family that commissioned the piece and is depicted in it. The paintings allow us to more fully understand the guitar's position within domestic settings as well as the qualities that were attached to the instrument by its owners. In addition, Baschenis's accuracy in representing such minute (but important) details as the guitar maker's label allows us to gauge the lasting value that was placed on these instruments, both as objects of sound and as *objets d'art* (Bayer 2001).

Although Baschenis is a household name in his native town of Bergamo, an important city for art north of Milan, he remains relatively unknown to the general public. He was not a prolific artist, and very few of his paintings are found outside private collections in Italy. His works are limited almost exclusively to still-life representations of instruments and food. Baschenis was never employed as a court artist, and therefore we do not find in his work the grandiose political and dynastic themes drawing on mythological or classical subjects that are typical of seventeenth-century courtly painting. On the contrary, in his portraits Baschenis concentrated on things that he owned—especially the instruments that he played, which were of such value to him that they become humanized through the art of portraiture. Baschenis captured the instruments as they aged, like a living person, with the passing of time. Today, his paintings are studied as a rich source of information about lute and guitar construction, instrumentation, and musical aesthetics.

Sixteenth- and seventeenth-century artists were aware of the rich symbolism that was attached to musical instruments, and this is why lutes, and occasionally guitars, are prominent in the genre known as the *natura morta,* or still life. With its usual representations of ripe and rotting fruit, wilting flowers, half-filled wine glasses, cobwebs, and absence of humans, the still-life genre was dedicated to exploring symbols. Common themes attached to lutes were death and Eros (the god of love), but also, in particular, *vanitas*—the transitory nature of life and the evanescence of vanity. This was most often represented by a broken string, by the lute strings facing down, or by the appearance of an old score lying unused. The symbolism of guitars is less complex. Like the lute, it was commonly associated with love. But its presence in a Baroque allegorical painting (and in opera) usually signified lust and licentiousness (once again a common connection with the modern electric guitar!). And for some conservative authors the guitar signified just that. The writer Pierre Trichet wondered in 1640 whether the guitar was so popular in France because "it has a certain something which is feminine and pleasing to women, flattering their hearts and making them inclined to voluptuousness?" (Trichet c. 1640, I: 94).

Metaphysical and sexual metaphors notwithstanding, in the end what makes the Agliardi Triptych so "musical" is Baschenis's experience as a practicing musician. The artist owned several lutes and guitars, among other instruments, and in the first panel of the triptych (Plate 18; Figure 8-5), he reveals himself autobiographically, not as a painter or even priest (though he is dressed like one), but as a competent keyboard player, perhaps playing an accompaniment. To the painter's left and playing the archlute is the twenty-year-old Ottavio Agliardi (b. 1645), the youngest son of Camillo Agliardi (1604–1674), commissioner of the portrait. The Agliardi family was of the oldest and most noble clans in Bergamo, and they had considerable influence in the city during the seventeenth century. As is typical of his approach, Baschenis provided an accurate and persuasive musical scene: Ottavio holds the lute correctly, with his right hand in a position that is recommended by all writers on lute technique.

Being a noble family, the Agliardi cultivated music as an important part of their education as well as their cultural identity. The other instruments lying on the table—a guitar, bass viol, and small mandola—suggest that Ottavio is skilled on these as well, and that these expensive instruments are owned by the family. Their inanimate position suggests the passing of time, in which the music is slowly being silenced as players leave the room. The music scores, with their folded edges and worn appearance, clearly indicating signs of use, also underscore this theme, as if the pieces have been played for the last time. Finally, the Anatolian rug covering the table adds an exotic flavor to the scene and represents yet another of the prized possessions owned by the Agliardi.

The guitar is painted with great care, with part of its vaulted back lying off of the table. Upon closer inspection one can notice other important details about the instrument's construction: the back is multiribbed (made up of many thin ribs), and the bridge has its two characteristic "moustaches" on either side. We also see the strings and the silk strap dangling listlessly. On the sheet of music protruding from the folder between the guitar and viol, a few lines of manuscript tablature are visible, perhaps indicating that these are original compositions. Even the music books are accurately painted with regard to format, proportion, and notation (Italian tablature, but not *alfabeto*).

Moving to the middle panel of the triptych (Figure 8-6), we encounter an especially haunting depiction of "silence." The instruments, including two lutes, a cittern, mandola, spinet, and guitar, all appear dead. They lie face down, the traces of their beautiful harmony memorialized by the distant echo of a few visible fragments of music. The piece of fruit on the spinet is beginning to spoil, and there is a fly (*mosca* in Italian, which is very similar to *musica,* music) on the music under the lute on the left. The fly's short lifespan may be another contribution to the *vanitas* conceit. This guitar, with its flat back without ribs, is differ-

Figure 8-5.   Evaristo Baschenis, Agliardi Triptych (c. 1665), Panel 1. Fotografia: Da Re Italy.

ent from the one on the first panel and may be a French model. Baschenis also provides a good view of the guitar's tied frets along the neck. One of the most brilliant effects the artist uses to convey the passing of time is the thin layer of dust that appears on the backs of each of the instruments. This dust includes visible tracks left from fingers streaking through it. On one level, this is a clear reference to the scriptural passage of "dust to dust." But on another level, the streaks also suggest the sensual caress of fingers against a lute's back, combining a tactile element to the senses of taste and smell, represented by the apples and flower stacked on top of the guitar.

The most elegant panel of the triptych is the third (Plate 19; Figure 8-7), which shows the remaining two Agliardi brothers, Alessandro (b. 1636) with the guitar, and the eldest, Bonifacio (b. 1635), "looking somewhat haughtily towards the painter and his brother" (Bayer 2001, 100). This scene offers a window into the cultured milieu shared by the two brothers, in which the guitar plays a central role in their pastimes and creative moments. Alessandro plays yet another type of guitar, an exquisitely made instrument with a thin neck, a style of early seventeenth-century guitar that was used more for strummed playing rather than for plucking. Indeed, Baschenis has captured Alessandro in the midst of executing an index-finger strum while forming a C-major chord with his left hand. The partly drawn curtains convey an atmosphere of intimacy, appropriate for a solo guitar. The gorgeous inlay on the guitar neck and elsewhere is itself a work of art, and, most importantly, Baschenis even reproduces the guitar maker's inscription, "Giorgio *Sellas* a la Stela in Venezia." This identifies the instrument as one built by the great seventeenth-century lute and guitar maker Giorgio Sellas, whose workshop was found "under the sign with a star" in Venice.

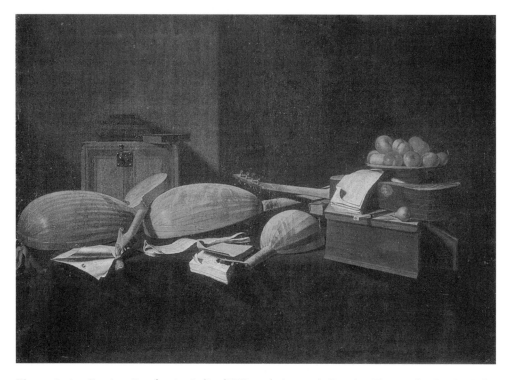

Figure 8-6. Evaristo Baschenis, Agliardi Triptych (c. 1665), Panel 2. Fotografia: Da Re Italy.

Along with the musical performance by Alessandro, Baschenis includes a still life setting on the table that includes yet another guitar, an archlute, and various books whose titles are visible. These demonstrate the range of possessions owned by the Agliardi brothers, and the things that were especially dear to them. With the titles of the books, one can further extrapolate the educational background of the Agliardi brothers and their extra-musical interests, giving us valuable information on the type of person who took up the guitar in the Baroque. Three of the books are poems by the seventeenth-century Roman Aurelio Orsi, the brother of the painter and acquaintance of Caravaggio, Prospero Orsi. Another book is a treatise on nobility by the author Andrea Tiraquellos, and a final volume is a legal tract by the authors Ubaldis and Canus (Bayer 2001, 98).

Guitar Music in France

By the time of Baschenis's triptych, the guitar had been fully in the mainstream of Italian music for over thirty years. The diversity of musical textures and the fluidity of the repertory were made possible by mixed tablature, which, as we have seen, combined the shorthand symbols of *alfabeto* with the longhand specificity of Italian tablature, resulting in a notation that was flexible enough to accommodate the various nuances of new compositional styles. The period 1630 to 1660 witnessed the publication of a great deal of outstanding guitar music, including impressive works by Foscarini (who was the first to use mixed tablature), Corbetta, Angelo Michele Bartolotti, Antonio Carbonchi (particularly his second guitar book of 1640), and Francesco Valdambrini. Over the last third of the seventeenth century, Italian guitarists continued their cultivation of the instrument. But aside from an extraordi-

Figure 8-7. Evaristo Baschenis, Agliardi Triptych (c. 1665), Panel 3. Fotografia: Da Re Italy.

nary collection of guitar solos published by Ludovico Roncalli in 1692, Italian guitar books of this period are marked by an increasing decline in originality. Indeed, in the last half of the century the focal point for guitar music shifted to France, through the endeavors of the Italian Francesco Corbetta.

Corbetta in France

Born in northern Italy around 1615, Francesco Corbetta had already made a career for himself as a guitarist and teacher in Bologna, a dignified university town that was an important center for the guitar (Pinnell 1976). Corbetta's fame landed him a position at the court in Mantua (a city whose days as an artistic center were by that time numbered), followed by a sojourn in Brussels. He began his association with the French court in the late 1640s, traveling there with other Italian musicians following the financially disastrous but artistically brilliant reign of Pope Urban VIII in 1644. Soon after his arrival, Corbetta was already instructing the young Louis XIV, thus planting the seeds for the golden age of the guitar at the French court that occurred when the Dauphin ascended to the throne as a fifteen-year-old in 1654 (see Chapter 5). After an interlude as court guitarist in Hanover from 1652 to 1653, Corbetta returned to France, where he became a fixture at the court and helped nourish what would soon be the most important guitar culture outside of Italy.

Corbetta's music was heard and praised by Jean-Baptiste Lully (an expatriate Italian who also played the guitar), and he published two excellent guitar books, in 1671 and 1674. In these publications, Corbetta disposed of both *alfabeto* and mixed tablature in favor of French lute tablature, a clear example of cultural "translation" as French music itself began to exhibit strong signs of nationalism. Sometime in the early 1660s, Corbetta settled in England in the entourage of the exiled Charles II, whose acquaintance with Corbetta in France had resulted in a deep appreciation for the guitar. Corbetta's arrival in England boosted an already active guitar culture, resulting in a vibrant musical scene in which he played a central role as player, teacher, and bon vivant gamester. The rise of the guitar in England was not embraced by everyone. By 1666, the composer and publisher John Playford lamented the decline of the English lute in the face of an instrument that had succeeded in capturing the spirits of the younger (and in Playford's view, unworthy) generation. And in a highly telling passage, the famous diarist Samuel Pepys, after hearing a performance by Corbetta on August 5, 1667, wrote: "After done, with the Duke of York; and coming out through his dressing room, I there espied Signor Francisco tuning his Guitar, and Monsieur du Puy with him, who did make him play to me; which he did most admirably, so well as I was mightily troubled that all that pains should have been taken on so bad an instrument" (quoted in Spring 2001, 413).

Corbetta's last printed guitar book, the *Guitarre royale* of 1674 (not to be confused with his other book of the same name of 1671, dedicated to Charles II), was dedicated to Louis XIV. Interestingly, in terms of style it returns to mostly strummed textures that were meant to be accessible, it seems, to the amateur courtier musicians of the French court.

The Global Travels of Santiago de Murcia

By Corbetta's death in 1681, the transmission of guitar styles from Italy to France and from France to England and the Low Countries had been set in motion. A few decades later, Santiago de Murcia carried the guitar full circle back to Spain as well as set it on a transatlantic itinerary to the New World—a journey whose impact continues to have ramifications to this day. In many ways, Murcia's career brings together many of the perspectives about the guitar we have mentioned above: the influence of Spain, the use of French courtly idioms, and, most of all, the fusion of styles—in this case, a fascinating assimilation of European and New World influences. Like bookends to the history of the guitar in the Baroque, we end where we began: with Spain.

The early eighteenth century witnessed a flowering of guitar music in Spain, spurred by composers whose works represent some of the most beautiful, melodic, and challenging pieces ever written for the instrument. Like other guitar composers before them, Gaspar Sanz, Francisco Gueráu, Santiago de Murcia, and others amalgamated popular tunes, national dances, and international courtly idioms, both French and Italian, to forge a new, eclectic style. The influence their publications had on the subsequent development of the guitar may be debatable, but the technical and stylistic models they provided strengthened the foundation for the emergence of the modern six-string guitar in Spain at the end of the century. Moreover, these works, especially those of Sanz, were virtually the only Baroque guitar music that was known by modern classical guitarists before the lute and early guitar revival that began in the 1970s.

The Spanish guitarist Santiago de Murcia (c. 1682–c. 1740) has been studied extensively in recent years because of the enormous breadth of his music—stylistically, technically, and culturally (Russell 1981). Born into a family of composers and instrument makers in Madrid, Murcia benefited from close ties to high-level patronage. His parents' connections to the Royal Chapel in Madrid may have provided him with the opportunity to study with the virtuoso guitarist and choir director Francisco Gueráu, whose only guitar book, the *Poema Harmonico* of 1694, contains works of astonishing invention and complexity. In his own treatise on guitar playing, *Resumen de acompañar* (Summary of Accompanying, 1714), Murcia has many words of praise for Gueráu. Moreover, there are stylistic connections between the two composers as well. By the early eighteenth century Murcia was engaged as the guitar teacher for the queen of Spain, María Luisa Gabriela, and this employment was followed by a string of valuable friendships with other noble patrons who served as the dedicatees of his guitar publications. Murcia's travels to France, Italy, Belgium, and Holland cannot be confirmed, but they are very likely, given the international traits, especially French, that appear in his compositions (Russell 1982; 1995, I: 131–133).

One trip that we are certain of ranks among the most important in the history of the guitar. Sometime after 1718, Murcia journeyed to Mexico, probably under the protection of one of his patrons in Spain, Joseph Alvarez de Saavedra, the dedicatee of the composer's *Passacalles y obras*. Murcia appears to have remained in Mexico until his death, and it was there that he composed the bulk of his output. His oeuvre consists of two separate manuscripts, written in Mexico, that were designed as a pair and presented to his patron Saavedra in 1732: the *Códice Saldívar, No. 4*, which is preserved in Mexico, and the *Passacalles y obras*, now owned by the British Library in London. These manuscripts contain many of the finest guitar works of the late Baroque Era and constitute the last great flowering of the Baroque guitar. Indeed, they provide a grand summary of Baroque guitar and the international styles it came to embrace.

Let us look at three works from the *Códice Saldívar* that demonstrate three different stylistic flavors: *La Jota, La Allemanda,* and *Marionas.* Of the sixty-nine pieces in the *Códice,* the majority are dances with variations, which fall into two categories. The first is the courtly and mannered *danzas,* which, when danced, used restrained hand motions. Most of the movement took place with the feet. The second is the vigorous *bailes,* which were enlivened with castanets and featured expressive hand and arm gestures together with fast movements of the feet. Murcia's *danzas* and *bailes* are both progressive and retrospective, revealing their writer's keen sense of history. Some of his pieces, such as the *españoleta,* reach back to sixteenth-century forms. Others, such as the *fandango* and *seguidilla,* became popular only in the nineteenth century. Another group of works in the manuscript represent French courtly dances, including several minuets which were part of the international instrumental language during this period. Italian influence can be observed as well, in the presence of a sonata in the fast-slow-fast Italian style.

La Jota (Sampler CD 2, track 7) is a Spanish folk dance from Aragon that was of recent vintage in the eighteenth century. It is related to both the *fandango* and perhaps even the *malagueña.* Through Spanish colonialism it became very popular in Mexico during the eighteenth and nineteenth centuries. The dance has been described as a mock combat between pairs of men and women playing castanets (which are, unfortunately, not scored) and challenging each other with aggressive advances and retreats (Russell 1995, 49). Murcia's setting portrays this scene by starting with a martial strumming section over tonic and dominant seventh chords, notated in the original with *alfabeto.* The hemiola rhythm produced by alternating 6/8 and 3/4 reflects a gesture found in other Spanish dances of the day, such as the *canario* (an exotic dance imported from the Canary Islands). Though the piece begins with strumming, a clear melody appears in the top voice, and this tune achieves full independence beginning with the arrival of a plucked section. Variations ensue. First the melody switches to the bass, followed by a passage of running notes and then a much quicker imitation between treble and bass, as the music gains speed. The final variations achieve an exciting conclusion through passages of parallel tenths and thirds combined with fast ascending and descending runs (Example 8-1).

By contrast, *La Allemanda* (Sampler CD 2, track 8) reflects the courtly French taste that is so integrated into Murcia's compositional style. In fact, the work is an arrangement of a French piece, André Campra's "L'Allemande" from the French court ballet *Ballet des frag-*

Example 8-1.   Murcia: *La Jota,* mm. 45–50.

ments de Mr. De Lully. Of German origin, the allemande was perhaps the most popular dance in eighteenth-century France, where it had long shed its popular Teutonic roots. In duple meter, it called for a moderately fast tempo and often began with an upbeat. The allemande appears to have been a popular dance in Mexico as well. Classic late-Baroque instrumental settings of the allemande, such as those of Bach, are normally in binary form and tend to have a thick, contrapuntal texture. Murcia's *La Allemanda* displays the binary form but little else. Beginning with the characteristic upbeat, the work evokes instead a country dance, with simple harmonies, droned bass notes, and strum-accented downbeats. The two-voice guitar texture is almost all in plucked style and demonstrates how the simplest work can be elaborated through the many textural possibilities offered by the guitar.

Marionas (Sampler CD 2, track 9), a triple-time dance that was popular in the Spanish theatre, was the second piece that Murcia entered into the *Códice Saldívar.* As a dance type, it appears in the guitar books of Sanz and Gueráu as well. It is one of the most rhythmically attractive *bailes,* with a halting accent on the second beat of every other measure. Like *La Jota, Marionas* begins with strummed chords over the repeated progression I–V–vi–(iv)–V–I, with some melodic movement in the upper note of the chords (Example 8-2). As the plucked variations begin, short four-note runs are interspersed with chords, so that the second-beat syncopations are retained. With the middle variations, however, the chords are replaced by repeated notes, scales, and a climactic section of rising sequences. In the concluding variations, a shift occurs from 3/4 to 6/8, which is followed by a few bursts of downward scales in the penultimate section. The work ends as it began, with a strummed statement of the *Marionas* progression.

Also of great interest in the collection are two works that draw on indigenous Afro-Mexican influences, *Cumbées* and *Zarambeques.* In the swinging, syncopated *Cumbées,* a work that was banned by the Inquisition as being lewd, lascivious, and indecent, Murcia asks the player to strike the guitar top with his hand for percussive effect (Example 8-3). The presence of *Cumbées* and *Zarambeques* within the context of the entire manuscript underlines

Example 8-2.   Murcia: *Marionas,* mm. 1–8.

Example 8-3. Murcia: *Cumbées,* mm. 1–7.

once again Murcia's sense of history, a sense that even seems to accommodate a *postmodern* view. In the *Códice* he assembles works from different styles, eras, and cultures without apology or hierarchy and without giving priority to any single tradition. Works from Europe appear outside of their courtly context, while new, local influences contribute to a vibrant sense of fusion and synthesis.

Conclusion: The Living Baroque Guitar

The thousands of pieces that survive for the Baroque guitar (which nevertheless probably represent only a fraction of the original repertory) reflect the musical contributions and tastes of a broad range of personalities. From short strummed dances on simple chord changes to complex, grandiose variations, this vast body of works reveals that Baroque guitarists, like their modern counterparts in popular music today, absorbed influences of many kinds. In so doing, they produced compositions that are much more inclusive in their stylistic and cultural mix than the music of other instrumental repertories. Guitarists' assimilation of fashionable courtly idioms as well as popular and even "world" music, as we have seen in the works of Santiago de Murcia, anticipates the fusion that has become the stylistic norm in music today (Russell 2003).

The study of popular music has now been validated as an academic pursuit. As a consequence, rock and rap are studied at universities together with Bach and Beethoven. Music by popular artists, from the Beatles and Stones, to Hendrix, Pink Floyd, and Radiohead has entered the repertoire of classical performers, and the once-impenetrable walls that used to separate "high" and "low" culture have all but crumbled. The Baroque guitar was not only a cultural equalizer in its own time. It also set an historical precedent for the stylistic reconciliation that has taken place in the music of today. With the revival of the Baroque guitar as a concert instrument over the past thirty years in the hands of such masterful players as Hopkinson Smith, James Tyler, Paul O'Dette, and Richard Savino (the performer on our CD), we are privileged to witness a fascinating reunion between two distant but very close cultural relatives.

BIBLIOGRAPHY

Bayer, Andrea, ed. 2001. *The Still Lifes of Evaristo Baschenis: The Music of Silence.* Milan: Olivares.
Boye, Gary. 2005. *The Baroque Guitar: Printed Music from 1606–1737* (www.library.appstate.edu/music/guitar/home.html)

Coelho, Victor. 1995. *The Manuscript Sources of Seventeenth-Century Italian Lute Music.* New York: Garland.

_____. 1997a. "Authority, Autonomy, and Interpretation in Seventeenth-Century Italian Lute Music." In *Performance on Lute, Guitar, and Vihuela: Historical Practice and Modern Interpretation,* ed. Victor Coelho, 108–141. Cambridge: Cambridge University Press.

_____. 1997b. "The Vihuela: Performance Practice, Style, and Context." In *Performance on Lute, Guitar, and Vihuela: Historical Practice and Modern Interpretation,* ed. Victor Coelho, 158–179. Cambridge: Cambridge University Press.

_____. 2000. "Picking through Cultures: A Guitarist's Music History." In *The Cambridge Companion to the Guitar,* ed. Victor Coelho, 1–15. Cambridge: Cambridge University Press.

Griffiths, John. 1989. "At Court and at Home with the Vihuela da mano: Current Perspectives on the Instrument, Its Music, and Its World." *Journal of the Lute Society of America* 22: 1–27.

Hudson, Richard. 1982. *The Folia, The Saraband, The Passacaglia, and the Chaconne: The Historical Evolution of Four Forms That Originated in Music for the Five-Course Spanish Guitar.* Stuttgart: Hänsler.

Pinnell, T. 1976. *Francesco Corbetta and the Baroque Guitar.* Ann Arbor, Mich.: UMI Research Press.

Russell, Craig H. 1981. "Santiago de Murcia: Spanish Theorist and Guitarist of the Early Eighteenth Century." Ph.D. dissertation, University of North Carolina.

_____. 1982. "Santiago de Murcia: The French Connection in Baroque Spain." *Journal of the Lute Society of America* 15: 40–51.

_____. 1995. *Santiago de Murcia's "Códice Saldívar No. 4": A Treasury of Guitar Music from Baroque Mexico,* 2 vols. Urbana: University of Illinois Press.

_____. 2003. "Radical Innovations, Social Revolution, and the Baroque Guitar." In *The Cambridge Companion to the Guitar,* ed. Victor Coelho, 153–181. Cambridge: Cambridge University Press.

Smith, Douglas Alton. 2002. *A History of the Lute from Antiquity to the Renaissance.* Lute Society of America.

Spring, Matthew. 2001. *The Lute in Britain.* Oxford: Oxford University Press.

Trichet, Pierre. c. 1640. *Traité des instruments de musique.* Paris: N.p.

Turnbull, Harvey, et al. 2001. "Guitar." In *The New Grove Dictionary of Music and Musicians,* ed. Stanley Sadie, 2nd ed., 10:551–578. London: Macmillan.

Tyler, James, and Paul Sparks. 2002. *The Guitar and Its Music: From the Renaissance to the Classical Period.* Oxford: Oxford University Press.

CHAPTER NINE

Seventeenth-Century Keyboard Music in Northern Europe: Germany, Austria, and the Netherlands

David Schulenberg

KEYBOARD MUSIC IS CENTRAL TO OUR understanding of the Baroque. During the early twentieth century, interest in the origins of the music of Johann Sebastian Bach led to extensive research on his predecessors in northern Europe, resulting in scholarly editions of much of the early Baroque keyboard repertory. In recent decades, however, music from France and Italy has received more attention, particularly in English-speaking countries, where the Lutheran chorales that form the basis of much of the seventeenth-century northern repertory have limited appeal. Even players specializing in Baroque keyboard music have tended to avoid the seventeenth-century repertory, in part because of the rarity of appropriate instruments and the inaccessibility of the old German editions, in part because much of this music, on paper, seems dry and colorless by comparison with earlier English and Italian or later French repertories—not to mention the familiar works of Bach himself.

Yet the keyboard composers of Germany, Austria, and the Netherlands were a powerful creative force during this period. Far more than mere prologue to Bach, their works reveal immense variety and expressive potential when interpreted within appropriate performance traditions. We can see this music as falling into two broad traditions, both taking their inspiration primarily from Italy until the widespread adoption of popular French features late in the century. One tradition, which incorporates an important English element as well, emerges in Holland and northwestern Germany and specializes in virtuoso public works for the organ. The other, centered in Austria and southern Germany, is more introspective and retains its predominantly Italian orientation longer, but with a distinctive Roman flavor due to the pervasive influence of Frescobaldi at the Viennese court.

Although it is customary to regard the seventeenth century as marking a new, Baroque style in European music, most traditions, including those of keyboard music, continued in an unbroken chain from those of the previous century. During the late Renaissance, major composers such as William Byrd (1543–1623) in England and Andrea Gabrieli (c. 1510–1586) in Italy created, for the first time in music history, keyboard pieces equal in stature to works in other genres. Such compositions joined improvised music and arrangements of vocal and instrumental works to form the foundations of keyboard players' repertories. Nevertheless, seventeenth-century keyboard playing continued to consist, in large part, of improvisation. Keyboard players routinely provided the basso continuo, a form of improvised accompaniment for other musicians. On the relatively rare occasions when solo keyboard music was heard in public, as in church services and the occasional public organ recital, one was as likely to hear improvisation as written compositions. Hence, much seventeenth-century keyboard music consists of idealized improvisations. Not only preludes and toccatas, but fugues and chorale settings reflect improvisational practices, taking a free, episodic approach to form and incorporating written-out examples of improvisatory figuration.

Yet the capacity of keyboard instruments for polyphonic playing made them uniquely suited for the teaching and study of composition. Thus ricercars, canzonas, and other models of learned counterpoint in an austere, unembellished style also form a large part of the seventeenth-century repertory. Between the extremes of freedom and rigor lay numerous types of composition that ranged from suites and variations on dance tunes to diverse types of chorale settings.

Instruments and Practices

INSTRUMENTS

The smallest, simplest, and most common keyboard instrument was the clavichord, whose strings are struck by small metal points, or tangents. Although small in sound, a good clavichord can produce a surprisingly full sonority while offering a sensitivity of touch—including the capacity for variable dynamics—not found on other seventeenth-century keyboard instruments. Most pre-eighteenth-century clavichords were fretted—that is, a single string serves for two, three, or even four different notes ($D\sharp$ and E, for instance), making certain chords and ornaments difficult or impossible to play, especially in keys whose scales involve numerous accidentals. Nevertheless, professionals as well as amateurs probably employed such instruments for the bulk of their practicing and private playing.

Keyboard instruments whose strings are plucked include not only the harpsichord but also smaller virginals and spinets. The strings are plucked by quills in each case, making the instruments in effect mechanical versions of the lute, which they gradually replaced as the preferred instrument for amateur music-making. Especially famous are the harpsichords and virginals built early in the seventeenth century by the Ruckers family of Antwerp. Exported throughout northern Europe, these were often depicted in paintings showing the interiors of prosperous Dutch households (Plate 20). Harpsichords generally contain two or three complete sets of strings, called ranks or registers, which can be played together or separately, thus permitting variations in tone color. Some seventeenth-century harpsichords even incorporate two keyboards, but the second keyboard sometimes served to provide only an alternate pitch level, as an aid to transposition when the player was accompanying other musicians (Figure 9-1). Few German harpsichords survive from the period, but their registers appear to have been marked by highly distinctive tone colors, even though composers never specified particular timbres (Koster 1999). In Austria and southern Germany, single-manual Italian-style harpsichords predominated. These had a more uniform but brighter sound than northern instruments.

Organs could produce far greater color variety, the largest instruments incorporating numerous ranks of pipes imitating flutes, reeds, and other instrumental sounds. Especially prized was the capacity of these sounds to blend in balanced combinations, particularly in the instruments of the North German master organ builder Arp Schnitger (1648–1719). A large northern organ typically had three or four keyboards, each controlling an ensemble of distinct ranks. One of these keyboards was a pedalboard, played with the feet and possessing its own distinctive stops, including powerful double-bass ranks. Organists could use the pedalboard to perform one or even two independent lines of music. But although pedal playing

Figure 9-1. Transposing keyboards from a 1638 harpsichord by Joannes Ruckers (1578–1642). The top keyboard includes a short octave whose apparent F-sharp and G-sharp keys engage the strings D and E, respectively. Russell Collection, Copyright University of Edinburgh. Used by permission of the Director of St. Cecilia's Hall.

was cultivated in the north, much seventeenth-century organ music, especially that from southern regions, lacked pedal parts.

Despite their considerable differences, the various keyboard instruments of the time share common features that are reflected in the music. Keyboard compasses rarely exceed four octaves (C–c'''), and the bottom octave is often incomplete or "short," lacking C♯, D, D♯, and E. The tuning systems of the day favored certain intervals, especially the major thirds on the notes A, C, D, E, F, G, B♭, and E♭, which were tuned more purely than in the equal temperament used today. This made the most commonly used consonant chords more resonant than chords built on other notes. Dissonances and chromatic intervals were even less sonorous, an effect often used for expressive purposes. Most keyboard music was confined to what we would call the keys closest to C major; key signatures of more than two accidentals were unusual.

The type of keyboard instrument required for a given piece was rarely specified by the composer. Sometimes the genre of a composition suggests an appropriate medium. Liturgical pieces, for instance, were presumably for organ. Keyboard compass and the presence of a pedal part can also furnish clues. But wide intervals between the lower voices do not necessarily imply use of organ pedals, for such intervals were sometimes playable with a short octave. In addition, some harpsichords and clavichords were fitted with pedalboards. A sustained melodic line, especially in an inner or lower voice, might point to the organ. But much of the repertory was probably not written with a specific instrument in mind, and players would have improvised adaptations as needed, as when a composition exceeded the available keyboard range.

A tradition of public performance of solo keyboard music existed only in the case of the organ. Regular concerts are known to have taken place in the Calvinist churches of the Dutch Republic, and the famous evening concerts (Abendmusiken) in Lübeck in northern Germany originated as organ recitals. Some organists, including Johann Pachelbel at Erfurt, were required to give annual public recitals. Indeed, repertory used today by church organists as preludes or interludes in church services often served pedagogical or concert functions in the seventeenth century. The organ introduced and accompanied congregational singing in many places, but this practice was by no means universal. Organists also provided continuo accompaniment in instrumental and vocal works.

The harpsichord was probably used primarily for accompaniment. Wealthy amateurs and professional court musicians might also have performed solo repertory on such instruments, but for this type of music most players would have had to be content with the smaller types of stringed keyboard instruments. During the second half of the seventeenth century, as German-speaking Europe recovered from the Thirty Years War and trade and communication with outlying lands increased, French music came increasingly into vogue. Stimulated by published collections of keyboard pieces by French composers, German musicians began to issue similar volumes. The dedications of these publications show that composers catered to wealthy amateurs, some of whom must have played the music themselves on both clavichord and harpsichord. The expense of printed music was such that professional musicians normally played from manuscripts copied from other manuscripts or from printed editions. Much of the keyboard music of the seventeenth century has been lost; what survives is preserved in a relatively small number of manuscripts that were assembled in painstaking fashion, one piece at a time. Examples include two large manuscripts prepared by Johann Christoph Bach (1671–1721), the older brother and teacher of Johann Sebastian Bach, who contributed a number of his early compositions to the collections.

NOTATION

Only in the late seventeenth century, under the influence of French publications, did German keyboard players adopt the modern system of keyboard notation on pairs of five-line staves. Pedal parts were normally included on the lower staff, not on a separate third staff as in modern organ scores. Some manuscripts, especially those containing music in the Italian or English style, still employed the staves of six or more lines used in those countries (Figure 9-2). In such manuscripts, the placement of notes on the upper or lower staff is an indication to use the right or left hand, respectively. A melodic line exchanged between the two hands, as in the inner voices of contrapuntal pieces, wanders between staves.

Many German musicians continued to employ the older form of notation known as tablature, which used letters instead of notes (Figure 9-3). Although more economical than staff notation—a composition could be copied on half as much paper—tablature was harder to read, and by 1700 it was going out of fashion. One of the few substantial German publications of keyboard music from the first half of the seventeenth century, Samuel Scheidt's *Tabulatura nova* (Hamburg, 1624), was printed in open score, using a separate staff for each contrapuntal line. This illustrated well the independence of each part. Scheidt nevertheless expected players to transcribe the music into tablature notation before performing it.

Figure 9-2. Notation on six-line staves. Autograph manuscript of the composer Matthias Weckmann (c. 1620–1674), showing the opening of a canzon with a "repercussive" subject. Note the double clefs in each staff, representing two of the traditional four voices. Lüneburg, Ratsbücherei, *Mus.ant.pract. KN 147*. Used with permission of the Ratsbücherei der Stadt Lüneburg.

PERFORMANCE PRACTICES

At a time when most players were professional musicians, relatively little was written about performance techniques, since this information was passed down directly from master to student. This is especially true in the realm of keyboard music, and as a consequence such fundamental issues as fingering, registration, and ornamentation must be addressed from scattered clues. Manuscripts occasionally provide fingerings, ornaments, and other performance markings, but these represent local practices from which it is difficult to draw broad conclusions. For example, German manuscripts containing works of Sweelinck and his contemporaries sometimes preserve "paired" fingerings for scales that alternate fingers 3 and 4 or 2 and 3. The right hand might finger an ascending C-major scale 3-4-3-4 3-4, etc., as in contemporary English practice. But it is difficult to fit such patterns to the irregular figuration found in the music of Froberger and others. Froberger's pieces might have called for the scale fingerings described in some Italian sources—2-3-4 3-4 3-4, etc.—or for more pragmatic approaches such as 2-3-4-5 2-3-4-5 or 1-2-3-4 1-2-3-4.

Paired fingerings do not necessarily have implications for touch or articulation. But even in contrapuntal pieces, which were modeled on vocal polyphony, players must have cultivated an articulate approach, to judge from the documented avoidance of the thumb and the frequent use of the same finger for successive notes in a melodic line. Accents would have been created chiefly through agogics—that is, by holding accented notes for their full written

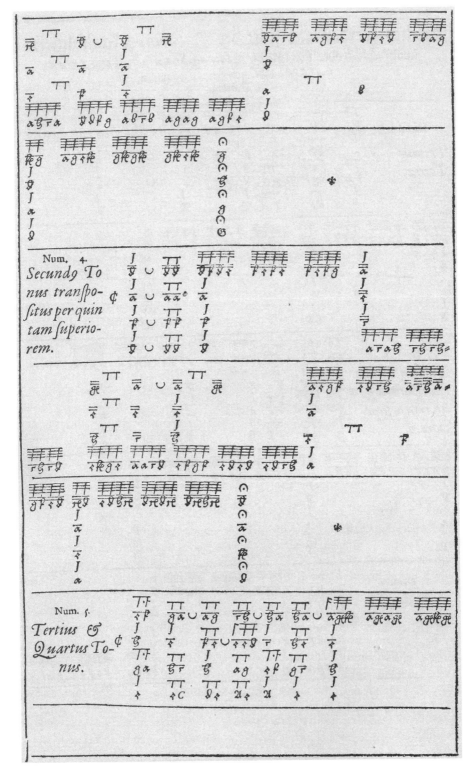

Figure 9-3. German keyboard tablature, using letters and other symbols instead of notes written on a staff, from Bernhard Schmid, *Tabulatur Buch von allerhand . . . Preludiis, Toccaten, Motteten, Canzonetten, Madrigalen und Fugen* (Strassburg, 1607). Reproduced courtesy of Broude Bros.

values and detaching others, especially upbeats and notes that precede emphasized ones. Similar conclusions are suggested by the short pedalboards of the period, which prevent the alternation of heel and toe used to create smooth legato lines in later organ music. Detached playing with the toe only was probably the rule, with the use of alternating feet in the liveliest pedal passages.

Ornamentation, an essential element of Baroque music, was heavily influenced by that of Italy. Thus Froberger followed Frescobaldi's use of the letter "t" to signify *tremolo* or *tremoletto,* that is, any of various short trill and mordent figures described by contemporary writers on vocal music. These figures, rarely indicated notationally, usually began on the main note; only the long cadential trill or *groppo* started on the upper auxiliary, and it was often written out until well into the seventeenth century. Equally important, although also rarely notated, were numerous types of *accenti*—passing notes inserted before or after the beat. Only toward the end of the century did composers introduce systems of ornament signs modeled on those being used in French publications. This coincided with the adoption of new types of ornaments that started with an expressive, accented dissonance—as in the trill starting from the upper note, which became the norm only in the late seventeenth century.

More elaborate embellishments, such as the cadenza-like passages used to decorate final cadences or to connect sections of a larger piece, were often written out in toccatas and similar works. Players must have improvised them in other contexts as well. The rhythm of such passages, and indeed rhythm generally, must have been treated more freely than the notation suggests. Tempo and rhythm were *à discrétion*—that is, at the discretion of the player, especially in genres such as the allemande and the organ praeludium. In a letter, a patron of Froberger expressed doubt that anyone could play his music with the same *discrétion* as his own. He nevertheless attempted to preserve through fairly precise rhythmic notation a style of playing that must have recalled recitative or the "modern madrigals" that Frescobaldi had mentioned as a model for performance.

Modern players do not always heed suggestions such as Frescobaldi's, sometimes employing excessively literal rhythm as well as anachronistic ornaments. Moreover, a dearth of usable instruments from the period and the scarcity of accurate modern copies force many performers to play the seventeenth-century repertory on inexact reconstructions. Hence players are only beginning to recreate the excitement that this music must have inspired in its original listeners.

Composers and Repertories

Keyboard music in late-Renaissance Germany is documented in several printed anthologies. The dances and transcriptions of vocal pieces in these sources seem to have been directed to players of middling ability (Butt 2004). Comparable pieces, together with settings of liturgical melodies in a similar style, had comprised the bulk of the surviving German repertory since as early as the fifteenth century. But by 1600 the best professional players were cultivating new genres imported from Italy, especially the toccata and ricercar as developed in Venice by Andrea Gabrieli and his nephew Giovanni Gabrieli (c. 1555–1612), who succeeded him as organist at St. Mark's Basilica. The Gabrieli tradition extended well into the seventeenth century through Giovanni's German pupil Heinrich Schütz (1585–1672) and Schütz's student Matthias Weckmann (1621–1674), who left important keyboard pieces.

HANS LEO HASSLER AND THE VENETIAN STYLE

An earlier recipient of the Venetian tradition was Hans Leo Hassler (1562–1612), who studied in Venice with Andrea Gabrieli before becoming court organist in 1586 in Augsburg in southern Germany. Hassler later served as a musician in his native city of Nuremberg and briefly as Capellmeister at the Saxon court in Dresden. Hassler is best known for his vocal music, yet the few dozen ricercars, toccatas, and other pieces securely attributed to him constitute the first important body of early Baroque keyboard music in Germany.

Most of Hassler's pieces, like those by other composers of his generation, are assigned to "tones" related to the modes of Gregorian chant. Thus his *Ricercar II. toni* (Ricercar of the Second Tone) is in what we would call the Dorian mode, transposed to G with one flat in the key signature. Like other late-Renaissance and Baroque ricercars, it is an extended exercise in imitative counterpoint in four voices; unlike earlier examples, it falls into clearly delineated sections of impressive dimensions, reflecting Baroque trends toward greater monumentality and clearer sectional divisions. Even more substantial are several pieces bearing the title "introitus." Hassler's *Introitus IV. Toni* (Introit of the Fourth Tone) is an extended example of the Venetian toccata, opening with massive homophonic chords (Example 9-1, a) and then proceeding to free figuration (Example 9-1, b) and imitative polyphony. Despite its old-fashioned title, the work uses an up-to-date tonal idiom derived from Giovanni Gabrieli. This permits the expressive juxtaposition of A-major and F-major chords in a passage that recalls Gabrieli's pieces for multiple choirs of instruments (Example 9-1, c).

Example 9-1. Hassler, *Introitus IV. toni,* a) mm. 1–4, b) mm. 16–18, c) mm. 130–135.

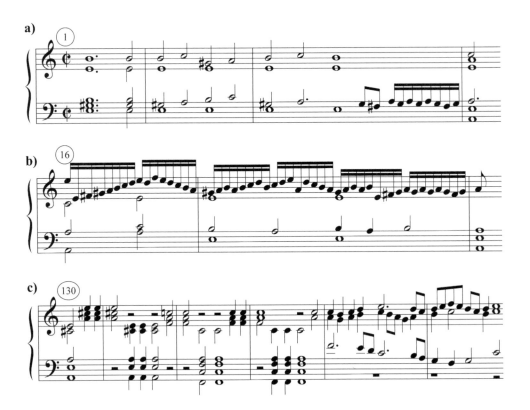

SWEELINCK AND HIS STUDENTS

Pieces similar to Hassler's were being composed under the title "fantasia" at about the same time by Jan Pieterszoon Sweelinck (1562–1621), organist at the Old Church (Oude Kerk) in Amsterdam from 1580 or so onward. Sweelinck also wrote short improvisatory toccatas, variations on popular tunes, settings of hymn melodies, and dances. Like Hassler, Sweelinck was a prolific composer of vocal music as well. But Sweelinck drew on a broader range of styles than Hassler, including French chansons and Elizabethan keyboard music. His relevance to the history of Baroque music would be assured by his teaching alone. His students included the most important German keyboard composers of the next two generations, and they used his keyboard works as models for their own. From 1632 to 1651, the organists in Hamburg's four principal churches were all Sweelinck students.

Sweelinck's variations are often regarded as harpsichord pieces, and indeed they owe much to the English virginalists. Sweelinck followed Byrd and other English composers in composing variations on the English tune "Fortune, my foe" (Sampler CD 2, track 10) and in writing an embellished keyboard arrangement of *Pavana lachrimae* by the lutenist John Dowland (1562–1626). But the consistently contrapuntal texture of Sweelinck's pieces, which often include sections in cantus firmus style with the tune sustained in long notes against lively counterpoint, suggests that even his secular variations were conceived for the organ. Perhaps Sweelinck played them in the recitals that he presented as municipal organist in Calvinist Amsterdam.

Among Sweelinck's most distinctive pieces are his so-called echo fantasias (PGM 117). Like Byrd's fantasias, these generally begin with a grave imitative section, then introduce livelier subjects and eventually virtuoso figuration, including the famous echo passages. The echoes involve exchanges of short motives in different registers (Example 9-2, a) or at different dynamic levels (Example 9-2, b). This effect became a favorite of Sweelinck's followers in Germany. These pieces also include solos for one active voice with simple accompaniment (also seen in Example 9-2, b). Fundamental to both types of passage is the fragmentation of the melodic line into short, lively motives that are then developed through sequence, a technique basic to later Baroque and Classical style.

This technique marked a shift from Renaissance polyphony, whose subjects, developed through imitation in strict counterpoint, were conceived as whole phrases (as would be found in a typical vocal melody of the period). Sweelinck continued to cultivate the older style in other, more conventional fantasias, which resemble Hassler's ricercars in their immense length and sectional divisions. These fantasias are monothematic, employing the same subject throughout but in a different rhythmic form in each section. Such a fantasia is an encyclopedic demonstration of how one can work out a given subject. The devices explored in one fantasia in the Dorian mode (PGM 117) include conventional imitative counterpoint, stretto, cantus-firmus technique (with the subject presented in rhythmic augmentation), and a lively bicinium in which the texture is reduced to two voices and the subject is fragmented into its component motives.

Over the course of these long pieces, the musical motion ebbs and flows, progressing gradually from the grave, sustained openings to more colorful and sometimes quite exciting passages. These works nevertheless have a somewhat neutral character, even when the thematic material is potentially expressive, as in the famous but atypical *Fantasia chromatica*. Yet the usefulness of such pieces for study may explain their preservation in numerous manuscript copies by Sweelinck's students, some of whom wrote fantasias and variations on the same subjects. Samuel Scheidt (1587–1654), who had studied with Sweelinck before becom-

Example 9-2. Sweelinck, Echo Fantasia in C Major, a) echo passage, mm. 75–85; b) "solo" (with echo dynamics), mm. 99–104.

ing organist at Halle in 1609, seems to have conceived his *Tabultatura nova* as a compendium of the types of pieces that Sweelinck had written. Thus it includes a hexachord fantasia (based on a six-note scale pattern), an echo fantasia, and variations on various liturgical and popular melodies. In each case, Scheidt trumps Sweelinck's models in length if not in variety of figuration.

Like Hassler, Scheidt occasionally reveals the influence of contemporary music for instrumental ensemble. Most famous are passages labeled *imitatio violistica,* referring to two- or four-note figures each marked with a slur, which on the viol or violin would signify performance with a single bow stroke. More impressive is the refined four-part counterpoint in the *Fuga quadruplicis*—a fantasia on subjects from Palestrina's madrigal *Io son ferito lasso*—which concludes by combining its four subjects contrapuntally. The fantasia on the chorale melody "Ich ruf zu dir, Herr Jesu Christ" belongs to a common seventeenth-century type in which each phrase of the tune becomes the basis of free imitative treatment. This technique was borrowed from vocal chorale settings of the time, such as those of Michael Praetorius (c. 1571–1621).

Later keyboard composers in northern Germany made freer use of the Sweelinck tradition, mingling it with other styles while avoiding its excesses. Particularly notable is Heinrich Scheidemann (c. 1595–1663), who became organist at St. Catherine's Church in Hamburg in 1625 after studying with Sweelinck from 1611 to 1614. Scheidemann's surviving output comprises toccatas, dances, and variations, as well as praeambula and *alternatim* settings of the Magnificat. Although much of this music, like Sweelinck's, is playable on any keyboard instrument, most was intended primarily for the organ, and it often includes the independent pedal part that was becoming a mark of organ music in North Germany.

Scheidemann's fourteen extant praeambula represent a genre which, under the similar title praeludium, would emerge as supremely important in later German keyboard music. Both words can be translated "prelude." Earlier German preludes were short, modestly contrapuntal pieces, sometimes incorporating brief passages of improvisatory figuration. They seem to have been literally preludial, meant to precede more extended works for keyboard or perhaps voices. Scheidemann's organ preludes are self-contained compositions equivalent to the sonata of the period, which was scored most frequently for one or two treble instruments and continuo. Most early seventeenth-century sonatas were still relatively brief pieces; many were intended principally for church performance. Not yet divided into distinct movements, as in the eighteenth century, they share with Scheidemann's praeambula a free, somewhat rhapsodic form, built phrase by phrase through the working out of short imitative motives and expressive chains of suspensions.

Scheidemann's Praeambulum in D Minor (no. 34 in the thematic catalog of Scheidemann's works) of 1637 opens with a four-note descending figure today associated with Dowland's *Pavana lachrimae*. In the 1630s, Dowland's music may still have been familiar in Hamburg. But Scheidemann's treatment of the figure is closer to that found at the opening of Giovanni Gabrieli's *Sonata con tre violini*, published in 1615. After its initial imitative treatment the figure is developed motivically in a series of sequences, becoming the basis of the entire opening section (Example 9-3, a). Like Gabrieli's sonata and other Italian violin music of the period, the piece then proceeds to more lively sections based on a variety of motives, including dotted figures and written-out trills and slides (Example 9-3, b).

Although sometimes resembling the so-called divisions with which Hassler, Sweelinck, and earlier composers had enlivened their keyboard pieces, Scheidemann's figuration avoids the even flow characteristic of sixteenth-century works. Instead, it exhibits a less regular type of continuity that we recognize as distinctly Baroque. This expressive irregularity, which Scheidemann might have found not only in Italian violin music but in the keyboard works of Frescobaldi, was an important part of the emerging *stylus fantasticus*. In this style, which came to dominate North German organ music later in the century, sudden bursts of virtuosity (often involving the organ pedals) mingle with harmonic and rhythmic surprises to evoke the character of a dramatic narrative or recitative.

The greatest number of Scheidemann's surviving works are settings of liturgical

Example 9-3. Scheidemann, Praeambulm in D Minor, WV 34, a) mm. 1–5, b) mm. 15–18.

melodies, mostly chorales but also the eight tones, or chant formulas, for the Magnificat. The Magnificat, a setting of Mary's hymn of exultation from Luke 1:46–55, was still sung at Vespers in Lutheran churches in the seventeenth century. Since the late Middle Ages it had been the practice for the choir to alternate with the organ in presenting individual verses of hymns and other liturgical songs. The Magnificat settings of Scheidemann and other German Baroque organists, however, appear to have functioned as independent interludes during the singing of the Magnificat, much like the Christmas interpolations that J. S. Bach composed for insertion within his own setting of this text. Scheidemann's organ settings are so extended and inventive that today they might be played as independent pieces. Each of his organ Magnificats consists of four settings based on the same chant melody that would have been sung by the choir.

FOREIGN INSPIRATIONS: TUNDER AND REINCKEN

Less survives of the music of Scheidemann's younger contemporary Franz Tunder (1614–1667), who became organist at St. Mary's in Lübeck in 1641. Tunder must have performed much of his surviving music during the Vespers concerts, or Abendmusiken, that he was presenting in Lübeck by 1646. His preludes fall more clearly than Scheidemann's into the sectional divisions that would become the norm for following generations. An introductory section graced by cadenza-like flourishes leads to one or more imitative sections, as in the Praeludium in G Minor (Sampler CD 2, track 11). The imitative section is archaic in style, recalling the generation of Hassler. But it soon gives way to a freer section with more flowing figuration. The most remarkable aspect of this piece—shared with many North German organ works—is the eloquent use of silence on the concluding page, where the counterpoint suddenly dissolves into a lovely homophonic progression broken up by rests (Example 9-4). These rests might have been understood as *sospiri,* or sighs, in the music-rhetorical language of the day.

Tunder's most important extant works are his chorale settings. Some are lengthy fantasias in which phrases of the chorale melody are subjected to the same forms of development that Sweelinck explored in his fantasias, including echoes. *Komm Heiliger Geist, Herre Gott* (PGM 104) opens with a monodic setting of the melody: the hymn tune, played in embellished form by the right hand, has a subdued accompaniment in the lower voices (Example 9-5, a). Eventually, motives from the chorale melody are developed in imitation and in sequence, including a series of quick echo effects. Particularly notable is the chromatic embellishment of the chorale melody during the first echo passage (Example 9-5, b). Such chromaticism had been understood since the mid-sixteenth century as having an intensely expressive effect. Although its exact significance here is difficult to judge, the pungent effect

Example 9-4.   Tunder, Praeludium in G Minor, mm. 74–81.

Example 9-5. Tunder, *Komm, Heiliger Geist, Herre Gott,* a) mm. 2–5, b) mm. 87–90.

which the chromatic steps would have created on an instrument tuned in an unequal temperament surely contributed to the intended "difficult" or "hard" effect of this passage.

Tunder's inspirations must have extended beyond the Venetian and English sources of earlier northern composers to the toccatas, partitas, and settings of liturgical melodies by Girolamo Frescobaldi (1583–1643), who worked primarily in Rome. Frescobaldi's numerous publications of keyboard music had a lasting impact throughout Germany. When Georg Muffat published a collection of keyboard music in 1690, he likened it in his preface to a Frescobaldi publication issued more than six decades earlier. An equally significant inspiration would soon come from France. By midcentury, German composers were writing dances in imitation of French harpsichord pieces. Because few French pieces survive from before the last third of the century, German imitations are among the earliest witnesses of the seventeenth-century French keyboard tradition. After the establishment of a permanent opera theater in Paris under Lully during the 1670s, the French influence on German music became pervasive as German rulers reorganized their courts along the lines of Louis XIV (see Chapter 5). Not surprisingly, transcriptions and imitations of airs and dances from Lully's operas became a mainstay of the German keyboard repertory.

Just as Frescobaldi and other Italians influenced the mercurial improvisations and the chromatic counterpoint of the *stylus fantasticus,* the French style is the source of an expressive type of melodic ornamentation as well as an increasingly refined use of idiomatic keyboard textures—not only the so-called *style brisé* or *luthée* on the harpsichord, but various types of trio scoring on the organ. One of the earliest northern German composers to combine both strands is Johann Adam Reincken, traditionally thought to have lived for nearly one hundred years (c. 1623–1722). Reincken is depicted at the harpsichord in a group portrait that is believed to represent two important contemporaries as well, Dieterich Buxtehude and Johann Theile (Plate 12).

Unfortunately, the paucity of Reincken's surviving music and the uncertainties of its dating make it difficult to reach a clear understanding of this figure, who is remembered today chiefly because of his longevity and his significance for Bach's career. Scheidemann's successor at St. Catherine's Church in Hamburg, Reincken may have improvised most of what he played. Certainly an improvisatory quality is evident in his one surviving toccata and in his fantasia on the chorale melody "An Wasserflüssen Babylon." The latter is often noted for its great length and for a slight resemblance to Bach's setting of the same melody (BWV

653). The toccata bears a more tangible relationship to Bach, for it is preserved in a manuscript copy that belonged to Bach's older brother Johann Christoph. Like the praeludia of his younger contemporaries, Reincken's toccata alternates between improvisatory and fugal sections. Its designation as a toccata reflects the virtuoso elaboration of a few prolonged harmonies in its opening section. This was an archaic device that Bach would abandon in most of his own toccatas.

Reincken also left a number of suites consisting of an allemande, courante, sarabande, and gigue unified by key. Now considered standard for the Baroque suite, such regularity was contrary to the practice of the French, whose collections of dances exhibited no uniform order or number of movements. The dances of the German suites were nevertheless French in origin. Those of Reincken reflect the pre-Lullian French style: discursive and rhetorical in tone, they lack Lully's tunefulness as well as the rhythmic subtlety of later French music. Their relatively rigorous counterpoint and motivic work are distinctly German, as are the flashes of virtuoso passagework. Reinken's suites also illustrate another German tradition, the so-called variation suite. Here the courante constitutes a reworking of the harmonic and melodic scheme of the allemande (see Example 9-9 below). Reincken's suites provided models for later North Germans while departing from the more restrained style of Froberger. The contrast between the two composers is clearest in their variations on the song "Schweiget mir vom Weiber nehmen," also known as *Die Mayerin*. Although both sets conclude with several dances such as one might find in a suite, Reincken's eighteen variations focus on inventive virtuoso figuration, whereas Froberger's shorter set tends toward more expressive types of writing.

DIETERICH BUXTEHUDE

A more striking and cosmopolitan integration of diverse styles and genres occurs in the music of Dieterich Buxtehude (c. 1637–1707), who succeeded Tunder in 1668 as organist at St. Mary's in Lübeck. Buxtehude's keyboard works survive in greater numbers than those of any other seventeenth-century German composer, perhaps reflecting the fame of the Abendmusik concerts at which they may have been played. They include toccatas, preludes, and chorale settings, as well as three important ostinato works—two chaconnes and a passacaglia.

Originally dances, the chaconne and passacaglia were each constructed over a short repeating ground bass line or ostinato. They occur in both the Italian tradition (Frescobaldi published several examples of each) and the French (where a grand chaconne or *passacaille* was often the climactic number of an opera or ballet). Treatises describing improvisation over ground basses were published in mid-seventeenth-century England and in northern Germany at the end of Buxtehude's lifetime. Not surprisingly, Buxtehude's pieces reveal a distinctly North German approach to the genre. This is evident above all in his placement of the ostinato in the pedals. This has led to the assumption that these pieces were meant for the organ, unlike Italian and French examples. (Recently a strong case has been made for the pedal clavichord as the intended instrument.) Although in the traditional triple meter, Buxtehude's chaconnes and passacaglia lack the characteristic rhythmic formulas of French examples, such as a two-note upbeat. Instead, they focus on Italianate running figuration. The relentless repetitions of the ostinato, coupled with improvisatory upper parts, might have led to a rambling piece without character. But Buxtehude projects a sense of architectural design, above all in the Passacaglia in D Minor, whose twenty-eight statements of the ostinato include seven in the tonic followed by seven in F major, seven in A minor, and seven more in the tonic.

Buxtehude's praeludia (there are eighteen or so) expand the genre as understood by Tunder. In most of the works the initial improvisatory section is followed by two fugues using variants of the same subject (typically in duple and triple time, respectively). These are not "preludes and fugues" in the eighteenth-century sense. As in earlier praeludia—and in contemporary sonatas for instrumental ensemble, including those of Buxtehude and Reincken—the fugues are not independent movements. Rather, they are integrated into a larger quasi-dramatic scheme. After the improvisatory opening section, the entry of the fugue subject and its subsequent contrapuntal development constitute a stentorian, orderly contradiction of the *stylus fantasticus*. But the "fantastic" style gradually returns in the course of each fugal section, which usually ends by relaxing into free motivic work that reverts to an improvisatory style.

The same conception is evident in the small number of works designated "toccata." Here the fugal passages are only one of several contrasting types of music that are heard in rapid succession. The Toccata in F Major, BuxWV 156 (PGM 104), opens with a section constructed over pedal points, then makes several quick alternations between 12/8 and 4/4 time while also introducing several short-lived imitative passages (Bach's Toccata in F Major, BWV 540, also opens with extended pedal points, suggesting that it was inspired by Buxtehude's work). A degree of coherence is assured by the recurrence of several motives which, although common property of the North German organ style, are worked out with great intensity in each section (Example 9-6, a–c). Particularly notable is the climactic appearance of one figure as an athletic pedal line (Example 9-6, d). Alternating between regular and irregular sections, this toccata calls to mind not only the contemporary sonata but also certain cantatas (or, as they were then designated, vocal concertos). Hence the alternation of arioso- and recitative-like sections creates for some modern listeners the impression of a vocally inspired piece of musical rhetoric (Butt 2004). Certainly the sheer size of such pieces, and especially the ultimate return to "fantastic" style at the end, gives the impression of an impressive architectural design, even if the plan is not as regular as that of the D-Minor Passacaglia.

The urge toward monumental yet "fantastic" writing led to a number of extended chorale fantasias which, as it turned out, represent some of the last examples of this tradition. Buxtehude's setting of the hymn "Nun freut euch lieben Christen g'mein," BuxWV 210 (PGM 104), is one of his longest chorale compositions. In the course of its 256 measures, Buxtehude treats each of the seven phrases of the melody in turn. Following the design used by Tunder, he presents the first two phrases as an ornamented monodic setting. But this proves to be only the introduction to a virtuoso demonstration of the possibilities of chorale elaboration, including extended contrapuntal and echo passages—Buxtehude's answer to Sweelinck's fantasias.

Also attributed to Buxtehude are a number of suites and variations on secular tunes (PGM 105). These were most likely intended for clavichord. Preserved in Scandinavian manuscripts, these may include the seven suites which, according to Bach's contemporary Johann Mattheson (1681–1764), Buxtehude composed "on the nature and qualities of the planets" (Mattheson 1739). But if so, the musical characterization of the planets is not distinctive enough to recognize them in the absence of explicit titles. The pieces fall into the same expressive but not particularly distinctive style that was typical of other German suites of the period—Froberger's excepted. At least two of the suites in question have conflicting attributions, raising the possibility that the group as a whole is by several composers. This would explain small inconsistencies in style and keyboard range.

Younger contemporaries of Buxtehude in northern Germany include Vincent Lübeck (1654–1740), Nicolaus Bruhns (1665–1697), and Georg Böhm (1661–1733). Lübeck and

Example 9-6. Buxtehude, Toccata in F Major, BuxWV 156, a) mm. 12–13, b) mm. 55–56, c) mm. 93–94, d) mm. 121–122.

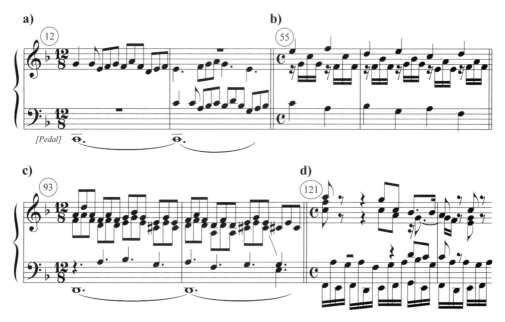

Böhm carried the North German tradition into the eighteenth century, and Böhm appears to have influenced the young Bach during the latter's student days in Lüneburg. Böhm's keyboard music incorporates up-to-date elements of the French and Italian styles. For instance, the unusual opening section of his Praeludium in G Minor (PGM 101), composed of repeated notes and arpeggios, seems to borrow ideas heard in the incipient Italian concerto.

Böhm's suites are more distinctive. Although stemming from the same tradition as Buxtehude's, they are closer to contemporary French compositions, including the early works of François Couperin. At the same time, they incorporate the drama and virtuosity of the North German style. The Chaconne of Böhm's Suite in F Minor—a remarkable key for this date—is in the full Lullian style, unlike the more Italianate chaconnes of Buxtehude. Yet it also incorporates the sweeping scales and other dramatic gestures of the *stylus fantasticus*. With Böhm, even the traditionally lyrical allemande is dramatized by bursts of arpeggiated figuration that span the complete keyboard. To be sure, a single allemande of Froberger, that of Suite 16 in G Major, contains comparable writing.

This last feature may confirm Böhm's authorship of a highly expressive suite in E♭ Major (no. 11 in the Beckmann edition) copied anonymously in one of Johann Christoph Bach's manuscripts. Although the work has been published as Froberger's, the key points to Böhm, for none of Froberger's authenticated works is in E♭ major. Johann Christoph Bach also owned a copy of a suite by Mattheson. J. S. Bach might have carried copies of both pieces back to Thuringia after his early sojourns in the north. He surely knew a later version of Mattheson's suite, published alongside eleven others by the composer in 1714. These suites include not only dance movements in the old tradition but distinctive preludes that Bach seems to have imitated in his English Suites and Partitas. The opening movement ("Fantasie") of Mattheson's Suite 5 resembles that of Bach's third English Suite in key and motivic material, and the "Symphonie" of Mattheson's Suite 10 furnishes an apparent model for the Sinfonia of Bach's C-Minor Partita.

One last composer to be mentioned in this context is George Frideric Handel (1685–1759), who worked in Hamburg for several years before departing for Italy in 1706. Handel had been trained in Halle by the capable organist-composer Friedrich Wilhelm Zachow (1663–1712), whose Variation Suite in B Minor appears alongside an early work of the same type by J. S. Bach in one of Johann Christoph Bach's manuscripts. Handel wrote several such suites, which, like the bulk of his keyboard music, were composed during his early years. Among them is the famous Suite in E Major, published as one of the eight "Great Suites" of 1720. The last movement, a set of variations, become known in the nineteenth century as "The Harmonious Blacksmith," after a musical artisan whom Handel supposedly overheard singing near Cannons (in England) in 1716 or 1717. But the movement harkens back to an earlier time, belonging to the seventeenth-century tradition of variations on short binary-form "arias." (The term "aria" in this case refers to the strophic songs popular at the time.) As in a chaconne or passacaglia, the variations are based less on the melody than on the bass line and its implied harmonic progressions. Bach's student Johann Philipp Kirnberger later quoted Handel's work to illustrate this type of variation technique.

FROBERGER

Outside northern Germany the central figure in mid-seventeenth-century keyboard music is Johann Jacob Froberger (1616–1667). Froberger traveled widely and was recognized during his lifetime as a master in both the French and the Italian styles. Although details of his life and output remain in dispute, by 1638 Froberger was in imperial service at Vienna and was almost immediately sent to Rome to study with Frescobaldi. He was back in Vienna from 1641 to 1645, but by 1649 had completed a second visit to Rome. After the death of his employer, the Holy Roman Emperor Ferdinand III, in 1657, Froberger was dismissed. He ended his career as teacher of Duchess Sibylla of Württemberg-Montbéliard, a small German enclave in what is now eastern France.

It was Dutchess Sibylla who wrote in a letter of the *discrétion* required to play Froberger's music. Despite her assertion that his music could not be properly performed by one who had not heard his own playing, the precision with which he notated the irregular, speech-like rhythms of his allemandes, toccatas, and other improvisatory movements underlines his determination to fix his practice in writing. It is odd, therefore, that Froberger did not also notate most of the ornaments—trills (*tremoli*), grace notes (*accenti*), and the like—that were an equally integral part of keyboard playing. The next generation of composers would indeed set them firmly in notation.

Froberger seems to have composed little besides keyboard music, much of which he gathered into manuscripts that he presented to his employers, the Austrian emperors. Three of these manuscripts survive, bearing the dates 1649, 1656, and 1658, respectively. The first two are designated volumes 2 and 4, showing that at least two others are missing. Each of the surviving manuscripts contains several sets of pieces grouped in half-dozens, as shown in Table 9-1.

Froberger's systematic organization was rare in earlier seventeenth-century sets, but it anticipated the practice of later Baroque composers, including Johann Kuhnau and J. S. Bach. This may be one reason for the importance attached to Froberger by music historians since the late nineteenth century. Another attribute, sensed already by his contemporaries, is the unusually expressive and personal character of much of his music, evident in the programmatic (and sometimes autobiographical) titles and rubrics attached to a number of his

Table 9-1.
Works by Johann Jacob Froberger in the Imperial Presentation Manuscripts

Volume	Pieces	Keys	Numbers*	Comments
II (1649)	6 toccatas	a-d-G-C-d-g	1–6	Nos. 5–6 are elevations
	6 fantasias	C-e-F-G-a-a	1–6	No. 1 published by Kircher
	6 canzoni	d-g-F-G-C-a	1–6	
	6 suites	a-d-G-F-C-G	1–6	No. 6 = variations *auf die Mayerin*
IV (1656)	6 toccatas	G-e-C-F-e-a	7–12	
	6 ricercari	d-g-e-G-d-f♯	7–12	
	6 capricci	G-g-e-F-F-a	7–8, 14–17	
	6 suites	e-A-g-a-D-C	7–12	No. 12 = lament for Ferdinand IV
V (1658)	6 capricci	G-a-d-F-g-C	1–6	
	6 ricercari	C-G-F-C-g-c♯	1–6	

*As numbered in *J. J. Froberger: Orgel- und* Klavierwerke, ed. Guido Adler (Denkmäler der Tonkunst in Österreich, 1897–1903).

works. In Book 4 this aspect extends to the famous emblematic images attached to the concluding suite, a lament for the late "King of the Romans" Ferdinand IV (Figure 9-4).

The collections suggest planning not only by genre but by "tone." Within groupings, tonalities are rarely repeated, and the exotic keys F-sharp and C-sharp minor come last in the two sets of ricercars. Except in the suites, Froberger borrowed the types, titles, and even notational styles of pieces published by Frescobaldi. The toccatas are written on Italian-style staves of six and seven lines, whereas the fantasias, ricercars, and other contrapuntal pieces are notated in open score. Froberger's contrapuntal pieces continued to circulate in manuscript copies in the eighteenth century, furnishing one model for Bach's Art of Fugue, which was similarly notated.

Froberger's toccatas resemble those of Roman composers—not only Frescobaldi but also Michelangelo Rossi (c. 1602–1656). Froberger shares with Rossi the common Baroque tendency toward clearer sectional divisions. Indeed, Froberger's later toccatas often consist of a distinct improvisatory section followed by two fugues, as in many of Buxtehude's praeludia. Froberger's toccatas are shorter than Buxtehude's praeludia, however, and they never call for pedals. This suggests that they were intended primarily for the harpsichord—no doubt a robust Italianate type. Exceptions include the last two toccatas of Book 2, which represent a special type of toccata performed during the elevation of the Host at Mass. The unusual dissonances, chromatic voice leading, and strangely wandering nature of these pieces—all common to Frescobaldi's elevation toccatas—are believed to have symbolized the mystery of the Incarnation. More typical is the final toccata in Book 4 (PGM 101), which strikes a balance between the rhapsodic freedom of the elevations and the schematic forms of some later works. This toccata alternates between free passages and imitative sections, of which the last alone is truly fugal. Although not all are variations of a single tune, as in Froberger's capricci,

Figure 9-4. Movement 1 (Lamento) from Johann Jacob Froberger, Suite 12 in C Major. Autograph manuscript (Vienna, Österreichische Nationalbibliothek, *HS 18707*). Froberger's musical notation is on five-line French keyboard staves; the added decoration is by Johann Friedrich Sautter. Used with permission.

Example 9-7. Froberger, Toccata 12 in A Minor, a) m. 10, b) m. 28, c) mm. 40–41, d) mm. 55–58.

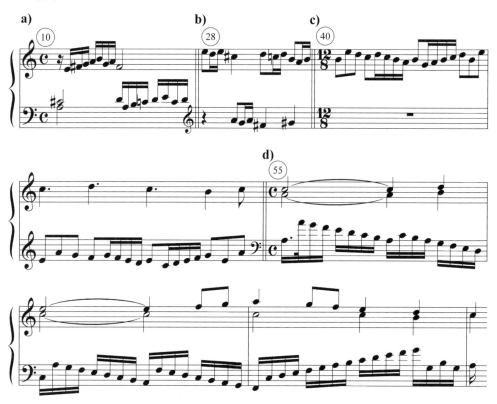

the imitative subjects of this toccata share a common intervalic structure (Example 9-7, a–c). This structure recurs in a sustained line that resounds, somewhat like a cantus firmus, over a rushing bass in a climactic final passage (Example 9-7, d).

The relatively impersonal nature of Froberger's contrapuntal pieces has discouraged interest from modern performers, despite their evident fascination for Froberger's patrons and fellow musicians. The canzoni and capricci, whose titles suggest things song-like and capricious, are in fact sober and sometimes strange pastiches of sixteenth-century modal counterpoint, spiced with frequent chromaticism. Although by no means unidiomatic for keyboard, they avoid the more flamboyant keyboard effects as well as the echoes of violin music found in Dutch and North German works. Most fall into several sections, each treating a variant of the opening subject or combining it with a distinctive countersubject. Brief improvisational transitions occasionally link sections, but even these are absent in the fantasias and ricercars. Clearly, these were pieces for connoisseurs of learned counterpoint. Yet they do not lack for striking ideas, as in the combination of lively, sonata-style subjects with chromatic *bizzarria* in Canzon 1 or Capriccio 8. In Canzon 1, the subject eventually is varied rhythmically to resemble that of one of Froberger's duple-time gigues (Example 9-8, a–b). In Capriccio 8 Froberger inverts the subject, then combines it in cantus-firmus style with livelier counterpoint (Example 9-8, c–d).

Froberger's suites are the earliest body of datable keyboard works of this type. Examples by Jacques Champion Chambonnières and other French composers, who presumably fur-

Example 9-8. Froberger, Canzon 1, a) mm. 1–4, b) mm. 100–101; Capriccio 8, c) mm. 1–4, d) mm. 63–65.

nished Froberger's models, generally survive only in later versions. Like the French keyboard pieces, Froberger's suites were eventually published (in this case posthumously) to meet popular demand for this increasingly fashionable music. Like Reincken's suites, however, Froberger's already follow a distinctly German tradition in the strict sequence of four movements (sometimes only three) and the frequent use of imitative counterpoint in the gigue. The gigue usually appears at the end of the suite, although in the suites of Book 4 it follows immediately after the allemande (in the early posthumous editions of these suites the gigues were moved to the end). Recently found manuscripts have added to the programmatic rubrics known for Froberger's works: the Allemande of Suite 27 represents a hazardous ferry crossing of the Rhine, that of Suite 16 depicts a "mountain path," and the Gigue of Suite 13 is entitled "La rusée mazarinique," referring to the chief minister of the young Louis XIV.

The early suites of Book 2 already reveal Froberger's mastery of the notation of the *brisé* style. More complicated in appearance than in sound, this notation provided a precise means of dictating the expressive arpeggiation that forms the basis of French harpsichord style, especially in the allemandes (Example 9-9, a). Although this element may have stemmed from French lute music, Froberger's suite style also owes something to Italian monody (see Chapter 2). One hears this in the frequent chromaticism and occasional quick repeated notes that may represent rapid declamation or perhaps the *trillo,* a common ornament in Italianate solo singing through the middle of the century (Example 9-9, a, m. 5).

Example 9-9. Froberger, Suite 1 in A Minor, a) Allemande, mm. 1–6; b) Courante, mm. 1–5.

Like most Baroque keyboard allemandes, Froberger's have little in common with the original dance apart from their binary form (adopted in all Froberger's dance movements). Instead, the allemandes resemble preludes, incorporating both improvisatory figuration and imitative passages, as at the opening of the Allemande of Suite 7 in E Minor (Sampler CD 2, track 12). This allemande is noteworthy for its extraordinary modulations, which include a passing tonicization of F-sharp minor, the same key represented earlier in the volume by Ricercar 12 (PGM 101). In such pieces the tuning problems that would have arisen on organs and clavichords of the period imply that Froberger performed the music on the harpsichord.

A few opening movements are designated laments, most famously in Suite 12 (PGM 101). There the imperial apotheosis, represented by the ascending scale at the end, is made explicit by the decoration in the Vienna manuscript (see Figure 9-4). The opposite effect, a downward scale, occurs at the end of the solitary Tombeau in C Minor for the lutenist Blanc-rocher, representing the musician's death in a drunken fall down a flight of stairs. Although potentially ludicrous by modern standards, this very concrete approach to musical representation was taken seriously by Froberger and his audiences. The extraordinarily expressive Allemande of Suite 14 in G Minor is designated "Lament sur ce que j'ay été volé" (Lament on What I Had Stolen from Me) in one manuscript, referring to an incident in which Froberger was robbed while traveling in what is now Belgium.

The gigues of Froberger's suites avoid the easy flow associated with the Italianate *giga* in the later Baroque. Many are serious contrapuntal exercises, inverting the subject in the second half, as in gigues by Reincken and Bach. Some gigues, like that of Suite 7 in E Minor (PGM 101), are in quadruple meter, without triplets. This notation was taken literally—it was not understood as an abbreviation for triplets, as was once thought—although like all of Froberger's music the movement would have been rendered expressive through unnotated ornaments and rhythmic *discrétion.* Froberger's courantes are relatively brief; the one in the E-minor Suite (Sampler CD 2, track 13) is less than a minute long. Yet they are among the few by German composers that attain the same metrical refinement as French examples. This is evident not only in the presence of hemiolas but also in subtle rhythms that may linger momentarily on broken chords but then move forward with impulsive figuration (as in Example 9-9b, m. 2). The sarabandes tend to be relatively simple in style. In Book 4 the sarabandes appear as final movements, serving as epigraphic conclusions to these lyrical, melancholic suites.

THE LATER FRESCOBALDI TRADITION: KERLL AND MUFFAT

Viennese composers maintained the Frescobaldi tradition after Froberger's departure. Johann Caspar Kerll (1627–1693) studied with Frescobaldi and, like Froberger, left toccatas and suites. These pieces combine devices used by the two older composers with more outwardly virtuosic gestures, including quick arpeggios and repeated notes. The result is more facile than impressive, however. More distinctive are Kerll's contributions to another Frescobaldian genre that Froberger neglected: the short fugue or verset on liturgical subjects. Kerll published a collection of these as the *Modulatio organica* (Vienna, 1686). Intended for *alternatim* performance of the Magnificat, the published versets point to the widespread use of such music in Roman Catholic contexts, especially in the churches and monasteries of the Habsburg empire.

Another figure active in Vienna, Alessandro Poglietti (d. 1683), recalls the English virginalist John Bull in combining astonishing virtuosity with flashes of wit. Poglietti's works include a learned ricercar on the songs of various birds and some bizarrely programmatic harpsichord pieces. Like Froberger, he presented a manuscript anthology to his imperial patrons. Entitled *Il rossignolo* (The Nightingale), it includes a set of twenty variations on a German aria dedicated to the Empress Eleanora. It is not always clear how seriously Poglietti intended his music to be taken. To modern ears it suggests the same sense of humor evident in programmatic pieces by the violinist Heinrich Biber. Among the variations are imitations of Bohemian bagpipes and other ethnic dances and instruments, as well as an "Old Women's Funeral Procession" that seems to parody the type of chromaticism that Froberger had included in one of his variations on *Die Mayerin.* Clearly the earnestness of the early Baroque was being set aside, despite such incidents as a rebellion in Hungary—also depicted in one of Poglietti's works—or the Turkish siege of Vienna, in which Poglietti died.

Other Austrian composers extended the Frescobaldi-Froberger tradition in a more serious manner. Johann Joseph Fux (1660–1741), first appointed organist at Vienna in 1696, is best known for his operas and theoretical writings. He was also an imaginative composer of suites, fugues, and other keyboard pieces. These strongly influenced the lively fugues and harpsichord suites published by his pupil and successor Gottlieb Muffat (1690–1770). Muffat's father, Georg (1653–1704), was also a major keyboard composer. Known primarily for his orchestral concertos and suites, the older Muffat became Capellmeister at Passau in southern Germany in 1690. In that year he also published his grandly titled *Apparatus musico-organisticus,* a collection of twelve large toccatas together with several variation works, playable on organ or harpsichord. In the preface, Muffat describes the work as the first of its type in seventy years—a reference to Frescobaldi's Second Book of Toccatas and Partitas of 1627. Muffat traces the formation of his style to his acquaintance with Lully in Paris and with Corelli in Rome, where he also met the composer and harpsichordist Bernardo Pasquini. Thus he was able to combine the best of the French and Italian styles in a "mixed" style that would soon be typical of Germany.

SOUTH AND CENTRAL GERMAN COMPOSERS AT THE TURN OF THE CENTURY: KRIEGER, KUHNAU, FISCHER, AND PACHELBEL

Other Germans also published keyboard music during the closing years of the seventeenth century. Although none emulated Frescobaldi as closely as Muffat, several maintained the tradition of demonstrating mastery of strict counterpoint in learned fugues and similar pieces while also exploring more fashionable genres. This presumably made their works attractive both to professionals and to students and well-off amateurs. But a nod toward less accomplished players is evident in the trends toward simpler counterpoint, lighter and more tuneful dance movements, and diminishing virtuosity—all features of what would soon be termed the *style galant.* Johann Krieger (1651–1739), organist at Zittau, issued collections of rather conventional suites or partitas (*Sechs musicalische Partien,* Nuremberg, 1697) as well as ricercars, fantasias, and other pieces in a somewhat simplistic contrapuntal style (*Anmuthige Clavier-Übung,* Nuremberg, 1698). In fact, this Krieger was a less original composer than his older brother Johann Philipp (1649–1725), whose works remained in manuscript. An important and prolific writer of cantatas, Johann Philipp was evidently a keyboard virtuoso during his early years, when he traveled to Venice and Rome. An immense, virtuosic passacaglia from early in his career is based on a haunting six-bar bass ostinato that later found its way into one of Telemann's Paris Quartets.

In southern Germany Johann Caspar Ferdinand Fischer (c. 1670–1746), Music Director to the Margrave of Baden, also followed a volume of suites with a contrapuntal collection. His suites (*Pièces de clavecin,* Schlackenwerth, 1696, reprinted as *Musicalische Blumen-Büschlein,* Augsburg, 1699) depart from those of Froberger and other German predecessors by opening with short praeludia. They also avoid the four usual dance movements—allemande, courante, sarabande, gigue—in favor of more colorful dances such as the bourrée and gavotte. Fischer's suites also contain several rondeaux and single examples of the branle, amener, and plainte. The titles and style of the pieces seem to reflect Fischer's familiarity with the current French theater. Indeed, some of these movements may have originated as transcriptions of theatrical dances.

Fischer's chief contrapuntal volume, the *Ariadne musica,* is a set of short preludes and fugues in the twenty most commonly used keys. The title refers to the mythological heroine who found her way out of the Minoan labyrinth—a symbol for the work's ranging through a wide variety of tonalities. The work is a predecessor of J. S. Bach's Well-Tempered Clavier, which quotes a number of Fischer's fugue subjects. But Fischer's fugues are short, close to the verset tradition. Pedal points in the preludes imply use of the organ, although the use of a pedal harpsichord or clavichord is, as always, also a possibility.

The best-known keyboard publications of the late seventeenth century are those of Johann Kuhnau (1660–1722), Bach's predecessor as Cantor at Leipzig's St. Thomas School. Kuhnau published two volumes of suites (Leipzig, 1689–1692), sharing with Krieger both the generic title *Partien* and the collective title *Clavierübung* (Keyboard Practice), which Bach would later borrow. Each suite incorporates the four usual movements together with a prelude and several additional dances, establishing a precedent followed by Bach. The preludes are often substantial pieces, comparable stylistically to the sonatas that Kuhnau published in two subsequent volumes (1696–1700).

Although Kuhnau's sonata volumes were the first such publications for keyboard instruments, their importance was exaggerated by nineteenth-century historians who viewed them as milestones in the development of the solo keyboard sonata. In fact, the solo keyboard sonata emerged as a genre only in the 1730s, in imitation of contemporary compositions for solo flute or violin with continuo. Kuhnau's works, by contrast, resemble the seventeenth-century ensemble sonatas written by Johann Rosenmüller, Johann Pachelbel, and other central German composers for four or five string instruments. Although these sonatas contain virtuoso solo passages for the leading violin part, the emphasis is on freely imitative sections framed by predominantly homophonic passages, as in the polyphonic sonatas that inspired the praeludia of the North German organists. But Kuhnau avoids the virtuosity and the most dramatic effects of the *stylus fantasticus*. He also has an unfortunate tendency to restate sequences and other patterns repeatedly, without modulating widely or maintaining a foreign key for very long. Evidently Kuhnau aspired to write imposing movements unified by the use of a limited number of distinct motivic ideas. But composers of his generation lacked the formal devices such as ritornello form through which Bach and other successors would create drama and contrast within compositions of sizable dimensions. Nor did Kuhnau lighten his learned writing with the airier styles of contemporary France and Italy. Instead, his music resembles his ostentatiously academic prose writings, a product of the university culture in Baroque Leipzig.

This is evident even in the six famous sonatas of the *Biblische Historien* of 1700, which nevertheless fulfill a novel programmatic conception. Each sonata represents a dramatic event from the Bible, which Kuhnau recounts in a German preface and summarizes in Italian headings above the various sections of each sonata. Rather than depicting actions and personalities, these works evoke the affects or emotional qualities associated with the events, often by borrowing gestures from vocal music. Thus Sonata VI, *La Tomba di Giacob* (Jacob's Death and Burial; PGM 101), suggests at the outset the "sadness of Jacob's children," opening with a freely imitative texture reminiscent of motet writing for a small vocal ensemble (Example 9-10, a). The "slight sweetening" of their feelings "at their father's blessing" is signified by interruptions in triple time, using broken chords (Example 9-10, b) that Kuhnau employed elsewhere to represent joyful harp playing. A four-part fugue represents their "thinking upon the consequences of this death"—pensiveness rather than death being depicted by the contrapuntal texture. Motet style returns to represent "the most sad lament of the assistants" at Jacob's burial, where the repeated notes of the imitative subject suggest recitative (Example 9-10, c; Sampler CD 2, track 14). The sonata ends by portraying "the consoled spirit of the survivors" in a lively movement in chaconne style, which Kuhnau used to conclude several other sonatas as well (Example 9-10, d).

Less ostentatious than Kuhnau, but of greater significance regionally and even for far-off

Example 9-10. Kuhnau, *Biblische Historien*, Sonata VI: a) "il dolore dei figlii di Giacob," mm. 1–3; b) ". . . raddolcito un poco dalla paterna benedittione" (same movement), mm. 29–31; c) "il lamento dolorisissimo fatto da gli assistenti," mm. 13–14; d) "l'animo consolato dei sopraviventi," mm. 1–4.

America, was Johann Pachelbel (1653–1706). In Pachelbel's works, elements of the Roman and Viennese keyboard traditions mingle with those of Central Germany. In some of his ruminative preludes and fantasias one hears echoes of Frescobaldi's elevation toccatas, and one senses Froberger in the background of Pachelbel's Ricercar in F♯ Minor. Yet Pachelbel's ricercar is more clearly tonal and more cogently structured—it is a regular double fugue—than the example by Froberger in the same key. A native of Nuremberg, Pachelbel studied in Vienna (possibly with Kerll), where he served for a time as organist at St. Stephen's Cathedral. After a series of further appointments he ended his career as organist in his hometown. His students included several members of the Bach family, among them Johann Sebastian's older brother and teacher Johann Christoph, as well as Pachelbel's own three sons, one of whom emigrated to America, eventually serving as organist in Charleston, South Carolina.

Pachelbel preceded Krieger and Kuhnau as a publisher of keyboard music, issuing a collection of chorale settings as early as 1678 and sets of variations in 1683 and 1699. The first set of variations also contained chorales. Its title, *Musicalische Sterbensgedancken* (Musical Contemplations of Death), is thought to reflect the composer's recent lost of both his wife and infant son. Unfortunately the work is lost, and although a number of pieces preserved in manuscript copies have been traced to the collection, their style is hardly as profound as the title would suggest. Rather, the elegant writing of a work such as the variations on "Was Gott tut, das ist wohlgetan" (What God Ordains Is Always Right; PGM 104) is what one might expect in something intended for amateur domestic performance. The 1699 collection is more sophisticated. Its title, *Hexachordum Apollinis* (Apollo's Hexachord), perhaps refers to the tonal ordering of the pieces, or at least of the first five, which are set in d, e, F, g, and a, respectively. Each work in the collection consists of an aria with variations. The last is in the rare key of F minor. Although some have noted the subtlety and "quiet virtuosity" of these pieces, the overall effect is one of modesty and refinement, as if the composer intentionally favored a certain "neutral" style, as opposed to the color and drama cultivated by his contemporaries in the north (Butt 2004).

The same is true of the many works that Pachelbel left unpublished, especially his chorales, for which this neutral style was evidently deemed appropriate. Older members of the Bach family, including the brothers Johann Christoph Bach (1642–1703) and Johann Michael Bach (1648–1694), composed similar pieces. But although composers of this generation did not yet reflect the meaning of the words in their chorale settings, Pachelbel did infuse them with lively figuration within a great variety of formal designs. Nevertheless, such music must have appealed primarily to students and connoisseurs. Addressed more to the public are several chaconnes in which, as in other German examples, the dance element is suppressed in favor of architectural designs whose climaxes are marked by virtuoso passagework.

Pachelbel also left a large number of works called *fuga,* or fugue. Rarely used in the seventeenth century as a title, the term suggests that these were intended as pedagogic examples of imitative technique. But the lively subjects and transparent textures distinguish them from the older type of learned ricercar. Although short by comparison to most eighteenth-century fugues, they are more extensive than the traditional verset. The largest group, often referred to as "Fugues on the Magnificat," contains few references to Magnificat melodies, although the pieces seem to have been intended for liturgical use. They appear to have consisted of two sets of thirty-two pieces each, with four fugues for every "tone." In this respect, they surpass Kerll's *Modulatio organica,* their likely model. The freely invented subjects range from old-fashioned vocal types to so-called repercussive themes, a popular German type of fugue subject in which the three or four reiterated notes typical of the sixteenth-century canzona are extended to a dozen or more quick repeated notes.

Here, as in the works of Poglietti, one discerns a sense of humor, or at least a fascination with *bizzaria,* that belies the present-day image of the seventeenth century as overwhelmingly serious and self-absorbed. In his capacity for wit or humor, Pachelbel shares something with his fashionable younger contemporaries, yet without sacrificing craft, originality, or seriousness of intent. Such qualities made him a fitting model for succeeding generations of German composers.

BIBLIOGRAPHY

Apel, Willi. 1972. *The History of Keyboard Music to 1700,* trans. Hans Tischler. Bloomington: Indiana University Press.

Butt, John. 2004. "Germany and the Netherlands. In *Keyboard Music before 1700,* ed. Alexander Silbiger, 2nd ed., 147–234. New York: Routledge.

Dirksen, Pieter. 1997. *The Keyboard Music of Jan Pieterszoon Sweelinck: Its Style, Significance, and Influence.* Utrecht: Koninklijke Vereniging voor Nederlandse Muziekgeschiedenis.

Hogwood, Christopher, ed. 2003. *The Keyboard in Baroque Europe.* Cambridge: Cambridge University Press.

J. J. Froberger, musicien européen: Colloque organisé par la ville et l'École nationale de musique de Montbéliard, Montbéliard, 2–4 novembre 1990. 1998. Centre de Musique Baroque de Versailles. Paris: Klincksieck.

Koster, John. 1999. "The Harpsichord Culture in Bach's Environs." In *Bach Perspectives 4: The Music of J. S. Bach: Analysis and Interpretation,* ed. David Schulenberg, 57–77. Lincoln: University of Nebraska Press.

Mattheson, Johann [1739] 1999. *Der volkommene Capellmeister.* Modern edition, ed. Friedrich Ramm. Kassel: Bärenreiter. English translation: *Johann Matheson's Der volkommene Capellmeister: A Revised Translation with Critical Commentary*, ed. Ernest C. Harriss. Ann Arbor, Mich.: UMI Research Press, 1981.

Niedt, Friedrich Erhardt. 1989 [1700–1721]. *The Musical Guide,* trans. Pamela Poulin and Irmgard C. Taylor. Oxford: Clarendon Press.

Snyder, Kerala J. 1987. *Dieterich Buxtehude: Organist in Lubeck.* New York: Schirmer Books.

Walker, Paul, ed. 1990. *Church, Stage, and Studio: Music and Its Contexts in Seventeenth-Century Germany.* Ann Arbor, Mich.: UMI Research Press.

Webber, Geoffrey. 1996. *North German Church Music in the Age of Buxtehude.* Oxford: Clarendon Press.

Williams, Peter. 1980–1984. *The Organ Music of J. S. Bach*, vol. 3: *A Background.* Cambridge: Cambridge University Press.

CHAPTER TEN

Bach and the Bounds of Originality

George B. Stauffer

WHEN JOHANN SEBASTIAN BACH DIED ON JULY 28, 1750, he went to the grave with a well-established reputation as one of the leading virtuoso keyboard performers and composers of his day. Indeed, the writers of the obituary that appeared shortly after his death were bold enough to assert that he was "the greatest organist and clavier player that we have ever had." The obituary authors described Bach's life and accomplishments and listed in broad outline his musical works, both published and in manuscript. Despite their promotional efforts, however, the bulk of this repertory soon fell into oblivion.

Although the keyboard pieces continued to be prized and championed by a small band of connoisseurs (chiefly composed of Bach's sons and students) and the motets remained in the active repertory of the St. Thomas School in Leipzig (where they were resented, because of their difficulty, by the choirboys), the cantatas, the Passions, the B-Minor Mass, the instrumental sonatas, the instrumental ensemble works, and other major portions of Bach's oeuvre disappeared almost completely from sight and were left to gather dust on the shelf for the next half century. The St. Matthew Passion, the Brandenburg Concertos, and other masterpieces were not heard between 1750 and 1800.

This changed in the nineteenth century with the arrival of the so-called "Bach movement." Spearheaded by Johann Nicolaus Forkel's ground-breaking biography *On Johann Sebastian Bach's Life, Genius, and Works* of 1802, Hoffmeister & Kühnel's attempt to print an *Oeuvres Complettes de Jean Sebastien Bach,* Carl Friedrich Zelter's readings of the choral works with the Berlin Singing Academy, and Mendelssohn's famous revival performance of the St. Matthew Passion in 1829, the Bach movement gathered momentum in the first half of the century and culminated with the formation of the Bach Society in 1850, the centennial of Bach's death. The subsequent publication over the next fifty years of the Bach-Gesamtausgabe, the first scholarly complete works edition, and Philipp Spitta's monumental *Johann Sebastian Bach,* published in two volumes in 1873 and 1880, represented the capstone of the revival and placed Bach firmly in the pantheon of German international cultural heroes.

Because the majority of Bach's works were first heard and evaluated in the nineteenth century, his music and compositional process were judged by the standard of the day—the works of Beethoven. Music from the B-Minor Mass, for instance, received one of its first performances alongside Beethoven's *Missa solemnis* in a public concert led by Gaspare Spontini in 1828. Spontini assembled an immense composite Romantic Mass by joining together the Kyrie and Gloria from the *Missa solemnis,* the Credo portion of the B-Minor Mass, and C.P.E. Bach's *Heilig,* or Sanctus (Stauffer 2003, 192).

With the Romantic view of Bach's music came the Romantic expectation, firmly established by Beethoven, that each work in a composer's output should represent a new and original creation, unveiled to the public in definitive form. Originality and innovation became the measure of success. The compositional procedures of Beethoven and Bach differed greatly, however, and as a consequence produced different results. In the case of Beethoven, a work was commonly years in the making. The Third Piano Concerto evolved over a period of three years, the *Missa solemnis* over a period of four years, *Fidelio* over a period of ten years. In the case of the Ninth Symphony, almost thirty years lay between Beethoven's initial consideration of Schiller's "Ode to Joy" and the completed composition (Levy 2003, 18–46). Beethoven labored mostly as an independent artist, and works were performed when they were ready.

In the case of Bach, circumstances were very different. Bach commonly completed works in a single week or day, and pieces were frequently performed for a specific purpose within a few days of completion. For instance, contemporary documents reveal that Bach completed Cantata 198, *Laß Fürstin, lass noch einen Strahl,* the large and magnificent "Trauer Ode" for Electress Christiane Eberhardine, on October 15, 1727. It was performed before a large assembly of townspeople and visiting dignitaries in the University Church just two days later.

The different demands called for different compositional approaches, which were summarized quite nicely by Robert L. Marshall in a discussion of Bach's compositional process: "A composer like Beethoven enjoyed a 'luxury of time' which allowed him to experiment with and assemble a large number of ideas from which he would ultimately choose the best one. Bach and his contemporaries had to invent or 'discover' their ideas quickly. The hectic pace of production did not tolerate passive reliance on the unpredictable arrival of Inspiration" (Marshall 1972, 235).

As a result of these circumstances, Bach was compelled to take an extremely proactive approach to composition, one that included the recycling of a great deal of earlier material, revised to fit new, pressing needs. Violin and oboe concertos became cantata movements and harpsichord concertos, secular cantatas became sacred cantatas (always in this order, it seems—see Schulze 1989, 17–18), cantata movements became Masses, keyboard pieces became instrumental works, and so forth, in a dazzling array of musical transmogrifications. Bach's extensive reliance on earlier compositions and his willingness to rework musical material became fully evident with the editing of the Bach-Gesamtausgabe in the second half of the nineteenth century, and even more so with the research accompanying the editing of the Neue Bach-Ausgabe (New Bach Edition) in the second half of the twentieth century. At least 20 percent of Bach's oeuvre stems from older music (Finscher 1969, 95), and many pieces that were written from scratch are handed down in multiple versions. For Bach, recycling and revising seem to have been the order of the day.

The initial "waves of indignation"—as Alfred Mann (1989, 177) has put it—in the nineteenth century over the Baroque practice of borrowing have subsided, and writers no longer use terms such as "plagiarism" or "appropriations" when discussing recyclings of earlier material. Nevertheless, Bach's reliance on old material and his ongoing revision of existing music continue to raise pressing questions of originality. When is a work "new"? When is it a different creation? What are the bounds of originality?

These questions are especially pertinent to the case of late "Big Works." Beethoven's *Missa solemnis,* Ninth Symphony, and late quartets stemmed from years of work. Each is highly original and breaks new ground. Bach's St. Mark Passion, Christmas Oratorio, and B-Minor Mass, by contrast, were "composed" relatively quickly and consist almost wholly of recycled music. Are they as original as Beethoven's late masterpieces?

Bach was not alone in transforming old music to new: borrowing was common to Baroque style, as we know from Handel and other contemporary composers. But how did Bach turn borrowing into high art?

Recycling in the Baroque

The precedents for recycling old music date from the earliest years of polyphony in Western music. Within the famous Medieval Notre Dame school of composition, Pérotin (c. 1160–1225), one of the founding fathers of notated polyphony, constructed new three- and four-part clausula, or polyphonic inserts, by adding voices to the pieces of his illustrious predecessor Léonin (c. 1135–1201).

In the Renaissance composers continued this tradition by writing Masses based on material borrowed from their own music or that of colleagues. These works were called parody Masses, though not in the satirical sense of the word parody. Quite the contrary, they were serious works, and the when the material was borrowed from another composer's music, it was viewed as an act of homage. Josquin des Prez's *Missa Malheur me bat,* for instance, is based on the chanson "Malheur me bat" (Misfortune Strikes Me), sometimes attributed to his illustrious forebear Johannes Ockeghem. Or Palestrina's *Missa Veni sponsa Christi* is derived from his own motet *Veni sponsa Christi,* which in turn is based on the antiphon of the same name.

In Renaissance keyboard music, too, borrowing was common practice. The Fitzwilliam Virginal Book, copied between 1609 and 1619, contains numerous keyboard arrangements of borrowed music, in the form of variations or dance movements composed in tribute to others, much like the parody Masses. The sequence Pavana and Galliard "Delight" by William Byrd is a setting of a song by Edward Johnson. John Dowland's popular "Lachrymae," from his *Second Booke of Songs or Ayres* of 1600, was transformed into keyboard pavane settings by William Byrd, Thomas Morley, and Giles Farnaby.

In the Renaissance, the borrowing of earlier music was more a question of art than practicality: it appears to have viewed as a type of musical conceit, a competition within musicians' circles to see who could write the most artful pieces based on earlier material. In the process, the familiarity of the model was critical to the success of the derived work. Far from hiding the model, composers proclaimed it in the title of the new piece.

In the Baroque Era borrowing became commonplace as a practical means for composers to meet the growing demands for new music, in both the sacred and the secular sphere. Much music was written for singular events, and composers understandably wished to recycle pieces performed only once to gain additional use of the material. But the increased amount of borrowing during the Baroque reflected more than commercial requirements: it was facilitated by new styles of composition that made musical recycling more feasible than ever.

One of the most important techniques was parody procedure, which in the eighteenth century denoted the retexting of a vocal composition to produce a new work. This was made possible by the use of madrigal poetry for librettos: the metrical schemes of the texts, with their regular strong and weak accents, were reflected in the meter and rhythm of the music. Local poets were able to produce parody texts based on the structure, diction, rhyme, and meter of the original libretto. The new text could then be inserted for the old in the music, thus producing a work for a new occasion (Melamed 1999, 357). This process could be carried out either after the fact or from the very beginning, in a premeditated way. In Baroque cantatas, oratorios, and Passions, madrigal poetry was generally used in the choruses and arias. Recitative, by contrast, was normally written in free verse; the music reflected the idiosyncratic nature of the original text and normally could not be reused. Thus choruses and arias could be recycled through the use of new parody texts. Recitatives, by contrast, had to be newly composed.

Bach's Easter Oratorio, *Kommt, eilet und laufet*, BWV 249, first performed on April 1, 1725, illustrates this process well. The bulk of the music stems from the secular cantata *Entfliehet, verschwindet, entweichet, ihr Sorgen*, BWV 249a, composed two months earlier, on February 23, for the birthday of Bach's patron Duke Christian of Saxon-Weissenfels. The opening chorus of the oratorio illustrates the clever retexting of the initial aria of the birthday cantata:

Birthday cantata:

Entfliehet, verschwindet, entweichet, ihr Sorgen
Verwirret die lustigen Regungen nicht!
   Lachen und Scherzen
   Erfüllet die Herzen
   Die Freude mallet das Gesicht.
(Pass quickly, disappear, vanish, O you worries,
Do not perplex the happy emotions!
   Laughing and joking
   Fill the heart
   And color the countenance.)

Easter Oratorio:

Kommt, eilet und laufet, ihr flüchtigen Füße,
Erreichet die Höhle, die Jesum bedeckt!
   Lachen und Scherzen
   Begleitet die Herzen,
   Denn unser Heil ist auferweckt.
(Come, hurry and run, you flying feet,
Reach the cave that shelters Jesus!
   Laughing and joking
   Accompany the heart,
   For our savior has awakened.)

The text of the birthday cantata was written by Bach's favorite Leipzig librettist, Johann Christian Henrici (known as "Picander"). It is likely that he was responsible for the text of the Easter Oratorio as well.

Although parody technique was common practice in Bach's day, it nevertheless met with criticism in some circles, because at times it involved the transformation of salacious opera arias and choruses into music for the church. Bach's Leipzig contemporary and occasional critic Johann Adolph Scheibe voiced concern about the process, for example: "He [Pater Präses] had a sheaf of Italian opera arias stocked up, so whenever he needed a sacred aria for a *Gloria*, he made a parody out of a lovesick and voluptuous opera aria and performed it with all devotion, just as if opera and church music were all one and the same, and as if one could sigh just as voluptuously, tenderly, and basely over the highest being as to an insensible beauty" (Schulze 1989, 12). In modern scholarship the term "parody" is often used more broadly, to describe the recycling of a preexisting composition either through new text underlay or through revision of the notes alone.

The advent of multimovement formats and sectional forms in the Baroque also facilitated the borrowing of material. Within operas, cantatas, oratorios, concertos, and sonatas, self-sufficient movements could be removed and used elsewhere, making borrowing a quick and easy procedure. As Daniel Melamed points out in Chapter 11, in 1736 Bach removed the chorus "O Mensch, bewein dein Sünde Groß" from the St. John Passion and recycled it as the closing movement of Part I of the St. Matthew Passion. Earlier, in the 1720s, Bach borrowed individual movements from Cöthen instrumental concertos to create introductory organ sinfonias for a number of Leipzig cantatas in his third annual cycle, as we shall see below. And for the second volume of the Well-Tempered Clavier, Bach was able to match up independent preludes and independent fugues to form new prelude and fugue pairs. Such carpentry work was made possible by the late-Baroque multimovement format.

Within movements, sectional designs such as the concerto form with discrete blocks of ritornello and episodic material and the da capo aria form with clearly articulated A and B sections also presented the opportunity for composers to lift entire sections from movements and recycle them elsewhere. The "Crucifixus" of Bach's B-Minor Mass, for example, is the revised version of the A section from the da capo opening chorus of Cantata 12, *Weinen, Klagen, Sorgen, Zagen.* Much of the B-Minor Mass, in fact, is composed of similarly recycled musical torsos.

Finally, the interchangeability of idioms also aided the borrowing process in the Baroque. In the first decades of the seventeenth century, the development of independent idioms for vocal, instrumental, and keyboard music was an essential element in defining the shift from Renaissance to Baroque style. By the eighteenth century, however, composers created a rich cosmopolitan language by freely exchanging the established idioms: one could write a keyboard piece in the manner of a vocal work, or a vocal piece in the manner of a keyboard work. This allowed for speedy adoption and reconfiguration. Within Bach's oeuvre, instrumental concertos became vocal movements (the third movement of Brandenburg Concerto No. 1 became the opening chorus movement of Cantata 207a, *Auf schmetternde Töne der muntern Trompeten,* for instance), organ trios became instrumental pieces (the second movement of Trio Sonata No. 3 in D Minor, BWV 527, became the middle movement of the Concerto in A Minor for Harpsichord, Flute, and Violin, BWV 1044), and cantata movements even became organ pieces (the closing fugal chorus of Cantata 131, *Aus der Tiefen rufe ich, Herr, zu dir,* became the Fugue in G Minor for Organ, BWV 131a). These exchanges reflect the exchangeability of idioms in late-Baroque style.

Ongoing Revisions

During the Baroque Era, most music remained in manuscript form. Publishing music with movable type was not yet practical, and the engraving process was expensive and could be used for limited press runs only. As a result, the majority of musical works circulated in manuscript. This tradition, and the fact that performance conditions constantly changed (the tenor available today might be replaced by a soprano tomorrow), freed composers from the urgency to create "definitive" versions of their music. Pieces commonly remained in a constant state of flux and revision. Whereas Beethoven created one version of the *Missa solemnis,* Bach created at least four versions of the St. John Passion (see Chapter 11).

In most cases, the concept of a definitive edition was foreign to Baroque composers. The open-endedness of the compositional process also created an atmosphere in which parody procedure and continuous revision were part and parcel of a composer's endeavor.

Bach and the Parody Process

Despite the presence of so many factors aiding the borrowing and revising process, Bach appears to have relied principally on new composition for his musical needs up to the Leipzig years. The works from his first four professional posts—Arnstadt (1703–1707), Mühlhausen (1707–1708), Weimar (1708–1717), and Cöthen (1717–1723)—seem to be almost exclusively newly composed. This is understandable, perhaps, since Bach needed to establish his reputation as a composer and to build a repertory of vocal, instrumental, and keyboard works for his professional duties, teaching, and personal use.

In addition, Bach was able to pursue this course by the relatively modest compositional demands of his first four positions. On the whole, he could work at a leisurely pace, and this pace is reflected in the clean appearance of his scores from the pre-Leipzig years. To be sure, in Weimar, after his elevation to the position of Concertmaster in March 1714 he was compelled to write a series of cantatas. But he composed them at a pace of one per month—a pace that was not considered taxing for a Baroque composer. Before the Leipzig years, Bach composed to fulfill ongoing but essentially occasional demands.

This pattern changed when Bach look up his duties as Cantor of the St. Thomas School and Director of Town Music in Leipzig in the spring of 1723 (Figure 10-1). As Cantor, he was required to supervise the music for the principal churches in town. More specifically, he was obligated to oversee personally the music for the main Sunday worship service that alternated between the two main churches, St. Thomas and St. Nicholas. The musical highpoint of the main service was the cantata, for which Bach was admonished to "so arrange the music that it shall not be too long, and shall be of such a nature as not to make an operatic impression, but rather incite the listeners to devotion" (David, Mendel, and Wolff 1998, 105).

Bach's predecessors depended heavily on the works of other composers to fulfill this weekly obligation. Bach, by contrast, decided to use pieces of his own composition—pieces that for the most part he had yet to compose. This was a tremendously ambitious undertaking, involving the production of approximately sixty works annually, for each Sunday (aside from those in Advent and Lent, when no instrumentally accompanied music was performed) and feast day of the year.

Bach approached his task with great industry, compiling between 1723 and 1729 five annual cycles of cantatas that he could then repeat in subsequent years (approximately one-third of these three hundred cantatas are lost, allowing only partial reconstruction of the fourth and fifth cycles). For the first annual cycle, compiled in 1723–1724, Bach cleared the shelf of cantatas created in Weimar and Cöthen and filled in the gaps with thirty-seven new works. As a result, the first annual cycle is heterogeneous in nature, displaying various forms and styles and utilizing texts by a numbers of authors. Some of the reperformed works show considerable revisions, pointing to the "openendedness" of Baroque music. But the number of true parodies is quite small: just four works for the entire cycle. Thus the first cantata cycle shows limited borrowing.

In the second cycle, assembled in 1724–1725, borrowing was nonexistent, since Bach decided to compose an entire year's worth of chorale cantatas to a unified series of texts apparently supplied by the retired conrector of the St. Thomas School, Andreas Stübel (Wolff 2000, 278). Stübel's death in January 1725 caused a libretto crisis for Bach. He nevertheless continued to write new works, though now based on texts by Leipzig poetess Marianne von Ziegler and other authors who remain anonymous. Borrowing and parody did not come into question in the second annual cycle.

It is in the third set, which took two years to compile (1725–1727), that we see a distinct shift in Bach's compositional habits. In the third cycle, he began to borrow from earlier

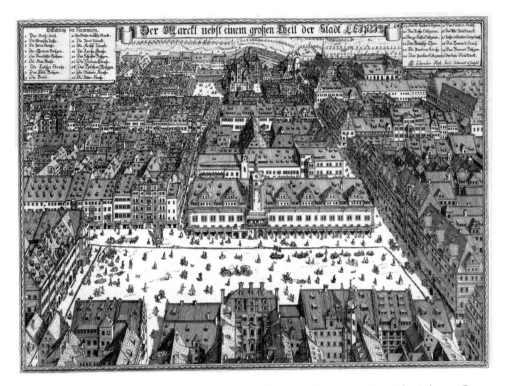

Figure 10-1.   Panorama of the Town Square in Leipzig. Engraving (1712) by Johann Georg Schreiber. Used by permission of Stadtgeschichtliches Museum Leipzig.

scores in a major way, and he continued this pattern for the rest of his life. Here Bach turned to heterogeneous texts and heterogeneous styles, as in the first cycle, and he wrote pieces at a much slower pace. Indeed, he composed new pieces also intermittently, filling in the gaps with repeat performances of old pieces and, in the winter, spring, and summer of 1726, a series of eighteen cantatas by his Meiningen cousin Johann Ludwig Bach.

The third cycle displays a deepened interest in new cantata types: solo and dialogue works, pieces with weighty instrumental preludes and interludes, and works with exceedingly colorful scoring. At the same time, this cycle shows a shift to a new and complex manner of borrowing, through Bach's heavy use of preexisting instrumental movements from Weimar and Cöthen. In a few cases these movements appear as straightforward sinfonias, or instrumental introductions, to the vocal movements of the cantatas (Cantatas 156 and 174, for instance). In other cases, Bach used an instrumental movement as the foundation for a vocal chorus, a procedure that called for considerable revamping of the music. In Cantata 110, *Unser Mund sei voll Lachens,* written for Christmas Day 1725, Bach layered newly composed voice parts over the opening Overture of the Orchestra Suite in D Major, BWV 1069; in Cantata 207, *Vereinigte Zwietracht der wechselnden Saiten,* a secular cantata composed a year later for the induction of Professor Gottlieb Kortte at the University, Bach added newly composed voice parts over the third movement of Brandenburg Concerto No. 1.

In the spring of 1726 Bach initiated a ground-breaking series of works incorporating organ solo. Between May and November of that year he penned six pieces—Cantatas 146,

170, 35, 47, 169, and 49—that display a rich array of sinfonias, choruses, and arias calling for obbligato organ. Almost all of these movements appear to be derived from preexisting violin and oboe concertos from his Cöthen years. Bach carefully revised the music, transferring the solo parts to the organ and, when fashioning choruses and arias, layering in vocal lines as well.

The obbligato movements represented a new use of the organ. In the obbligato movements Bach moved the instrument from the background of the ensemble, where it played as a member of the continuo group, to the foreground, where it appeared as a center-stage soloist. This laid the foundation for his further exploration of the keyboard as solo instrument in the harpsichord concertos of the 1730s, which we will discuss shortly. But it also introduced a new and complex parody style, one involving comprehensive synthesis and amalgamation. This extremely sophisticated process of carefully selected borrowing and artful reworking became the norm for Bach in the final two decades of his life.

The Organ Trio Sonatas

One of the direct results of Bach's numerous reworkings in the third cantata cycle was the Six Trio Sonatas for Organ, BWV 525–530 (Figure 10-2). The Sonatas date from around 1727 or so—that is, from the period directly following Bach's intense involvement with obbligato organ writing in the third cantata cycle. Like the obbligato cantata movements, the six sonatas break new ground in the organ repertory: they are chamber music transferred to the organ and illustrate, once again, the interchangeability of instrumental and keyboard idioms. The trio sonatas could not have been written without the cantata movements, which brought the organ into the sphere of chamber music as a full-fledged solo instrument.

The trio sonatas are a hybrid of trio and concerto styles. The texture is that of the Italian trio sonata (see Chapter 3), with the two violin parts taken by the right and left hands of the organist playing on separate manuals. The basso continuo part is taken by the feet on the pedalboard. Bach treats the pedal part as an equal partner to the manual lines and frequently assigns it the same musical motives as those found in the upper voices. At the same time, the three-movement format of the trio sonatas—fast-slow-fast—and much of the thematic material, which displays the alternation between tutti and episode, reflects the concerto writing of Antonio Vivaldi.

It is clear that a good deal of the music in the Six Trio Sonatas is borrowed from preexisting compositions, in the spirit of the third cantata cycle. The second movement of the Sonata No. 3 in D Minor is derived from a lost instrumental trio (which later served as the model for the middle movement of the Concerto in A Minor for Violin, Flute, and Harpsichord, BWV 1044), and the first movement of the Sonata No. 4 in E Minor stems from the Sinfonia to Part II of Cantata 76, *Die Himmel erzählen die Ehre Gottes,* of 1723. In addition, there are early versions of the first movement of Sonata No. 3, the second movement of Sonata No. 4, and the second movement of Sonata No. 5 in C Major, suggesting that this music, too, was recycled from earlier scores.

Still, the progressive style of the trio sonatas leads one to believe that much of the remaining music is new, especially that of Sonata No. 1 in E-Flat Major and Sonata No. 6 in G Major, the most modern of the works. Thus the Six Trio Sonatas appear to be a tasteful blend of old music arranged from preexisting compositions and new music written just for the collection. This, too, mirrors the eclectic nature of the third cantata cycle and foreshadows by a decade Bach's approach in Book 2 of the Well-Tempered Clavier.

A seventh work, the Trio Sonata in G Major, BWV 1027a (PGM 115), provides a fascinating glimpse into Bach's organ-composition workshop of the time. During his Cöthen years it seems, Bach composed a four-movement trio sonata for two violins and continuo. At

Figure 10-2. J. S. Bach, Six Trio Sonatas for Organ, BWV 525–530, First page of Sonata No. 1 in E-Flat Major. Autograph manuscript (Berlin State Library, *P 271*).

a later point, probably during his Leipzig years, in the 1730s, as Director of the University Collegium Musicum ensemble, he rearranged the music, first as the Sonata for Two Flutes and Continuo, BWV 1039, and then as the Sonata for Viola da Gamba and Harpsichord, BWV 1027. But Bach, or possibly his students, also arranged the first, second, and fourth movements of the music for organ, in the manner of the Six Trio Sonatas. Joined with a transcription of the third movement made in recent times by Russell Stinson for PGM 115, the arrangements make an impressive four-movement trio sonata.

The first movement, an imitative Adagio (Sampler CD 2, track 15), could be transferred to the organ almost without change, since the treble parts serve nicely as keyboard figures and the continuo bass line can be assigned to the pedal with only slight modification, mainly to avoid the note d', which was not found on the pedalboard of the organ in question (Example 10-1, a-b; CD: 0:00). The sustained quality of the organ also imitates well the sustained tone of two flutes—a feature that would have been even more pronounced in Bach's time, when the hand-pumping of the organ simulated the uneven breathing of human lungs.

The second movement, Allegro ma non tanto, reflects the imitative style of Italian trio sonata writing. Here Bach brings back the principal theme toward the end almost in the manner of the recapitulation of the later Classical sonata form. The third movement, Andante, is a languid duet for the two upper voices over a slowly descending line. The music is reminiscent of a lyrical pastoral.

The final movement is a vigorous fugue-like piece (Sampler CD 2, track 16). It is marked Presto in the flute sonata and Allegro moderato in the gamba sonata but carries no tempo marking in the organ version—suggesting perhaps a straightforward Allegro. Bach (or his student transcriber) was compelled to make a number of changes in the bass line to accommodate the limitations of pedal playing. This can be seen toward the end of the movement, where the scalar notes of the continuo line in the two-flute sonata are transformed into chordal figures that can be performed more readily by the feet (Example 10-2, a-b; CD: 2:05).

The Trio Sonata in G Major illustrates the parody process and underscores the remarkable flexibility of late-Baroque idioms. Music for two violins and continuo could serve as the basis for works for two flutes and continuo, gamba and obbligato harpsichord, and organ with two manuals and pedal. The organ version is not "original" in the Beethovenian sense of a new creation. But the changes that were made to the score in the course of adopting the music to the organ gave it new life. One must grant creativity to the arranger for envisioning the possibilities inherent in recycling the music in a new guise.

The Collegium Musicum Works of the 1730s

In the spring of 1729, shortly after completing the Six Trio Sonatas, Bach assumed the directorship of the University Collegium Musicum ensemble in Leipzig. There was no precedent for this move, and it represented a remarkable career change for the forty-four-year-old composer. None of Bach's cantorial predecessors had shown any interest in the group, which consisted of amateur student performers who convened weekly in Gottfried Zimmermann's Coffee House (in the winter) or Coffee Garden (in the summer) for a sort of "musical seminar" before an audience of coffee-drinking, tobacco-smoking "cavaliers et dames." By this time, Bach had completed the bulk of the five annual cantata cycles. The Collegium directorship appears to have represented a new artistic challenge.

Bach directed the Collegium ensemble from 1729 to 1737, and then again from 1739 to 1742 or so. The weekly concerts were two hours long (in the winter they took place on Fridays from 8 to 10 P.M.; in the summer they took place on Wednesdays from 4 to 6 P.M., and during the annual Leipzig trade fairs (St. Michael's, New Year's, and Easter) they occurred

Example 10-1. a) Bach: Sonata in G Major for Two Flutes and Continuo, BWV 1039, movement 1, mm. 1–3; b) Bach: Trio Sonata in G Major for Organ, BWV 1027a, movement 1, mm. 1–3 (from Stinson 1992, 3).

Example 10-2. a) Bach: Sonata in G Major for Two Flutes and Continuo, BWV 1039, movement 4, mm. 88–91; b) Bach: Trio Sonata in G Major for Organ, BWV 1027a, movement 4, mm. 88–91 (from Stinson 1992, 17).

twice a week. The trade fair concerts seem to have featured special music with trumpets and drums and other festive forces. As far as we can tell, the Collegium concerts were reading sessions, during which the performers played through the music *a prima vista*—that is, for the first time. In addition to the students from the University, the ensemble included the professional Town Pipers and Art Fiddlers, members of Bach's family and circle of students, and visiting guest musicians from Dresden, Berlin, and elsewhere.

According to several eyewitnesses, the Collegium ensemble contained forty-to-fifty performers, and there can be no doubt that Bach found the large size of the group attractive. His ensemble in Cöthen had been much smaller, and the more expansive forces of the Collegium group gave him the opportunity to return to instrumental genres such as the French overture (see Chapter 5) and Italian concerto grosso and solo concerto (see Chapter 3) and explore them afresh. The compositional demands on Bach during the Collegium years were possibly even greater than they had been during the period of intense cantata composition (Stauffer 2007). When Bach focused on cantata writing in the 1720s, he was responsible for supplying one half-hour of music per week. As Collegium director in the 1730s, he was obligated to provide two hours of music per week (and four hours during the trade fairs).

To meet the new demands, Bach turned to a wide variety of music. The programs included fashionable works by contemporary composers—concertos by Giovanni Legrenzi, orchestral overtures by Bach's cousin Johann Bernhard Bach (in a parallel to using the cantatas by his cousin Johann Ludwig Bach), secular cantatas by Nicholas Porpora, and other pieces. But for the most part Bach seems to have used his own music, including keyboard and lute pieces, chamber duets and trios, large ensemble works, and secular cantatas. And for the bulk of this music he borrowed from earlier compositions on a grand scale.

This can be observed in Book 2 of the Well-Tempered Clavier, which Bach completed around 1742 but compiled earlier, during the Collegium years. Unlike Book 1, which is handed down in a reference-book-like format (which may or may not have been bound in Bach's day), Book 2 is transmitted as a series of independent pages in orchestral-sheet format, each containing a prelude on one side and a fugue on the other. This made for practical page turning in performance, which would have been necessary in the Collegium concerts.

For the music of Book 2, Bach turned to a core group of five prelude-and-fughetta pairs (BWV 870a and BWV 899–902), written in the 1720s or even earlier, and four fughettas that were preserved in a manuscript written by his student Johann Friedrich Agricola. Bach expanded, filled in, and refined these pieces to produce larger, more mature works. He added fugues to the four independent fughettas and transposed the music where necessary to fit the encompassing key scheme of the Well-Tempered Clavier project. For instance, Bach transformed the Fughetta in F Major, BWV 901/1, of twenty-four measures length, into the Fugue in A-Flat Major, BWV 886/2, of fifty measures length. After converting the prelude-and-fughetta pairs, the four fughettas, and other pieces, he added a brilliant series of new works to fill in the gaps.

The result was a heterogeneous blend of old and new that gives Book 2 of the Well-Tempered Clavier a very different character from that of Book 1, which despite its variety is more uniform in nature. This blend hints at a new form of "originality" in Bach's late works: early and late styles and old and new music are woven together to produce a rich, seamless fabric.

The chamber works that Bach used for the Collegium performances display a similar gathering process. They include sonatas for flute and continuo or obbligato harpsichord, sonatas for gamba and obbligato harpsichord, and a series of miscellaneous pieces for lute. Many of these pieces, too, are reworkings of earlier compositions. The well-known Sonata in B Minor for Flute and Harpsichord, BWV 1030, appears to be the rearrangement of a Sonata in G Minor for Oboe and Harpsichord, probably from Cöthen. The Sonata in G Major for Gamba and Harpsichord, BWV 1027, is a thorough reworking of the Sonata in G Major for Two Flutes and Continuo, BWV 1039, as we have mentioned. Among the lute works, the Suite in G Minor, BWV 995, is a polyphonic arrangement of the Suite in C Minor for Cello, BWV 1011, and the Fugue in G Minor, BWV 1000, is derived from the fugue of the Sonata in G Minor for Unaccompanied Violin, BWV 1001. The full extent of borrowing is surely much greater than this: One suspects that there are many other models from Cöthen that are now lost.

Viewed as a whole, the chamber works show a marked tendency toward the use of obbligato harpsichord rather than continuo. In many works the keyboard no longer stands in the background in the continuo group, providing a bass line and filling in chords, but rather emerges as an equal participant with the solo melody instrument (or instruments), providing a bass line in traditional fashion but now also adding an obbligato right-hand line. In such works, the cello that is normally found in the continuo group is dropped from the ensemble, setting the stage for the true piano duets and trios of the Classical Era. This "keyboardization" may stand behind Bach's extensive use of preexisting material. Drawing from old music allowed him to focus sharply and efficiently on the invention of a new genre, the sonata with obbligato harpsichord, without having to start from scratch.

Bach's infatuation with parody and solo harpsichord is nowhere clearer than in the large body of concertos for one, two, three, and four harpsichords written for the Collegium ensemble. Bach had planted the seeds for the keyboard concerto a decade earlier in Cöthen, where he composed Brandenburg Concerto No. 5 in D Major, BWV 1050, the first "keyboard concerto" on record. The fourteen Collegium works—eight concertos for one harpsichord, three concertos for two harpsichords, two concertos for three harpsichords, and one concerto for four harpsichords—bring the Cöthen experiment to full fruition. The concertos represented a great novelty, and it is evident that Bach and his host Gottfried Zimmermann must have viewed the repertory as an attractive draw for Leipzig citizens and trade-fair visitors. As Collegium director, Bach had a small army of gifted harpsichordists at his disposal. In addition to himself, he could turn to his sons as well as a sizable group of talented keyboard students. All were trained in his rigorous school of harpsichord and organ playing. With the harpsichord concertos, especially, Bach combined practical considerations—the availability of a pool of skilled players—with artistic invention. And the springboard for the new genre was Bach's approach to recycling.

The harpsichord concertos appear to be derived almost completely from earlier compositions, mostly concertos for violin, oboe, and other instruments that were completed during the Cöthen years. The eight solo concertos (the last work, the Concerto No. 8 in D Minor, BWV 1059, is a fragment) seem to have composed one by one between 1729 and 1738, when Bach gathered them into a single manuscript. The multiple harpsichord concertos also appear to have been written little by little, but they were never assembled into a collection.

Extant models have been preserved or can be proposed for all of the Collegium harpsichord concertos. In some cases the original model has been lost, but parallel "sister" versions of the music have been handed down in the organ obbligato movements from the third cantata cycle (Table 10-1).

When creating harpsichord concertos from violin concertos, Bach normally transposed the music down a step, to bring it into better range for his keyboard instruments (which normally went no higher than c''' or d'''). The great challenge in creating the harpsichord concertos was to create a new solo part for the keyboard instrument, complete with its own bass line. In a number of the earliest works (Concerto No. 7 and Concerto No. 8 for one harpsichord, which were actually written before Concerto Nos. 1–6), Bach transferred the original solo part to the right hand of the harpsichord and the original continuo part to the left hand, much as he had done in the 1726 with the obbligato organ arrangements for his cantatas. In Concerto No. 1 for one harpsichord, he preserved this procedure but embellished considerably both the bass and treble lines. In Concerto Nos. 2–5 he became more adventurous, rewriting the bass line of the harpsichord to produce a part that has great independence from the continuo line. In so doing, he fully emancipated the harpsichord from the continuo group and set the stage for the Classical and Romantic protagonists of the piano concertos of Mozart, Beethoven, Mendelssohn, and Brahms.

Concerto No. 6 in F Major is the most adventurous in this regard. In transcribing the music from Brandenburg Concerto No. 4 in G Major, Bach completely reconsidered the relationship between the harpsichord and the two recorders. The Brandenburg version featured a solo group consisting of three fairly equal members: violin and two recorders. In the revised version, the harpsichord basks fully in the limelight, with increased virtuoso writing, and the two recorders stand to a greater extent in the background, with the strings and continuo. Bach achieved this by completely rescoring the piece, changing the balance among the three solo instruments and between the solo instruments and the tutti ensemble.

Work	Model
Table 10-1. Borrowing in Bach's Harpsichord Concertos	

Work	Model
Concertos for One Harpsichord	
Concerto No. 1 in D Minor, BWV 1052	Lost concerto for violin; music also appears in Cantatas 146 and 188
Concerto No. 2 in E Major, BWV 1053	Lost concerto for oboe; music also appears in Cantatas 49 and 169
Concerto No. 3 in D Major, BWV 1054	Concerto in E Major for Violin, BWV 1042
Concerto No. 4 in A Major, BWV 1055	Lost concerto for oboe d'amore
Concerto No. 5 in F Minor, BWV 1056	Lost concerto for oboe; movement 2 derived from Cantata 156
Concerto No. 6 in F Major, BWV 1057	Brandenburg Concerto No. 4 in G Major, BWV 1049
Concerto No. 7 in G Minor, BWV 1058	Concerto in A Minor for Violin, BWV 1041
Concerto No. 8 in D Minor, BWV 1059 (fragment)	Lost concerto for oboe; music also appears in Cantata 35
Concertos for Two Harpsichords	
Concerto in C Minor, BWV 1060	Lost concerto for oboe and violin
Concerto in C Major, BWV 1061	Concerto in C Major for Two Unaccompanied Harpsichords, BWV 1061a
Concerto in C Minor, BWV 1062	Concerto in D Minor for Two Violins, BWV 1043
Concertos for Three Harpsichords	
Concerto in D Minor, BWV 1063	Source uncertain
Concerto in C Major, BWV 1064	Lost concerto for three violins
Concerto for Four Harpsichords	
Concerto in A Minor, BWV 1065	Vivaldi: Concerto in B Minor for Four Violins, opus 3, no. 10

The writing at m. 141 of the first movement illustrates this well. In the Brandenburg version, the violin has single-line arpeggiated figures against a sustained note and an arpeggio, in a higher range, in the recorders. The violin then continues the single line alone (Example 10-3).

In the revised version, the flute parts remain the same (though now transposed down to F major), but the harpsichord now sounds *above* the recorders, and in parallel thirds, and as it continues on alone, it presents more animated, thirty-second-note arpeggios as well as

Example 10-3. Bach: Brandenburg Concerto No. 4 in G Major, BWV 1049, movement 1, mm. 241–245.

Example 10-4. Bach: Concerto No. 6 in F Major for Harpsichord and Two Recorders, BWV 1057, movement 1, mm. 241–245.

sixteenth-note figures (Example 10-4). In this way, and in many others, Bach manages to transform the piece from a group concerto to a solo work.

Such transmogrifications, carried out in the parody process, are equally fateful in the Concerto in A Minor for Four Harpsichords, BWV 1065. Here Bach took as his model the music of Vivaldi, whose *Estro armonico* (Harmonic Whim) collection of violin concertos of c. 1712 Bach had used in Weimar for a series of organ transcriptions. For the A-Minor Concerto, Bach took Vivaldi's Concerto in B Minor for Four Violins and transformed it into an extravaganza work for four harpsichords. He probably earmarked the four solo parts for himself and his three oldest sons, Wilhelm Friedemann (1710–1784), Carl Philipp Emanuel (1714–1788), and Johann Gottfried Bernhard (1715–1739), who were all budding keyboard players at the time. This distribution seems to be reflected in the parts, since harpsichord 1 is noticeably more virtuosic than harpsichords 2, 3, and 4 and requires a larger instrument with a wider keyboard compass.

In transforming the solo parts from four violins to four harpsichords, Bach showed special concern for creating new bass parts for the harpsichords that would preserve the independent character of each instrument. His inventiveness carries contrapuntal composition to new heights, as can be seen in the cadential measures of the opening tutti theme of movement 3, where each of the harpsichords has an independent bass line, none of which coincides with the original bass line of the continuo. In a sense, Bach has created four new bass lines that can be combined in perfect counterpoint with each other and Vivaldi's original bass part, which is preserved in the string band. But equally impressive is the way Bach fashioned new contrapuntal lines for the upper voices, producing a denser, more complex texture than Vivaldi's simpler, repeated-note chords (Examples 10-5 and 10-6).

Although the Concerto in A Minor for Four Harpsichords is not an "original" work—the fundamental text stems from Vivaldi—it illustrates the "new" nature of Bach's recycled pieces. As Walter Blankenburg once observed, in such refashionings, Bach seems to have awakened sleeping potential that resided in scores written at an earlier time (Blankenburg 1974, 97).

It is also interesting to note that such music can be effectively transcribed to the key-

Example 10-5. Vivaldi: Concerto in B Minor for Four Violins and Strings, movement 3, mm. 19–22.

board, despite its complexity. The organist Joan Lippincott has recently arranged the A-Minor Concerto for solo organ with commendable success, taking the harpsichord and string parts and transferring them to two manuals and pedal (compare movement 3, Allegro, on Sampler CD 2, track 17).

During his last years, Bach returned to organ music for a final time. In the "Great Eighteen" Collection of chorale preludes he went back to Weimar works, revising them and setting them in good order. In *An Wasserflüssen Babylon*, BWV 653b (By the Waters of Babylon; Sampler CD 2, track 18), he thinned out the five-part texture, dropping the virtuosic but old-fashioned double pedal in favor or a more up-to-date single-line part.

The Late Vocal Works

Bach's pattern of borrowing is equally prevalent in his vocal works of the 1730s and 1740s. The music for the St. Mark Passion of 1731, Bach's last Passion setting and his first sizable sacred vocal work after turning his back on cantata writing in 1729, has not survived. But its published libretto suggests that it was a large-scale parody undertaking. To judge from its text, five movements were drawn from Cantata 198, *Laß, Fürstin, laß noch einen Strahl*, the so-called "Trauer-Ode," composed in 1727 for the Leipzig memorial service for Christiane Eberhardine, Electress of Saxony. The listing of the Passion in the Breitkopf music catalog of

Example 10-6. Bach: Concerto in A Minor for Four Harpsichords and Strings, BWV 1065, movement 3, mm. 19–22.

1764 also shows that it had the same scoring as the "Trauer-Ode": four-part chorus, two flutes, two oboes, gambas, strings, and continuo. Other movements of the Passion appear to be reworkings of pieces from Cantata 54, *Wiederstehe doch der Sünde,* Cantata 204, *Ich bin in mir vergnügt,* and possibly Cantata 120a, *Herr Gott, Beherrscher aller Dinge.* Only the recitatives, narrative choruses, and chorales appear to have been newly composed.

The Christmas Oratorio, written for the holiday season of 1734–1735, is also based largely on parody technique. Almost all the arias and choruses from Parts I to V are drawn from three secular works, Cantata 213, *Lasst uns sorgen, lasst uns wachen* ("Hercules at the

Crossroads"), Cantata 214, *Tönet, ihr Pauken!,* and Cantata 215, *Preise dein Glücke,* composed in 1733 and 1734. The close chronological proximity of the secular works to the Christmas Oratorio and the extensive—indeed, almost exhaustive—nature of the parodying has led scholars to suspect that Bach may have written the three secular cantatas with an eye to re-working the music in sacred form soon thereafter. Part VI of the Oratorio appears to be the parody of a now-lost cantata.

Bach's borrowing in the Christmas Oratorio occasionally shows the shortcomings of the parody procedure. The extended vocal echoes in the aria "Flößt, mein Heiland, flößt dein Name" (Let Flow, My Savior, Let Flow Thy Name) can be explained only by the parody model, "Treues Echo, dieser Orten" (Trusted Echo of This Region), from the Hercules cantata. And the timpani solo that opens Part I, "Jauchzet, frohlocket, auf, preiset die Tage" (Shout for Joy, Rejoice, Rise and Praise the Day) lacks the textual allusion it enjoyed in Cantata 214, "Tönet, ihr Pauken!" (Sound Forth, You Timpini!). But the ingenious transformation of the aria "Schlafe, mein Liebster, und pflege der Ruh" (Sleep, My Dear One, and Care for Your Rest), in which Hercules is seduced by Pleasure, into a cradle song for the infant Jesus, "Schlafe, mein Liebster, genieße der Ruh" (Sleep, My Dear One, Enjoy Your Rest), and other adaptations demonstrate the skill with which Bach recycled the earlier music.

The four short Masses, BWV 233–236, of c. 1737 to c. 1747 also consist of parody material. Of the twenty-four movements, twenty stem from extant works, and it is presumed that the remaining four movements are derived from cantata music now lost. Bach may have composed the four short Masses for the Dresden court, as part of his obligations as "Royal Polish and Electoral Saxon Court Composer," a title he gained in the fall of 1736. If so, he certainly would have taken his submissions to the court seriously, and he must have viewed parody technique as a worthy method of producing appropriate musical offerings for the Saxon Elector, August II.

Finally, we must consider the B-Minor Mass. Compiled during the last three years of Bach's life, the work stands as one of the great achievements of Western music, transcending the traditional boundaries of Lutheran and Catholic practice to become a "universal Mass," in the sense of Beethoven's *Missa solemnis* (with which, as we noted earlier, it was revived in the nineteenth century). When Bach decided to write the B-Minor Mass, seemingly during the summer of 1748, he began by recycling without significant change the *Missa,* or Kyrie and Gloria, that he had composed in 1733 for submission to the Dresden court. To this he added newly compiled Credo, Sanctus, and Agnus Dei portions to complete the large-scale work (Figure 10-3).

As with the St. Mark Passion, Bach retained the ambitious scoring of the parody model, the *Missa,* for portions of the "new" work, the Credo and Agnus Dei: five-part chorus (the standard for a festive Dresden Mass), three trumpets and timpani, two oboes, two flutes, strings, and continuo. For the Sanctus, he expanded the chorus to eight parts (six voice parts for the "Sanctus" and two four-part choruses for the polychoral "Osanna") and added an alto oboe to the orchestra. The change in forces reflects the fact that Bach borrowed preexisting music for the Sanctus, music calling for the larger chorus and orchestra. Parody models can be pinpointed or proposed for thirteen of the B-Minor Mass's twenty-seven movements (Table 10-2), but it is likely that all the music in the work, aside from the introduction to the opening "Kyrie" and the bridge between the "Confiteor" and "Et expecto" movements, is derived from preexisting scores (Stauffer 2003, 49).

Bach's revision of the earlier music is remarkable not only for its artful details, such as the instrumental rescoring in the "Patrem Omnipotentem" and "Crucifixus" movements, but also for the boldness of its wholesale carpentry. In three instances, the "Crucifixus," "Os-

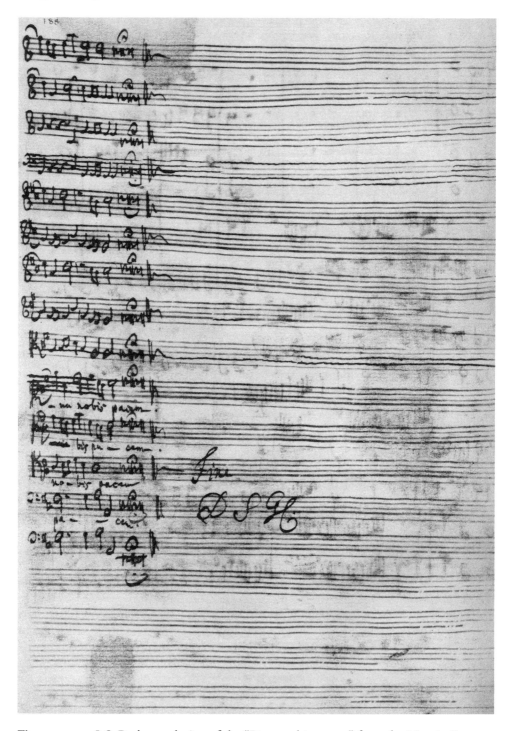

Figure 10-3. J. S. Bach, conclusion of the "Dona nobis pacem" from the Mass in B Minor. Autograph manuscript (Berlin State Library, *P 180*).

Table 10-2.
Borrowing in Bach's B-Minor Mass

Movement	Model
"Gratias agimus tibi"	Chorus "Wir danken dir, Gott," BWV 29/2 (or from an earlier common model)
"Domine Deus"	Probably from duet "Ich will rühmen" from lost Cantata 193a
"Qui tollis"	The A section of the chorus "Schauet doch, und sehet" from Cantata 46
"Credo in unum Deum"	Chorus "Credo in unum Deum" in G Major
"Patrem Omnipotenem"	Chorus "Gott, wie dein Name" from Cantata 171
"Et in unum Dominum"	Lost duet, considered for the aria "Ich bin deine" from Cantata 213
"Crucifixus"	The A section of the chorus "Weinen, Klagen, Sorgen, Zagen" from Cantata 12
"Et resurrexit"	Probably from the A section of chorus "Entfernet euch, ihr heitern Sterne" from lost Cantata BWV Anh. 9/1
"Et expecto"	Chorus "Jauchzet, ihr erfreuten Stimmen" from Cantata 120
"Sanctus"	Sanctus setting, BWV 232^{III}, of 1724
"Osanna"	The A section of the chorus "Preise dein Glücke" from Cantata 215 (or from an earlier common model)
"Agnus Dei"	Aria "Ach, bleibe doch" from Cantata 11 (or from an earlier common model)
"Dona nobis pacem"	Chorus "Gratias agimus tibi" from Gloria

anna," and "Et resurrexit," Bach excised the A sections from A–B–A da capo forms to produce highly concise, complete movements. Although the model is lost, the "Benedictus" is undoubtedly the A section of a vanished da capo piece as well. These "torsos" work well within the B-Minor Mass, which was cast in the multimovement Neapolitan Mass format that was in use at the Dresden court. But the torsos also underline Bach's willingness to take extreme measures—the wresting of material from a carefully shaped form—to create a new composition. Most of the music for the B-Minor Mass stems from Leipzig cantatas, sacred and secular. That he could take music of such high quality and lift it to further heights is a supreme testament to his creative powers.

In this sense, the B-Minor Mass may have been even more challenging to compose than Beethoven's *Missa solemnis,* for it involved the reshaping and further polishing of music that was already highly refined. Like Bach's other parody works, the B-Minor Mass displays extraordinarily reinvention—reinvention that broadened the bounds of originality.

BIBLIOGRAPHY

Blankenburg, Walter. 1974. *Einführung in Bachs h-moll-Messe.* Kassel: Bärenreiter.

David, Hans T., Arthur Mendel, and Christoph Wolff, eds. 1998. *The New Bach Reader.* New York: W. W. Norton.

Finscher, Ludwig. 1969. "Zum Parodieproblem bei Bach." In *Bach Interpretationen,* ed. Martin Geck, 94–105. Göttingen: Vandenhoeck & Ruprecht.

Levy, David. 2003. *Beethoven: The Ninth Symphony.* Rev. ed. New Haven, Conn.: Yale University Press.

Mann, Alfred. 1989. "Bach's Parody Technique and Its Frontiers." In *Bach Studies,* ed. Don O. Franklin, 115–124. Cambridge: Cambridge University Press.

Marshall, Robert L. 1972. *The Compositional Process of J. S. Bach: A Study of the Autograph Scores of the Vocal Works.* Princeton, N.J.: Princeton University Press.

Melamed, Daniel R. 1999. "Parody." In *J. S. Bach,* ed. Malcolm Boyd, 356–357. The Oxford Composer Companions. Oxford: Oxford University Press.

Neumann, Werner. 1965. "Über Ausmaß und Wesen des Bachschen Parodieverfahrens." *Bach-Jahrbuch* 51: 63–85.

Schering, Arnold. 1921. "Über Bachs Parodieverfahren." *Bach-Jahrbuch* 18: 49–95.

Schulze, Hans-Joachim. 1989. "The Parody Process in Bach's Music: An Old Problem Reconsidered." *Bach: The Journal of the Riemenschneider Bach Institute* 20, no. 1: 7–21.

Smend, Friedrich. 1985. *Bach in Köthen,* trans. John Page. St. Louis: Concordia Publishing House.

Stauffer, George B. 1998. "Die Sinfonien." In *Die Welt der Bach Kantaten,* ed. Christoph Wolff, vol. 3, 157–175. Kassel: Metzler/Bärenreiter.

———. 2003. *Bach: The Mass in B Minor.* New Haven, Conn.: Yale University Press.

———. 2007. "Music for 'Cavaliers et Dames': Bach and the Repertoire Performed by His Collegium Musicum." In *About Bach,* ed. Gregory G. Butler, Mary Dalton Greer, and George B. Stauffer, in press. Urbana: University of Illinois Press.

Stinson, Russell. 1989. *The Bach Manuscripts of Johann Peter Kellner and His Circle: A Case Study in Reception History.* Durham, N.C.: Duke University Press.

———, ed. 1992. *Keyboard Transcriptions from the Bach Circle.* Madison, Wis.: A-R Editions.

Wolff, Christoph. 1991. "The Agnus Dei of the B Minor Mass: Parody and New Composition Reconciled." In *Bach: Essays on His Life and Music,* 332–339. Cambridge, Mass.: Harvard University Press.

———. 2000. *Johann Sebastian Bach: The Learned Musician.* New York: W. W. Norton.

CHAPTER ELEVEN

Bach's St. John Passion: Can We Really Still Hear the Work—and Which One?

Daniel R. Melamed

THE WITTIEST REMARK IN THE ARGUMENTS about the performance of early music is attributed to the conductor and Bach specialist Helmuth Rilling, who reportedly once said that it was all very well that we have original instruments and original performance practices, but unfortunate that we have no original listeners. Rilling had a fat target: the often overblown claims that "authentic" performances present pieces "as the composer intended them" or "as they originally sounded." The technical skills and historical awareness of players and singers have come a long way since the rise of early music in the 1960s and 1970s, but today the word "authentic" is often viewed with suspicion and even a little embarrassment, and the claims made for period-instrument or historically informed performances (note the change in terminology) tend to be more modest than they once were.

Moreover, with early- and modern-instrument performances sounding more and more alike, and with the advent of superstar period-instrument conductors and bands, the sound of Baroque instruments is a little less alien—the personal threat many people felt from the performance practice movement has receded. What little steam is left in the debate is largely concentrated on the issue of how close to the present these "early" instruments and practices will creep (Brahms? Mahler? Stravinsky?).

But Rilling's comment, defused as it might be, still raises an extremely important question: Is it ever possible for us to hear a centuries-old piece of music as it was heard when it was composed? To put it another way, when we listen to a Bach Passion, is it really the same piece Bach wrote in the early eighteenth century? This is an extreme way of expressing the problem, to be sure, but the question is legitimate and the answer probably is "No": we hear a different piece today than Bach's first listeners did. Even leaving aside the use of modern instruments, voices, and performance techniques, our backgrounds and experiences (musical and otherwise) are so different and the context of performances so changed that we can never hear a piece as an early listener would have. This is a potentially upsetting result, and we have to ask whether this makes any difference in our enjoyment of a composition.

Performing Forces

We can start, of course, with modern versus eighteenth-century performing forces. First of all, our choruses are usually bigger: the sixty or so singers used in a typical performance today are perfectly ordinary for a twenty-first-century choir, but such an ensemble little resembles Bach's. The original sources make it clear to many interpreters that Bach reckoned with one principal singer for each line—meaning four with four additional voices for the St. John Passion, and eight for the St. Matthew Passion—plus a few extras to sing certain small dramatic roles and sometimes certain chorale melodies. Even those who doubt the validity of this interpretation (largely, it seems, for ideological reasons) usually suggest an outer limit of about twelve singers for the St. John Passion and twenty-four for the St. Matthew.

Beyond the difference in size this represents, the voices in typical modern performances are different, too. Leaving aside imponderables like changes in physiology caused by climate, health, nutrition, and the like, Bach's singers were all male: boys sang the soprano and alto parts (some altos might be male falsettists), both in the chorus and in solo numbers. That difference alone affects the color and strength of the voices and the balance within the ensemble, compared to today's typical practice of employing women on the upper parts. We do not know much about Bach's vocal coaching and rehearsals, but we can be sure that musical training in the early eighteenth century was different from that today, and that ideals of vocal production were also different. Overall, the sound of the vocal ensemble was certainly not identical to that of today's typical modern choir.

Instruments were different, too. Strings were gut, violin necks were shorter, flutes were wooden, oboes included now-obsolete family members, and organs were hand-pumped tracker-action instruments, to say nothing of the substantial differences in brass instruments (not called for in Passion settings, however). Playing techniques also differed in matters of phrasing, articulation, bowing, breathing, ornamentation, vibrato, fingering, tuning, temperament, and the like.

Opinions vary on the size of Bach's instrumental ensemble, just as they do on his vocal ensemble, but today's orchestras, with their typical multiple doublings of string parts, far exceed the forces Bach used. This means a different balance between strings on the one hand and woodwinds and continuo on the other. Overall, with a larger orchestra and larger chorus, a typical modern performance involves many more musicians than even the most generous estimates of Bach's own. This can lead, in turn, to a view of Bach's Passions as monumental works deserving a suitably powerful presentation. This is not necessarily wrong, but it is not the early eighteenth-century view of the pieces.

And there are still more differences: In Bach's time, there were two (or three) different pitch standards in use, neither of which conforms to our concert pitch of A = 440 Hz, itself not a universally observed standard. And even if we attempt to use "Baroque pitch" (a dubious concept), we are still in trouble, because almost every one of Bach's Leipzig church performances used two pitch standards simultaneously with the result that some instrumentalists played from parts in different keys—not just *notated* differently, like modern clarinet and horn parts, but actually *in* different keys. This led to combinations of keys and sounding pitches that we cannot reproduce today on modern instruments and that until recently have presented problems even with copies of older instruments.

I could go on with contrasts in performance practice: players generally stood, not sat; everyone, including the singers, read from individual parts, not scores (this certainly changes a singer's view of the piece); performances were often led from the organ and first violin, not from a conductor's podium (though a work like a Passion setting is likely to have been an exception); Bach's singers were almost all from Saxony and Thuringia, and so spoke a dialect very different from the modern High German one typically hears today. The chorus and orchestra were a motley group, mixing schoolboys, graduates, university students, town musicians, Bach family members, and private music students. At the very least, this probably meant that they were underrehearsed. We should not underestimate their skills, but the technical standards of performance were probably very different from the one we have adopted in our own time, an age saturated with note-perfect recordings assembled from multiple takes made in a studio.

Modern performances also tend to deploy their forces according to practices that differ from Bach's. Today, soloists and choir members are distinct people, but all the evidence suggests that Bach's aria singers (the "soloists") *were* the chorus. Instrumentalists' duties are determined today by modern custom and sometimes by union rules, but Bach's practices were often different from ours. For example, the accompanied recitative "O Schmerz" (O Anguish) in the St. Matthew Passion calls for recorders. Today these parts are likely to be played by the two flute players assigned to Chorus 1 (for which union musicians get a so-called doubling fee for playing a second instrument). But in Bach's original performing parts the recorder lines are in the violin parts, clearly indicating that they were played by the violinists. This might not seem like a big deal until one asks how many violinists Bach used. Given that the recorder parts are in both copies of each of the two violin parts in Chorus 1, it looks as though Bach expected the recorder lines to be played by two people each. In sum, it becomes clear that the way we think about performing forces is different, and that this can lead to differences both in conception and in practice.

Another physical aspect of a Passion performance that is substantially different today concerns the kind of building in which it usually takes place. Modern concert halls are very different places from either the St. Thomas Church or the St. Nicholas Church in Leipzig, the two houses of worship in which Bach's annual Passion performances alternated. Concert halls are typically deeper and almost always wider than these churches (St. Thomas is substantially narrower than St. Nicholas, and the St. Matthew Passion, at least, appears to have been designed for St. Thomas). More importantly, a concert hall is laid out completely differently. We often hear Bach's Passions performed from an elevated stage to an audience sitting in seats facing the performers. In the Leipzig churches, the performers would have been in the organ loft and musicians' galleries above and behind (or to the side) of the listeners. As a result, most people would have had their backs or sides to the singers and instrumentalists (St. Thomas has been remodeled since Bach's time, so its layout is different today). Even modern performances in churches typically place the performers at the front of the nave, directly before most of the audience and in full view, just as in a concert hall. The sound is likely to be different in such an arrangement, but so, too, is the focus on the performers.

Most of these differences are physical and practical, and most could be—and in recent years have been—overcome. We can listen to a performance of a Bach Passion in the St. Thomas Church or St. Nicholas Church in Leipzig performed by a small choir of men and boys and an orchestra playing eighteenth-century instruments, all well schooled in Baroque performance practice. Such a rendition can be instructive and beautiful, but even though it arguably comes closer to reproducing the physical conditions of Bach's time than many modern performances, it does not solve our problem. In an important way it does no better in reproducing the experience of hearing the piece in Bach's time than does a typical modern performance because the real obstacles to hearing as Bach's listeners did have nothing to do with instruments or performance practices or buildings. Instead, they concern the music's liturgical context and significance and the experience, knowledge, assumptions, and conventions that listeners brought to a performance.

Liturgical Context

Almost all modern performances of Bach Passions, even those around Holy Week and those that take place in churches, are concert presentations. In Bach's Leipzig, by contrast, the composition filled a specific liturgical requirement: the presentation of a musical Passion setting during Vespers on Good Friday. Beginning late in the cantorate of Bach's predecessor, Johann Kuhnau, the Passion took the form represented by Bach's settings. The context was a church service, not a concert, and the main point was the detailed and affective telling of the Passion story according to the words of one of the four Gospels, together with its enhancement by newly written words of commentary. It is possible, of course, that some eighteenth-century Leipzig citizens went to church just for the music, but at least in principle the liturgical context made for a very different kind of listening. Presumably the attentive listener was prepared to be moved by the story and instructed by the commentary that was added in the framing and interpolated movements.

The Passion's place in a liturgy had other consequences. For example, Bach's Passions are long—the St. Matthew Passion may be the longest nonstaged musical composition that modern audiences regularly sit through—but in Bach's time they were part of a service that was even longer. Aside from the Passion performance, the longest element of the service was a sermon, lasting more than an hour, that was preached between Parts I and II of the Passion. Modern audiences stretch their legs, use the rest room, and eat M&Ms for fortification between the parts of a Passion. Bach's listeners instead heard the themes of the story elaborated upon at length in the sermon, which was often based on a subject raised by the point in the narrative at which composer and librettist chose to end Part I (the capture of Jesus in the St. Matthew Passion; Peter's bemoaning of his act of betrayal in the St. John).

The service contained other music, as well, and the Passion was heard within its context. To cite one of the most striking examples, just after the Passion was performed the choir sang a Latin setting of Isaiah 57:1–2, "Ecce, quomodo moritur justus" (Behold, the Righteous Man Perishes) in a four-voice setting by Jacob Handl (known also as Gallus) widely published in Germany since the early seventeenth century. In the case of the St. Matthew Passion, this little work directly followed the final chorus "Wir setzen uns mit Tränen nieder" (We Sit Down with Tears). Today, that chorus is usually followed by silence, then applause and curtain calls. The thought of listening to still more music is usually inconceivable. But Bach's Passions were designed to be followed by "Ecce, quomodo moritur justus." Who among us has heard them this way, or notes the absence of this piece?

The Passion setting was also the first concerted music (that is, music using voices and independent instruments) the congregation had heard in a long time because the Leipzig churches observed a so-called *tempus clausum,* or closed period, during Lent, just as they did during Advent. No instrumental music was permitted from the beginning of Lent until Easter Sunday, with the exceptions of a Marian feast that occasionally fell in this time and the Good Friday Passion performance. So the congregation, having heard no cantatas, concerted Mass movements, or even organ music for a month, listened to the Passion after a long musical drought. (This meant that Easter was a particularly brilliant explosion of festive music, usually made even more striking by the inclusion of trumpets and drums in the instrumental ensemble.)

Today, by contrast, some listeners prepare for a Passion performance by listening to a recording of it beforehand, not to mention all the other music they probably encounter in the weeks before. In fact, in modern society it is hard, if not impossible, to go a day—never mind weeks—without being exposed to musical performances.

The liturgical context of Passion performances also points to other essential differences in the way a listener in Bach's time would have approached a musical setting. The Passion story and its messages were of the deepest significance in the Lutheran creed—indeed, the cross is arguably the central symbol in Martin Luther's theology. The biblical text and the commentary on it would have been a focus of the contemporary listener's engagement with a Bach Passion setting, perhaps well ahead of Bach's music. The ubiquitous presence of crucifixion and deposition scenes in contemporary art verifies that the story of Jesus's Passion, death, and resurrection held central significance for Bach's audience (Plate 21). The theologically well-informed listener would have been far more aware than today's typical listener of the interpretive themes that Bach and his librettists emphasized in their text and music, themes that presumably resonated with the topic of the preacher's sermon. Understanding these themes requires knowledge of early eighteenth-century theology that few concertgoers have today.

The Text

Bach's listeners would have been aided, of course, by the presentation of this material in their native language, whereas many listeners today do not understand German. They can always follow the text in a program—actually, so could those in Leipzig willing to pay for one of the printed librettos offered for sale—but most non-German speakers experience the work one step removed, because they must rely on a translation.

Even those who do read German have to face the additional obstacle of the Passion's old-fashioned and stylized language. A Passion libretto of Bach's type consists of three textual elements: (1) Gospel narrative sung by the Evangelist, various characters, and the chorus; (2) hymn stanzas (chorales), often chosen for their connection to the biblical text, inserted at important moments to reflect on the action; and (3) free poems presented mostly by soloists in recitatives and arias. (The opening and closing choruses of both of Bach's Passions are also poetic texts of this type. They are essentially arias for chorus.) The old-fashioned aspect of the text is not so much the biblical language, where most of us expect a kind of elegant archaism, but in the free poetry and to some extent in the chorale verses. Although no one spoke in the style of liturgical church poetry in everyday life in Leipzig in the early eighteenth century, this kind of language was the accepted ecclesiastical style of the time. The members of Bach's congregation were accustomed to it. Modern listeners are not. They have to contend with an archaic poetic style and the figurative distance it can create, a distance not completely made up by the familiarity of the biblical text.

The poetry in Bach's Passions is elaborate and highly stylized, and like all poetry and most theology, it is subject to fashion. In fact, changing taste in religious poetry is one of the reasons Bach's church cantatas and Passion settings ceased to be performed regularly a few years after his death. They were revived not by theologians in liturgical presentations (where their poetic language would have seemed embarrassing), but by musicians in concert performances (in the case of the St. Matthew Passion, by Felix Mendelssohn, in 1829). The Passion story continued to be sung in churches after Bach's death, but preferences in theology and language shifted to the point that his St. Matthew and St. John Passions became unusable.

The chorales in the Passion would also have been heard very differently by Bach's listeners, and not just for their language. The melodies and texts of these chorales were intimately familiar because they were regularly sung in church, and probably also in less formal devotions at home and elsewhere. It is more than likely Bach's Passions were not designed to have the congregation sing the chorales. The chorales in these works call for a different performance than the normal congregational hymn, using one or occasionally two stanzas whose text was carefully selected to complement particular moments in the story. Congregational hymnody, by contrast, involved the singing of every stanza of a hymn, one after the other. This kind of chorale performance is sometimes found in contemporary Passion settings, but not in Bach's works. Nevertheless, Bach's listeners, who knew and sang the chorales on other occasions, must have felt especially connected to the Passion presentation through the chorales in a way that most modern listeners do not.

One special feature of the chorale stanzas and aria texts in Bach's Passions (and in the St. Matthew Passion, in particular) must have strengthened their attraction to the contemporary listener: many of them are in the first person. This choice on the part of the librettist is meant not only to draw the hearer into the story but also to make a broad theological point, namely, the central importance of the individual's personal relationship to the Passion story in Lutheran theology. This should remind us of the larger difficulty for modern listeners: most have not been raised with the theological ideas Bach and his librettists emphasized in their Passion settings and so are bound to approach them differently. Even the listener who approaches the works today from the standpoint of faith almost certainly has a modern theological perspective rather than one from the eighteenth century. That does not render the work meaningless, of course—just different.

The Music

So far we have considered performing forces, the liturgical context, and the text of Bach's Passions but have not dealt with the music and the way we hear it compared to Bach's listeners. One might think that finally we have found common ground with them: Bach's music is universal, we are often told. But for several reasons that is not really so. In the realm of music, too, we must hear this piece differently from a listener in the eighteenth century because our musical experiences are both richer and poorer than those of Bach's audience.

Think first about the kind of work a Bach Passion represents. The modern term for this type of piece, which has an Evangelist narrator, characters, and interspersed arias and chorales, is "oratorio Passion," so called because its framework—narration by a Gospel voice—resembles that of a biblical oratorio. The reaction of Bach's listeners to an oratorio Passion, to the extent we can generalize, was probably complex. On the one hand, it was the kind of piece they grew accustomed to hearing in the main Leipzig churches and elsewhere, and thus it would have been familiar. On the other hand, the oratorio Passion was a relatively recent development, having been used in the principal Leipzig churches only since 1721, when it was introduced by Bach's predecessor Johann Kuhnau. In the 1720s, many (if not most) of the listeners to Bach's Passions would have considered the oratorio Passion fairly newfangled. We are in no position to appreciate the newness of this kind of piece because few other kinds of Passions—indeed, few Passions at all other than Bach's two surviving settings—have been much performed until very recently.

In addition, we also do not have the repertorial context for this piece that the average Leipzig listener might have had. Besides his own settings, Bach performed Passions by other composers in some years, exposing the congregations to a setting he attributed to Reinhard Keiser and to some music from a setting by George Frideric Handel. Bach's listeners had points of reference and comparison that most of us do not.

But however problematic our ignorance of other Passion settings might be, it is minor compared to the difficulties raised by our familiarity with other music. In the broadest sense we can never hear as Bach's listeners did because we have heard not only Bach and Handel and Vivaldi, but also Mozart and Beethoven and Wagner and Stravinsky and Cage, to say nothing of popular and vernacular music of this culture and others. We bring completely different ears to this music. We should remember that many people in Bach's time found his music strange, overly complex, and generally difficult. Our familiarity with his music (and with arguably much more difficult pieces) makes it harder to hear Bach that way today. Some thought Bach's musical style was out-of-date and old-fashioned; we recognize it as historical and belonging to another era—but that is a different reaction.

I can demonstrate the problem of our unfamiliarity with the musical context of Bach's Passions with an example. An oratorio Passion like Bach's works presents the Gospel narrative in speech-like recitative sung by an Evangelist and various characters (Jesus, Pilate, groups of witnesses, etc.) and interpolates extended moments of reflection and commentary in the form of hymn stanzas and free poetry. The narrative is set in a fairly graspable way that emphasizes the grammar and sense of the narrative, and in a musical style that shares features with traditional and musically simpler ways of singing biblical texts. The chorales are also in a recognizable musical style: they are mostly simple four-part syllabic arrangements with no independent instrumental parts. The chorale movements are prototypical hymn settings, in fact, and musically were probably the most familiar element to Bach's listeners.

But our reaction to the settings of the free poetry is certainly different from that of an early listener. The free poems often come in pairs, especially in the St. Matthew Passion—a poem in blank verse followed by another in lyric verse—and are generally set as instrumentally accompanied recitatives and arias for vocal soloists. Most listeners today associate these musical types with church cantatas and Passions, but recitative-aria pairs using poetry of this type meant exactly one thing in Bach's time: opera. Recitatives and arias were the building blocks of musical theater. In fact, the oratorio Passion and the kind of church cantata Bach composed in Leipzig were acknowledged to be a poetic and musical adaptation of Italian operatic style. Most of us listen to very little eighteenth-century opera today, so we are relatively unlikely to hear Bach's Passions in this way without prompting.

Even if we do, it is hard for us to react to these musical types in the visceral way that some of Bach's listeners apparently did. To many in Bach's time, opera was the polar opposite of church music, and the intrusion of a decadent, secular musical style into the church was suspect at best. (Complaints about the corrosive incursion of secular musical styles into the realm of church music pop up regularly, so this one should come as no great surprise.) Bach himself had promised, when he was hired, not to present music that would make "an operatic impression" (David, Mendel, and Wolff 1998, 105), and eventually he came under criticism from the Leipzig town authorities for the text (and presumably its musical setting) of the St. John Passion. Nonetheless, we are hardly in a position to appreciate the significance of operatic style to Bach's listeners, because for the most part we no longer hear the theatrical influence and probably are not scandalized if we do.

Sometimes the borrowings from operatic conventions go beyond the structure of the text and music to its very substance. For example, consider the bass aria "Gebt mir meinen Jesum wieder" (Give Me Back My Jesus) from the St. Matthew Passion, sung after Judas has betrayed Jesus for money. The vehement, rhythmically irregular declamation of the text, the singer's wide-ranging line and rapid runs, and the furious virtuosity of the solo violin part sound to us like appropriate musical gestures for this moment in the Passion. But the informed listener in the eighteenth century would have recognized this piece as a rage aria of a kind often given to bass singers in operas whose characters were particularly upset. The Passion aria thus arguably brings with it the rage of operatic basses, representing an intensity of emotion that the modern listener might miss.

The significance of other musical features has faded as well for most listeners, especially in colorful and unusual scorings: the aria without a bass line, "Aus Liebe will mein Heiland sterben" (My Savior Would Die for the Sake of Love) from the St. Matthew Passion or the aria with viola da gamba "Es ist vollbracht" (It is Finished!) from the St. John Passion, for example. Then there are the expressive harmonies that strike us less, given our familiarity with late-nineteenth-century music but that sometimes strain the limits of early eighteenth-century musical language; the use of two orchestras and choirs in the version of the St. Matthew Passion most often heard; and so on. The more one investigates Bach's rich and complex Passion scores, the more one realizes that behind every musical decision on Bach's part was a wealth of conventions, expectations, and associations that we can reconstruct and appreciate but that are not part of our direct experience.

The Passion Today

The task of hearing Bach's Passions "right" begins to look a little hopeless, and we must eventually concede that we cannot hear them as they were heard in Bach's time. We bring such different experiences to them, in fact, that they may not even be the same pieces heard in the eighteenth century. Yet these works continue to be performed despite the resources they require, the demands they make of their listeners, and their fundamentally alien character. Why? And does it matter that today's Passions are different pieces than were heard in Leipzig? Isn't the bottom line that people still enjoy them? (Actually, here is another problem: Bach would probably have been puzzled if not suspicious at the idea that one would listen to pieces like these to "enjoy" them, not because they are church music but because enjoyment was not the chief way the musical experience was thought of in his day. Music could uplift or instruct or move, but the idea of enjoying a piece of music as the point of listening to it was a feature of later eighteenth-century aesthetics.)

There is no clear answer to our questions, but there is compelling evidence that it does not matter that Bach's Passions are different pieces today: listeners have flocked to performances since their revival in the nineteenth century. They may be different pieces than Bach's listeners heard, but they are still considered great works. Perhaps that is part of what makes a piece of music "timeless" or "transcendent": not that it keeps all of its meaning and significance over the years and in changing modes of performance, but that it is capable of constantly drawing new listeners, whatever they know or do not know as they approach it.

The Manuscript Sources of the St. John Passion

Most people's sense that there is a single work identifiable as "the St. John Passion" is confirmed by Wolfgang Schmieder's assignment of a single Bach catalog number—BVW 245—to it. But the situation is more complicated: there are multiple St. John Passions, some of which can be recovered and some of which cannot. There is even one that may not really qualify as a version, depending on how one defines the concept.

Understanding this problem requires knowing something about the sources that transmit Bach's piece. We know the St. John Passion, first of all, from a large stack of vocal and instrumental parts Bach used in his various performances, which are now preserved in the Berlin State Library (Figure 11-1). It turns out that there are four layers, each representing a different performance and identified in the modern literature by Roman numerals: I (1724, Bach's first Passion season in Leipzig), II (1725), III (c. 1732), and IV (c. 1749, near the end of Bach's life). The layers of parts and the performances they represent suggest a useful working definition of "version" of the St. John Passion: a form of the work as it was performed under Bach's direction and as documented in a set of parts..

In truth, this is not so simple, because what survives is not four complete sets of parts but the set-aside remnants of one set and a second set that was doctored several times. In 1724 Bach must have had a complete set of parts copied for the work's first performance, but for some reason he did not reuse most of that set the next year. Rather, he had most of the material for the work recopied in 1725 for the second performance. The bulk of the surviving

Figure 11-1. J. S. Bach, "Es ist vollbracht" from St. John Passion. First page of the gamba performance part (Berlin State Library, *St. III*). Bildarchiv Preussischer Kulturbesitz/Art Resource, New York.

material is thus not from version I but from version II, which is represented by an essentially complete set. Most of the parts from version I are missing, though a few were retained and used in version II.

Further, Bach did not make new parts for versions III or IV but instead marked up the parts from 1725 (version II). Version III is documented by paste-overs, inserts, and corrections in the parts for version II; version IV is represented by further alterations to the version III parts, plus a few new ones. A version, then, does not necessarily correspond to a set of parts, but often merely to the state of a set of parts at a certain moment.

Perhaps the strangest thing is the survival of some parts—but not a full set—from version I. Most, as mentioned, are lost. But those that do survive are a curious assortment consisting of four ripieno vocal parts (for the singers who did not sing the dramatic roles and arias) that were reused for version II, and a few instrumental parts that we can deduce were duplicates: violin I, violin II, and basso continuo, of which Bach and his assistants typically made two copies for church performances. What is strange is not that these parts were reused in 1725, but that the others from version I (1724)—the bulk of the parts—were not.

Why did Bach not simply reuse the original parts, altering them to reflect changes in the work, as he often did in similar situations? We do not know, but suspect that the first set was unavailable for some reason. Perhaps Bach had lent the parts to someone, retaining for himself the duplicates and somewhat redundant ripieno vocal parts, only to realize that he needed to perform the St. John Passion in 1725 after all and forcing him to copy out a new set. (If so, here is a tantalizing question: what had Bach planned to perform in 1725 before deciding to reuse the St. John Passion?) We know of a possible parallel: Bach had loaned a set of parts for the large Sanctus setting that later became a part of the B-Minor Mass to a count in Bohemia only to be forced to copy a new set when he performed the piece once again in Leipzig because his materials had not been returned.

For our purposes, the reason for Bach's decision is less important than the result: we cannot fully reconstruct version I, the original form of the piece, because most of the parts that document it are missing. We know the order of its movements from the few surviving parts, and we can deduce that in most musical respects the 1724 Passion was like its successor versions, but there are unknowns, especially in orchestration. Bach also recomposed one short recitative in the second version, and the original is now lost.

Version II, by contrast, survives essentially complete. The only missing material consists of a few instruments in one chorus, and because Bach later recycled this piece in yet another work we can reliably fill in the missing lines from the sources for that composition (The movement in question is the chorale setting "O Mensch, bewein dein Sünde groß" (O Humankind, Bewail Your Great Sin), which in 1736 became the closing movement of Part I of the St. Matthew Passion). For version III we know the order of movements and have most of the music, but two movements new to this version were lost to us when Bach removed them again in version IV. Version IV is well documented and can be almost entirely specified. Overall, then, we have two versions about which we know a great deal (II and IV) and two with gaps (I and III).

So far we have considered only performing parts, but Bach's music is often preserved in scores as well, so we can turn next to the original scores of the St. John Passion and what they tell us about versions of the work. To begin with, we do not have the manuscript that would tell us a great deal about the work's early form: Bach's composing score. We know it existed and can safely assume that the performing parts for version I were copied from it, as were those for the replacement set for version II. But because versions I and II differ, we can guess that that Bach must have annotated and marked up his composing score in preparing version

II. If we still had the original score, we would still have to sort out its layers carefully in reconstructing the history of the piece and its versions.

Let us imagine for a moment that Bach's composing score did survive and that we were able to compare it with the parts for versions I and II. To judge from many parallel cases in Bach's music we would almost certainly find differences between the score and the parts, even though the parts were copied from the score. That is, the score and the supposedly matching original parts made from it would almost certainly not agree.

This sounds contradictory, but there are two good reasons that it would be so. The first is that scores and parts give us different kinds of information about a composition. Many aspects of a work that are directly related to performance (details of instrumentation, basso continuo figures, ornamentation, and the distribution of lines among singers and players, for example) tend to be reflected only in performing parts. They represent decisions Bach made in realizing a work for performance and are usually not reflected in a score. The second reason is that Bach could (and often did) make revisions in the process of copying parts, occasionally changing his mind about certain matters. He might make changes as he copied or edited the parts prepared by an assistant without bothering to notate these changes in the score. This could lead to a situation in which the score and parts of the "same" version transmit different readings.

If we did find differences in our imaginary comparison of the composing score and original parts of the St. John Passion, would the readings in the score represent a "version" with the same status as those in the parts? We could argue that the score reflects Bach's conception of the work just as much as (or even more than) the parts do; on the other hand, he never performed the work as notated in a score, only as written in parts. If the readings in a score do represent a version, it is somehow different from the ones we know from the performing parts.

In a way we do have to face this problem with the St. John Passion. Although Bach's composing score for the work does not survive, we do have a later, beautiful fair copy of the score, partly in Bach's hand and partly in the hand of an assistant (Figure 11-2). It is a complex document indeed. From paper and handwriting we can deduce that Bach began to write it sometime in the late 1730s—that is, between the documented performances of versions III and IV. (We should keep in mind that there may have been other performances that did not leave any trace in the parts.) In his copying, Bach got only as far as the tenth number in the Passion, stopping after twenty pages, most of the way through the recitative "Derselbige Jünger war dem Hohenpriester bekannt" (The Same Disciple Was Known to the High Priest). We know neither why he started a new fair copy nor why he broke off writing it.

Some ten years later, around the time of the performance of version IV, one of Bach's assistants, Johann Nathanael Bammler, completed the score. Presumably Bach and Bammler used Bach's composing score (the one now lost) as a model for the new one, but each carried out his work differently. Bach's assistant made a literal copy of the original score when he started on page 21, but Bach, apparently not content simply to copy music he had composed almost fifteen years earlier, revised the piece as he wrote pages 1–20, making changes to the first ten numbers in the Passion. His changes affect details of every aspect of the work. Some of the most striking are found in the four-part chorales, which Bach enriched with the chromatic and contrapuntal language characteristic of his later chorale settings, like those in the Christmas Oratorio of 1734–1735.

This score, then, represents a revision of the St. John Passion by the composer and is arguably yet another version of the piece. More precisely, it represents a fragment of a version, because Bach never got past the first ten numbers—the assistant's later work simply repre-

Figure 11-2. J. S. Bach, St. John Passion. First page of the revised score (Berlin State Library, *P 28*). Bildarchiv Preussischer Kulturbesitz/Art Resource, New York.

sents a copy of the original. Here is the truly knotty aspect of this problem: the revisions were never heard in Bach's time. The new readings never found their way into any of Bach's performing parts, even those of version IV, which took place after the revisions were made. The performing parts used for it were, of course, merely adaptations of the older parts, and so retained the readings from the older versions. We thus have to ask whether the fragmentary revised version represented by Bach's portion of the recopied score is comparable to the four versions we know from the parts, not only because it is transmitted in a score but also because it was never heard under Bach.

Perhaps Bach's partial revision represents a kind of abstract version of the piece, in contrast to the practical versions represented by the performing parts. But this is not necessarily a good distinction, because for Bach (and most composers) the line between the artistic and the practical was fuzzy, or even meaningless. If we like the idea of Bach's returning to his great compositions near the end of his life, assembling, revising, and refining them in a kind of valedictory act (consider the assembling of the Mass in B Minor and the preparation of the Art of Fugue for publication), then perhaps his recopying of the St. John Passion is part of this process and this "version" of the work holds a similar place in his output. But, of course, Bach began the St. John revisions in the late 1730s, not his final years, and he never bothered finishing the project.

The Versions of the St. John Passion

Whether or not we regard the music in the later score as a true version, we have a wealth of choices in performing the St. John Passion. The version that most modern listeners know today resembles version I of 1724. It opens with the chorus—a choral aria really—"Herr, unser Herrscher" (Lord, Our Master), whose text is a poetic paraphrase of a Psalm, and it ends with the choral aria "Ruht wohl" (Rest Well) and a simple chorale setting, "Ach Herr, laß dein lieb Engelein" (O Lord, Let Your Dear Little Angels; PGM III). It includes a number of accompanied recitatives and arias among its interpolated commentary movements.

When Bach performed version II in 1725 he made some important changes that altered the character of the composition while retaining its Gospel narrative and many of its commentary movements. The opening poetic chorus, "Herr, unser Herrscher," was replaced by an elaborate chorale setting, "O Mensch, bewein dein Sünde groß," the same movement that in 1736 would close the first half of Bach's St. Matthew Passion. There is some thought that this piece was not newly composed for version II of the St. John Passion, but its original context is a matter of debate in Bach scholarship. The closing chorale of the Passion was replaced by a different hymn setting, "Christe, du Lamm Gottes" (O Christ, Lamb of God) in an arrangement not newly composed but borrowed from the cantata Bach had performed at his Leipzig audition in 1723, *Du wahrer Gott und Davids Sohn*, BWV 23.

Bach added or replaced some of the work's solo arias as well. The chorale "Wer hat dich so geschlagen" (Who Has Beaten You So; PGM III) was followed in version II by a new (or possibly recycled) aria with chorale, "Himmel reiße, Welt erbebe" (Heaven, Open, Earth, Quake). The aria "Ach, mein Sinn" (O My Disposition; PGM III) was replaced by an aria in concitato (or agitated) style, "Zerschmettert mich, ihr Felsen und ihr Hügel" (Crush Me, You Rocks and You Mountains). The soothing and reflective arioso "Betrachte, meine Seel" (Consider, My Soul; PGM III) and its companion aria "Erwäge, wie sein blutgefärbter Rücken" (Consider How His Bloodstained Back; PGM III) were replaced by a new aria, "Ach, windet euch nicht so, geplagte Seelen" (Ah, Do Not Writhe So, Tormented Souls). Finally, the recitative that describes the cataclysms in the immediate aftermath of Jesus' death, "Und siehe da, der Vorhang im Temple zerriß" (And See, the Curtain of the Temple Was

Torn; Sampler CD 2, track 19), whose words had actually been borrowed from Mark's gospel, was replaced by a new version, this time using the parallel text from Matthew that describes the event in even greater detail. Apparently, this moment was of great dramatic and theological interest to Bach and his Leipzig congregation, because he and his unknown librettist twice went outside John's gospel for this passage.

What was the effect of these changes? Most of the revisions in version II are to the poetic portions of the Passion, the commentaries that guide the listener through the messages of the story. The opening chorus, which establishes the theological tone of the work, provides a particularly good example. The opening number in version I, "Herr, unser Herrscher" (Sampler CD 2, track 20), focuses on Jesus' paradoxical glorification in the abasement of the crucifixion. Its text begins with a poetic adaptation of a Psalm glorifying God as ruler. This aspect of the text is reflected musically in Bach's setting: in the threefold invocation "Lord" when the voices enter, in the busy, ornamental vocal parts, and in the repetitive phrases that rise in pitch toward a series of small climaxes (Figure 11-3). The text also invokes Jesus' crucifixion, and to reflect this aspect of the text Bach casts the movement in a minor key and presents much of the movement over portentous bass lines that hold one note despite all the activity going on above them. What is more, Bach adds an instrumental layer—a pair of oboes—whose lines form a series of grating dissonances. These serious elements are heard together with the quasi-celebratory ones in a way that sets the tone for the entire Passion story.

The replacement movement in version II uses instead a hymn stanza that emphasizes humankind's sinfulness, representing a different perspective of the meaning of the Passion. Given that the two opening choruses orient the listener in different ways, they represent a real shift in the way the work was meant to be heard. The replacement chorale at the end of version II follows suit, intensifying the call for mercy heard in the chorale that had ended version I. The three new arias emphasize elements of violence and torment present in the original but intensified in version II. Particularly prominent are apocalyptic images, extending even to the ordinarily fixed Gospel narrative. Version II, then, offers different interpretive messages, focusing on humankind's errant ways and the consequences for individuals.

This means, of course, that even movements that are common to the two versions would have been heard in different ways. For example, the aria "Es ist vollbracht" (Sampler CD 2, track 21), which occurs shortly before the moment of Jesus' death on the cross, is in two strongly contrasting sections. The first section is a slow lament that uses a viola da gamba—perhaps the most personally expressive instrument used in the Passion—together with a solo voice. But the second section is a literal call to arms to the "hero of Judah," using the modern string instruments in the accompanimental band in a much faster tempo to invoke battle trumpets. Version II of the St. John Passion, with its emphasis on violence and apocalypse, would certainly have thrown more emphasis on this second section of the aria.

All of this raises two questions: Why did Bach make these changes, and do they represent a new Passion setting? We do not know the answer to the first question, except that it seems likely that Bach did not wish to present exactly the same work in 1724 and in 1725, the first two years of his Leipzig tenure. It has also been proposed that the revision, particularly the incorporation of the enormous new opening chorale setting, was connected with Bach's project in 1724–1725 of creating a cycle of cantatas for Sundays and feast days based on a seasonal hymns, each typically opening with a large vocal and instrumental movement that sets the chosen chorale. Version II of the St. John Passion, with its opening setting of "O Mensch, bewein," begins much like Bach's cantatas from the church year in which it fell.

Given the particular movements that Bach replaced or added, I would argue that version II of the St. John Passion indeed does represent a new setting. It differs from the 1724 version

Figure 11-3. J. S. Bach, "Herr, unser Herrscher, dessen Ruhm" from the St. John Passion. First entrance of the chorus. From the revised score, in Bach's hand (Berlin State Library, *P 28*). Bildarchiv Preussicher Kulturbesitz/Art Resource, New York.

in precisely the ways that would have been most important to listeners and interpreters in Bach's time: in its tone, and in the theological themes it introduces and emphasizes in its commentary movements. It is true that most of the music of version II is the same as that in version I, but Bach's changes fall primarily in the interpolated poetic pieces and chorales, not in the settings of the Gospel text. This makes for a new interpretation of the Gospel text.

Of course the telling of the story was the essential liturgical purpose of a musical Passion setting, but that could have been accomplished (and often was, even in Bach's time) by a simple presentation of the Passion in chant. What made a musical setting individual was its commentary movements. The opening movement, especially, set the tone for the interpretation of the familiar story, and together with the arias and chorales presented a perspective of the story in much the same way that a sermon offered a particular angle of interpretation. We regard the 1725 St. John Passion as a version of the 1724 piece, but in many ways it was a new work.

Whatever Bach's reasons for making the changes, he did not let them stand. Version III, from the early 1730s, shows additional revisions. Bach restored the opening chorus, "Herr unser Herrscher," from version I and the recitative and arioso "Betrachte, meine Seel" and aria "Erwäge, wie sein blutgefärbter Rücken," though with lute and violas d'amore in the arioso replaced by keyboard and muted violins. He also removed the violent aria "Himmel reiße" he had added in 1725. In these respects, the first part of version III resembles that of version I. Bach also removed the closing chorale altogether, ending the work with the lullaby chorus "Ruht wohl" instead. For the spot occupied by the aria "Ach, mein Sinn" in version I and its even more tormented replacement "Zerschmettert mich" in version II, Bach used yet another aria. This piece is now lost, so we do not know the nature of its text or music. The movements that reflected on Jesus' death, including the arioso "Mein Herz, indem die ganze Welt" and the aria "Zerfließe, mein Herz," were replaced by an instrumental sinfonia, also now lost.

On the whole, version III appears to represent a softening of the tone of version II, partly by a return to the material of version I and partly by the addition or substitution of new music. Unfortunately we do not know the text or notes of some of the new pieces, so we cannot say for certain exactly how they affected the Passion's tone or interpretive message. We can note that in addition to the all-important opening, Bach continued to tinker with two especially important spots in the narrative: the aftermath of Peter's betrayal of Jesus, and the moment of Jesus' death.

Musically speaking, version IV, undertaken many years later, was essentially a return to version I except that it retained the curtain-tearing passage from Matthew that had surfaced in version II. It added a contrabassoon to the orchestra and used harpsichord continuo rather than organ, though this might have been a last-minute substitution more attributable to practical circumstances than to any interpretive purpose. But this version also provided revised texts for some of the poetic movements: the aria "Ich folge dir gleichfals" (I Follow You With Joyful Stride) and the arioso "Betrachte, meine Seel" (some of whose lines were altered) and the aria "Erwäge, wie sein blutgefärbter Rücken" (which received an entirely new text beginning "Mein Jesu" [My Jesus]).

Commentators have described the revised texts as more rationalistic than the original versions, and it has been speculated that the changes were prompted by official dissatisfaction with theological aspects of the St. John Passion. (Revisions to the text of the chorus "Ruht wohl" found in the sources are now thought to date from after Bach's death but are similar in their effect.) Once again, we should probably recall that the language and messages of the commentary movements substantially defined Passion settings, and that these small textual revisions would have been extremely important. This means that the "return" to version I was not total in Bach's last years—the revised texts slightly but distinctly changed the tone of the work.

What emerges from our survey of the four known versions is a picture of a work to which Bach returned often, revising it each time in different respects and probably for different reasons. We do not know which changes he made for "good" reasons and which he might have made under duress (for example, in response to complaints from religious authorities about his texts), or how we should interpret his striking return in version IV to essentially the composition as he first created it in 1724, at least in musical terms. We do know, in surprising detail, several versions that Bach performed in Leipzig along with the never-realized revisions made in his copying of the score, and we can choose to perform any of them except version III, which has unavoidable gaps.

The St. John Passion Today

Which St. John Passion do we usually hear today? The most influential modern editions are those by Arthur Mendel, who prepared the work for the New Bach Edition and who also produced a widely used vocal score published by G. Schirmer. Mendel's editions give primacy to Bach's revised version of the first ten numbers, using the readings from the score Bach partly copied in the 1730s. As we have mentioned, this exists as a fragment, and Mendel filled out his editions with readings largely from version IV. But he did not use the revised texts from version IV, choosing instead the original texts of version I. Movements from version II are presented as alternatives in an appendix, as are the original readings of the first ten numbers and the revised texts. (The performance on PGM III follows Mendel's New Bach Edition.)

From the strictest point of view, of course, the New Bach Edition is no version at all but rather a modern pastiche. The edition relies simultaneously on several editorial philosophies: (1) the principle that final revisions are best (in its use of "improved" readings from the autograph portion of the recopied score), (2) the preference for the first form of a composition, setting aside revisions made ostensibly under pressure or as an afterthought (in the use of the original aria texts), and (3) the love of the most interesting elements (in the favoring of the colorful original orchestration using lute and violas d'amore). The typical modern St. John Passion, then, is an editorial creation, mixing readings from several versions and corresponding to nothing heard in Bach's time.

Lest we be too harsh on the editor or on performers who perpetuate this form of the piece we should recall that in many respects their choices are limited in performing the work, despite all we know. We can approach certain versions only if we tolerate gaps and fragments: versions I and III are not fully recoverable. There is also no question that Bach's revisions to the first ten numbers from his fair copy of the score are worth hearing. But we need to remember that the original readings for these movements were good enough for Bach to use for his entire career in Leipzig—he never went to the trouble of putting his revisions to use. At the same time, the movements unique to version II include some stunning music, and there is fascinating insight to be gained in hearing a St. John Passion that begins, like version II, with "O Mensch, bewein" and that takes a different theological approach to the story.

At the least we need to avoid the trap of thinking of the editorial pastiche—or any version or compilation—as "the" St. John Passion. Each time we perform the work we need to choose. Indeed, only on a recording can we indulge multiple choices, and even then we can listen to only one at a time. There will always be guesswork in realizing many elements of

Bach's performances, whichever version we choose. But multiple perspectives of a work that survives in several versions can be immensely illuminating.

We are increasingly interested in the meanings and messages of compositions like Bach's Passions, and different versions from the composer's hand, with their different outlooks, remind us that we can find multiple significance in any great work. Bach's own rethinking of his piece should inspire us to rethink it, too, even if we end up favoring one version of the composition above others. And if we feel enriched by Bach's setting of the St. John Passion, imagine the treasure represented by four (or more) of them.

BIBLIOGRAPHY

Boyd, Malcolm. 1997. *Bach.* 3rd ed. New York: Oxford University Press.

David, Hans T., Arthur Mendel, and Christoph Wolff, eds. 1998. *The New Bach Reader.* New York: W. W. Norton.

Dürr, Alfred. 2000. *Johann Sebastian Bach's "St. John Passion": Genesis, Transmission, and Meaning,* trans. Alfred Clayton. New York: Oxford University Press.

Leaver, Robin A. 1997. "The Mature Vocal Works and Their Theological and Liturgical Context." In *The Cambridge Companion to Bach,* ed. John Butt, 86–122. Cambridge: Cambridge University Press.

Marissen, Michael. 1998. *Lutheranism, Anti-Judaism, and Bach's St. John Passion.* New York: Oxford University Press.

Melamed, Daniel R. 2005. *Hearing Bach's Passions.* New York: Oxford University Press.

Smallman, Basil. 1970. *The Background of Passion Music: J. S. Bach and His Predecessors.* 2nd ed. New York: Dover.

CHAPTER TWELVE

Music in the "New World": The Baroque in Mexico and Brazil

Gerard Béhague

THE BAROQUE CARRIES SPECIAL MEANINGS of great significance in Latin American art and culture. The concept of Baroque as an expression of extravagance, ostentation, complex fantasy, and mystery has been a constant throughout Latin American history. The famous Cuban creative writer and music historian Alejo Carpentier (1904–1980), speaking in *El reino de este mundo* (1949), believed that "Our art has always been Baroque, from the splendid pre-Columbian sculpture to the best modern narrative, and the colonial cathedrals and monasteries of our continent." Carpentier also raised the question "For what is the history of Latin America but a chronicle of magical realism?" Although the term "magical realism" was first applied to a category of visual art, it became particularly suitable to designate a trend in Latin American twentieth-century literature, represented by Carpentier himself along other well-known figures such as Gabriel García Marquez, Isabel Allende, and Mario Vargas Llosa.

In his novel *Concierto Barroco* (Baroque Concert, 1974), Carpentier considers the cultural synthesis of Latin America through the imagined story of a wealthy Mexican's journey to eighteenth-century Venice, where he meets Vivaldi, Handel, and Alessandro Scarlatti. For Carpentier, Latin America represented the native Baroque based on the reality of its history but viewed in numerous imaginative and fantastic manners. Thus the linkage of magical realism and the Baroque is very appropriate, since both stress the hybrid nature of Latin American culture, which resulted from the incorporation and assimilation of European, indigenous, and African-related cultures in unique and frequently magical and entrancing ways.

Therefore, if this magical realism pervades the whole history of Latin America, is it possible to identify a specific "Baroque Period" in that history? The post-Conquest time corresponds to the colonial period that extended from the early sixteenth to the early nineteenth centuries. As an extension of Western European trends, Latin American high art follows Baroque ideals mostly from the latter part of the seventeenth century to the end of the eighteenth century, with some notable exceptions in music composition. Thus this time period—the late seventeenth century to approximately 1800—can be considered the Baroque Period in Latin America.

It is also quite germane to remember that it was the Portuguese word *barroco,* first applied to irregular, "imperfect" pearls, that ended up designating a whole period of artistic achievement in both Europe and Latin America and the philosophical, religious, and political configuration of the same period. In Latin America particularly that configuration consisted of strong, showy, and spectacular contrasts expressed in highly dramatic, sumptuous fashion. In *Barroco, A Alma do Brasil* (Baroque, the Soul of Brazil), poet and writer Affonso

Romano de Sant'Anna details the "circuitous" history of the word "Baroque," which he considers indeed a "Baroque history, for it is disorderly, full of comings and goings, patches of shadow and light" (Sant'Anna 1997, 29). Despite many pejorative interpretations, such as that of the poet Wieland who called some women Baroque "because they had ugly faces but beautiful legs," the term acquired the universal prestige of the artistic aesthetics that flourished for over two centuries.

Cultural Context

The music of the Latin American Baroque Period inevitably reflects the heritage of the European colonization, but it also discloses the differences of the social and ethnic makeup of musicians between the colonies and the Iberian nations. From the very beginning of colonization, European music assumed a paramount role in the catechization of the native populations. The enormous success of the conversion process was due in great part to the astute use of music by the missionaries, who quickly recognized and then praised the Indian aptitude for assimilating European music. Indian participation in church and mission musical activities proved to be one of the most effective tools of conversion, since it promoted the acculturation process. The most significant ecclesiastic orders in charge of missionary work were the Franciscans, Dominicans, and Augustinians, with the Jesuits predominating later in Hispanic America. In Brazil, the Jesuits were the first missionaries to arrive, and by the early eighteenth century they had become such strong leaders in educational and religious matters and protectors of the Indians that the Portuguese government saw them as a real threat to its central power. They were subsequently expelled from Brazil in 1759. Spanish America followed suit in 1767.

From the very beginning missionary activity included the establishment of music schools such as the San Francisco School, founded in Mexico by the layman Pedro de Gante (Pierre de Gand), or the Colegio de San Andrés in Quito (Ecuador) established by two Belgian monks. Jesuit missionary musicians particularly influential in South American colonies during the seventeenth and early eighteenth centuries, especially in Peru and Bolivia and parts of Chile, Paraguay, Argentina, and Brazil. Some of the best-known Jesuit figures were the early seventeenth-century Franco-Flemish Jean Vaisseau and Louis Berger, then the Austrian Anton Sepp in Paraguay, and even the famous Italian composer Domenico Zipoli, active in Córdoba, Argentina. In Brazil José de Anchieta and Manoel da Nóbrega laid the foundation of Jesuit mission music in the latter part of the sixteenth century.

The significance of mission life in general cannot be overstated, for it represents one of the primary sources of the new civilization referred to as *la raza,* which emerged from the coexistence and eventual integration of European and native expressive culture of which music is one powerful marker. In particular, religious music in the missions seems to have been conducive to cultural synthesis. Indian music and dances were permitted to be a part of religious services, especially in the various processions commemorating the most important feasts. Besides the singing of psalms, hymns, and antiphons, the Indians learned to sing *alabanzas* and *alabados,* songs of religious praise in the vernacular that remained popular throughout the continent and were eventually retained as folk songs. Such song genres form part of the contemporary Mexican and Mexican-American repertory of the *conchero* associations in their annual religious pilgrimage.

The missionaries' conciliatory attitude toward the Indians and African slaves promoted the rapprochement of different worldviews. In the words of the Brazilian anthropologist Gilberto Freyre, the Jesuits' liturgy in Brazil was "social rather than [strictly] religious, a softened, lyric Christianity with many phallic and animistic reminiscences of the pagan cults"

(Freyre 1964, 97). Despite the prohibition of such reminiscences from the Church authorities at various periods (especially during the Inquisition), the enforcement at the mission or parish church levels proved rather laborious. But actual examples of church music composition in a likely *mestizo,* a mixed or simultaneous style, have not been found because of such bans. However, the widespread adoption of Hispanic popular religious songs and their styles in contemporary *mestizo* folk music traditions attests to the effectiveness of the colonial missionary activity.

The strong social stratification in colonial Latin America undoubtedly prevented Indians from holding positions of leadership in the musical life of the early period. In Spanish America, only during the middle colonial period (c. 1650–1750) did a few *mestizo* musicians hold significant positions. In Mexico and Guatemala documentary evidence points to the existence of Indian composers in the seventeenth century, whereas Brazilian mulatto composers appeared quite frequently during the eighteenth century.

In Spanish America, the organization of cathedral life reflected Spanish traditions adapted to the new conditions. Most cathedrals were modeled after those of Seville (as in the case of Mexico City) or Toledo (as in Puebla and Durango in Mexico). The distinction of having the finest cathedral in the region was a matter of great civic pride. Normally located in the main city square, the cathedral was the focus of most religious fiestas and processions as well as many political events. Each cathedral was governed by an archbishop and a council of clergymen known as the *cabildo,* or chapter.

The *cabildo* supervised all activities of the cathedral, appointed musicians, set their salaries, determined the music budget in general, and drew up job descriptions. In all major cathedrals the chapter governed through a set of more or less strict rules known as choir constitutions. The most elaborate of these provided detailed instructions regarding the duties of the chapelmaster, the repertory to be sung and played at specific feasts, and the manner in which it was to be performed. Professional musicians got most of their training in the music chapels, which formed an integral part of the cathedral life, but cathedral authorities were not concerned with the training of Indian musicians. With very few exceptions, Europeans or European-trained musicians filled the most important positions of chapelmaster and organist. However, many cathedrals had to rely on Indian singers and instrumentalists, since Spanish musicians were not plentiful. Members of some Indian or *mestizo* families practiced the music profession for several generations, enjoying a definite monopoly in certain areas of performance.

The level of musical competence and creativity in a cathedral depended primarily on the benevolence of its chapter and, to a greater degree, the support of the archbishop. Throughout the colonial period, many archbishops in major centers nurtured the musical life in their cathedrals. Actions to improve cathedral music generally included recruitment of better musicians, with a consequent raising of salaries, enlargement of music libraries and archives (with the necessary repair and replacement of damaged or stolen manuscripts or printed collections), and the upkeep of musical instruments.

The transfer of European musical styles to the American colonies in both sacred and secular music resulted in the gradual development of a very rich repertory. Polyphonic music of the late Renaissance influenced the sacred Latin music composed in Hispanic America up until the early eighteenth century. During the seventeenth and eighteenth centuries, Baroque musical styles and practices were felt especially in solo cantatas, duets, arias, and villancicos, with figured or unfigured basso continuo and separate instrumental parts. A homophonic, pre-Classic style commonly appeared in the sacred music written during the latter part of the eighteenth century. Since the European musical idioms were considered the only models suitable for Christian worship, the church music of the Baroque Period in Latin America exhibits little native stylistic orientation.

However, genres such as villancicos, *chanzonetas,* and *juguetes,* often set to texts in indigenous languages or local dialects, incorporate elements related to a more secular Hispanic tradition while generally maintaining the sacred music idiom of the period. The subgenres of villancicos that seem to have enjoyed particular preference with composers and listeners alike were the *negrilla* or *negro* and *xácara/jácara* types. The *negrilla* was a narrative and devotional villancico in supposedly black dialect. In reality it was a caricatured imitation of black Africans' mispronunciation of the Spanish language. (One could interpret the so-called dialect as a rather racist jab of poking fun, and some writers have. There is no direct evidence that composers and chapelmasters bore any contempt toward blacks or "gypsies," however.) Musically, both *negrilla* and *jácara* present specific musical features that can be related easily to contemporary folk music. In indirect fashion, then, these sacred villancicos can be considered as early sources of the development of *mestizo* folk song and dance genres.

The official attitude of the church to these types of villancicos was to condemn them as unsuitable for worship because the pieces were exceedingly provocative. But in practice the works were tolerated in church, even if only for black *cofradías* (brotherhoods), in some cases. In his famous treatise *El Melopeo y Maestro* (1613), Pietro Cerone described the presence of the villancico in Spanish churches as widespread and enormously popular, even with lazy congregants who were otherwise indifferent worshippers. Obviously the native elements in church music resonated with local citizens, even in Cerone's time. In Mexican churches, the same situation prevailed. In discussing the literary history of the villancico in his engaging and informative volume *Christmas Music from Baroque Mexico,* Robert Stevenson cites the study of Mexican scholar Alfonso Méndez Plancarte, who edited the complete works of the nun Sor Juana Inés de la Cruz, including her villancico sets:

> In principal churches and convents each of the three nocturns celebrated at first-class vespers consisted of three psalms or three lessons, each of which was in turn followed by a polyphonic responsory. After each of the responsories, a villancico served as entr'acte, diverting the people. To enliven these entr'actes all kind of licences were allowed— comic characters, actors singing rustic, provincial, Gypsy, Indian, and Negro dialects, or even burlesque skits. (Stevenson 1974, 5)

The precise nature of the music of the "rustic" skits is impossible to reconstruct with accuracy, but the highly rhythmic, joyful, and dance-like character of such music is confirmed by numerous villancicos written by church-music composers. In Puebla, for example, the chapelmaster Juan García de Zéspedes (Céspedes; c. 1619–1678) composed a villancico, *Convidando está la noche,* whose refrain (*estribillo*) is entitled *guaracha,* which has been interpreted as the earliest example of the Afro-Cuban dance genre of the same name. Although the term *guaracha* is mentioned twice in the text of this villancico, in the generic sense of dance, it does not follow that this is the same modern-day Cuban *guaracha.* Actually, it may very well be an archaic spelling of *huaracha* (as mentioned in Gabriel Pareyón, *Diccionario de música en México* 1995, 253).

It seems highly probably that *huaracha* (derived from the Purépecha Indian language *huarari,* meaning dancer) was the intended folk dance and song of possible Michoacán origin that Juan García had in mind as a model and not the Afro-Cuban *guaracha.* In their eagerness for exotic display, many directors of early music ensembles view such pieces as the opportunity to reinvent a performance tradition, adding numerous percussion instruments, Baroque guitars, sackbut, shawms, and the Cuban folk guitar known as *tres* (three courses of double strings), and stressing a "gypsy-like" vocal style involving overzealous portamento. Although the resulting sound can be quite enticing, common sense must prevail so as not to confuse colonial church *villancicos* and *jácaras* with post–Vatican II folk songs.

Since it is not feasible to consider the whole world of Latin American Baroque music in one short chapter, the present examination of Mexican and Brazilian colonial music is meant as a contrasting representative illustration of the unique creative activity in Latin America based on the Baroque heritage of Spain and Portugal.

Baroque Mexico ("New Spain")

The two major centers of music activities in New Spain during the seventeenth and eighteenth centuries were undoubtedly Mexico City and Puebla, with other provincial centers, such as Oaxaca and Morelia, also showing some substantial music-making.

MEXICO CITY

As one of the two main administrative centers of the Spanish colonial empire (the other being Lima), Mexico City developed into a major artistic center. The city enjoyed a substantial artistic history since its founding by the Mexicas/Aztecs in 1325, with a particularly successful cultural development in the fifteenth century. By the 1560s, under Spanish rule, the city had begun to erect a permanent cathedral on the site of Aztec ruins. The first phase of building was completed by 1667. Although its first exterior follows the restrained and somber Spanish style of the Renaissance, its interior eventually combined various aspects of the very rich Baroque of subsequent periods (Figure 12-1; Plate 22). The highly decorative elements of its stone façade stand as the prime example of early eighteenth-century Mexican Baroque art and architecture. Next to the Cathedral stood the palace-fort that served as the seat of the viceroys. After being destroyed by fire in the seventeenth century, the palace was rebuilt and enlarged in the eighteenth century, retaining its essentially Baroque style. Both of these landmarks, together with several theatres, were the main sites of public music-making.

In 1625 the British traveler Thomas Gage referred to the music he heard in Mexico City as being so exquisite "that I dare be bold to say that the people are drawn to their churches more for the delight of the music than for any delight in the service of God" (Gage 1958, 72). From a European perspective these comments are indicative of the achievements of colonial church music, if only in performance skill, at such an early period. They also suggest that the "people," presumably made up of *criollos, mestizos,* and Indians, were involved in the making and enjoyment of a music entirely European in style and function. For lack of documentation, it is not known if parish church music differed in any way from the main polyphonic compositions of the cathedrals of New Spain. The two Aztec *chanzonetas* to the Virgin, with Nahuatl text (c. 1599) ascribed to a "Don" Hernando Franco, identified by Robert Stevenson as an Indian of noble descent, could be considered an illustration of the simpler, less elaborate style of parish church music (Stevenson 1968b, 204–219).

At any rate, by the early seventeenth century, the music chapel of the Mexico City Cathedral enjoyed the services of the priest Juan Hernández, chapelmaster from 1586 to about 1620. Hernández was believed at one time to have been the composer Juan de Lienas, whose works occupy some sixty pages of the famous Carmen Codex and also figure prominently in the manuscripts of Mexican choirbooks at the Newberry Library in Chicago. In the latter Lienas is mentioned by apparently gossipy scribes as *el cornudo Lienas* (the cuckold Lienas), among other similar names, suggesting that he was married, thereby eliminating the speculative fusion of the two men. Lienas's works belong to the best tradition of the "golden century" of Spanish polyphony.

Figure 12-1. Cathedral, Mexico City, exterior. Reproduced with permission from *Catedrales de México.*

Among the various seventeenth- and early eighteenth-century chapelmasters at the Cathedral, Francisco López Capillas and Antonio de Salazar attract our attention. López Capillas (c. 1608–1674), the first Mexican-born chapelmaster, has been singled out as the "most profound and prolific composer of Masses in Mexican history" (Stevenson 1967). He was appointed in 1654 by unanimous vote and without public competition, after having served the Puebla Cathedral since 1641 as second, then first organist, bassoonist, and singer. In the Puebla chapter minutes for early 1648, he is referred to as *licenciado,* which implies that he must have earned an advanced degree locally, perhaps at the University of Mexico, founded in 1553. He clearly attached such importance to the chapelmastership that he added the word *Capillas* to his name Francisco López. His significance as a composer is attested by the number of works ascribed to him in four of the nine Mexico Cathedral choirbooks, two of which are almost entirely of his composition.

López Capillas's reputation as a creative composer is illustrated by the proposal in January 1656 of the New Spain 22nd Viceroy, the Duke of Albuquerque, to request López Capillas to write a Mass for four choruses on the occasion of the July 1656 consecration of four bishops of New Spain. The Viceroy further suggested that each chorus (with its own organ and instrumentalists) would be placed in different areas of the Cathedral and would sing a complete Mass, but different from the other three. And yet the four compositions were to function as a perfect whole. Indeed, a very Baroque idea! Whether the resulting composition was performed at the intended consecration is not known, but the public reaction at a performance in the Cathedral was described at the time as perplexed but full of awe and admiration. It is impossible to ascertain if the mentioned work really turned out to be a real tour de force, since the manuscript of this Mass has never been found. By means of a 1673 royal warrant, the chapelmaster was promoted to a full prebend. A full book at the Madrid National Library (M 2428) containing Masses and Magnificats by López Capillas may have been part of credentials presentation for his candidacy to the full prebend position. According to Robert Stevenson, this is the most lavish and splendid Mexican colonial manuscript owned by a library outside Mexico (Stevenson 1970).

The work of López Capillas reveals a talented, knowledgeable, and imaginative composer, especially of Latin compositions, which number eight Masses, nine settings of the Magnificat, motets, hymns, and a St. Matthew Passion. One of his four-part Magnificat settings in the Carmen Codex shows a sober, elegant polyphony which at times pits static parts against very active ones (Example 12-1).

The Mexico City Cathedral Choirbook No. VIII contains the *Missa Re Sol,* a four-part

Example 12-1. López Capillas: Magnificat, "Gloria patri," mm. 1–14.

parody Mass based on the song of the same title by the Spanish composer Juan de Riscos. This fact led Stevenson to wonder if López Capillas might not have studied with Riscos during his visit to Jaén, Spain, and if he was perhaps trying to pay him homage, since this Mass appears at the beginning of his collection of Masses, and Riscos appears to have been unknown in New Spain. Choirbook No. VII includes two of López Capillas's best-known Masses, the *Missa super Scalam Aretinam* and the *Missa Batalla*. The former Mass has been shown to be the most "hexachordal" of all such Masses and of a deliberately archaic flavor. The latter, also a parody Mass, is based on the famous polyphonic chanson *La guerre* of Clément Janequin. Two other parody Masses by López Capillas are based on Palestrina material. The high quality of López Capillas's compositions is undeniable, even though the style he cultivated tends to be on the conservative side.

The *Missa Super Scalam Aretinam* is preceded in Choirbook No. VII by a *Declaración de la missa,* whose aim was to explain to the performers some of the rather obsolete mensural procedures used in the work, such as the "tempus perfectum." The singers complained about the performance difficulty resulting from mensural problems of having the entire Mass in ternary meter. Indeed, López Capillas explains at the beginning that this ternary meter apparently caused "novelty for some of my singers, and dispute over [the resulting figures]." He concludes the first paragraph of his *Declaración* by warning that "to satisfy [those who criticized this work], I shall put here the authorities of great masters from whom I learned what has been achieved" (Brothers 1989). These great masters are sixteenth-century figures such as Morales and Palestrina, revealing Capillas's deep theoretical knowledge and his own intellectual and artistic affinity with the late Renaissance. At the same time, one can also see a number of Baroque elements in some of his works, such as the dramatic and expressive treatment (often in duets) of solo parts in the St. Matthew Passion and perhaps the new sense of "sound space" particularly evident in the *Missa Batalla.*

By the time of López Capillas's death in 1674, instrumental music at the Cathedral was flourishing, and by the end of the century the Cathedral orchestra included fifteen different instruments within four sections—strings, woodwinds, brass, and organ. In 1695 a new organ made in Spain was brought to the Cathedral, and its installation required more than two years of work. With seventy-eight stops and a monumental, locally made case, it greatly enhanced the musical splendor of the new cathedral. A second monumental organ, built entirely in Mexico by the master José Nazarre and considered in Spain as one of the wonders of the New World, was dedicated on August 15 at the Feast of the Assumption, 1735. Still in place, it originally had no fewer than approximately eighty-six stops and 3,350 pipes (Plate 22).

The next chapelmaster with influence in the Cathedral's musical life was Antonio de Salazar (c. 1650–1715), appointed in 1688 after serving in the same capacity at the Puebla Cathedral from 1679. One of his first undertakings in Mexico City was to recover, restore, and put in order the various holdings of the music archive (choirbooks and loose music manuscripts and scores) and to supervise the installation of the Nazarre organ. During his twenty-seven years of service as chapelmaster, Salazar wrote some of the best polychoral motets of his time and many sets of villancicos. His works, which show a solid contrapuntal technique, were known throughout New Spain (Puebla, Morelia, Oaxaca) and Guatemala. In some of his motets, such as *O sacrum convivium* and *In veni David,* one finds extensive antiphonal effects, contrasting alternation between solo voices and chorus, and the unusual presence of two continuos, one for the soloist, the other for the chorus. Salazar is known to have written a multitude of *chanzonetas* and villancicos, including seventy-two villancico texts of the famous feminist poetess of Puebla, Sor Juana Inés de la Cruz. Unfortunately these works are no longer extant.

Salazar wrote villancicos for various religious feasts, from Christmas, Assumption, and Saint Peter to Our Lady of Guadalupe, and relied in some sections on popular music types of the period, such as the *jácara,* the *negrilla,* the *folía,* and the *juguete.* Curiously, although none of his music was printed during his lifetime, the text of no fewer than thirty-six of his villancicos was published. The manuscript scores of some of his works bear witness to the fact that they were performed by women as well as men. Indeed, the score of the villancico *Angélicos coros con gozo cantad* for double choir even carries the names of the nuns in a Puebla convent who sang the music and performed the instrumental accompaniment. Among the many students that Salazar taught in Mexico City was Manuel de Zumaya (or Sumaya), of Indian and European ancestry. Zumaya took over the chapelmaster's teaching responsibilities in 1710, when Salazar became ill and almost blind.

Born in Mexico City around 1680, Zumaya's training took place in the Cathedral, first as a choirboy (by the time he was around ten), and then as a pupil of the official cathedral organist Joseph de Idiáquez. Zumaya received the financial support of the chapter. From Salazar he learned counterpoint and composition. Zumaya was ordained by the time he reached his twentieth birthday. He won the competition for the chapelmastership by unanimous vote on June 7, 1715. The manuscript of the villancico he composed for that occasion, *Solfa de Pedro es el llanto,* is now in the music archive of the Guatemala Cathedral. For the next twenty-four years, Zumaya contributed to the splendor of the Cathedral's music chapel not only through his own compositions and effective teaching but also through the recruitment of high-quality singers and instrumentalists. By the mid-1730s the chapel boasted an orchestra of considerable size, with varied string, woodwind, and brass instruments. The unprecedented high level of musical competence resulted from Zumaya's demands and from the financial backing of the *Cabildo.* In light of this, Zumaya's transfer to Oaxaca in August 1739 at the invitation of the new bishop of that city was totally unforeseen by the Mexico City chapter. At Oaxaca, Zumaya was initially placed in charge of purely religious matters. Only in 1745 was he appointed chapelmaster, a function he fulfilled until his death in 1755.

A prolific composer, Zumaya wrote mostly for church services, providing Vespers music, psalm settings, sets of Lamentations, Misereres, and Masses, and numerous villancicos (especially for the Feast of St. Peter). But he is also well known for being the author of scenic music for *El Rodrigo* (1708) and *La Parténope,* the second opera to be produced in the New World. Set to a libretto by Silvio Stampiglia, *La Parténope* was produced at the vice-royal palace on May 1, 1711. Cast in three acts, the rather convoluted plot presents seven characters, two of them rival princesses. The new viceroy, the Duke of Linares, arrived in Mexico earlier that year and was known to be fond of Italian opera. Although the music of *La Parténope* and *El Rodrigo* is not extant, it probably followed the prevailing Italian style, since it evidently pleased the Duke.

Zumaya's music shows a stylistic dichotomy between the sacred Latin works and the villancicos and *cantadas,* especially when compared to the works of his predecessors at the Cathedral. Zumaya's Masses and Lamentations, in particular, reveal his total command of late-Renaissance polyphonic style, softened with an exquisite, sensitive expression that was highly personal. In the villancicos and *cantadas,* he tends to break away from the *prima prattica* of the seventeenth century, showing a clear Italian Baroque influence in the use of concertato style and cantata form (with opening choruses, numerous recitatives and arias, and choral finales). In the late polychoral villancicos, which are preserved mainly in the music archive of the Oaxaca Cathedral, the orchestral scoring shows an unmistakably Baroque character, with a string body of first and second violins, viola, and bass, plus oboe, clarion trumpet (*clarín*), and continuo. Polychoral style was commonly employed in sacred music composed in Spain during the Baroque, from the early seventeenth century onward. That tradition was practiced in Mexico City, Puebla, and Oaxaca. Zumaya's villancico *Celebren, publiquen, entonen y canten* (Praise, Proclaim, Intone, and Sing) illustrates pertinently this particular style. Written for two choirs (the first with alto, tenor, and bass, the second with *tiple* [treble, or soprano], alto, tenor, and bass), cornet, three violins, and basso continuo (partially figured), the villancico exudes a celebratory character that is made clear in the unison call of the violins and the trumpet at the very beginning of the *estribillo* (refrain). This is immediately followed by the three vocal parts of the first chorus, which complete the theme (Example 12-2).

This beginning already indicates the close dynamic interaction between instrumental and vocal writing that is so pervasive in Zumaya's works. As suggested by musicologist Aurelio Tello, the transcriber of the piece, the text may have been written for the Assumption of the Virgin Mary, which explains the music's festive nature. Indeed, this is expressed through the energetic drive that results from a rather fast tempo, the constant dialogue between the two choruses imitating or complementing each other, the brief but forceful string and cornet punctuation, and the contrasting dynamics. The last section of the refrain displays a vivid stretto of rich and intricate polyphony that underscores the words "por Pura, por Reina, por Virgen, por Madre" ([each one awaits reverently] as the Pure One, as Queen, as Virgin, as Mother; Example 12-3). This passage displays many typical Baroque features of the early eighteenth century, such as melodic sequences of small fragments, isometric figures, throbbing rhythm, and perfect integration of the vocal and instrumental parts. This passage illustrates well Zumaya's brand of *stile moderno,* or modern Baroque style.

The four-line *coplas,* or stanzas, are set for an imitative vocal duet of alto and tenor. An instrumental bridge cadencing in the dominant separates the first two lines from the last two lines of the initial stanza. This is followed by an instrumental interlude. This time, however, the music cadences in the tonic, which forms a transition to the *estribillo,* or refrain. Zumaya adhered to the traditional alternation of *estribillo* and *coplas,* in this case producing the sequence *estribillo, coplas* (one and two), *estribillo, coplas* (three and four), *estribillo.*

The presence of Domenico Scarlatti and several other significant Italian composers at the court in Madrid during the first half of the eighteenth century had repercussions in Mexico. With the appointment of Ignacio Jerusalem (1707–1769) to the chapelmaster position of the Mexico City Cathedral in 1749 and the hiring of an Italian assistant, organist and rival Matteo Tollis de la Roca (c. 1710–1781), late-Baroque style came into its own in Mexico. Jerusalem was the first Italian to hold the chapelmaster post. A native of Lecce (Puglia, Italy), he was initially invited to Mexico to work in the new theater, the Coliseo de México, where he directed the orchestra. His theatrical expertise had a decisive influence on church music in Mexico City. During his tenure the Cathedral orchestra grew in strength—its string section, in particular, became large and impressive. In Jerusalem's works, the orchestral accompaniment normally calls for two violins, woodwinds and brass in pairs, an occasional timpani, and continuo with a distinct organ part. Called a "musical miracle" in his own time because he was a child prodigy, violin virtuoso, and prolific and imaginative composer, Jerusalem left over two hundred works, many known as far south as Guatemala and as far north as the Santa Barbara and San Fernando California missions. Besides Masses and other Latin works, his compositions include arias, cantatas, *pastorelas, loas,* and villancicos.

Jerusalem cultivated a predominantly homophonic style based on the *galant* idiom of the eighteenth century. His writing features highly embellished melodies and rhythmic flexibility. Jerusalem also favored dynamic and textural contrasts, and the virtuoso violin passages in the accompaniment of his most elaborate settings underscore the worldly spirit of cathe-

Example 12-2.   Zumaya: *Celebren, publiquen, entonen y canten,* mm. 1–5.

Example 12-3. Zumaya: *Celebren, publiquen, entonen y canten,* mm. 37–41.

Example 12-3 (continued).   Zumaya: *Celebren, publiquen, entonen y canten,* mm. 37–41.

dral music of the time. In his cantatas and villancicos, such as *Cuando la primavera* or *A la milagrosa escuela,* his creative melodies, counterpoint, and attractive homophonic textures provide evidence of his technical proficiency. Referring to the Masses found in the San Fernando Mission of California, musicologist Craig Russell has remarked: "When these masses embark into the realm of Baroque counterpoint, the writing is never angular or 'heavy.' For instance, the 'Christe Eleison' and 'Amen' sections are often fugal—but in spite of their adherence to the rigors of Baroque counterpoint, they always sound smooth, elegant and unforced" (Russell 1993, 102–103). The polychoral Mass in D Major in the San Fernando Mission discovered by John Koegel in the late 1980s and attributed to Jerusalem is a particularly remarkable illustration of the composer's writing. Indeed, this Mass reveals Jerusalem's brilliant combination of Baroque structures, expressive *galant* melodic invention (particularly evident in the "Gratias agimus tibi" of the Gloria), and a smart sense of construction and energetic progression.

PUEBLA

Siendo de Ángeles la Puebla
en el título y el todo
no pudo menos que ser
de Ángeles también el coro.

As Puebla belongs to angels
by name and all the rest
there could be no other but angels
also in its choir.

—Sor Juana Inés de la Cruz

The city of Puebla de los Ángeles, or Angelópolis (as it was called until 1867) was founded in 1531 and by the end of the sixteenth century had developed a very active musical life. Soon thereafter it grew into an important artistic center of New Spain. During the seventeenth century it boasted some thirty magnificent churches, several schools for middle and advanced studies, and the first public library in the Western Hemisphere, with a collection of five thousand volumes donated by the extraordinary Viceroy of New Spain, Archbishop of Mexico (1642–1643), and Bishop of Puebla, Juan de Palafox y Mendoza. A patron of the arts, Mendoza lived in Puebla from 1640 to 1649 and had a far-reaching influence on the artistic achievements of the city. Several painters and creative writers, including poetess Sor Juana Inés de la Cruz, contributed to the city's intellectual atmosphere. In addition, Puebla was home to as many as nineteen printers.

Puebla's first church, built by the Indians between 1536 and 1539, became a cathedral in 1550. By the 1560s the architect who had designed the Mexico City Cathedral undertook the planning of a second cathedral. Begun in 1575, the edifice was consecrated on April 18, 1649, by Bishop Palafox; it remains standing to this day. Considered one of the most magnificent Baroque cathedrals in the Hispanic world, it followed the typical architectural plan of Spanish churches, with the choir bisecting the central nave and enclosed on three sides (Figure 12-2). Organs were located within the choir on side panels. The musicians sat in the choir, facing each other. This arrangement favored antiphonal effects, either by the alternation of plainchant and polyphony or by polyphony alone sung by double choirs. The choir organs can be traced back to 1536, and the instruments went through several major repairs over the next century and a half. A new Spanish organ was installed in 1700 (Figure 12-3). For a time during the mid-seventeenth century, the Puebla Cathedral surpassed Mexico City's in wealth and grandeur.

A number of major figures served as the Cathedral's chapelmasters in the seventeenth century, beginning with Pedro Bermúdez (chapelmaster from 1603–1606), who was followed by the Portuguese-born Gaspar Fernandes (1606–1629), Juan Gutiérrez de Padilla (1629–

Figure 12-2.   Cathedral, Puebla, nave and choir exterior. Reproduced with permission from *Catedrales de México.*

1664), Juan García de Zéspedes (1664–1678), Antonio de Salazar (1679–1688), and Matheo de Dallas y Lana (1689–1712). Of these, Fernandes and Padilla are particularly significant representatives of the vital creative activity at Puebla. Fernandes (c. 1570–1629), who first served as cathedral organist in his hometown of Évora, went to Guatemala as organist and later served as chapelmaster. In September 1606 he was appointed chapelmaster at the Puebla Cathedral, where he served until his death. During his tenure, Fernandez was able to increase the number of singers and instrumentalists, considerably enhancing the music program of the Cathedral. He was also able to convince the chapter that one could not hold the positions of organist and chapelmaster without assistance. As a result, the Cathedral hired Juan Gutíerrez de Padilla to serve as assistant chapelmaster in 1622.

Fernandes's music is found in Guatemala and Oaxaca, but not Puebla. At the Guatemala Cathedral are preserved a group of Benedicamus Domino settings in the eight tones, a Magnificat, and some organ pieces. Gabriel Ruiz de Morga, a disciple of Fernandes's, was apparently responsible for the transfer to Oaxaca of a 284-folio volume containing Latin works and 250 villancicos and chanzonetas by Fernandes, written between 1609 and 1616. The variety and liveliness of the villancicos, designated as *negro, negrito, guineo,* or *negrilla,* reveal the composer's close ties with native folk idioms. With Spanish, Portuguese, pseudo-black dialects, and even Tlaxcala Indian texts, these pieces constitute an early and highly valuable

Figure 12-3. Cathedral, Puebla, organ (1700). Reproduced with permission from *Catedrales de México.*

corpus of vernacular polyphony. As noted by Aurelio Tello, the texts shrewdly "combine wisely the religious and the secular, the divine and the human, the severe and the humoristic" (Tello 1999, 26). Indeed, *Eso Rigor e repente,* a villancico referred to as *guineo* (from African Guinea), is scored for five voices—*tiple,* two altos, tenor, and bass. It was recorded as early as 1975 by the Roger Wagner Chorale and the Sinfonia Chamber Orchestra (LP USR 7746) and stands as a perfect example of this style. Robert Stevenson, writing on the Afro-American Musical Legacy to 1800, used *Eso Rigor e repente* to illustrate what he considered standard musical features of the seventeenth-century *guineo* or *negro,* namely a vivid rhythm in 6/8 meter with constant hemiola shifts to 3/4 time, F or C major as the almost exclusive keys, and responsorial scoring of soloist versus chorus (Stevenson 1968a, 496–497). The text, in pseudo-black dialect, reads in part as follows:

ESTRIBILLO: "Play the little drum, dear black man, sing, brother. Play, oh, play the sarabanda with your noisy talkative guitar. Tonight we shall all be white. Oh, Jesus, what laughter we shall share, oh, what laughter, Saint Thomas!"

COPLAS: "Black men of Guinea, let's go to the manger, let's not [allow] the Angolan blacks to go, for they are all ugly blacks. We want the Child to see only polished and handsome blacks such as are our brothers, who already have "fine clothes." Play the villano and the folia and let's dance happily."

The refrain begins with a solo tenor line that sets the playful character of the piece through rhythm and tempo. Then the various voices create a rich texture through rapid successive answers. This is enhanced by hemiola shifts that are typical of a saraband. The onomatopoeic effects of the syllables "tenge que tenge" and the African-sounding words "sum ba casum cu-cumbe" in contrasting homophonic texture add to the popular character of the work (Example 12-4). In addition to its high quality, Fernandes's music represents a very significant transition in New Spain from Renaissance polyphony to Baroque style.

The composer who took best advantage of the acoustical properties of the Puebla Cathedral was Gutiérrez de Padilla (c. 1590–1664). Padilla occupied the chapelmaster position from 1629 to the end of his life, and he is undoubtedly the most significant figure of seventeenth-century composition in New Spain. Born at Málaga, Padilla was first trained by the local chapelmaster, Francisco Vásquez. He then studied with Jérez de la Frontera at the collegiate church. In 1616, already ordained, Padilla became the chapelmaster of the Cádiz Cathedral, where his excellent services were acknowledged by the local chapter. The first written record of his presence in New Spain dates from 1622, when he was named a coadjutor maestro at Puebla, and then chapelmaster at the death of Gaspar Fernandes.

By the middle of the century Padilla had succeeded in bringing very competent composers and performers to the Puebla Cathedral: Francisco López Capillas (until 1654), the organist Pedro Simón, the bassoonist Simón Martínez, the harp virtuoso Nicolás Grinón, the cathedral succentor Francisco de Olivera, and Juan García de Zéspedes, Padilla's eventual successor. Under Padilla's leadership, the chapel ensemble grew significantly in size. The instruments considered most important were those in the continuo group: organ, harp, and bass viol. Next in rank were recorders, shawms, sackbuts, cornetts, and the soprano, tenor, and bass *bajones* (bassoons), whose function was to double or substitute for the vocal parts. By the early eighteenth century the orchestra began to encompass violins, string bass, trumpets, and horns, as in the Mexico City Cathedral.

Padilla's extensive output survives in several sources. The most important collection is Choirbook XV of the Puebla Cathedral, which contains Masses, motets, hymns, psalms, Lamentations, responsories, antiphons, a litany, and a St. Matthew Passion. Padilla's villancico cycles are found in loose sheets. He wrote in all genres of the Spanish Baroque except the Magnificat and Requiem. His Latin music reveals a marked preference for double choir, which he treats with considerable diversity. Both imitative techniques and antiphonal effects are combined very effectively, and sometimes used simultaneously. Padilla conceives each choir as a four-part unit, using the two groups in alternation, in both polyphonic and homophonic sections. His polyphony is derived from the conservative Renaissance *stile antico* style, which remained in common use in Spanish church music until the end of the seventeenth century. Clarity of form and polyphonic texture enhances the mystical character of

Example 12-4. Fernandes: *Guineo, Eso Rigor e repente,* mm. 25–33.

this music. The basso continuo is not indicated in the music sources. It was easily produced, however, by having the organ or harp double the bass line, in the Spanish tradition (Catalyne 1966). *Exultate Justi in Domino* illustrates well the expressive force of Padilla's double-choir techniques, which include polyphonic, homophonic (although infrequent), and homophonic-antiphonal textures (Example 12-5, a-b). All were common in his polyphonic church works.

Padilla's Masses for double choir, such as the *Ave Regina* and *Ego flos campi,* achieve formal unity through the use of a motto phrase that occurs in each movement and through the use of thematic material that was announced in the previous movement. *Ego flos campi,* a parody Mass based on an unknown model, displays the composer's skill in dealing with the formal constraints of the genre by adding vital dance-like rhythms here and there. The antiphonal dialogue between the two choirs (with some echo effects and the sudden alternation of major and minor harmonies), combined with full-sounding homophonic passages, reminds one of the early Italian Baroque works of Giovanni Gabrieli and Claudio Merulo.

The polyphonic villancico reached its peak of popularity in New Spain during Padilla's time. Padilla himself wrote many different types of villancico, such as *negrilla, calenda, gallego, jácara,* and *juguete.* All were characterized by references to popular dance or folk music, which explains in part the presence of so many ostinato patterns. By the mid-1600s, villancicos were composed especially for the feast of Corpus Christi, and, to an even greater extent, Christmas. They were also employed in Matins for specific saints' days. The villancicos were a genre of rejoicing, and thus linked with special celebrations. In Spain and New Spain cathedral chapelmasters were required to compose new villancicos each year, for which they had to find suitable poetry. The texts were frequently written in sets or cycles. Perhaps the most famous of these are the villancicos of Sor Juana Inés de la Cruz, whose Christmas sets of 1678, 1680, and 1689 were written for Puebla. They include literary imitations of dialects described as *gallego, portugués, indio, vizcaíno,* and *puerto rico.*

The Lilly Library at Indiana University owns the printed texts of the villancicos performed at the Puebla Cathedral for various festivities in 1649, 1652, 1654, 1656, and 1659. Although no composer is mentioned in these prints, the texts were most likely set by Padilla. Among the texts are found *ensaladillas, batallas, jácaras, negrillas,* and local genres such as the *tocotín* (in a Nahuatl-related language). The collection even includes a *guasteco.* Four Christmas villancico cycles by Padilla survive. His 1653 Christmas cycle includes the regular nine villancicos (three for each nocturne of the Matins) and represents one of the most impressive sets of New World villancicos, in terms of expressive diversity and quality. From this cycle come the two most frequently cited villancicos by Padilla: *A la jácara, jacarilla,* a *jácara* type, and *¡Ah, siolo Flasiquillo!,* a *negrilla.* These two pieces appear to have been known in the Portuguese royal chapel. The villancico is unusually long, with twelve coplas full of syncopated patterns reminiscent of folk music of the Mexican Pacific coast. The coplas call for alternating solo voices: copla 1 is sung by alto, copla 2 by tenor, copla 3 by *tiple,* and so forth. The presentation by solo voices gives the appearance of a dramatization of the text, as in an oratorio or opera.

The *negrilla ¡Ah, siolo Flasiquilla!* represents the most festive item of the cycle. Written *a 4* and *a 6,* with three coplas in duet, this villancico provides a clear idea of the type of theatrical representation that the performance of these works entailed. The text is set as a normal conversation, with questions, answers, descriptions, and the mention of specific characters. Thus Francisco, Tomás, Anton, Andrea, Munglavé, Miguel, and Antonio all interact on this joyful occasion, making preparation for their music and dance in celebration of the birth of Jesus. Some of the terms in the text are clear indications of the black musical and dance her-

Gerard Béhague

Example 12-5. Padilla: *Exultate,* a) mm. 1–4; b) mm. 16–18.

Example 12-6. Padilla: *¡Ah, siolo Flasiquillo!, responsión*, mm. 38–41.

itage in the peninsula as well as the Spanish colonies: *zambamba,* a generic term for drum, and *guacambe, canario, villano,* all dance designations. As in Gaspar Fernandes's *guineo* mentioned above, the African-sounding words "Tumbucutú, cutú, cutú" in the responsión *a 6,* the systematic syncopated rhythmic ostinato in 6/8 meter, and the responsorial-like vocal structure add to the popular, quasi-black traits of this *negrilla* (Example 12-6).

A late-seventeenth-century Puebla chapelmaster whose villancicos won him wide recognition not only in New Spain but throughout the Spanish American colonies was Miguel Matheo de Dallo y Lana (c. 1650–1705), who was appointed to the Cathedral in 1688 and served there until his death. Three of his villancicos cycles were set to texts by Sor Juana Inés de la Cruz and performed in the cathedral in 1689 and 1690. Many of Dallo de Lana's Latin-texted works are polychoral.

During the eighteenth century the Cathedral suffered a decline in the creative accomplishments of its composers. The Cathedral orchestra, however, was larger and more diverse than during the previous century, and it continued to present splendid musical performances. Indeed, the interest in instrumental music seems to have increased during the course of the eighteenth century. It is possible that the famous Spanish guitarist-composer Santiago de Murcia (see Chapter 8) could have settled in Puebla during the 1740s, since a copy of his *Passacalles y obras de guitarra* of 1732 was purchased in Puebla by the English collector Julian

Marshall in 1881 (it was subsequently sold to the British Museum). In 1937 Mexican music historian Gabriel Saldívar purchased what came to be known as the *Códice Saldívar n° 2* that contains a *Método de cítara* that was compiled in Puebla at the beginning of the eighteenth century by Sebastián de Aguirre, a local guitar player. This Códice n° 2 contains interesting pieces of popular dance character—*pavana, pasacalle, zarabanda, panamá,* and others. Of special interest are eight dance pieces entitled *portorricos.* One of these bears the heading *Puerto Rico de la Puebla.* While purely instrumental music was certainly cultivated in New Spain during the seventeenth and eighteenth centuries, very few examples have survived.

Baroque Brazil

Compared to the musical activities in Mexico and Spanish America in general, the transfer of European culture to the Portuguese colony of Brazil during the sixteenth and seventeenth centuries was slow. In Brazil, the organization of churches lagged behind that of Mexico. A bishop was appointed in 1551 in Salvador, Bahia, the capital of the colony until 1763, but additional bishoprics were not created until the mid-seventeenth century. Bahia did not become the seat of an archbishop until 1676. Eventually bishoprics were established in Pernambuco, Maranhão, Minas Gerais, Rio de Janeiro, and São Paulo. With the possible exception of the work of the Jesuits, the church in Brazil was unable to develop the moral and political stature of its Spanish American counterpart. While the church provided education for the privileged few, most artists and intellectuals had to rely on Portugal's educational institutions. No university was established in Brazil during the colonial period. This was in stark contrast with Mexico City, Lima, and other South American cities, where distinguished universities were founded. Printing presses were forbidden until 1808, and the colony imported few books. In spite of these handicaps, colonial Brazil produced a very significant body of literature, authored by Antonio de Vieira, Gregório de Matos, Antonio José da Silva, Cláudio Manoel da Costa, and others.

Relatively little is known about art-music activities until the first part of the eighteenth century or so. Throughout the colonial period most music-making took place in church services. Thus the extant repertory is mainly sacred music, with a few isolated exceptions. Substantial historical documentation has been uncovered since the 1960s that attests to musical activities in Pernambuco (Olinda, Recife) and Bahia (Salvador; Lange 1966). In Brazil the post of chapelmaster was not limited to cathedrals but extended to parish churches (*matrizes*) as well. The qualifications and duties of the chapelmaster did not differ in either jurisdiction. Besides teaching, conducting the choir, and composing music, the chapelmaster was expected to be a good singer and able to play one or more instruments. He acted as contractor for musical services both within and without the church, and he established artistic standards. The chapelmaster controlled all music matters in his jurisdiction. Indeed, no one could conduct any group without his permission. This widely practiced system of control and monopoly, although illegal, precipitated a kind of musical stagnation in some places (Duprat and Orbino 1968).

MINAS GERAIS PROVINCE

Thanks to the prodigious efforts of the late researcher Francisco Curt Lange, the importance of the colonial music life of Minas Gerais (General Mines) has been gradually assessed since the early 1940s. The exploration and subsequent development of this wealthy province began in the late seventeenth century. The discovery of gold around 1693 and diamonds and other precious stones around 1727 led to a period of great prosperity. Elevated to the rank of General Captaincy in 1720, the province developed rapidly. The news of potential wealth initiated the second major gold rush in the history of the Americas. People came from Portugal and other European countries and from all regions of Brazil. Together with Indians and a fairly large number of black slaves, the immigrants constituted a rather heterogeneous population.

By the middle of the eighteenth century, however, mulattos and blacks formed the majority of the population. Free mulattos held important positions among the clergy and dedicated themselves to craftsmanship and art. The development of the splendid local Baroque architecture and sculpture was due in large part to *mestizo* artists, such as the famous Aleijadinho (Antonio Francisco Lisboa) and his imposing Sanctuary in the town of Congonhas do Campo. The practice of music similarly fell to a majority of mulatto artists, a fact that prompted Curt Lange to refer to this phenomenon as *mulatismo musical* (Lange 1946; Plate 23). Substantial documentation reveals a unique musical development that reached its peak during the last quarter of the eighteenth century. Lange has calculated that about a thousand musicians were active in Minas between 1760 and 1800 or so, especially in the cities of Vila Rica (present-day Ouro Peto), Sabará, Mariana, Arraial do Tejuco (present-day Diamantina), São João del Rei, and São José de Rei (present-day Tiradentes).

Following Portuguese models, musical life in Minas was organized around various brotherhoods (*irmandades*) rather than the Church. All practicing musicians belonged to one music brotherhood or another, such as Saint Cecilia, Holy Sacrament, or St. Joseph of Black Men. These organizations supplied music and musicians to the Church or municipality, which commonly commissioned specific works or performances for religious festivities. The brotherhoods also established their own music archives, but a substantial amount of music is also found in orchestra or band archives. There is also evidence of local organ builders, the use of harpsichord in the church, and the existence of manuscript copies and prints of European music.

Little information is available concerning music instruction in Minas. The earliest musicians were probably secular priests from Bahia, Pernambuco, and Rio de Janeiro. Monks were rarely in evidence in Minas Gerais, since the building of convents or monasteries was forbidden by royal decree to prevent the smuggling of gold and precious stones. It is likely that composers received their training in costal cities of the colony, if they were not self-taught.

To understand the style of church music in Minas Gerais, one must remember that local composers normally assimilated the prevailing European styles of the time. Curiously enough, they did not mimic the Neapolitan style that was invading the Iberian Peninsula. Instead, almost all composers whose works are extant seem to have adopted late-Italian Baroque and pre-Classical homophonic styles. Thus the term "Baroque" is only partially appropriate for this music. The majority of compositions are liturgical works for four-part mixed chorus, with solo sections and an orchestral accompaniment of two violins, viola (or cello), bass, and two French horns. The works are more chamber-like than symphonic in character. The use of continuo is not consistent. Double choruses appear infrequently, and counterpoint is eschewed for the most part in favor of homophony (Neves 1997, 10–20).

The most significant composers active in Minas Gerais during the eighteenth century were José Joaquim Emerico Lobo de Mesquita, Marcos Coelho Netto, Francisco Gomes da Rocha, Ignacio Parreiras Neves, and Manoel Dias de Oliveira. The oldest known manuscripts bear dates from the 1760s, and copies from as late as the early twentieth century reveal that the eighteenth-century repertory remained in almost constant use in Minas and the neighboring provinces, especially São Paulo. Earlier manuscripts seem to have been discarded.

To judge from the repertory that survives, Lobo de Mesquita (1745–1805) was the most prolific composer of the province. He spent most of his life at Arrail do Tejuco and Vila Rica. He entered the brotherhood of Nossa Senhora das Mercês dos Homens Crioulos (Our Lady of Mercy of Black Men of Tejuco), which indicates that he was a mulatto. Mesquita worked as the organist of several other brotherhoods and then moved in 1795 to Vila Rica, where he served as a composer, conductor, and organist for the Ordem Terceira do Carmo brotherhood. He consequently moved to Rio de Janeiro, where his professional activities have not been determined. One of his earliest works is the antiphon *Regina Caeli Laetare* (1779), whose first few measures illustrate the composer's well-balanced choral writing (Example 12-7).

The beginning of the solo soprano's melodic line constitutes the antecedent (a) of the opening phrase, which is followed by a consequent (b) of equal length, performed by the tutti ensemble. The tenor remains on the dominant while the altos and basses proceed by contrary motion. This procedure is maintained in m. 4, with the parts inverted. The harmonic progressions and modulations in this opening passage are typical of the composer's sober style—namely, the use of simple chords with frequent tonic, dominant, and subdominant harmonies.

Lobo de Mesquita's Mass in E-Flat Major, for mixed chorus and orchestra (strings, flutes, oboes, and horns), consists of the Kyrie and Gloria only. But it is of very large proportions and belongs to the concertante genre, with eight choral numbers, a duet, and three arias. Although the work reveals an excessive use of homophony and isometric rhythmic figures, it also provides rare examples of Lobo de Mesquita's contrapuntal writing. Imitation appears in the "Christe eleison," where it alternates with contrasting homophonic passages. The instruments double the vocal parts, in the *colla parte* practice that was customary in European church music of the time. Lobo de Mesquita casts his arias in da capo form (the "Quoniam," an aria for soprano, for example), and he even includes a short motivic development section in the "Domine Deus." All these stylistic components mirror European classic practices.

Marcos Coelho Netto (1746–1806) was a composer, conductor, and French horn player, and a member of the Vila Rica Brotherhood of São José dos Homens Pardos. Among Coelho Netto's works is a hymn, *Maria Mater Gratiae* of 1787, for mixed chorus and an orchestra of strings and French horns. The work effectively combines late-Baroque and early Classical stylistic traits. Francisco Gomes da Rocha (c. 1754–1808) entered the same brotherhood as a mulatto composer and singer. The records of the brotherhood also refer to him as kettle drummer in the local regiment of the dragoons, hinting at the different types of income sought by colonial musicians in Brazil. Among Gomes da Rocha's works are a four-part *Novena de Nossa Senhora do Pilar* (1789) and an eight-part *Spiritus Domini* (1795). These and other pieces display the composer's inventive assimilation of Classical stylistic practices both in the choral treatment and the instrumental accompaniment. The *Spiritus Domini* treats the responsory polyphonically in three sections—Andante, Allegro, Andante. The first movement, a thirty-seven-measure-long Andante, illustrates very well the composer's chorale writing. Set for double chorus, it uses antiphonal imitation and much textural variety. The final Andante exhibits a more dramatic character, created through the use of chromatic tension and contracting dynamics (piano and forte, with mezza voce and sforzando).

Ignacio Parreiras Neves (c. 1729–1794) was also a member of the São José Brotherhood for Black Men. The two works bearing his name include an incomplete *Oratoria ao Menino Deos para a Noite de Natal* (Oratorio to the Young Jesus for Christmas Night, 1789), discovered in 1967. Its importance is enhanced by the fact that it was hitherto the only known sec-

Example 12-7.   Mesquita: *Regina Caeli Laetare,* mm. 1–7.

ular choral work from Minas Gerais. The extant performance parts (Figure 12-4) suggest that this Christmas oratorio, originally conceived for solo voices, chorus, and orchestra, was a work of large proportions (Béhague 1971, 25–26).

Theatrical activities in Minas Gerais are well documented, but not a single work survives. The first Casa da Opera was built in Vila Rica in 1770. It consisted of a large room with scenery and appropriate accoutrements. The opera repertory, known through an expense report of the Vila Rica municipality, included Portuguese operas as well as works composed locally. The author Cláudio Manuel da Costa, from the group "Arcadia Ultramarina," wrote the play *O Parnaso obsequioso* (based on Molière's *Le bourgeois gentilhomme*), referring to it as an "opera to be narrated with music." He probably had a composer in mind for the endeavor. In 1786 the Vila Rica Municipal Chamber commissioned three operas on the occasion of the festivities held to celebrate the engagement of the royal infants of Portugal and Spain. Marcos Coelho Netto is mentioned as the musical director and a Francisco Furtado da Silveira as the "composer of the music" (Lange 1946, 3–11). Local opera troupes consisting of blacks and mulattos are reported not only in Minas, Bahia, and Rio de Janeiro, but also in places as re-

a)

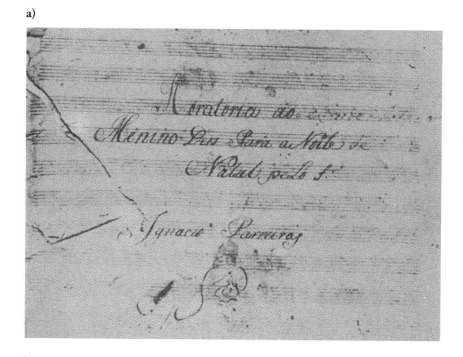

b)

Figure 12-4. Ignacio Parreiras Neves (c. 1729–1794), *Oratoria ao Menino Deos para a Noite de Natal* (Oratorio to the Young Jesus for Christmas Night), 1789. a) Title page, b) soprano performance part.

c)

Figure 12-4 (continued). c) alto performance part.

mote from the coastal area as Cuiabá, where in 1790 the opera *Erzo in Roma* (probably by Jommelli) was produced by an all-mulatto cast.

The colonial art music of Mexico and Brazil, then, resulted from a unique combination of European and local styles. This gave the Baroque in the New World a unique flavor that distinguished it from European music of the same period.

BIBLIOGRAPHY

Béhague, Gerard. 1971. "Música 'Barroca' mineira à luz de novos manuscritos." *Barroco* 3: 6–39.

Brothers, Lester. 1989. "Francisco López Capillas, First Great Native New World Composer: Reflections on the Discovery of His Will." *Inter-American Music Review* 10, no. 2: 101–118.

Catalyne, Alice Ray. 1966. "Music of the Sixteenth through the Eighteenth Centuries in the Cathedral of Puebla, Mexico." *Yearbook, Inter-American Institute for Musical Research* (Tulane University) 2: 75–90.

Duprat, Régis, and Nise Poggi Orbino. 1968. "O estanco da música no Brasil colonial," in *Yearbook, Inter-American Institute for Musical Research* (Tulane University) 4: 98–109.

Estrada, Jesús. 1973. *Música y Músicos de la Época Virreinal.* Mexico: Secretaría de Educación Pública.

Freyre, Gilberto. 1964. *The Masters and the Slaves.* New York: Alfred A. Knopf.

Gage, Thomas. 1958. *Travels in the New World,* ed. J.E.S. Thompson. Norman: University of Oklahoma Press.

Lange, Francisco Curt. 1946. "La música en Minas Gerais. Un informe preliminary." *Boletín Latino-Americano de Música* 6: 409–494.

_____. 1966. *A organização musical durante o período colonial brasileiro.* Coimbra: N.p.

Neves, José Maria. 1997. *Música Sacra Mineira (Catálogo de Obras).* Rio de Janeiro: FUNARTE.

Ray, Alice. 1953. "The Double Choir Music of Juan de Padilla." Ph.D. dissertation, University of Southern California.

Russell, Craig H. 1993. "The Mexican Cathedral Music of Ignacio de Jerúsalem: Lost Treasures, Royal Roads, and New Worlds." *Revista de Musicologia* 16: 102–103.

_____. 1995. *Santiago de Murcia's Códice Saldívar n°4: A Treasury of Secular Guitar Music from Baroque Mexico.* 2 vols. Urbana: University of Illinois Press.

Sant'Anna, Affonso Romano de. 1997. *Barroco, A Alma do Brasil.* Rio de Janeiro: Comunicação Máxima.

Stevenson, Robert. 1967. "López Capillas Francisco." In *New Catholic Encyclopedia,* 8:986. New York: McGraw Hill.

_____. 1968a. "The Afro-American Musical Legacy to 1800." *Musical Quarterly* 54: 475–502.

_____. 1968b. *Music in Aztec and Inca Territory.* Berkeley: University of California Press.

_____. 1970. "The First New World Composers: Fresh Data from Peninsular Archives." *Journal of the American Musicological Society* 23: 95–106.

_____. 1974. *Christmas Music from Baroque Mexico.* Berkeley: University of California Press.

Tello, Aurelio. 1999. "Fernandes, Gaspar." In *Diccionario de la Música Española e Hispanomericana,* 5:25–27. Madrid: Sociedad Unipersonal de Grupo Anaya.

SELECTED COMPACT DISCS

A la Milagrosa Escuela. URTEXT 1998.

Mexican Baroque: Music from New Spain. TELDEC Classics International, 4509-96353-2, 1994.

México Barroco/Puebla I (Maitines de Natividad, 1653. Juan Gutiérrez de Padilla). URTEXT/UMA 2004/1996.

México barroco/Puebla II. URTEXT/UMA 2005/1996.

México Barroco Vol. I. Schola Cantorum URTEXT/UMA 2001/1995.

Missa Mexicana. Harmonia Mundi HMU 907293, 2002.

Música do Brasil Colonial. Compositores Mineiros. Paulus 11652-2, 1997.

Nueva España: Close Encounters in the New World, 1590–1690. Erato no. 2292-45977-2, 1993.

Sacred Music from 18th Century Brazil. Claves Records CD 50-9521, 1995.

Sampler CDs Track List

15–16. J. S. Bach: Trio Sonata in G Major for Organ, BWV 1027a (PGM 115,   7:22
    tracks 3 and 6)
    15. Movement 1, Adagio
    16. Movement 4, Allegro moderato
17. J. S. Bach: Concerto in A Minor for Four Harpsichords, BWV 1065, transcribed for   3:42
    organ by Joan Lippincott, movement 3, Allegro (PGM 115, track 18)
18. J. S. Bach: *An Wasserflüssen Babylon,* BWV 653b (PGM 115, track 8)   5:07
19. J. S. Bach: St. John Passion, Recitative "Und siehe da, der Vorhang im Temple   :27
    zerriß" (PGM 111, CD 2, track 13)
20. J. S. Bach: St. John Passion, Chorus "Herr, unser Herrscher" (PGM 111, CD 1, track 1)   8:45
21. J. S. Bach: St. John Passion, Aria "Es ist vollbracht" (PGM 111, CD 2, track 10)   5:35

TOTAL TIME   76:56

THE WORLD OF BAROQUE MUSIC
New Perspectives
EDITED BY GEORGE B. STAUFFER

Errata

Some errors in the Sampler CDs Track List and PGM Recordings Catalog were printed in the original edition of *The World of Baroque Music,* pages 281–284.

For correct times of the recordings, please refer to the liner notes enclosed with the Sampler CDs.

The Art of the Trio Sonata, performed by The Public Musick and listed as PGM 114 is not a PGM recording. It was recorded privately and has not been previously published.

The recordings PGM 116 through PGM 119 were made and produced by David Oliver and Eric Wagner, members of the PGM Recordings staff, after Gabe Wiener's death. They have been previously released as PGM Archive recordings.

PGM 116, *Barbara Strozzi Arias and Duets,* was previously released as Dorian Recordings DOR-93218.

PGM 117, *Keyboard Music of Jan Pieterszoon Sweelink,* is only available as a PGM Archive recording.

PGM 118, *Rossi and His Circle,* was previously released as Dorian Recordings DOR-93184.

PGM 119, *Santiago de Murcia: Danza y Differencias,* was previously released as Koch International KIC CD-7445.

PGM and PGM Archive recordings are available for purchase at www.pgm.com.

PGM Recordings: Catalog

PGM 101   *Ricercar: Keyboard Music in Germany before Bach*
Gavin Black, harpsichord
Works by Froberger, Böhm, and Kuhnau

PGM 102   *The Buxtehude Project, volume I: Sacred Cantatas*
Sarum Consort and the Chamber Choir of St. Peter's in the Great Valley, Martha N. Johnson, director
Buxtehude: Seven cantatas

PGM 103   *Lagrime Mie: Early Songs of Love and Torment*
Jennifer Lane, mezzo-soprano; Timothy Burris, theorbo
Songs by Caccini, Kapsberger, d'India, Monteverdi, Strozzi, and Frescobaldi

PGM 104   *Praeludium: Origins of Bach's Genius*
Gavin Black, organ
Works by Lübeck, Tunder, Pachelbel, and Buxtehude

PGM 105   *The Buxtehude Project, volume II: Harpsichord Music*
Gavin Black, harpsichord
Buxtehude: Suites in C Major, D Minor, and E Minor, Variations on *More Palatino* and *La Capricciosa*

PGM 106   *Divoti Affetti: Early Music at the Court at Dresden*
New York Baroque, Eric Milnes, director
Works by Ristori, Heinichen, and Fux

PGM 107   *Francesco Maria Veracini: The Recorder Sonatas, volume I*
Gwyn Robert, recorder, with Tempesta di Mare
Works by Veracini

PGM 108   *Salamone Rossi: The Songs of Solomon, volume I*
New York Baroque, Eric Milnes, director
Rossi: Music for the Sabbath

PGM 109   *Heinrich Schütz: Kleine geistliche Konzerte, volume I*
New York Baroque, Eric Milnes, director
Sixteen sacred songs

PGM 111   *J. S. Bach: The St. John Passion*
Trinity Cathedral Choir and Baroque Orchestra
Eric Milnes, director

PGM 112   *The Summe of All Delights: Songs and Ayres of Shakespeare's England*
Jennifer Lane, mezzo-soprano, with A Deux Viole Esgales
Works by Tobias Hume and Robert Jones

PGM 113   *Salamone Rossi: The Songs of Solomon, volume II*
New York Baroque, Eric Milnes, director
Rossi: Holiday and Festival Music

PGM 114   *The Art of the Trio Sonata*
The Publick Musick
Trio sonatas by Telemann, Castello, and Bach

PGM 115   *The Uncommon Bach: Johann Sebastian Bach Organ Works—Variants, Rarities, and Transcriptions*
Joan Lippincott and George Ritchie, organists
Bach: Prelude and Fugue in G Minor, BWV 535a, Trio Sonata in G Major, BWV 1027a, Toccata in D Major, BWV 912, and other works

PGM 116   *Barbara Strozzi: Cantatas and Arias*
           New York Baroque, Eric Milnes, director
           Strozzi: selected cantatas and arias
PGM 117   Keyboard Music of Jan Pieterszoon Sweelinck (Produced but not issued)
           Gavin Black, harpsichord
           Keyboard works by Sweelinck
PGM 118   *Rossi and His Circle* (Released on Dorian Recordings)
           Rebel, Jörg-Michael Schwarz, director
           Instrumental works by Rossi, Buonamente, and Marini
PGM 119   *Santiago de Murcia: Danza y Diferencias* (Released on Koch Recordings)
           Richard Savino, Baroque guitar
           Guitar works by de Murcia

Contributors

Michael Beckerman is Professor of Music and Chair of the Department of Music at New York University. His most recent books include *Janáček and His World* and *New Worlds of Dvořák*. He is currently publishing a collection of essays on Martinů, working on a monograph on music and the idyllic, and researching the music of Gideon Klein. He is a frequent contributor to *The New York Times* and many other publications.

The late **Gerard Béhague** was Professor of Ethnomusicology at the University of Texas, Austin. A past president of the Society for Ethnomusicology and editor of its journal for many years, he published extensively on the music of Latin America, South America (especially Brazil), the Spanish Caribbean, and West Africa. He is author of *The Music of Latin America: An Introduction* and contributor to *The New Grove Dictionary of Music and Musicians* and many other publications.

Victor Coelho is Professor of Music at Boston University, as well as lutenist and director of the ensemble *Il Furioso*. He has authored and edited many books on lute and guitar practices (both historical and modern), including *The Cambridge Companion to the Guitar, Music and Science in the Age of Galileo, Manuscript Sources of Seventeenth-Century Italian Lute Music,* and *Performance on Lute, Guitar, and Vihuela.* His recordings appear on the Stradivarius, Toccata Classics, and UCM labels.

Barbara Russano Hanning, Professor of Music at City College and The Graduate Center of the City University of New York, is author of a book on early opera and various articles and reviews on seventeenth- and eighteenth-century Italian and French music. She is a past president of the Society for Seventeenth-Century Music and chaired the Music Department at The City College of New York for fifteen years. Her well-known volume, *The Concise History of Western Music,* will receive its third edition in 2006.

Wendy Heller is Associate Professor of Music at Princeton University. She has won numerous fellowships, including the Rome Prize from the American Academy in Rome. Her book *Emblems of Eloquence: Opera and Women's Voices in Seventeenth-Century Venice* received the book award from the Society for the Study of Early Modern Women and was named a finalist for the Otto Kinkeldey Prize by the American Musicological Society. She is currently writing a book on Baroque opera and the reception of antiquity.

Daniel R. Melamed is Associate Professor at the Indiana University School of Music. He is author of *J. S. Bach and the German Motet,* co-author (with Michael Marissen) of *An Introduction to Bach Studies,* and editor of *Bach Studies 2.* He has published numerous articles, reviews, and musical editions on J. S. Bach and members of the Bach family. His latest book is for general readers: *Hearing Bach's Passions.*

Craig Monson is Professor of Music and former Chair of the Department of Music at Washington University in St. Louis. His wide-ranging musical interests include Elizabethan and

Jacobean music (notably four volumes of *The Byrd Edition*), Baroque keyboard music and opera, convent music (including two books: *Disembodied Voices: Music and Culture in an Early Modern Italian Convent* and *The Crannied Wall: Women, Religion, and the Arts in Early Modern Europe*), and Native American music.

Mary Oleskiewicz, Assistant Professor of Music at the University of Massachusetts/Boston, is known internationally as a performer on historical flutes and a scholar of seventeenth- and eighteenth-century music, performance practice, and organology. Her articles have appeared in *Early Music,* the *Journal of the American Musical Instrument Society,* and other publications. She is currently editing the solo sonatas of C.P.E. Bach for the Packard Humanities Institute.

David Schulenberg is Professor of Music and Chair of the Music Department at Wagner College. Author of *Music of the Baroque* and *The Keyboard Music of J. S. Bach,* he is also editor of *Bach Perspectives 4: The Music of J. S. Bach, Analysis and Interpretation.* He is recognized internationally as a performer on the harpsichord and other historical keyboard instruments.

Kerala J. Snyder is Professor Emerita of Musicology at the Eastman School of Music, University of Rochester. She is widely acknowledged as a leading expert on German Baroque music, and the life and works of Dieterich Buxtehude, in particular. She is author of *Dieterich Buxtehude: Organist in Lübeck* and served as founding editor-in-chief of the online *Journal of Seventeenth-Century Music* from 1995 to 2003. She is presently a consulting editor of the same journal.

George B. Stauffer is Dean of the Mason Gross School of the Arts and Professor of Music History at Rutgers University. He has written extensively on the music and culture of the Baroque Era, and the life and music of J. S. Bach in particular. He is author, most recently, of *Bach: The Mass in B Minor* and contributor to numerous American, European, and Asian publications. He has held Guggenheim, Fulbright, and ACLS fellowships and is a past president of the American Bach Society.

Index

Page numbers in **bold** indicate the entry is the principal topic of discussion.

Index